THE
BIG BOOK OF
BREAD

ANNE SHEASBY

THE BIG BOOK OF BREAD

365 RECIPES FOR BREAD MACHINES AND HOME-BAKING

BLUE HERON BOOKS

Vancouver

The Big Book of Bread
Anne Sheasby

First published in Canada in 2004 by
Blue Heron Books
9050 Shaughnessy Street
Vancouver, B.C
V6P 6E5
www.raincoast.com

Conceived, created and designed by
Duncan Baird Publishers Ltd
Sixth Floor
Castle House
75–76 Wells Street
London W1T 3QH

Library and Archives Canada Cataloguing in Publication:
Sheasby, Anne
        The big book of bread : 365 recipes for bread machines
and home baking / Anne Sheasby.
ISBN 1-897035-15-2
        1. Bread. 2. Automatic bread machines. I. Title.
TX769.S44 2004   641.8'15   C2004-903458-8

Typeset in Univers Condensed
Color reproduction by Scanhouse, Malaysia
Printed in China by Imago

Managing Editor: Julia Charles
Editor: Rachel Connolly
Managing Designer: Manisha Patel
Designer: Megan Smith
Studio photography: William Lingwood
Food stylist: Bridget Sargeson
Assistant food stylist: Jayne Cross
Prop stylist: Helen Trent

10 9 8 7 6 5 4 3 2 1

Contents

Introduction   6

Bread basics   8

Everyday breads and rolls   22

Specialty and festive breads   72

Flat breads   106

Quick breads   124

Breadmaker recipes   170

Gluten-free breads   190

Bread dishes   208

Index   238

Introduction

BREAD OVER THE CENTURIES

Bread has been part of the staple diet of many countries around the world for thousands of years and it is still held in high esteem within many cultures. Bread forms an important part of our everyday diet, providing a good, basic food which is both nutritious and delicious.

In centuries gone by, bread was initially baked over open fires, but gradually traditional ovens of brick or stone were built into homes or bakeries. Such ovens are still in use in the more rural areas of countries such as Italy and Greece, and can be seen in many other parts of the world. Older properties sometimes still have such ovens, but they are more for decoration than practical use today. The advance of technology and the development of modern ovens has seen the traditional types much less used. Over time, an increasing range of breads has been created. New ingredients and flavorings have been discovered and added to basic recipes, resulting in the vast range of delicious loaves available to us today. Breads come in all shapes and sizes, with many different tastes and textures.

Today, bakers, grocers, delicatessens, and supermarkets all stock an array of traditional loaves as well as many popular regional loaves, and local farmers' markets also have a good selection of tasty breads on offer. We can choose from sweet or savory breads, some plain, others flavored with ingredients such as seeds, olives, cheese, herbs, sun-dried tomatoes, spices, or dried fruit.

Breads from all over the world, including countries and regions such as France, Italy, Spain, Germany, Scandinavia, Turkey, Greece, and India, are all popular and widely available. These days, many supermarkets, and an increasing number of corner or village shops, have in-store bakeries, producing a tempting range of tasty freshly baked savory and sweet loaves, rolls, buns, and other delights. An increasing range of organic and specialist breads, such as gluten-free or dairy-free breads, is also readily available. Not to be outdone, small, independent and local bakers also produce a wide selection of these freshly baked loaves, and craft bakers offer traditional loaves as well as creating new and interesting breads.

HOME-BAKED BREAD

Nevertheless, it is hard to beat the rich aroma and full flavor of freshly baked home-made bread, and making your own bread can be very enjoyable as well as simple to do. Breadmaking doesn't have to be time consuming or complicated, and it is immensely satisfying to bake your own bread using fresh and nourishing ingredients. By mastering a simple basic bread dough, you can then flavor and shape the dough in a multitude of ways. Bread recipes vary from simple, basic or rustic doughs to the more fancy or sophisticated enriched or specialty doughs. Breadmakers (bread machines) are also increasingly popular appliances and help us to make fresh bread even more quickly, especially for those of us with little spare time on our hands.

OUR DAILY BREAD

Bread is an appetizing food as well as being nutritious, and we should try to include a good proportion of starchy foods, such as bread, in our everyday diet. Many basic breads are low in fat, and bread provides an excellent source of starch—the more complex carbohydrate which provides the body with a sustained energy source, as well as some protein. All breads provide dietary fiber, and wholewheat varieties contain nearly four times more than white loaves, in addition to lots of B vitamins and some iron. White flour is generally fortified with calcium, so in fact, white bread can contribute significantly to calcium intake.

Obviously, some of the more elaborate enriched breads and doughs contain more calories and fat than basic loaves, but these too can be enjoyed as special occasion breads or treats within a balanced diet. Many of the quick breads such as English muffins and scones also provide healthy snacks.

TEMPTING RECIPES FOR ALL TYPES OF BREAD

This book by no means includes all bread recipes, but it aims to cover many of the different types of tasty breads available from all over the world, enabling you to create and enjoy these in your own home, at a fraction of the cost of commercially produced loaves. Many of the recipes are simply prepared by hand, but we also include a good selection of recipes that can be partly or fully prepared in a breadmaker.

The book starts with a section on everything you need to know about the basics of breadmaking, including key ingredients, breadmaking techniques, bread shapes and finishes, and so on. We then move on to the seven recipe chapters, which each include a wide range of tempting breads, so you can choose which recipes to try, whether it be a simple basic bread dough, a more challenging enriched bread dough, a traditional flat bread recipe, or a quick and easy quick bread or English muffin recipe. We also include a chapter on gluten-free bread recipes, for those with a sensitivity to gluten. The final chapter provides a tempting selection of recipes which use bread as an ingredient, so creating a wide range of savory and sweet delights such as croutons, bruschetta, burgers, pasta dishes, stuffing mixes, tarts, puddings, and ice cream.

Each recipe is clearly written and easy to follow, and includes guidance tips such as preparation and cooking times, as well as the number of servings. Many also include ingredient variations if you want to try something different. The enticing full color photographs incorporated throughout the book are sure to tempt you into trying many of the different recipes.

So, we invite you to take a leisurely journey through this eclectic collection of mouth-watering recipes from all over the world, and hope that you will be inspired to try some for yourself, your family and friends. Enjoy the experience of making, creating, and baking your own bread at home; once you begin to bake bread, you will soon discover the endless varieties available at your fingertips.

Bread basics

TYPES OF BREAD

Bread comes in all shapes and sizes and in many different colors, textures, and flavors. By mastering the basic technique of breadmaking, there are endless ways to experiment with recipes and to create numerous delicious home-made breads, including everyday basic breads, specialty (enriched) breads, flat breads, quick breads, and gluten-free breads. With breadmakers on the increase, the variety of breads that can be created using a breadmaker provide additional recipes and ideas. Bread itself is also versatile and can be used as an ingredient in other recipes.

BASIC INGREDIENTS FOR BREADMAKING

Bread has four essential ingredients: flour, yeast, liquid, and salt. Other ingredients such as sugar, fat, and eggs may be added to produce different types of bread.

Flour

Types of Flour

For traditional yeasted breads, choose strong wheat flour, also known as breadmaking flour or bread flour. It is available in several varieties, the most common being white, brown, wholewheat, malted grain, and soft grain white. Strong or bread flour has a high gluten content, which stretches the dough and traps in air as it cooks, to give a well-shaped loaf with a good rise and a light, open texture.

Strong flour is recommended for use when making bread by hand and also when making bread in a breadmaker. Flours vary between brands but choose organic, unbleached strong flour, if possible. All-purpose or self-rising flours should only be used in yeast-free breads (although some yeasted doughs use a mixture of flours, such as French Baguettes), and all of the quick bread recipes in this book are made using these types of flour. Quick breads tend to have a closer, more crumbly texture.

Breads made with strong wholewheat flour may take a little longer to rise than those made with white flour, as the bran in wholewheat flour inhibits the gluten. They also tend to be slightly denser and coarser in texture than white breads, though they are very flavorful and nutritious. An alternative idea is to use half strong white and half strong wholewheat flour for a lighter-textured loaf.

Strong brown flour will produce a lighter brown loaf, whereas strong malted grain flour, which is a mixture of strong brown flour and malted wheat flakes or grains, produces loaves with a nutty, malted flavor. Strong malted grain flour may also be made from a combination of strong wholewheat and white flours, sometimes with rye flour added, and malted grains. Stoneground flour (available in wholewheat and brown varieties) is ground between stones, hence the name, and this gives the flour a slightly roasted, nutty flavor. Strong soft grain flour is strong white flour with kibbled grains of wheat and rye added, and this also produces a tasty loaf.

Other flours such as barley, millet, and spelt flours have a low gluten content, but can be combined with strong bread flours to make delicious loaves. Rye flour is also used in breadmaking and although it has a good gluten content, rye doughs are often sticky and difficult to handle, so for this reason it is frequently mixed with other flours to create a more manageable dough.

Gluten-Free Flours

If you have an intolerance or sensitivity to gluten, then you will need to avoid flours which contain gluten. Because gluten is the protein that strengthens and binds dough in baking, you may need to find alternative binding agents when using gluten-free flours. A combination of starches often works better than a single type, and adding ingredients such as egg, grated apple, or mashed banana may also help. It should be noted that gluten-free flours tend to make denser loaves with a closer texture.

A range of gluten-free flours including gluten-free white and bread flours (as well as gluten-free all-purpose flour) are available from many supermarkets or healthfood shops. Alternately, you can combine a selection of gluten-free flours yourself. Other naturally gluten-free flours include rice flour, gram (garbanzo) flour, buckwheat flour, cornmeal, tapioca flour, and potato flour.

When using gluten-free flours in recipes, it is important to remember that they tend to absorb more liquid than ordinary flours, so you may need to add a little more liquid to all your recipes (we have accounted for this in the recipes in this book), if you are adapting/changing standard recipes into gluten-free recipes.

It is important to remember when making bread by hand or using a breadmaker, that all utensils should be washed thoroughly before and after use, as even the slightest trace of wheat may cause an allergic reaction in someone who suffers with celiac disease or who has an intolerance to wheat. If you are baking a batch of breads, be careful to keep ingredients separate so that there is no risk of wheat flour contaminating the gluten-free foods. If you do a lot of gluten-free baking, it may be sensible to always use separate baking pans and cooking utensils.

Gluten-free bread mixes are also available from healthfood shops, and these are suitable for making bread by hand on in the breadmaker.

Some recipes also contain gluten-free self-rising white flour—if this is not available, simply use gluten-free all-purpose flour and add 1 teaspoon gluten-free baking powder to each 1½ cups of all-purpose flour used. Other brands of gluten-free flours are also available.

Yeast

Yeast is an essential ingredient in breadmaking as it causes the bread to rise. It is a living organism, which requires food and moisture to grow and survive. Fresh yeast is alive but inactive when you buy it, and it will only become active once it is mixed with a warm liquid such as milk or water. Dried yeast is also inactive and it will remain so until it becomes activated during the process of fermentation.

Yeast feeds on the sugar and later the starches in the flour and it then releases a gas (carbon dioxide) that makes dough rise. Warmth encourages the yeast to grow more quickly, but it is not essential. Bread dough will rise in a refrigerator overnight and this slow, cool rise produces a good, well-shaped loaf.

Types of Yeast

Yeast is available in several different forms including fresh yeast, traditional or ordinary dried active yeast, and easy-blend, easy-bake, quick or fast-action dried yeast. All forms of yeast can be used and interchanged in the recipes, so long as the general guidelines are followed. It is important to treat yeast with care. As soon as it comes into contact with moisture of any kind it will activate and start to feed on the starch and sugars in the dough.

Easy-Blend (Easy-Bake) or Fast-Action (Quick) Dried Yeast Easy-blend (easy-bake) or fast-action (quick) dried yeast is a combination of dried yeast and the bread improver ascorbic acid (vitamin C), which accelerates the action of the yeast during the fermentation process, allowing a quick rise, and eliminating the need to "punch down" the dough and rise it for a second time. This type of yeast is available in handy ¼-oz sachets, or it can be bought in resealable foil packages of 4½oz, which need to be kept in the refrigerator once opened and used within 10–12 weeks. Easy-blend (easy-bake) or fast-action (quick) dried yeast is sprinkled and mixed directly into the flour or dry ingredients, before adding the warm liquid to make the dough. It is a fast-action yeast, so that often only one kneading and rising is required, making yeast cookery quicker and easier. It is important to remember that yeast won't work if it is stale, so always follow instructions for storage and adhere to the use-by date on the package. This type of yeast is recommended for use in a breadmaker.

Traditional or Ordinary Dried Active Yeast Traditional or ordinary dried active yeast is compressed yeast from which the moisture has been removed. It is available in granules. This type of yeast will need to be reactivated with water prior to use. It is usually available in 4½-oz tubs and will keep for up to 2 months once opened. Traditional or ordinary dried active yeast is simply blended with warm liquid (with a pinch or so of sugar to help activate it), covered and set aside in a warm place for about 15 minutes or until a frothy head develops. Once reactivated, it is then used like fresh yeast, to make hand-made breads and doughs which require two rising periods. It is not recommended for use in a breadmaker.

Fresh Yeast Fresh yeast is available to buy in some baker's, healthfood shops or delicatessens. It should look firm, moist and creamy-colored and should have a good "yeasty" smell when you buy it. Fresh yeast is simply blended with the warm water or liquid specified in the recipe and then mixed with the flour to make a dough. It can be kept, wrapped, for up to 3 days in the refrigerator or in the freezer for up to 3 months. Fresh yeast is not suitable for use in a breadmaker.

Sourdough Starter A sourdough starter is another traditional method of leavening, which produces a close-textured loaf with a distinctive flavor. To make a sourdough starter, a mixture of yeast, flour, and water is left to ferment for several days before it is added to the dough.

A Note About the Yeast Used in the Recipes in this Book For this cookbook, in the majority of recipes that contain yeast, we have used easy-blend dried yeast, for convenience and ease of use. This type of dried yeast is simply added straight to the flour, with no need to reconstitute or activate it in water first.

    With many of the plainer, more basic bread doughs (which specify using easy-blend dried yeast) we also include two rises. Although this is not necessary when using this type of yeast, it tends to give a better overall result (i.e. the doughs have one rise after the initial kneading and one rise after the dough has been punched down and shaped, before baking).

There is also a selection of yeasted doughs included in this book that only require one rising, and for these recipes we have specified using fast-action dried yeast (although in fact, easy-blend, easy-bake, quick and fast-action dried yeasts are similar products with different names). This is so that, at a glance, you are able to see if a recipe requires one or two rises.

For many of the enriched or specialty doughs, we have also specified using easy-blend dried yeast and these doughs have two rises. Enriched doughs such as Brioche, Chelsea Buns, and Stollen, which contain ingredients such as fat, sugar, and/or eggs, take more time to rise than plainer doughs, so this type of dough must be allowed to rise before and after shaping to achieve the best results. However, there is also a small selection of enriched doughs where we have specified using fast-action dried yeast, as these are slightly lighter doughs which require only one rising.

Doughs made using fresh yeast or ordinary dried yeast granules always require two rises to produce bread with a light, even texture. There are a couple of recipes in this book—Ciabatta and Pugliese—where we have specified using fresh yeast, as for these recipes fresh yeast really gives the best results.

As a rough guide, one sachet (¼oz) easy-blend or fast-action dried yeast (1 sachet = about 2 teaspoons) is equivalent to ½oz fresh yeast or 1 tablespoon ordinary dried yeast. This quantity of yeast is enough to rise up to 5 cups flour.

For doughs enriched with butter, sugar, eggs, fruit, etc, you will usually need to add a little more yeast to ensure a good rise—please refer to the recipes in this book for guidance.

Other Leavening Agents

While yeast is the most popular and most common leavening ingredient used in breadmaking, other raising agents such as baking powder and baking soda are also used for making some breads, including quick breads such as Irish Soda Bread and Wheaten Bread.

Sugar and Other Sweeteners

Sugar helps to feed the yeast and make it more active, hence encouraging fermentation to take place more quickly. Modern types of yeast (such as easy-blend or fast-action dried yeast) no longer need sugar as the flour provides them with enough food, but for good measure it is usual to add a little sugar in breadmaking.

White, light soft brown, or dark soft brown sugars can all be used in breadmaking and 1 teaspoon sugar is enough to activate the yeast in a 1lb 2oz loaf, although more sugar will be added to sweet and some enriched doughs.

In some bread recipes, honey, light corn syrup, maple syrup, malt extract, or molasses are used to add flavor and color. Sugar also helps delay the staling process in baked bread because it attracts moisture. However, too much sugar can cause the dough to rise too much and collapse, so follow the recipes carefully. Artificial sweeteners are not suitable for breadmaking.

Salt

Salt improves the flavor of bread. However, salt also slows down the action of yeast, so be careful not to add too much, and do not add salt directly to the yeast. Salt helps the dough to rise in a controlled and even way, resulting in a well-risen, even loaf. Too little salt means the loaf will stale more quickly; too much and the crust will harden.

Liquids

The liquid used in breadmaking is usually water, although milk or a mixture of milk and water is used in some recipes. Milk tends to give the bread a softer, lighter texture and a soft crust. The temperature of the liquid used is important. It should be warm (tepid) or hand-hot (about 38°C/100°F); if it is too hot it may destroy the yeast, and if it is too cold it will slow down the action of the yeast.

When adding liquid in a yeasted bread recipe, in many recipes the quantities of liquid given should be used as a guide, because the absorbency of flour varies according to type and brand, and also depends on the surrounding conditions such as heat and humidity. For example, doughs made with wholewheat flours tend to need more liquid than those made with white flour. Always add the liquid gradually, rather than all at once, so that you only add as much as is needed. However, with some yeasted bread recipes, all the liquid needs to be added to the dough to achieve the correct consistency, so always read through the recipe carefully before you begin, as this will be indicated in the text. Other liquids including buttermilk, plain yogurt, coconut milk, beer, cold tea, or fruit juices such as orange juice, may also be used to make some bread doughs.

Fats

Some recipes include a little fat, such as butter, to be rubbed into the flour before or after the yeast is added. Other recipes may include the addition of oil or melted butter. We have specified using butter in most of the recipes (where applicable), but in many of these recipes, vegetable margarine or a similar alternative fat may be used instead of butter, if preferred. Fats add flavor to breads as well as improving their keeping qualities, but too much fat will slow down the action of the yeast. Some enriched doughs such as Lardy Cake and Danish Pastries contain a large amount of fat, which helps to produce these delicious breads and pastries. The rising times on recipes such as these may be a little longer than with basic bread doughs.

Bread Mixes

There is a good range of bread mixes available that are ideal for making bread by hand or in a breadmaker, enabling you to make and bake flavorful breads with very little effort. They include white, wholewheat, or malted grain bread mixes as well as a range of flavored mixes, and specialty bread mixes such as ciabatta or focaccia.

We have used a basic white bread mix for a selection of recipes in this book, to create some tempting, flavorful breads. Once bread mixes have been mixed, kneaded and shaped, they only require one rising, so are ideal if you would like to create a tasty loaf but are a little short of time.

ESSENTIAL BREADMAKING TECHNIQUES FOR YEASTED DOUGHS

Mixing and Kneading the Dough

Once the yeast and liquid (and sometimes other ingredients, depending on the recipe) have been added to the dry ingredients, they are mixed together to form a soft, pliable dough. The dough then needs to be kneaded vigorously to strengthen and work the gluten in the flour and to create a smooth, stretchy, elastic dough to achieve a good rise. Kneading is vital for good, even-textured, well-shaped bread and it ensures that the yeast is distributed throughout the dough so that the loaf rises evenly. Remember, if yeasted dough has not been kneaded it will not rise.

If you are kneading the dough by hand this will usually take about 10 minutes. Turn the dough onto a lightly floured worktop and pull and stretch it firmly away from you using the heel of your hand, then fold it toward you, press it down again and away from you using the heel of your hand, giving it a small turn as you do so. Continue pulling, stretching, folding, pressing, and turning the dough like this until it becomes smooth and elastic.

Alternately, you can use a large mixer with a dough hook attachment, or a food processor, to mix and knead the dough for you. Kneading in a mixer (on a low speed) usually only takes about 5 minutes. Many domestic food processors will only allow you to knead moderate amounts of dough per batch and for a limited time. However, be careful not to over-knead the dough if using an electric mixer or food processor, and remember that not all doughs are suitable for kneading in a mixer, e.g. doughs containing dried fruit, where the fruit is added with the flour, may result in the fruit becoming too broken down by the kneading action of the machine.

First-rising the Dough

Once the dough has been kneaded, place it in a large, lightly oiled bowl (leaving plenty of room for expansion) and cover with a clean dish towel or oiled plastic wrap. This will help the dough to rise and will prevent a skin from forming on the top. Set aside in a warm place until the dough has risen and doubled in size, and springs back slowly when you press it with your fingertips.

The time dough takes to rise will depend on several factors including the temperature of the room, the temperature of the ingredients, type of recipe, etc. The first rising of bread doughs usually takes the longest, on average between 1–2 hours. Enriched doughs tend to take longer to rise, e.g. the Chocolate Bread recipe takes between 2–3 hours to rise sufficiently. The ideal temperature for rising dough is about 75–80°F/24–27°C—this is a similar temperature to central heating radiator or near a warm oven. However, don't be tempted to speed up the rising process by putting the dough somewhere hot, as this may kill the yeast and will result in misshapen bread with a poor texture.

Some people prefer to rise their dough more slowly (in a cool, unheated room, for example) as they feel cool rising produces a better tasting loaf. Avoid rising dough in a draughty room, though, as this may cause the bread to bake unevenly.

Punching Down and Second-rising the Dough

Once the dough has risen, it is then "punched down". This process will smooth out any large air pockets and ensure an even texture in the bread. To "punch down" the dough, remove the cover and punch the risen dough in the bowl with your fist to deflate it and knock out the air. Turn the collapsed dough onto a lightly floured worktop and knead it briefly—for about 2–3 minutes—to redistribute the yeast and the gases formed by fermentation. Sometimes, at this stage, other ingredients such as olives, chopped herbs, chopped sun-dried tomatoes, chopped nuts, seeds, or dried fruit may be kneaded into the dough.

The dough is then shaped or molded as required, and then covered once again and left in a warm place until it has doubled in size. This is known as the second-rising stage; it is quicker than the first rising and usually takes about 30–60 minutes, depending on the recipe.

It is important not to over-rise the dough at this stage, otherwise the bread may collapse during baking—make sure the dough only rises until it is doubled in size. However, if it does not rise enough at this stage the loaf will be dense and flat.

To test if the dough has risen enough, simply press it lightly with your fingertip. It should feel springy and the indentation made by your finger should slowly spring back and fill.

For professional-looking bread, rising (proving) baskets (often used by professional bakers) may be used for rising (proving) the dough. Rising baskets are wicker baskets lined with linen or canvas, which are lightly floured, and they provide extra support to the bread during its final rising. They are available in round or long (baguette) shapes from good kitchenware shops. Once the dough has risen in a basket, simply turn it out onto a cookie sheet and bake as normal.

Shaping Bread

Once the bread dough has been punched down, it may be shaped in various ways. Common bread shapes include traditional loaf, cottage loaf, large round or oval, braid or baton, while bread rolls can be shaped into rounds, knots, long rolls, and rings, for example. Dough can also be slashed with a sharp knife in various ways before or after rising: slash the top of the loaf along its length (this is the traditional finish for a loaf); make criss-cross lines over the top of the loaf; cut a deep cross across the center of the loaf; cut several diagonal slashes across the top of the loaf.

Slashing the tops of loaves is not only done for visual effect but can also be done for practical reasons, to provide escape routes for the air and to control the direction and extent of the rise during baking. The earlier you slash the dough the wider the splits in the baked loaf, and the deeper the slashes the more the bread will open during baking. Use a sharp knife and a swift, smooth action when slashing the dough, to avoid tearing it.

Glazing Bread

Brushing a loaf with a glaze before baking will enhance the color of the bread, as well as adding flavor to the crust. Glazes not only help to give the baked bread an attractive finish, they also add moisture to the loaf (by producing steam which helps to expand the loaf and ensure even cooking). Additionally, glazes help toppings, decorations, or garnishes to stick to the surface of the dough.

Breads may be glazed before, during or just after baking. The most common ingredients used to glaze loaves are water, milk, or beaten egg, but you can also try melted butter, olive oil, light cream, warmed clear honey, sugar syrup, or a thin candied frosting for a variety of different finishes.

Finishing Touches for Bread

Various ingredients can be used for topping or finishing bread before it is baked, and each ingredient will create a different effect. Try sprinkling with seeds, cracked or kibbled wheat, rolled oats, salt flakes, grated cheese, or fresh herbs before baking, or dust with a little flour. For sweet breads, try dusting with confectioners' sugar or sprinkling bread with crushed sugar cubes, chopped nuts, flaked almonds, dried fruits, or grated or chopped chocolate, usually after baking.

A Note About Enriched Doughs During baking, some of the enriched doughs (or doughs containing chocolate, more sugar, etc) in this book may need covering to prevent them browning too much. If the bread shows signs of browning too quickly, simply cover it loosely with foil toward the end of the cooking time.

Storing Bread

Most home-made bread is at its best when served freshly baked and on the day it is made, and it should be eaten within 1–2 days as it stales quite quickly. Bread with a high fat or sugar content, such as enriched doughs, are also best eaten when freshly baked, but will keep longer, for up to 2–3 days.

Bread is best stored in a cool, dry, well-ventilated bread bin or an earthenware bread crock, and not in the refrigerator (the cold draws moisture out of the loaf, making it dry and stale). Wrap bread in foil or a plastic bag if it has a soft crust, and in a paper or fabric bag if it is crusty.

Bread also freezes well for a short time—up to about 1 month. Simply seal the bread in a polythene freezer bag, or alternately, cut the loaf in half or into slices and freeze in convenient portions, ideal for defrosting when required. Defrost frozen breads at room temperature.

Quick (yeast-less) breads tend to stale quickly and these are often best eaten freshly baked and warm from the oven.

Many shop-bought breads contain preservatives or flour improvers, hence they have a longer storage life than home-made breads.

BREADMAKING UTENSILS

The various utensils useful for breadmaking are too numerous to mention here, but most modern kitchens will have sufficient equipment to make bread.

A Note About Bread Pans and Molds If using a loaf pan or other shaped pan to bake your bread, it is important to choose one that is the correct size for the amount of dough you have made. As a general guide, the pan should be about twice the size of the dough.

Regular loaf pans came in two sizes—1lb and 2lb. However, nowadays there is a wider choice of loaf pan sizes to choose from. For this book, when we refer to 1lb and 2lb loaf pans we have used pans with the following approximate dimensions (the measurements are the *internal* measurements of each pan):

1lb loaf pan = 7¼ inches = length; 3½ inches = width;
2¼ inches = depth.
2lb loaf pan = 8½ inches = length; 4¼ inches = width;
2¾ inches = depth.

We also occasionally use a slightly larger 2½lb loaf pan in some recipes, with the following approximate *internal* measurements:

2½lb loaf pan = 10in = length; 4¼in = width;
3in = depth.

We have used several other pans for some of the recipes in this book, such as springform pans, deep round cake pans, square cake pans, and English muffin pans, some with loose bases, others not, as well as more specialist shaped pans or molds such as brioche and kugelhopf pans. We have included the appropriate pan size or capacity on the relevant recipes.

Pans, such as those mentioned above, should be greased before use—simply wiping vegetable oil over the surface with absorbent paper towel should suffice. For breads baked on a cookie sheet, either grease or flour the cookie sheet before use, whichever you prefer. Some high fat recipes such as Danish Pastries are better baked on a greased rather than a floured cookie sheet, to avoid sticking. With each recipe, we include instructions on preparing the pans or cookie sheets.

BREADMAKERS

There is a wide range of breadmakers to choose from and selecting a model to suit you will depend on several factors, including size or capacity required and budget. Do some research before buying a breadmaker to ensure it is the right model to suit you.

We have included a whole chapter on breadmaker recipes in this book, but throughout the book we also include a selection of other recipes which are suitable for making both by hand and in the breadmaker.

We have given ingredient quantities and cooking instructions for each breadmaker recipe, but it is very important that you thoroughly read the manufacturer's instruction book for your particular breadmaker before embarking on any of the recipes. Breadmakers vary, so you may find, for example, that you have to add the ingredients to the bread pan in a slightly different order to that given in these recipes. Simply add the ingredients to the bread pan in the order specified in your instruction booklet.

Breadmakers will save time and effort and they are relatively simple to use. Before you begin, it is well worth familiarizing yourself with your machine and experimenting with the different settings and options. Practice makes perfect and you will soon master how to use and program your machine. The names of the settings used, such as Rapid Bake or Basic White, may also differ slightly from one model to another. The delay timer facility is useful for when you are not at home or are asleep—it's hard to beat the aroma of freshly baked bread as you walk through the door at the end of a hard day or when you wake up in the morning!

When making bread in a breadmaker it is vital that the salt, sugar, and yeast are kept apart from each other. This is less important if you are making some breads using the Rapid Bake or Fast Bake program, as the ingredients are mixed as soon as the program begins.

Breadmaker pans vary in size between models and on large models you may have the option of making up to three different sizes of loaf. We have selected a medium-sized loaf for these recipes, which should suit most breadmakers.

Programs vary between models, but many include a Basic White or Normal, Wholewheat, Multigrain, Rapid Bake or Fast Bake, Sweet, Raisin Bake or Raisin Beep, Dough Only, Raisin Dough, and Bake Only programs. Some models may also include more specialized programs such as French, Cake, Sandwich, Pizza, and Jelly. Again, please refer to your manufacturer's instruction booklet for more details of the programs included with your machine.

Some machines also offer a choice of three crust colors: light, medium, or dark. However, if your machine does not have this option or you would prefer a darker crust once the loaf has been baked, simply brush the top of the baked loaf with a little melted butter or egg yolk mixed with water and brown under a hot broiler or in a preheated oven at 200°C/400°F/gas mark 6 for 5–10 minutes.

Adapting Recipes For Use in a Breadmaker

Having mastered your breadmaker, you may decide that you would like to try and adapt some of your own recipes to make in it. There is no easy formula for adapting conventional recipes for the breadmaker, but the best advice is to look through the recipes in this book and find one that is similar and use it as a rough guide. It is also worth checking your manufacturer's instruction book as this may give advice for adapting your own recipes to suit that particular model. Once you have tried a few recipes in your breadmaker, you will soon get the feel for how to adapt your own.

Quick Tips For Adapting Your Own Recipes

- Firstly make sure you use the correct quantities for the breadmaker, ensuring that the total quantity of ingredients will fit into your bread pan. Do not exceed the recommended maximum. If necessary, reduce the flour and liquid quantities to match those in a similar recipe.
- Use the flour and water quantities given in the recipes in this book as a guide and always refer to your manufacturer's instruction book. Keep the flour and liquid in the correct proportions. You may find that you need to add a little more water than the amount given in hand-made recipes, but this will vary depending on several factors, such as the type of recipe itself, other ingredients used, etc. With a bit of practice, you will soon get the feel for approximately how much liquid to add to different basic quantities of flour.
- Keep the yeast dry and separate from any liquids added to the pan, until mixing commences. Separate the yeast from the liquid by adding the yeast before or after the flour (or according to your instruction booklet).
- Always keep salt, sugar, butter, and yeast separate from each other until mixing commences.
- Always replace fresh yeast with an appropriate amount of easy-blend (easy-bake) or fast-action (quick) dried yeast (for more details refer to your manufacturer's guidelines). As a rough guide for wholewheat bread, try using 1 teaspoon easy-blend or fast-action dried yeast for up to 13oz flour or 1½ teaspoons yeast for up to 4½ cups flour.
- If you are using the timer delay setting, use skim milk powder and water instead of fresh milk.
- If your conventional recipe uses egg, add the egg as part of the total liquid measurement.
- Check the consistency of the dough during the first few minutes of mixing. Remember that breadmakers require a slightly softer dough than with hand-made doughs, so you may need to add a little extra liquid. The dough should be wet enough to gradually relax back. If it is crumbly or the machine seems to be laboring, add a little extra water. If it is sticking to the sides of the pan and doesn't form a ball, add a little extra flour.

Gluten-Free Breads

When making gluten-free breads in the breadmaker, the Rapid Bake or Fast Bake program will usually produce the best results. Refer to your manufacturer's guidelines for details of the specific setting(s) recommended for gluten-free breads made in your particular breadmaker.

A NOTE ABOUT THE RECIPES

- The sachets of easy-blend dried yeast are ¼oz in size.
- All spoon measures are level unless otherwise stated. Sets of measuring spoons are available for accurate measurements.
- Medium eggs should be used in the recipes, except where otherwise specified.
- We have included cooking temperatures for electric and gas ovens. Remember if you have a fan-assisted oven that you need to reduce the oven temperature slightly (usually by around 20 degrees) and/or adjust the cooking times. Please refer to manufacturer's guidelines for more specific information on adjusting the temperature and time for your cooker, if applicable.
- Some of the recipes in this book may contain raw or lightly cooked eggs—these recipes are not recommended for babies and young children, pregnant mums, the elderly, and those convalescing.
- The 🍞 icon indicates that the recipe can be made in a breadmaker.

CHAPTER 1
Everyday breads and rolls

In this chapter you will find a selection of delicious breads and rolls that are ideal for regular baking. We include basic loaves and rolls, as well as a collection of slightly more unusual breads that are enjoyed all over the world, many on a daily basis.

Choose from rustic, homely bread recipes such as Quick Country Wholewheat Bread, Oatmeal Bread, Cottage Loaf, Milk Loaf, or Flowerpot Bread, or try authentic recipes from Europe such as French Baguettes, Ciabatta, Pugliese, or Greek Olive Bread. Alternately, travel further afield and enjoy recipes such as Seeded Moroccan Bread, Coconut Bread, Sourdough Bread, Bagels, or Garlic Bubble Ring. Or select from a tempting range of bread rolls, including Rustic Wholewheat Rolls, Malted Country Rolls, Panini Rolls, or Petit Pains au Lait, as well as Golden Cheddar Twists, Sesame Breadsticks, or Seeded Knots.

001 Basic white bread

PREPARATION TIME *20 minutes, plus rising* **COOKING TIME** *30–35 minutes*
MAKES *2 loaves (each loaf serves 12–14)*

4¾ cups strong white flour	**1½ teaspoons easy-blend dried yeast**
2 teaspoons salt	**2 tablespoons butter, diced**
1 teaspoon superfine sugar	**About 2 cups warm water**

1   Grease two 2lb loaf pans and set aside. Sift the flour and salt into a large bowl, stir in the sugar and yeast, then rub in the butter. Make a well in the center, then add enough water, mixing to form a soft dough.
2   Turn the dough onto a lightly floured worktop and knead until smooth and elastic. Shape the dough into a round, then place it in a lightly oiled bowl, cover and let rise in a warm place until doubled in size.
3   Punch down the dough on a lightly floured worktop, then divide it in half and shape each portion into an oblong. Press into the loaf pans, cover and let rise again for about 30 minutes, or until doubled in size.
4   Meanwhile, preheat the oven to 230°C/450°F/gas mark 8. Bake the loaves for 15 minutes, then reduce the oven temperature to 200°C/400°F/gas mark 6 and bake for a further 15–20 minutes, or until the bread is risen, golden brown, and sounds hollow when tapped underneath. Turn out and cool on a wire rack. Serve in slices.

VARIATION *If you do not have any suitable loaf pans, simply shape the punched down dough into a large round or oval (or divide the dough in half and shape each portion into a round or oval), place on a greased cookie sheet, let rise, then bake as above.*

002 Basic wholewheat bread

PREPARATION TIME *20 minutes, plus rising* **COOKING TIME** *30–35 minutes*
MAKES *2 loaves (each loaf serves 12–14)*

1½ cups strong white flour	**2 teaspoons easy-blend dried yeast**
3 cups strong wholewheat flour	**2 tablespoons butter, diced**
2 teaspoons salt	**About 2 cups warm water**
1 teaspoon superfine sugar	

1   Grease two 2lb loaf pans and set aside. Sift the white flour into a large bowl, then stir in the wholewheat flour, salt, sugar, and yeast. Rub the butter into the flour mixture. Make a well in the center, then add enough water, mixing to form a soft dough.
2   Turn the dough onto a lightly floured worktop and knead until smooth and elastic. Shape the dough into a round, then place it in a lightly oiled bowl, cover and let rise in a warm place until doubled in size.
3   Punch down the dough on a lightly floured worktop, then divide it in half and shape each portion into an oblong. Press into the loaf pans, cover and let rise again for about 30 minutes, or until doubled in size.
4   Meanwhile, preheat the oven to 230°C/450°F/gas mark 8. Bake the loaves for 15 minutes, then reduce the oven temperature to 200°C/400°F/gas mark 6 and bake for a further 15–20 minutes, or until the bread is risen, lightly browned, and sounds hollow when tapped underneath. Turn out and cool on a wire rack. Serve in slices.

003 🍞 Farmhouse wholewheat loaf

PREPARATION TIME *20 minutes, plus rising* **COOKING TIME** *30–35 minutes*
MAKES *1 loaf (serves 10–12)*

3 cups strong brown flour, plus extra
    for dusting
⅔ cup wheat bran
1 sachet (¼oz) fast-action dried yeast

1 teaspoon salt
2 tablespoons butter, diced
1 tablespoon clear honey
About 1¼ cups warm milk

1   Grease a 2lb loaf pan and set aside. Mix the flour, wheat bran, yeast, and salt in
a large bowl, then rub in the butter. Make a well in the center, then add the honey and
enough milk, mixing to form a soft dough.

2   Turn the dough onto a lightly floured worktop and knead until smooth and elastic. Shape
the dough into an oblong, then place it in the loaf pan. Using a sharp knife, score a pattern
over the top surface of the dough, if desired. Cover and let rise in a warm place until
doubled in size.

3   Meanwhile, preheat the oven to 230°C/450°F/gas mark 8. Dust the top of the loaf with
a little flour. Bake for 15 minutes, then reduce the oven temperature to 200°C/400°F/gas
mark 6 and bake for a further 15–20 minutes, or until the bread is risen, lightly browned,
and sounds hollow when tapped underneath. Turn out and cool on a wire rack.

TO MAKE IN BREADMAKER, *use quantities as listed in main recipe but amend following ingredients*
and use 1¼ cups milk, 1¼ teaspoons salt, and 2 teaspoons fast-action dried yeast, and add
2 teaspoons light soft brown sugar. Add ingredients to breadmaker in order specified in your
instruction book. Use Wholewheat or similar setting for this recipe.

004 Home-style malted grain bread

PREPARATION TIME *20 minutes, plus rising* **COOKING TIME** *30–35 minutes*
MAKES *1 large loaf (serves 14–16)*

2½ cups strong malted grain flour
2½ cups strong wholewheat flour, plus
    extra for dusting
2 teaspoons salt
2 tablespoons butter, diced

2 teaspoons easy-blend dried yeast
1 tablespoon malt extract
⅔ cup warm milk
About 1¼ cups warm water

1   Grease or flour a cookie sheet and set aside. Mix the flours and salt in a large bowl, then
rub in the butter. Stir in the yeast. Make a well in the center, then add the malt extract,
milk, and enough water, mixing to form a soft dough.

2   Turn the dough onto a lightly floured worktop and knead until smooth and elastic. Shape
the dough into a round, then place it in a lightly oiled bowl, cover and let rise in a warm
place until doubled in size.

3   Punch down the dough on a lightly floured worktop and shape into a large round. Place on
the cookie sheet, cover and let rise again for about 30 minutes, or until doubled in size.
Using a sharp knife, cut a cross on the top of the loaf and dust with a little flour.

4   Meanwhile, preheat the oven to 230°C/450°F/gas mark 8. Bake the loaf for 15 minutes,
then reduce the oven temperature to 200°C/400°F/gas mark 6 and bake for a further
15–20 minutes, or until the bread is risen, lightly browned, and sounds hollow when
tapped underneath. Transfer to a wire rack to cool. Serve in slices.

VARIATIONS *Use all strong malted grain flour in place of the mixed flours, if preferred.*
Alternatively, use all-purpose flour in place of wholewheat flour.

005 Family white bread

PREPARATION TIME *20 minutes, plus rising* **COOKING TIME** *30–35 minutes*
MAKES *1 large loaf (serves 14–16)*

4¾ cups strong white flour, plus extra
    for dusting
2 teaspoons salt
2 tablespoons butter, diced

1 sachet (¼oz) easy-blend dried yeast
1 teaspoon superfine sugar
⅔ cup warm milk
About 1¼ cups warm water

1   Grease or flour a cookie sheet and set aside. Sift the flour and salt into a large bowl, then rub in the butter. Stir in the yeast and sugar. Make a well in the center, then add the milk and enough water, mixing to form a soft dough.

2   Turn the dough onto a lightly floured worktop and knead until smooth and elastic. Shape the dough into a round, then place it in a lightly oiled bowl, cover and let rise in a warm place until doubled in size.

3   Punch down the dough on a lightly floured worktop and shape into a large oval. Place on the cookie sheet, cover and let rise again for about 30 minutes, or until doubled in size.

4   Meanwhile, preheat the oven to 230°C/450°F/gas mark 8. Using a sharp knife, slash the top of the loaf diagonally 3 or 4 times, then dust with a little flour. Bake the loaf for 10 minutes, then reduce the oven temperature to 200°C/400°F/gas mark 6 and bake for a further 20–25 minutes, or until the bread is risen, golden brown, and sounds hollow when tapped underneath. Transfer to a wire rack to cool. Serve in slices.

006 Quick country wholewheat bread

PREPARATION TIME *20 minutes, plus rising* **COOKING TIME** *30–35 minutes*
MAKES *2 loaves (each loaf serves 12–14)*

4¾ cups strong wholewheat flour
2 teaspoons salt
1 teaspoon superfine sugar
2 tablespoons butter, diced

1 sachet (¼oz) fast-action dried yeast
About 2 cups warm water
A little milk, for glazing
2 tablespoons cracked wheat

1   Grease or flour 2 cookie sheets or two 2lb loaf pans and set aside. Mix the flour, salt, and sugar in a large bowl, then rub in the butter. Stir in the yeast. Make a well in the center, then add enough water, mixing to form a soft dough.

2   Turn the dough onto a lightly floured worktop and knead until smooth and elastic. Divide the dough in half and either shape each portion into a round and place on the cookie sheets, or shape each portion into an oblong and place in the loaf pans. Cover and let rise in a warm place until doubled in size.

3   Meanwhile, preheat the oven to 230°C/450°F/gas mark 8. Lightly brush the top of each loaf with a little milk, then sprinkle with cracked wheat. Bake the loaves for 15 minutes, then reduce the oven temperature to 200°C/400°F/gas mark 6 and bake for a further 15–20 minutes, or until the bread is risen, lightly browned, and sounds hollow when tapped underneath. Transfer or turn out onto a wire rack and let cool. Serve in slices.

007 Malted wholegrain cobb

PREPARATION TIME *20 minutes, plus rising* **COOKING TIME** *30–35 minutes*
MAKES *1 large loaf (serves 14–16)*

3 cups strong malted grain flour
1½ cups strong wholewheat flour
2 teaspoons salt
2 tablespoons butter, diced
2 teaspoons easy-blend dried yeast

⅔ cup warm milk, plus extra for glazing
2 tablespoons malt extract
About 1¼ cups warm water
Kibbled or cracked wheat, for sprinkling

1 Grease or flour a cookie sheet and set aside. Mix the flours and salt in a large bowl, then rub in the butter. Stir in the yeast. Make a well in the center, then add the milk, malt extract, and enough water, mixing to form a soft dough.

2 Turn the dough onto a lightly floured worktop and knead until smooth and elastic. Shape the dough into a round, then place it in a lightly oiled bowl, cover and let rise in a warm place until doubled in size.

3 Punch down the dough on a floured worktop and shape into a large round. Place on the cookie sheet, cover and let rise again for about 30 minutes, or until doubled in size.

4 Meanwhile, preheat the oven to 230°C/450°F/gas mark 8. Using a sharp knife, slash the top of the loaf into a cross shape, brush with a little milk, and sprinkle with kibbled wheat.

5 Bake for 10 minutes, then reduce the oven temperature to 200°C/400°F/gas mark 6 and bake for a further 20–25 minutes, or until the bread is risen, lightly browned, and sounds hollow when tapped underneath. Transfer to a wire rack to cool. Serve in slices.

008 Multigrain harvest loaf

PREPARATION TIME *25 minutes, plus rising* **COOKING TIME** *30–35 minutes*
MAKES *2 loaves (each loaf serves 10–12)*

2 cups strong wholewheat flour
2 cups strong malted grain flour
⅔ cup rye flour
2 teaspoons salt
2 tablespoons butter, diced
1 teaspoon light soft brown sugar
1 sachet (¼oz) easy-blend dried yeast
½ cup rolled oats

⅓ cup mixed seeds, such as sesame, sunflower, and poppy seeds, plus extra for sprinkling
2 tablespoons malt extract
⅔ cup warm milk, plus extra for glazing
About 1½ cups warm water

1   Grease or flour 2 cookie sheets and set aside. Mix the flours and salt in a large bowl, then rub in the butter. Stir in the sugar, yeast, oats, and mixed seeds. Make a well in the center, then add the malt extract, milk, and enough water, mixing to form a soft dough.

2   Turn the dough onto a lightly floured worktop and knead until smooth and elastic. Shape the dough into a round, then place it in a lightly oiled bowl, cover and let rise in a warm place until doubled in size.

3   Punch down the dough on a lightly floured worktop, divide it in half and shape each portion into a round or oval. Place on the cookie sheets, cover and let rise again for about 30 minutes, or until doubled in size.

4   Meanwhile, preheat the oven to 220°C/425°F/gas mark 7. Gently brush the top of each loaf with a little milk and sprinkle with some extra mixed seeds. Using a sharp knife, cut a slash down the center of each loaf, if desired.

5   Bake the loaves for 15 minutes, then reduce the oven temperature to 190°C/375°F/gas mark 5 and bake for a further 15–20 minutes, or until the bread is risen, lightly browned, and sounds hollow when tapped underneath. Transfer to a wire rack to cool.

VARIATION *Use two 2lb loaf pans in place of cookie sheets. Divide the punched down dough in half, shape each portion into an oblong, and place in the pans. Let rise, then bake as above.*

009 Oatmeal bread

PREPARATION TIME *20 minutes, plus rising* **COOKING TIME** *30–35 minutes*
MAKES *1 loaf (serves 12–14)*

3 cups strong wholewheat flour
1½ cups medium oatmeal
⅔ cup pinhead or fine oatmeal
1 sachet (¼oz) fast-action dried yeast
2 teaspoons salt

1 tablespoon clear honey
⅔ cup warm milk
About 1 cup warm water
Rolled oats, for sprinkling

1   Grease a cookie sheet and set aside. Mix the flour, oatmeals, yeast, and salt in a bowl. Make a well in the center, then add the honey, milk, and enough water, mixing to form a soft dough.

2   Turn the dough onto a lightly floured worktop and knead until smooth and elastic. Shape the dough into a round or oval and place on the cookie sheet. Cover and let rise in a warm place until doubled in size.

3   Meanwhile, preheat the oven to 230°C/450°F/gas mark 8. Lightly brush the top of the loaf with water and sprinkle with rolled oats. Bake for 15 minutes, then reduce the oven temperature to 200°C/400°F/gas mark 6 and bake for a further 15–20 minutes, or until the bread is risen, golden brown, and sounds hollow when tapped underneath. Transfer to a wire rack to cool. Serve in slices.

010 Traditional loaf

PREPARATION TIME *20 minutes, plus rising* COOKING TIME *30–35 minutes*
MAKES *2 loaves (each loaf serves 12–14)*

2½ cups strong white flour
2½ cups strong wholewheat flour, plus
   extra for dusting
2 teaspoons salt

1 teaspoon superfine sugar
1 sachet (¼oz) fast-action dried yeast
1 egg, lightly beaten
About 1½ cups warm milk

1 Grease two 2lb loaf pans and set aside. Sift the white flour into a large bowl, then stir in the wholewheat flour, salt, sugar, and yeast. Make a well in the center, then add the egg and enough milk, mixing to form a soft dough.

2 Turn the dough onto a lightly floured worktop and knead until smooth and elastic. Divide it in half, then pat each portion into a rectangle shape the length of the pans. Roll up each portion of dough from one short end. Place into the loaf pans, seam-sides down, and tuck the ends under. Cover and let rise in a warm place until doubled in size.

3 Meanwhile, preheat the oven to 230°C/450°F/gas mark 8. Lightly dust the tops of the loaves with a little wholewheat flour. Using a sharp knife, cut a deep slash lengthwise along the center of the top of each loaf.

4 Bake the loaves for 15 minutes, then reduce the oven temperature to 200°C/400°F/gas mark 6 and bake for a further 15–20 minutes, or until the bread is risen, lightly browned, and sounds hollow when tapped underneath. Turn out and cool on a wire rack.

VARIATION *If you do not have suitable loaf pans, simply shape the dough into 2 rounds, ovals, or shapes of your choice and place on greased cookie sheets. Let rise and bake as above.*

011 Bloomer

PREPARATION TIME *25 minutes, plus rising* COOKING TIME *40–50 minutes*
MAKES *1 large loaf (serves 14–16)*

4¾ cups strong white flour
2 teaspoons salt
1 teaspoon superfine sugar
1½ teaspoons easy-blend dried yeast

2 tablespoons butter, diced
⅔ cup warm milk
About 1¼ cups warm water
1 egg

1 Grease or flour a cookie sheet and set aside. Sift the flour and salt into a large bowl, stir in the sugar and yeast, then rub in the butter. Make a well in the center, then add the milk and enough water, mixing to form a soft dough.

2 Turn the dough onto a lightly floured worktop and knead until smooth and elastic. Shape the dough into a round, then place it in a lightly oiled bowl, cover and let rise in a warm place until doubled in size.

3 Punch down the dough on a lightly floured worktop, then roll out to form a rectangle about 1in thick. Starting from a short side, roll up the dough like a jelly roll, to make a short, thick roll, pinching it together along the seam after each roll. On the final seam, pinch the dough together, then neatly tuck the ends under. Place the loaf on the cookie sheet, seam-side down, cover and let rise again until doubled in size.

4 Meanwhile, preheat the oven to 230°C/450°F/gas mark 8. In a small bowl, beat the egg with 1–2 tablespoons water, then brush over the top of the dough. Using a sharp knife, make 5 or 6 deep slashes diagonally across the top of the loaf at regular intervals. Brush the slits with egg glaze.

5 Bake the loaf for 15 minutes, then reduce the oven temperature to 200°C/400°F/gas mark 6 and bake for a further 25–35 minutes, or until the bread is risen, golden brown, and sounds hollow when tapped underneath. Transfer to a wire rack to cool. Serve in slices.

VARIATION *Brush with salted water before baking instead of using the egg glaze, if desired.*

Cottage loaf

PREPARATION TIME *20 minutes, plus rising* **COOKING TIME** *30–35 minutes*
MAKES *1 large loaf (serves 14–16)*

**4¾ cups strong white flour, plus extra
    for dusting**
2 teaspoons salt
2 tablespoons butter, diced

1 sachet (¼oz) easy-blend dried yeast
1 teaspoon superfine sugar
About 1¾ cups warm water
Beaten egg, to glaze

1   Grease or flour 2 cookie sheets and set aside. Sift the flour and salt into a large bowl,
    then rub in the butter. Stir in the yeast and sugar. Make a well in the center, then add
    enough water, mixing to form a fairly firm dough. To ensure a good-shaped cottage loaf,
    the bread dough for this recipe needs to be firm enough so that the bottom round of dough
    can support the weight of the top piece of dough without sagging. However, if you do end
    up with a slightly misshapen loaf, don't worry, it will still taste delicious!

2   Turn the dough onto a lightly floured worktop and knead until smooth and elastic. Shape
    the dough into a round, then place it in a lightly oiled bowl, cover and let rise in a warm
    place until doubled in size.

3   Punch down the dough on a lightly floured worktop, then cut off one third of the dough.
    Shape both pieces of dough into plump balls and place each one on a cookie sheet. Cover
    and let rise in a warm place until doubled in size.

4   Meanwhile, preheat the oven to 220°C/425°F/gas mark 7. Gently flatten each ball of
    dough and carefully place the smaller ball on top of the larger. Gently push the floured
    handle of a wooden spoon down through the center of the dough to join both pieces
    together, then slightly enlarge the hole with your fingers. Let rest for 5–10 minutes.

5   Lightly brush the loaf with beaten egg and dust with a little flour. Using a very sharp knife,
    make slashes at regular intervals around the top of the bread and around the base. Bake
    the loaf for about 30–35 minutes, or until the bread is golden brown, and sounds hollow
    when tapped underneath. Transfer to a wire rack to cool. Serve in slices.

013 Soft grain cobb

PREPARATION TIME *20 minutes, plus rising* **COOKING TIME** *30–35 minutes*
MAKES *2 loaves (each loaf serves 8–10)*

4¾ cups strong soft-grain white flour,
   plus extra for dusting
2 teaspoons salt
1 tablespoon butter, diced

2 teaspoons easy-blend dried yeast
1 teaspoon superfine sugar
About 2 cups warm water

1   Grease or flour 2 cookie sheets and set aside. Sift the flour and salt into a large bowl, then rub in the butter. Stir in the yeast and sugar. Make a well in the center, then add enough water, mixing to form a soft dough.

2   Turn the dough onto a lightly floured worktop and knead until smooth and elastic. Shape the dough into a round, then place it in a lightly oiled bowl, cover and let rise in a warm place until doubled in size.

3   Punch down the dough on a lightly floured worktop, then divide it in half. Shape each piece of dough into a round cobb shape, then place each one on a cookie sheet. Cover and let rise again for about 30 minutes, or until doubled in size.

4   Meanwhile, preheat the oven to 230°C/450°F/gas mark 8. Dust each loaf with flour. Bake the loaves for 15 minutes, then reduce the oven temperature to 200°C/400°F/gas mark 6 and bake for a further 15–20 minutes, or until the bread is golden brown, and sounds hollow when tapped underneath. Transfer to a wire rack to cool. Serve in slices.

014 Milk loaf

PREPARATION TIME *20 minutes, plus rising* **COOKING TIME** *30–40 minutes*
MAKES *2 loaves (each loaf serves 12–14)*

4¾ cups strong white flour
2 teaspoons salt
2 tablespoons butter, diced

1 teaspoon superfine sugar
1 sachet (¼oz) easy-blend dried yeast
About 2 cups warm milk

1   Grease two 2lb loaf pans (or 2 cookie sheets) and set aside. Sift the flour and salt into a large bowl, then rub in the butter. Stir in the sugar and yeast. Make a well in the center, then add enough milk, mixing to form a soft dough.

2   Turn the dough onto a lightly floured worktop and knead until smooth and elastic. Shape the dough into a round, then place it in a lightly oiled bowl, cover and let rise in a warm place until doubled in size.

3   Punch down the dough on a lightly floured worktop, divide the dough in half, and shape each half into an oblong (or round). Press into the pans (or place on the cookie sheets), cover and let rise again for about 30 minutes, or until doubled in size.

4   Meanwhile, preheat the oven to 200°C/400°F/gas mark 6. Bake the loaves for 30–40 minutes, or until the bread is risen, golden brown, and sounds hollow when tapped underneath. Turn out and cool on a wire rack. Serve in slices.

015 Crown loaf

PREPARATION TIME *25 minutes, plus rising* COOKING TIME *30–40 minutes* MAKES *1 loaf (serves 10)*

4¾ cups strong wholewheat flour, plus
 extra for dusting
2 teaspoons salt
2 tablespoons butter, diced

1 teaspoon superfine sugar
2 teaspoons easy-blend dried yeast
⅔ cup warm milk
About 1¼ cups warm water

1 Grease a deep 9-inch round cake pan and set aside. Mix the flour and salt in a large bowl, then rub in the butter. Stir in the sugar and yeast. Make a well in the center, then add the milk and enough water, mixing to form a soft dough.

2 Turn the dough onto a lightly floured worktop and knead until smooth and elastic. Shape the dough into a round, then place it in a lightly oiled bowl, cover and let rise in a warm place until doubled in size.

3 Punch down the dough on a lightly floured worktop and divide into 10 equal pieces. Roll each portion of dough into a ball. Arrange 7 dough balls around the inside edge of the pan, then fit the remaining 3 into the center. Cover and let rise again for about 30 minutes, or until doubled in size.

4 Meanwhile, preheat the oven to 200°C/400°F/gas mark 6. Dust the top of the loaf with a little flour. Bake the loaf for 30–40 minutes, or until the bread is risen, lightly browned, and sounds hollow when tapped underneath. Cool in the pan for a few minutes, then turn out and cool completely on a wire rack. Break into portions to serve.

VARIATION *Brush the top of the risen loaf with a little milk and sprinkle with poppy seeds or sesame seeds before baking.*

016 ⌂Malted grain herb round

PREPARATION TIME *25 minutes, plus rising* COOKING TIME *30–35 minutes*
MAKES *1 loaf (serves 8–10)*

3 cups strong malted grain flour
1 teaspoon salt
2 tablespoons butter, diced
1½ teaspoons fast-action dried yeast
½ teaspoon superfine sugar
1 tablespoon chopped fresh mixed herbs,
 such as chives, sage, and marjoram

1 tablespoon chopped fresh parsley
1½ teaspoons freshly ground black
 pepper
About 1¼ cups warm water
Milk, to glaze
Sesame seeds, to sprinkle

1 Grease or flour a cookie sheet and set aside. Mix the flour and salt in a large bowl, then rub in the butter. Stir in the yeast, sugar, chopped herbs, and black pepper. Make a well in the center, then add enough water, mixing to form a soft dough.

2 Turn the dough onto a lightly floured worktop and knead until smooth and elastic. Shape the dough into a round and place it on the cookie sheet. Cover and let rise in a warm place for about 1 hour, or until doubled in size.

3 Meanwhile, preheat the oven to 230°C/450°F/gas mark 8. Brush the top of the loaf with a little milk and sprinkle with sesame seeds. Bake the loaf for 10 minutes, then reduce the oven temperature to 200°C/400°F/gas mark 6 and bake for a further 20–25 minutes, or until the bread is risen, golden brown, and sounds hollow when tapped underneath. Transfer to a wire rack to cool. Serve in slices.

TO MAKE IN BREADMAKER, *use quantities as listed in main recipe but amend following ingredients and use 1¼ cups water, 2 teaspoons salt, and 2 teaspoons superfine sugar, and add 1 tablespoon dried skim milk powder. Add ingredients to breadmaker in order specified in your instruction book. Use Wholewheat or similar setting for this recipe.*

017 Braided three-seed ring

PREPARATION TIME *25 minutes, plus rising* **COOKING TIME** *30–35 minutes*
MAKES *1 large loaf (serves 14–16)*

4¾ cups strong white flour
2 teaspoons salt
2 tablespoons butter, diced
1 teaspoon superfine sugar
2 teaspoons easy-blend dried yeast
3 tablespoons sesame seeds

3 tablespoons sunflower seeds
3 tablespoons poppy seeds or linseeds
About 2 cups warm water
A little milk, for glazing
Extra mixed seeds, for sprinkling

1 Grease or flour a cookie sheet and set aside. Sift the flour and salt into a large bowl, then rub in the butter. Stir in the sugar, yeast, and seeds. Make a well in the center, then add enough water, mixing to form a soft dough.

2 Turn the dough onto a lightly floured worktop and knead until smooth and elastic. Shape the dough into a round, then place it in a lightly oiled bowl, cover and let rise in a warm place until doubled in size.

3 Punch down the dough on a lightly floured worktop and divide into three equal portions. Roll each portion into a long sausage or rope shape, each about 12 inches long, and place them side by side, pinching them together at one end to seal. Loosely braid the ropes of dough together, then pinch them together at the other end. Brush both ends with a little milk, then shape the braided dough into a ring, pressing the ends together to seal.

4 Place the braided ring on the cookie sheet, cover and let rise again for about 30 minutes, or until doubled in size.

5 Meanwhile, preheat the oven to 200°C/400°F/gas mark 6. Brush the braided ring with a little milk and sprinkle with some extra seeds. Bake the loaf for 30–35 minutes, or until the bread ring is risen, golden brown, and sounds hollow when tapped underneath. Transfer to a wire rack to cool. Serve in slices.

018 Spelt bread

PREPARATION TIME *20 minutes, plus rising* **COOKING TIME** *40–50 minutes*
MAKES *2 loaves (each loaf serves 12–14)*

5½ cups spelt flour
2 teaspoons salt
1 sachet (¼oz) fast-action dried yeast
2 tablespoons light olive oil

1 teaspoon clear honey
2½ cups warm water
Sesame seeds, for sprinkling (optional)

1 Grease two 2lb loaf pans and set aside. Mix the flour and salt in a large bowl, then stir in the yeast. Make a well in the center, then add the oil, honey, and water and mix vigorously using your hand for about 5–10 minutes, or until the dough begins to leave the sides of the bowl clean—the dough may still be slightly sticky at this stage.

2 Transfer the dough to the loaf pans, filling each pan about half full and pushing the dough into the corners. Sprinkle with sesame seeds, if desired. Cover and let rise in a warm place for about 1 hour, or until the dough just reaches the top of the pan.

3 Meanwhile, preheat the oven to 200°C/400°F/gas mark 6. Bake the loaves for 40–50 minutes, or until the bread is lightly browned, and sounds hollow when tapped underneath. The bread will have a flattish top, rather than a high rise. Turn out and cool on a wire rack. Serve in slices.

019 Potato bread

PREPARATION TIME *25 minutes, plus rising* COOKING TIME *30–40 minutes*
MAKES *1 loaf (serves 8–10)*

**1 large floury potato such as Yellow Finn
or California long white, about
12oz in weight
3⅔ cups strong white or wholewheat
flour, plus extra for dusting
1 sachet (¼oz) easy-blend dried yeast
2 teaspoons salt**

**½ cup mature cheddar cheese, finely
grated
1½ teaspoons dried herbes de Provence
A few turns of freshly ground black
pepper
About ¾ cup warm water**

1 Grease or flour a cookie sheet and set aside. Peel and dice the potato, then cook it in a saucepan of boiling water for 10–15 minutes, or until tender. Drain well, mash thoroughly, and set aside to cool slightly.

2 Mix the flour, yeast, salt, cheese, dried herbs, and black pepper in a large bowl. Add the mashed potatoes and work into the flour mixture using your fingers. Make a well in the center, then gradually add enough water, mixing to form a soft dough.

3 Turn the dough onto a lightly floured worktop and knead until smooth and elastic. Shape the dough into a round, then place it in a lightly oiled bowl, cover and let rise in a warm place until doubled in size.

4 Punch down the dough on a lightly floured worktop, then shape into an oval or round and place it on the cookie sheet. Cover and let rise again until doubled in size.

5 Meanwhile, preheat the oven to 200°C/400°F/gas mark 6. Dust the top of the loaf with a little flour. Bake the loaf for 30–40 minutes, or until the bread is risen, golden brown, and sounds hollow when tapped underneath. Transfer to a wire rack to cool. Serve in slices.

VARIATIONS *Use emmental or fresh Parmesan cheese in place of the cheddar. Stir ½–1 teaspoon ground caraway seeds into the dry ingredients in place of the dried herbs.*

020 ▣ Barley bread

PREPARATION TIME *20 minutes, plus rising* COOKING TIME *30–35 minutes*
MAKES *1 loaf (serves 10–12)*

**1½ cups strong wholewheat flour
1⅓ cups barley flour
2 teaspoons salt**

**1 teaspoon superfine sugar
3 teaspoons easy-blend dried yeast
About 1¼ cups warm water**

1 Grease a 2lb loaf pan and set aside. Mix the flours and salt in a large bowl, then stir in the sugar and yeast. Make a well in the center, then add enough water, mixing to form a soft dough.

2 Turn the dough onto a lightly floured worktop and knead until smooth and elastic. Shape the dough into a round, then place it in a lightly oiled bowl, cover and let rise in a warm place until doubled in size (this may take up to 2–3 hours).

3 Punch down the dough on a lightly floured worktop and shape into an oblong. Place in the loaf pan, cover and let rise again for about 1 hour, or until doubled in size.

4 Meanwhile, preheat the oven to 230°C/450°F/gas mark 8. Bake the loaf for 10 minutes, then reduce the oven temperature to 200°C/400°F/gas mark 6 and bake for a further 20–25 minutes, or until the bread is risen, lightly browned, and sounds hollow when tapped underneath. Turn out and cool on a wire rack. Serve in slices.

TO MAKE IN BREADMAKER, *use quantities as listed in main recipe but amend following ingredients and use 1½ cups water, 2¾ cups strong brown flour, ¾ cup barley flour, 2 teaspoons superfine sugar, and 1½ teaspoons fast-action dried yeast. Add ingredients to breadmaker in order specified in your instruction book. Use Dough setting for this recipe, then continue as above from Step 3 of main recipe.*

021 ▣ Flowerpot bread

PREPARATION TIME *20 minutes, plus rising* **COOKING TIME** *35–40 minutes* **MAKES** *2 loaves*

3 cups strong wholewheat flour
1½ teaspoons salt
2 tablespoons butter, diced
2 teaspoons easy-blend dried yeast
1 teaspoon superfine sugar
⅓ cup barley flakes,

plus extra for sprinkling
1–2 tablespoons chopped fresh mixed herbs
1 tablespoon malt extract
About 1 cup warm water
Milk, for glazing

1 You will need 2 tempered earthenware/terracotta flowerpots (about 5½ inches in diameter and 4½ inches high), to mold the bread. To temper (seal) the new perfectly clean pots, brush liberally with vegetable oil inside and out, then place in a hot oven (200°C/400°F/gas mark 6) for about 30 minutes. Let cool, then repeat this procedure until the pots are impregnated with oil. They should now only need a little greasing before use. Do not wash them after use, simply wipe clean with paper towels.

2 Grease the flowerpots; set aside. Mix the flour and salt in a bowl; rub in the butter. Add the yeast, sugar, barley flakes, and herbs. Mix in the malt extract and enough water to form a soft dough.

3 Turn the dough onto a floured worktop and knead until smooth. Shape into a round, then place in a lightly oiled bowl, cover and let rise in a warm place until doubled in size.

4 Punch down the dough on a floured worktop and divide in half. Shape and fit each piece of dough into a flowerpot—the dough should roughly half-fill the pot. Cover and let rise again for 45–60 minutes, or until the dough almost reaches the top of the flowerpots.

5 Meanwhile, preheat the oven to 200°C/400°F/gas mark 6. Brush the tops of the loaves with a little milk and sprinkle with extra barley flakes.

6 Bake for about 35–40 minutes, or until the bread is risen and sounds hollow when tapped underneath. Turn the loaves out and place on a wire rack to cool. Serve in slices.

TO MAKE IN BREADMAKER, *use quantities as listed in main recipe but amend following ingredients and use 1½ cups water, 2 teaspoons superfine sugar, and use fast-action dried yeast. Add ingredients to breadmaker in order specified in your instruction book. Use Dough setting, then continue as above from Step 4 of main recipe.*

022 Sweet potato bread

PREPARATION TIME *35 minutes, plus rising* COOKING TIME *30–35 minutes*
MAKES *1 large loaf (serves 14–16)*

1 large sweet potato
3⅔ cups strong white flour
2 teaspoons salt
1 sachet (¼oz) easy-blend dried yeast

1½ teaspoons caraway seeds, plus extra
  for sprinkling
A few turns of freshly ground black
  pepper
About ¾ cup warm water

1 Grease or flour a cookie sheet and set aside. Peel and dice the sweet potato, then cook it in a saucepan of boiling water for about 15 minutes, or until tender. Drain well, mash thoroughly, and set aside to cool.

2 Sift the flour and salt into a large bowl, then add the mashed sweet potato, rubbing it loosely into the flour. Stir in the yeast, caraway seeds, and black pepper, then make a well in the center and add enough water, mixing to form a soft dough.

3 Turn the dough onto a lightly floured worktop and knead until smooth and elastic. Shape the dough into a round, then place it in a lightly oiled bowl, cover and let rise in a warm place until doubled in size.

4 Punch down the dough on a lightly floured worktop and shape into a large round or oval loaf. Place on the cookie sheet, cover and let rise again for about 30 minutes, or until doubled in size.

5 Meanwhile, preheat the oven to 200°C/400°F/gas mark 6. Lightly brush the top of the loaf with water and sprinkle with caraway seeds. Using a sharp knife, slash the top of the loaf with 3–4 diagonal cuts to make a criss-cross effect.

6 Bake the loaf for 30–35 minutes, or until the bread is risen, golden brown, and sounds hollow when tapped underneath. Transfer to a wire rack to cool. Serve in slices.

023 Pumpkin seed bread

PREPARATION TIME *20 minutes, plus rising* COOKING TIME *30–35 minutes*
MAKES *1 loaf (serves 12–14)*

2½ cups strong white flour
2 teaspoons salt
1½ cups rye flour
1 sachet (¼oz) fast-action dried yeast
2 tablespoons olive oil
⅔ cup warm milk

About ⅔ cup warm water
¾ cup pumpkin seeds, roughly chopped
2 teaspoons coriander seeds, roughly
  crushed
1 tablespoon fennel seeds

1 Grease or flour a cookie sheet and set aside. Sift the white flour and salt into a bowl, then stir in the rye flour. Stir in the yeast. Make a well in the center, then add the oil, milk, and enough water, mixing to form a soft dough.

2 Turn the dough onto a lightly floured worktop and knead until smooth and elastic. Sprinkle the pumpkin, coriander, and fennel seeds over the dough, then gently knead them into the dough until evenly distributed.

3 Shape the dough into a round or oval and place it on the cookie sheet. Cover and let rise in a warm place until doubled in size.

4 Meanwhile, preheat the oven to 220°C/425°F/gas mark 7. Using a sharp knife, cut several criss-cross slashes in the top of the dough to make a diamond pattern. Bake the loaf for 15 minutes, then reduce the oven temperature to 190°C/375°F/gas mark 5 and bake for a further 15–20 minutes, or until the bread is risen, lightly browned, and sounds hollow when tapped underneath. Transfer to a wire rack to cool. Serve in slices.

024 🄰 Braided herb bread

PREPARATION TIME *30 minutes, plus rising* **COOKING TIME** *35–45 minutes* **MAKES** *1 loaf (serves 10)*

3 cups strong white flour
1½ teaspoons salt
2 tablespoons butter, diced
1 sachet (¼oz) easy-blend dried yeast
¾ cup mature cheddar cheese,
    finely grated

1 tablespoon dried herbes de Provence
⅔ cup warm milk, plus extra for glazing
About ⅔ cup warm water

1. Grease or flour a cookie sheet and set aside. Sift the flour and salt into a large bowl, then rub in the butter. Stir in the yeast, cheese, and dried herbs. Make a well in the center, then add the milk and enough water, mixing to form a soft dough.
2. Turn the dough onto a lightly floured worktop and knead until smooth and elastic. Shape the dough into a round, then place it in a lightly oiled bowl, cover and let rise in a warm place until doubled in size.
3. Punch down the dough on a lightly floured worktop, then divide it in half. Roll each piece of dough into a long sausage or rope shape and place them side by side, pinching them together at one end to seal. Loosely braid the ropes of dough together, then pinch them together at the other end.
4. Place the braid on the cookie sheet. Cover and let rise again for about 30 minutes, or until doubled in size.
5. Meanwhile, preheat the oven to 190°C/375°F/gas mark 5. Lightly brush the braid with a little extra milk. Bake for 35–45 minutes, or until the bread is risen, golden brown, and sounds hollow when tapped underneath. Transfer to a wire rack to cool. Serve in slices.

TO MAKE IN BREADMAKER, *use quantities as listed in main recipe but amend following ingredients and use ⅔ cup milk, ⅓ cup water, 1¼ teaspoons salt, and 1½ teaspoons fast-action dried yeast, and add 1½ teaspoons superfine sugar. Add ingredients to breadmaker in order specified in your instruction book. Use Dough setting for this recipe, then continue as above from Step 3 of main recipe.*

025 Rustic walnut bread

PREPARATION TIME *25 minutes, plus rising* **COOKING TIME** *30–35 minutes*
MAKES *2 loaves (each loaf serves 10–12)*

4¾ cups strong white flour, plus extra
    for dusting
2 teaspoons salt
2 tablespoons butter, diced
2 teaspoons easy-blend dried yeast

1¼ cups walnut halves, roughly chopped
3 tablespoons chopped fresh flat-leaf
    parsley
About 2 cups warm water

1. Grease or flour 2 cookie sheets and set aside. Sift the flour and salt into a bowl, then rub in the butter. Stir in the yeast, chopped walnuts and parsley. Make a well in the center, then add enough water, mixing to form a soft dough.
2. Turn the dough onto a lightly floured worktop and knead until smooth and elastic. Shape the dough into a round, then place it in a lightly oiled bowl, cover and let rise in a warm place until doubled in size.
3. Punch down the dough on a lightly floured worktop, then divide it in half. Shape each portion of dough into a round or oval and place on the cookie sheets. Cover and let rise again for about 30 minutes, or until doubled in size.
4. Preheat the oven to 220°C/425°F/gas mark 7. Lightly dust the loaves with a little extra flour and cut several slashes in the tops of the loaves to make a criss-cross pattern.
5. Bake the loaves for 10 minutes, then reduce the oven temperature to 190°C/375°F/gas mark 5 and bake for a further 20–25 minutes, or until the bread is risen, golden brown, and sounds hollow when tapped underneath. Transfer to a wire rack to cool. Serve in slices.

026 Farmer's rye loaf

PREPARATION TIME *20 minutes, plus rising* **COOKING TIME** *35–40 minutes* **MAKES** *1 loaf (serves 10)*

2½ cups strong white flour	1 sachet (¼oz) easy-blend dried yeast
2 teaspoons salt	1 tablespoon molasses
1½ cups rye flour	⅔ cup warm milk
2 tablespoons butter, diced	About ⅔ cup warm water

1 Grease or flour a cookie sheet and set aside. Sift the white flour and salt into a bowl, then stir in the rye flour. Rub the butter into the flour, then stir in the yeast. Make a well in the center, then add the molasses, milk, and enough water, mixing to form a soft dough.
2 Turn the dough onto a lightly floured worktop and knead until smooth and elastic. Shape the dough into a round, then place it in a lightly oiled bowl, cover and let rise in a warm place until doubled in size.
3 Punch down the dough on a lightly floured worktop, then shape into an oval or round and place it on the cookie sheet. Cover and let rise again until doubled in size.
4 Meanwhile, preheat the oven to 200°C/400°F/gas mark 6. Using a sharp knife, cut several slashes in the top of the dough.
5 Bake the loaf for 35–40 minutes, or until the bread is risen, lightly browned, and sounds hollow when tapped underneath. Transfer to a wire rack to cool. Serve in slices.

VARIATION *Just before baking, lightly brush the top of the loaf with milk and sprinkle with caraway, fennel, or sesame seeds, if desired.*

027 ▣ Rustic rye bread

PREPARATION TIME *20 minutes, plus rising* **COOKING TIME** *35–40 minutes* **MAKES** *1 loaf (serves 10)*

2¾ cups strong wholewheat flour, plus extra for dusting	2 teaspoons easy-blend dried yeast
1¼ cups rye flour	1 tablespoon molasses
2 teaspoons salt	About 1¼ cups warm milk

1 Grease or flour a cookie sheet and set aside. Mix the flours, salt, and yeast in a large bowl. Make a well in the center, then add the molasses and enough milk, mixing to form a soft dough.
2 Turn the dough onto a lightly floured worktop and knead until smooth, firm, and elastic. Shape the dough into a round, then place it in a lightly oiled bowl, cover and let rise in a warm place until doubled in size.
3 Punch down the dough on a lightly floured worktop, then shape into a round or oval and place it on the cookie sheet. Cover and let rise again for about 1 hour, or until doubled in size.
4 Meanwhile, preheat the oven to 200°C/400°F/gas mark 6. Lightly dust the top of the loaf with a little flour. Bake the loaf for 35–40 minutes, or until the bread is risen, lightly browned, and sounds hollow when tapped underneath. Transfer to a wire rack to cool. Serve in slices.

TO MAKE IN BREADMAKER, *use quantities as listed in main recipe but amend following ingredients and use 1¾ cups milk, use fast-action dried yeast, and add 2 teaspoons light soft brown sugar. Add ingredients to breadmaker in order specified in your instruction book. Use Wholewheat or similar setting for this recipe.*

028 Rye and caraway bread

PREPARATION TIME *20 minutes, plus rising* **COOKING TIME** *30–40 minutes*
MAKES *1 loaf (serves 12–14)*

2½ cups rye flour
1½ cups strong white flour
2 teaspoons salt
2 tablespoons butter, diced
2 teaspoons easy-blend dried yeast
2 teaspoons caraway seeds

1 tablespoon molasses
1 tablespoon malt extract
⅔ cup warm milk
About ⅔ cup warm water
Wholewheat flour, for dusting (optional)

1 Grease or flour a cookie sheet and set aside. Mix the rye and white flours and salt in a large bowl, then rub in the butter. Stir in the yeast and caraway seeds. Make a well in the center, then add the molasses, malt extract, milk, and enough water, mixing to form a soft dough.

2 Turn the dough onto a lightly floured worktop and knead until smooth and elastic. Shape the dough into a round, then place it in a lightly oiled bowl, cover and let rise in a warm place until doubled in size.

3 Punch down the dough on a lightly floured worktop and shape into an oval. Place on the cookie sheet, cover and let rise again until doubled in size.

4 Meanwhile, preheat the oven to 200°C/400°F/gas mark 6. Using a sharp knife, cut several slashes in the top of the dough, then dust with a little wholewheat flour, if desired.

5 Bake for 30–40 minutes, or until the loaf sounds hollow when tapped underneath. Transfer to a wire rack to cool. Serve in slices.

029 Soy bread

PREPARATION TIME *20 minutes, plus rising* **COOKING TIME** *35–40 minutes*
MAKES *1 loaf (serves 10–12)*

3 cups strong white flour
½ cup soy flour
1 teaspoon salt
1 sachet (¼oz) fast-action dried yeast
½ cup mature cheddar cheese,
   finely grated

2 tablespoons sunflower oil
About 1¼ cups warm milk
Beaten egg, to glaze
Sesame seeds, for sprinkling

1   Grease a 2lb loaf pan and set aside. Mix the flours and salt in a large bowl, then stir in
    the yeast and cheese. Make a well in the center, then add the oil and enough milk, mixing
    to form a soft dough.
2   Turn the dough onto a lightly floured worktop and knead until smooth and elastic. Shape
    the dough into an oblong and place it in the loaf pan. Cover and let rise in a warm place
    until doubled in size.
3   Meanwhile, preheat the oven to 200°C/400°F/gas mark 6. Lightly brush the top of the loaf
    with beaten egg and sprinkle with sesame seeds. Using a pair of clean kitchen scissors,
    snip 3 or 4 crosses decoratively in the top of the dough, if desired.
4   Bake the loaf for 35–40 minutes, or until the bread is risen, golden brown, and sounds
    hollow when tapped underneath. Turn out and cool on a wire rack. Serve in slices.

VARIATION *Sprinkle the egg-glazed loaf with roasted peanut halves in place of sesame seeds.*

030 ◧ Caraway cheese loaf

PREPARATION TIME *25 minutes, plus rising* **COOKING TIME** *30 minutes*
MAKES *1 loaf (serves 10–12)*

3 cups strong white flour
1 teaspoon salt
1 cup mature cheddar cheese, finely
   grated
¼ cup fresh Parmesan cheese, grated

2 teaspoons mustard powder
3 teaspoons caraway seeds
1 sachet (¼oz) easy-blend dried yeast
About 1½ cups warm milk, plus
   extra for glazing

1   Grease or flour a cookie sheet and set aside. Sift the flour and salt into a large bowl, then
    stir in ¾ cup cheddar cheese, the Parmesan cheese, mustard powder, 2 teaspoons
    caraway seeds, and the yeast. Make a well in the center, then add enough milk, mixing to
    form a soft dough.
2   Turn the dough onto a lightly floured worktop and knead until smooth and elastic. Shape
    the dough into a round, then place it in a lightly oiled bowl, cover and let rise in a warm
    place until doubled in size.
3   Punch down the dough on a floured worktop and shape into a 6-inch round. Place on the
    cookie sheet, cover and let rise again for about 30 minutes, or until doubled in size.
4   Meanwhile, preheat the oven to 230°C/450°F/gas mark 8. Using a sharp knife, cut a
    shallow cross in the top of the loaf, then brush with a little milk. Mix together the
    remaining cheese and caraway seeds and sprinkle over the top of the loaf.
5   Bake the loaf for 10 minutes, then reduce the oven temperature to 200°C/400°F/gas mark
    6 and bake for a further 20 minutes, or until the bread is risen, golden brown, and sounds
    hollow when tapped underneath. Cover the loaf loosely with foil halfway through the
    cooking time if it is browning too much. Transfer to a wire rack to cool. Serve in slices.

TO MAKE IN BREADMAKER, *use quantities as listed in main recipe but amend following ingredients
and use 1¼ cups milk, 1¼ teaspoons salt, and 1½ teaspoons fast-action dried yeast, and add 1½
teaspoons superfine sugar. Use ¾ cup cheddar cheese and 2 teaspoons caraway seeds in dough;
use remaining cheese and seeds as instructed in Step 4 of main recipe. Add ingredients to
breadmaker in order specified in your instruction book. Use Dough setting, then continue as above
from Step 3 of main recipe.*

031 ▣ Cheese and grain cobb

PREPARATION TIME *25 minutes, plus rising* **COOKING TIME** *35–45 minutes*
MAKES *1 loaf (serves 10–12)*

3 cups strong malted grain flour
1½ teaspoons salt
2 tablespoons butter, diced
2 teaspoons easy-blend dried yeast
¾ cup mature cheddar, finely grated
2 teaspoons mustard powder

A few turns of freshly ground
 black pepper
About 1¼ cups warm milk, plus extra
 for glazing
Kibbled or cracked wheat, for sprinkling

1 Grease or flour a cookie sheet and set aside. Mix the flour and salt in a large bowl, then rub in the butter. Stir in the yeast, cheese, mustard powder, and black pepper. Make a well in the center, then add enough milk, mixing to form a soft dough.
2 Turn the dough onto a lightly floured worktop and knead until smooth and elastic. Shape the dough into a round, then place it in a lightly oiled bowl, cover and let rise in a warm place until doubled in size.
3 Punch down the dough on a floured worktop, then shape into a round cobb and place on the cookie sheet. Cover and let rise again for 30–45 minutes, or until doubled in size.
4 Meanwhile, preheat the oven to 190°C/375°F/gas mark 5. Lightly brush the top of the loaf with milk, then sprinkle with kibbled or cracked wheat. Bake the loaf for 35–45 minutes, or until the bread is risen, golden brown, and sounds hollow when tapped underneath. Transfer to a wire rack to cool. Serve in slices.

TO MAKE IN BREADMAKER, *use quantities as listed in main recipe but amend following ingredients and use 1¼ cups milk and 1½ teaspoons fast-action dried yeast, and add 1½ teaspoons granulated sugar. Add ingredients to breadmaker in order specified in your instruction book. Use Dough setting, then continue as above from Step 3 of main recipe.*

032 ▣ Cheese and sesame seed cobb

PREPARATION TIME *25 minutes, plus rising* **COOKING TIME** *35–45 minutes* **MAKES** *1 loaf (serves 10)*

3 cups strong white flour
1½ teaspoons salt
2 tablespoons butter, diced
2 teaspoons easy-blend dried yeast
¾ cup gruyère or emmental cheese,
 finely grated

2 teaspoons mustard powder
A few turns of freshly ground black
 pepper
About 1¼ cups warm milk, plus extra
 for glazing
Sesame seeds, for sprinkling

1 Grease or flour a cookie sheet and set aside. Sift the flour and salt into a large bowl, then rub in the butter. Stir in the yeast, cheese, mustard powder, and black pepper. Make a well in the center, then add enough milk, mixing to form a soft dough.
2 Turn the dough onto a lightly floured worktop and knead until smooth and elastic. Shape the dough into a round, then place it in a lightly oiled bowl, cover and let rise in a warm place until doubled in size.
3 Punch down the dough on a lightly floured worktop, then shape into a round cobb shape and place on the cookie sheet. Cover and let rise again for about 30 minutes, or until doubled in size.
4 Meanwhile, preheat the oven to 190°C/375°F/gas mark 5. Lightly brush the dough with a little milk and sprinkle with sesame seeds. Bake for 35–45 minutes, or until the bread is risen, golden brown, and sounds hollow when tapped underneath. Transfer to a wire rack to cool. Serve in slices.

TO MAKE IN BREADMAKER, *use quantities as listed in main recipe but amend following ingredients and use 1¼ cups milk, 1¼ teaspoons salt, and 1½ teaspoons fast-action dried yeast, and add 1½ teaspoons superfine sugar. Add ingredients to breadmaker in order specified in your instruction book. Use Dough setting for this recipe, then continue as above from Step 3 of main recipe.*

033 🔲 Cheese and poppyseed braid

PREPARATION TIME *30 minutes, plus rising* **COOKING TIME** *30–40 minutes* **MAKES** *1 loaf (serves 10)*

3 cups strong white flour
1½ teaspoons salt
2 tablespoons butter, diced
1 sachet (¼oz) easy-blend dried yeast
¾ cup mature cheddar cheese, finely
   grated

2 teaspoons mustard powder
A few turns of freshly ground
   black pepper
About 1¼ cups warm milk, plus extra
   for glazing
Poppy seeds, for sprinkling

1   Grease or flour a cookie sheet and set aside. Sift the flour and salt into a large bowl, then rub in the butter. Stir in the yeast, cheese, mustard powder, and black pepper. Make a well in the center, then add enough milk, mixing to form a soft dough.

2   Turn the dough onto a floured worktop and knead until smooth. Shape into a round, then place in a lightly oiled bowl, cover and let rise in a warm place until doubled in size.

3   Punch down the dough on a lightly floured worktop, then divide it in half. Roll each piece of dough into a long sausage or rope shape and place them side by side, pinching them together at one end to seal. Loosely braid the ropes of dough together, then pinch them together at the other end. Place the braid on the cookie sheet. Cover and let rise again for about 30 minutes, or until doubled in size.

4   Meanwhile, preheat the oven to 190°C/375°F/gas mark 5. Brush the braid with a little milk and sprinkle with poppy seeds. Bake for 30–40 minutes, or until the bread is risen, golden brown, and sounds hollow when tapped underneath. Cover the loaf loosely with foil toward the end of the cooking time if it is browning too much. Transfer to a wire rack to cool. Serve in slices.

TO MAKE IN BREADMAKER, *use quantities as listed in main recipe but amend following ingredients and use 1¼ cups milk, 1¼ teaspoons salt, and 1½ teaspoons fast-action dried yeast, and add 1½ teaspoons superfine sugar. Add ingredients to breadmaker in order specified in your instruction book. Use Dough setting for this recipe, then continue as above from Step 3 of main recipe.*

034 Bacon and cheese bread

PREPARATION TIME *30 minutes, plus rising* **COOKING TIME** *35–40 minutes*
MAKES *1 loaf (serves 10–12)*

6 slices lean smoked back bacon
2 cups strong white flour, plus extra
  for dusting
1 teaspoon salt
1 cup strong wholewheat flour
2 teaspoons fast-action dried yeast

2 teaspoons light soft brown sugar
1 tablespoon caraway seeds (optional)
1 cup Farmers cheese
1 egg
About ½ cup warm milk

1 Grease or flour a cookie sheet and set aside. Preheat the broiler to high. Place the bacon slices on the rack in the broiler pan, then broil for about 4–6 minutes, turning once, until cooked. Remove from the heat, drain on paper towels, and cool slightly, then snip into small pieces using a clean pair of kitchen scissors.

2 Sift the white flour and salt into a bowl, then stir in the wholewheat flour, yeast, sugar, and caraway seeds, if using. Place the Farmers cheese and egg into a blender or food processor and blend until smooth. Make a well in the center of the dry ingredients, stir in the cooked bacon, then stir in the Farmers cheese mixture and add enough milk, mixing to form a soft dough.

3 Turn the dough onto a lightly floured worktop and knead until smooth and elastic. Shape the dough into an oval and place on the cookie sheet. Cover and let rise in a warm place until doubled in size.

4 Meanwhile, preheat the oven to 190°C/375°F/gas mark 5. Using a sharp knife, cut a deep slash along the center of the top of the dough, then dust with a little flour.

5 Bake the loaf for 35–40 minutes, or until the bread is risen, lightly browned, and sounds hollow when tapped underneath. Transfer to a wire rack to cool. Serve in slices.

VARIATION *Use sesame, poppy, or fennel seeds in place of the caraway seeds.*

035 ▣ Golden cheesy breads

PREPARATION TIME *20 minutes, plus rising* **COOKING TIME** *20–25 minutes*
MAKES *4 small loaves (each loaf serves 1–2)*

3 cups strong white flour
1 teaspoon salt
2 tablespoons butter, diced
2 teaspoons fast-action dried yeast

1 teaspoon mustard powder
1¾ cups gouda or Dutch cheese, grated
About 1¼ cups warm milk, plus extra
  for glazing

1 Grease or flour 2 cookie sheets and set aside. Sift the flour and salt into a large bowl, then rub in the butter. Stir in the yeast, mustard powder, and two-thirds of the cheese. Make a well in the center, then add enough milk, mixing to form a soft dough.

2 Turn the dough onto a lightly floured worktop and knead until smooth and elastic. Divide into 4 equal portions and shape each piece into a round or oval and place on the cookie sheets. Cover and let rise in a warm place until doubled in size.

3 Meanwhile, preheat the oven to 200°C/400°F/gas mark 6. Lightly brush the tops of the loaves with a little extra milk, then sprinkle over the remaining cheese.

4 Bake the loaves for 20–25 minutes, or until the bread is risen, and golden brown, and sounds hollow when tapped underneath. Cover the loaves loosely with foil toward the end of the cooking time if they are browning too much. Transfer to a wire rack to cool.

TO MAKE IN BREADMAKER, *use quantities as listed in main recipe but amend following ingredients and use 1¼ cups milk, 1¼ teaspoons salt, and 1½ teaspoons fast-action dried yeast, and add 1½ teaspoons superfine sugar. Use two-thirds of cheese in dough; use remaining cheese as instructed in Step 3 of main recipe. Add ingredients to breadmaker in order specified in your instruction book. Use Dough setting, then continue as above from Step 2 of main recipe (punching down rather than kneading dough, then divide and shape dough and continue as directed).*

036 Golden raisin and hazelnut bread

PREPARATION TIME *35 minutes, plus rising* COOKING TIME *30 minutes*
MAKES *2 loaves (each loaf serves 10)*

3 cups strong white flour
1½ cups strong wholewheat flour, plus
    extra for dusting
2 teaspoons salt
2 tablespoons butter, diced

⅔ cup golden raisins
⅓ cup toasted hazelnuts, chopped
2 teaspoons easy-blend dried yeast
2 tablespoons malt extract
About 1½ cups warm water

1   Grease or flour 2 cookie sheets and set aside. Mix the flours and salt in a large bowl, then rub in the butter. Stir in the golden raisins, hazelnuts, and yeast. Make a well in the center, then add the malt extract and enough water, mixing to form a soft dough.

2   Turn the dough onto a lightly floured worktop and knead until smooth and elastic. Shape the dough into a round, then place it in a lightly oiled bowl, cover and let rise in a warm place until doubled in size.

3   Punch down the dough on a lightly floured worktop, divide it in half and shape each portion into a round about 5½ inches in diameter. Place on the cookie sheets, cover and let rise again for about 30 minutes, or until doubled in size.

4   Meanwhile, preheat the oven to 220°C/425°F/gas mark 7. Dust each loaf with a little wholewheat flour, then, using a sharp knife, slash the tops in a criss-cross pattern.

5   Bake the loaves for 10 minutes, then reduce the oven temperature to 190°C/375°F/gas mark 5 and bake for a further 20 minutes, or until the bread is risen, lightly browned, and sounds hollow when tapped underneath. Transfer to a wire rack to cool. Serve in slices.

VARIATIONS *Use chopped ready-to-eat dried apricots or peaches in place of golden raisins. Use toasted almonds in place of hazelnuts. Use two 2lb loaf pans in place of cookie sheets, if preferred (and do not slash the tops of the loaves before baking).*

037 Savory sesame loaf

PREPARATION TIME *25 minutes, plus rising* COOKING TIME *40–50 minutes*
MAKES *1 loaf (serves 14–16)*

3⅔ cups strong white flour
1 teaspoon salt
1 sachet (¼oz) easy-blend dried yeast
1 teaspoon mustard powder
1 cup mature cheddar cheese,
    grated

About 1¼ cups warm water
2 tablespoons butter
1 onion, chopped
2 tablespoons sesame seeds

1   Grease a 2lb loaf pan or a cookie sheet and set aside. Sift the flour and salt into a bowl, then stir in the yeast, mustard powder, and cheese. Make a well in the center, then add enough water, mixing to form a soft dough.

2   Turn the dough onto a lightly floured worktop and knead until smooth and elastic. Shape the dough into a round, then place it in a lightly oiled bowl, cover and let rise in a warm place until doubled in size. Meanwhile, melt the butter in a skillet, add the onion and sauté for about 5 minutes, or until the onion is softened.

3   Punch down the dough on a lightly floured worktop, then knead the onions evenly into the dough. Shape into an oblong and press into the loaf pan, or shape into an oval and place on the cookie sheet, then cover and let rise again until doubled in size.

4   Meanwhile, preheat the oven to 190°C/375°F/gas mark 5. Brush the top of the loaf with water and sprinkle with sesame seeds. Bake the loaf for 40–50 minutes, or until the bread is risen, golden brown, and sounds hollow when tapped underneath. Turn out and cool on a wire rack. Serve in slices.

VARIATION *Use poppy seeds in place of sesame seeds.*

038 Rustic zucchini loaf

PREPARATION TIME *25 minutes, plus rising* **COOKING TIME** *30–35 minutes*
MAKES *1 large loaf (serves 12–14)*

2½ cups strong white flour
2 teaspoons salt
2 cups strong wholewheat flour
1 sachet (¼oz) fast-action dried yeast
1 teaspoon superfine sugar

A few turns of freshly ground
  black pepper
2 teaspoons chopped fresh thyme
2 medium-large zucchini, trimmed and
  coarsely grated
About 1¼ cups warm water
Olive oil, for brushing

1 Grease or flour a cookie sheet and set aside. Sift the white flour and salt into a bowl, then stir in the wholewheat flour, yeast, sugar, black pepper, and chopped thyme. Stir the grated zucchini into the flour mixture. Make a well in the center, then add enough water, mixing to form a soft dough.
2 Turn the dough onto a lightly floured worktop and knead until smooth and elastic. Shape the dough into a large round and place on the cookie sheet. Cover and let rise in a warm place until doubled in size.
3 Meanwhile, preheat the oven to 220°C/425°F/gas mark 7. Lightly brush the top of the loaf with a little oil. Bake the loaf for 15 minutes, then reduce the oven temperature to 190°C/375°F/gas mark 5 and bake for a further 15–20 minutes, or until the bread is risen, golden brown, and sounds hollow when tapped underneath. Transfer to a wire rack to cool. Serve in slices.

VARIATIONS *Use grated carrots in place of zucchini. Use finely chopped fresh rosemary or oregano in place of thyme.*

039 Tomato and fresh basil loaf

PREPARATION TIME *15 minutes, plus rising* **COOKING TIME** *25–30 minutes*
MAKES *1 loaf (serves 8–10)*

1⅔ cups packed white bread mix
1 teaspoon superfine sugar
1 teaspoon salt
1–2 tablespoons chopped fresh basil
2 tablespoons olive oil

2 tablespoons tomato paste
About ¾ cup warm water
¼ cup fresh Parmesan cheese,
  finely grated

1 Grease or flour a cookie sheet and set aside. Place the bread mix in a bowl and stir in the sugar, salt, and chopped basil. Mix the oil and tomato paste together. Add the oil mixture to the bread mix, then add enough water, mixing to form a soft dough.
2 Sprinkle the Parmesan cheese onto a clean, dry worktop. Turn the dough onto the cheese surface and knead until the cheese is incorporated and the dough is smooth and elastic. Shape the dough into a round and place on the cookie sheet. Cover and let rise in a warm place for about 30 minutes, or until doubled in size.
3 Meanwhile, preheat the oven to 220°C/425°F/gas mark 7. Using a sharp knife, cut a large cross on the top of the loaf. Bake the loaf for 15 minutes, then reduce the oven temperature to 190°C/375°F/gas mark 5 and bake for a further 10–15 minutes, or until the bread is risen, lightly browned, and sounds hollow when tapped underneath. Transfer to a wire rack to cool. Serve in slices.

040 🞀 Herb baguettes

PREPARATION TIME *25 minutes, plus rising* **COOKING TIME** *25 minutes*
MAKES *2 loaves (each loaf serves 4–6)*

**3 cups strong white flour, plus extra
   for dusting**
1 teaspoon salt
1 teaspoon easy-blend dried yeast

1 tablespoon dried herbes de Provence
½ cup fresh Parmesan cheese, grated
2 tablespoons olive oil
About 1 cup warm water

1   Grease or flour a large cookie sheet and set aside. Sift the flour and salt into a large bowl, then stir in the yeast, dried herbs, and Parmesan cheese. Make a well in the center, then add the oil and enough water, mixing to form a soft dough.

2   Turn the dough onto a floured worktop and knead until smooth. Shape into a round, then place in a lightly oiled bowl, cover and let rise in a warm place until doubled in size.

3   Punch down the dough on a lightly floured worktop, divide it in half and shape each half into a baton about 12 inches in length. Place on the cookie sheet, cover and let rise again for about 45 minutes, or until doubled in size.

4   Preheat the oven to 220°C/425°F/gas mark 7. Dust each loaf with a little flour, then, using a sharp knife, slash across the top of each loaf 4 times diagonally at regular intervals.

5   Bake the loaves for about 25 minutes, or until the bread is risen, golden brown, and sounds hollow when tapped underneath. Transfer to a wire rack to cool. Serve warm or cold.

TO MAKE IN BREADMAKER, *use quantities as listed in main recipe but amend following ingredients and use 1¼ cups water, 1¼ teaspoons salt, and 1½ teaspoons fast-action dried yeast, and add 1½ teaspoons superfine sugar. Add ingredients to breadmaker in order specified in your instruction book. Use Dough setting, then continue as above from Step 3 of main recipe.*

041 Pugliese

PREPARATION TIME *25 minutes, plus rising* **COOKING TIME** *30–35 minutes*
MAKES *1 large loaf (serves 12–14)*

For the** Biga **starter
1 cup strong white flour
¼ x 1oz fresh yeast cake, crumbled
6 tablespoons warm water

For the dough
**1½ cups strong white flour, plus extra
   for dusting**

2 teaspoons salt
1½ cups strong wholewheat flour
1 teaspoon superfine sugar
½ x 1oz fresh yeast cake, crumbled
1¼ cups warm water
4–5 tablespoons extra-virgin olive oil

1   Make the *biga* starter. Sift the flour into a large bowl and make a well in the center. In a small bowl, cream the yeast with the water, then pour into the center of the flour. Gradually mix the flour into the liquid to form a firm dough.

2   Turn the dough onto a floured worktop and knead until smooth. Return to the bowl, cover and let rise in a warm place for 8–10 hours, or until risen and starting to collapse.

3   Lightly flour a cookie sheet and set aside. Make the dough. Sift the white flour and salt into a large bowl, then stir in the wholewheat flour and sugar. Cream the yeast and water together in a separate bowl, then stir in the *biga* and mix well until combined. Gradually stir the flour mixture into the *biga* mixture, adding a little at a time, then gradually add enough olive oil, mixing to form a soft dough.

4   Turn the dough onto a floured worktop and knead until smooth. Shape into a round, then place in a lightly oiled bowl, cover and let rise in a warm place until doubled in size.

5   Punch down the dough on a lightly floured worktop, then shape into a round. Place on the cookie sheet, cover and let rise again for 1–1½ hours, or until almost doubled in size.

6   Meanwhile, preheat the oven to 230°C/450°F/gas mark 8. Lightly dust the loaf with a little flour. Bake for 15 minutes, then reduce the oven temperature to 200°C/400°F/gas mark 6 and bake for a further 15–20 minutes, or until risen and golden brown. Transfer to a wire rack to cool. Serve warm or cold in slices.

042 🍞 French baguettes

PREPARATION TIME *35 minutes, plus rising* **COOKING TIME** *35–40 minutes*
MAKES *3 baguettes (each baguette serves 2–3)*

3 cups strong white flour
1 cup all-purpose flour
2½ teaspoons salt

1 sachet (¼oz) easy-blend dried yeast
About 1¼ cups warm water
1 teaspoon cornstarch

1 Flour a large cookie sheet; set aside. Sift the flours and 1½ teaspoons salt into a large bowl, then stir in the yeast. Add enough water, mixing to form a soft dough.

2 Turn the dough onto a floured worktop and knead until smooth. Shape into a round, then place in an oiled bowl, cover and let rise in a warm place until doubled in size.

3 Punch down the dough on a lightly floured worktop, then divide it into 3 equal portions; shape each portion into a roll or baton about 10 inches in length.

4 Place between the folds of a pleated dish towel for support, cover and let rise again until doubled in size.

5 Meanwhile, preheat the oven to 200°C/400°F/gas mark 6. Place a roasting pan of water on the bottom shelf of the oven. Make the glaze. Blend the remaining salt and the cornstarch with 1 tablespoon water. Pour ½ cup water into a small saucepan and stir in the cornstarch mixture. Bring to the boil, stirring, then remove from the heat.

6 Roll the loaves onto the cookie sheet; brush the baguettes with some of the salt solution. Using a sharp knife, cut several diagonal slashes in the top of each loaf at regular intervals. Bake the baguettes for 35–40 minutes, brushing the surfaces of the loaves with the salt solution every 10 minutes or so, until the baguettes are brown, crisp, and sound hollow when tapped underneath. Transfer to a wire rack. Serve warm or cold.

TO MAKE IN BREADMAKER, *use quantities as listed in main recipe but amend following ingredients and use 3 cups strong white flour, omit the all-purpose flour, use 1¼ cups water, and 1½ teaspoons fast-action dried yeast. Use 1½ teaspoons salt in dough; use remaining salt as instructed in Step 5 of main recipe. Add ingredients to breadmaker in order specified in your instruction book. Use French Dough or Dough setting, then continue from Step 3 of main recipe.*

043 Greek black olive bread

PREPARATION TIME *30 minutes, plus rising* **COOKING TIME** *30–35 minutes*
MAKES *1 loaf (serves 10–12)*

1 cup whole black olives
3⅔ cups strong white flour, plus extra
for dusting
1 teaspoon salt

2 teaspoons easy-blend dried yeast
5 tablespoons extra virgin olive oil
About 1¼ cups warm water

1 Grease or flour a cookie sheet and set aside. Using a sharp knife, remove and discard the pits from the olives and chop the flesh, then set aside. Sift the flour and salt into a large bowl, then stir in the yeast. Make a well in the center, then add half the chopped olives, the oil and enough water, mixing to form a soft dough.

2 Turn the dough onto a lightly floured worktop and knead until smooth and elastic. Shape the dough into a round, then place it in a lightly oiled bowl, cover and let rise in a warm place until doubled in size.

3 Punch down the dough on a lightly floured worktop, then roll out to form a rectangle about 14 x 10 inches. Sprinkle the surface of the dough evenly with the remaining chopped olives, then roll up the dough tightly like a jelly roll, starting from a short side. Pinch the edges of each end of the roll together to seal.

4 Place the loaf, seam-side down, on the cookie sheet. Using a sharp knife, cut a slash down the length of the center of the loaf, if desired. Cover and let rise again for about 1 hour, or until doubled in size.

5 Meanwhile, preheat the oven to 220°C/425°F/gas mark 7. Dust the loaf with a little sifted flour. Bake for 10 minutes, then reduce the oven temperature to 190°C/375°F/gas mark 5 and bake for a further 20–25 minutes, or until the bread is risen, golden brown, and sounds hollow when tapped underneath. Transfer to a wire rack. Serve warm or cold in slices.

044 Ciabatta

PREPARATION TIME *45 minutes, plus rising* **COOKING TIME** *25–30 minutes*
MAKES *2 loaves (each loaf serves 6–8)*

For the **Biga** *starter*
2½ cups all-purpose flour
¼ x 1oz fresh yeast cake, crumbled
About ¾ cup warm water

For the dough
3⅔ cups strong white flour, plus extra
for dusting

½ x 1oz fresh yeast cake, crumbled
1¾ cups warm water
4 tablespoons warm milk
2 teaspoons salt
3 tablespoons extra-virgin olive oil

1   Make the *biga* starter. Sift the flour into a large bowl and make a well in the center. In a small bowl, cream the yeast with the water, then pour into the center of the flour. Gradually mix the flour into the liquid to form a firm dough.

2   Turn the dough onto a lightly floured worktop and knead until smooth and elastic. Return the dough to the large bowl, cover and let rise in a warm place for about 12 hours, or until the dough has risen and is starting to collapse.

3   Flour 2 cookie sheets and set aside. Make the dough. Sift the flour into a bowl. Cream the yeast and water together in a separate bowl, then gradually add to the *biga*, mixing well until combined. Mix in the milk, beating thoroughly with a wooden spoon.

4   Using your hand, gradually beat in the flour, lifting the dough as you mix, to eventually form a very wet mix (this will take about 15 minutes). Beat in the salt and olive oil, then cover and leave in a warm place until doubled in size.

5   Using a large spoon, carefully tip half of the dough onto each of the cookie sheets (try to avoid punching down the dough as you are doing this). Using floured hands, shape the dough into rough oblong shapes, flattening them slightly until they are each about 1 inch thick. Sprinkle with flour and let rise again for about 30 minutes.

6   Meanwhile, preheat the oven to 220°C/425°F/gas mark 7. Bake the loaves for 25–30 minutes, or until the bread is golden brown, and sounds hollow when tapped underneath. Transfer to a wire rack to cool. Serve warm or cold in slices or chunks.

045 Olive potato bread

PREPARATION TIME *30 minutes, plus rising* **COOKING TIME** *30 minutes*
MAKES *2 loaves (each loaf serves 8–10)*

3⅔ cups strong white flour, plus extra
for dusting
1 teaspoon salt
2 tablespoons butter, diced
1 cup packed cold cooked mashed
potatoes

1½ teaspoons easy-blend dried yeast
1 cup pitted black olives, finely chopped
1 teaspoon fresh rosemary, finely
chopped
About 1¼ cups warm water

1   Grease or flour 2 cookie sheets and set aside. Sift the flour and salt into a large bowl, then rub in the butter. Add the mashed potatoes, rubbing it loosely into the flour, then stir in the yeast, olives, and rosemary. Make a well in the center, then add enough water, mixing to form a soft dough.

2   Turn the dough onto a floured worktop and knead until smooth. Shape into a round, then place in a lightly oiled bowl, cover and let rise in a warm place until doubled in size.

3   Punch down the dough on a lightly floured worktop, divide it in half and shape each half into a small oval about 6½ x 3½ inches. Place on the cookie sheets, cover and let rise again for about 30 minutes, or until doubled in size.

4   Meanwhile, preheat the oven to 230°C/450°F/gas mark 8. Using a sharp knife, cut a shallow slash along the length of each loaf. Bake the loaves for 10 minutes, then reduce the oven temperature to 200°C/400°F/gas mark 6 and bake for a further 20 minutes, or until the bread is risen, golden brown, and sounds hollow when tapped underneath. Transfer to a wire rack to cool. Serve in slices.

046 Seeded Moroccan bread

PREPARATION TIME *30 minutes, plus rising* **COOKING TIME** *30–35 minutes*
MAKES *1 loaf (serves 10–12)*

2½ cups strong white flour
1 teaspoon salt
1½ teaspoons easy-blend dried yeast
1 tablespoon clear honey
About 1 cup warm milk

3 tablespoons mixed seeds such as
    sunflower, pumpkin, and sesame seeds
Beaten egg, to glaze
Extra sesame or sunflower seeds, for
    sprinkling

1 Grease or flour a cookie sheet and set aside. Sift the flour and salt into a large bowl, then stir in the yeast. Make a well in the center, then add the honey and enough milk, mixing to form a soft dough.

2 Turn the dough onto a lightly floured worktop and knead until smooth and elastic. Shape the dough into a round, then place it in a lightly oiled bowl, cover and let rise in a warm place until doubled in size.

3 Punch down the dough on a lightly floured worktop, then gently knead in the mixed seeds. Shape the dough into a round ball and flatten slightly. Place on the cookie sheet, cover and let rise again for about 45 minutes, or until doubled in size.

4 Meanwhile, preheat the oven to 200°C/400°F/gas mark 6. Brush the top of the loaf with beaten egg and sprinkle with the extra sesame or sunflower seeds.

5 Bake the loaf for 30–35 minutes, or until the bread is risen, golden, and sounds hollow when tapped underneath. Transfer to a wire rack to cool. Serve in slices.

047 Pumpernickel

PREPARATION TIME *30 minutes, plus rising* **COOKING TIME** *30 minutes*
MAKES *2 loaves (each loaf serves 10)*

2 cups rye flour
1 cup strong stoneground wholewheat
    flour
1 cup strong white flour
1½ teaspoons salt

1 sachet (¼oz) easy-blend dried yeast
1 tablespoon dark soft brown sugar
About 1½ tablespoons molasses
1 tablespoon sunflower oil
1½ cups warm water

1 Grease two 1lb loaf pans and set aside. Mix the flours and salt in a bowl, then stir in the yeast and sugar. Make a well in the center, then add the molasses, oil, and water, and mix well to form a soft, slightly sticky dough, which may be difficult to work with.

2 Turn the dough onto a lightly floured worktop and knead for about 10 minutes, or until it becomes firmer, smooth, and elastic. Shape into a round, then place it in a lightly oiled bowl, cover and let rise in a warm place for 1–1½ hours, or until doubled in size.

3 Punch down the dough on a lightly floured worktop, then divide it in half. Shape each portion into a small oblong and press into the loaf pans. Cover and let rise again for about 30 minutes or until doubled in size.

4 Meanwhile, preheat the oven to 200°C/400°F/gas mark 6. Bake the loaves for about 30 minutes, or until the bread is dark brown and sounds hollow when tapped underneath. Turn out and cool on a wire rack. Wrap in waxed paper and foil for at least 24 hours before serving. Serve in thin slices.

048 Pumpkin bread

PREPARATION TIME *25 minutes* COOKING TIME *1–1¼ hours* MAKES *1 loaf (serves 12–14)*

2 cups all-purpose flour
1½ teaspoons baking powder
½ teaspoon salt
2 teaspoons ground pudding spice
1 stick butter, softened

1 cup light soft brown sugar
2 eggs, beaten
1 cup canned pumpkin purée (see
  Variation)
¼ cup pumpkin seeds

1   Preheat the oven to 170°C/325°F/gas mark 3. Grease a 2lb loaf pan and set aside. Sift the flour, baking powder, salt, and pudding spice into a bowl and set aside.
2   Place the butter and sugar in a bowl and cream together until light and fluffy. Gradually beat in the eggs. Stir in the pumpkin purée, then fold in the flour mixture, followed by the pumpkin seeds.
3   Transfer the mixture to the loaf pan and level the surface. Bake for 1–1¼ hours, or until golden and a skewer inserted in the center comes out clean. Turn out and cool on a wire rack. Serve in slices.

VARIATION *If you can't buy canned pumpkin purée, use fresh pumpkin instead. Simply peel, seed, and dice pumpkin flesh, then cook it in boiling water for about 15 minutes, or until tender. Drain well, mash or purée until smooth, then use in place of the canned purée. You will need about 10oz prepared (peeled and seeded) pumpkin flesh to make about 1 cup purée.*

049 Sourdough bread

PREPARATION TIME *30 minutes, plus fermenting and rising* COOKING TIME *35–40 minutes*
MAKES *1 large loaf (serves 14–16)*

For the sourdough starter
1 cup strong white flour
2 teaspoons superfine sugar
1 cup water

For the bread dough
1¼ cups warm water

1 tablespoon ordinary dried yeast (NOT
  fast-action or easy-blend yeast)
2 teaspoons superfine sugar
4¼ cups strong white flour
2 teaspoons salt
½ teaspoon baking soda

1   Make the sourdough starter. Place the flour and sugar in a bowl, then gradually add the water, mixing to form a smooth batter. Cover and leave in a warm place for about 2 days, stirring the mixture after 24 hours, until it begins to bubble and rise.
2   Grease or flour a cookie sheet and set aside. Make the bread dough. Pour the water into a large bowl, then sprinkle over the yeast and add 1 teaspoon sugar. Whisk thoroughly, then let stand in a warm place for 10–15 minutes, or until the yeast starts to froth.
3   Stir the sourdough starter into the yeast mixture, then add 3 cups flour, the remaining sugar, and the salt, and beat the mixture with a wooden spoon for 2–3 minutes to form a thick, elasticy batter. Cover and let rise in a warm place for about 2 hours, or until doubled in size.
4   Mix 1 cup of the remaining flour with the baking soda, then stir this into the risen dough. Add the remaining flour and knead into the dough. Turn the dough onto a well-floured worktop and knead for about 5 minutes, or until smooth, soft, and elastic.
5   Shape the dough into a large round and place on the cookie sheet. Cover and let rise again for 20–30 minutes.
6   Meanwhile, preheat the oven to 200°C/400°F/gas mark 6. Bake the loaf for 35–40 minutes, or until the bread is golden brown, and sounds hollow when tapped underneath. Transfer to a wire rack to cool. Serve in slices.

050 Currant bread

PREPARATION TIME *25 minutes, plus rising* COOKING TIME *35–40 minutes*
MAKES *2 loaves (each loaf serves 8–10)*

3 cups strong white flour
1 teaspoon salt
1 teaspoon ground pudding spice
2 tablespoons butter, diced
2 teaspoons easy-blend dried yeast

2 tablespoons superfine sugar
About 1 cup warm milk
1 cup dried currants
2 tablespoons clear honey, to glaze

1 Grease two 1lb loaf pans and set aside. Sift the flour, salt, and pudding spice into a large bowl, then rub in the butter. Stir in the yeast and sugar. Make a well in the center, then add enough milk, mixing to form a soft dough.
2 Turn the dough onto a lightly floured worktop and knead until smooth and elastic. Shape the dough into a round, then place it in a lightly oiled bowl, cover and let rise in a warm place until doubled in size.
3 Punch down the dough on a lightly floured worktop, then gently knead in the currants until evenly distributed. Divide the dough in half and shape each half into an oblong. Place in the loaf pans, cover and let rise again until the dough reaches the top of the pans.
4 Meanwhile, preheat the oven to 200°C/400°F/gas mark 6. Bake the loaves for 35–40 minutes, or until the bread is risen, golden brown, and sounds hollow when tapped underneath.
5 Turn out and cool on a wire rack. While still warm, brush the loaves all over twice with honey to glaze. Let cool. Serve in slices.

VARIATIONS *Use ground cinnamon in place of pudding spice. Use golden raisins or chopped dried cranberries or cherries in place of dried currants.*

051 Spiced rye bread

PREPARATION TIME *20 minutes, plus rising* COOKING TIME *35–40 minutes*
MAKES *1 loaf (serves 10–12)*

2½ cups strong wholewheat flour, plus
 extra for dusting
1½ cups rye flour
1 teaspoon salt
1 teaspoon ground cinnamon

1 teaspoon ground pudding spice
2 tablespoons butter, diced
2 teaspoons easy-blend dried yeast
1 tablespoon clear honey
About 1¼ cups warm milk

1 Grease or flour a cookie sheet and set aside. Mix the flours, salt, and ground spices in a large bowl, then rub in the butter. Stir in the yeast. Make a well in the center, then add the honey and enough milk, mixing to form a soft dough.
2 Turn the dough onto a lightly floured worktop and knead until smooth and elastic. Shape the dough into a round, then place it in a lightly oiled bowl, cover and let rise in a warm place until doubled in size.
3 Punch down the dough on a lightly floured worktop, then shape it into a round or oval and place on the cookie sheet. Cover and let rise again until doubled in size.
4 Meanwhile, preheat the oven to 200°C/400°F/gas mark 6. Using a sharp knife, cut 1 or 2 slashes across the top of the loaf, then lightly dust with flour. Bake the loaf for 35–40 minutes, or until the bread is risen, lightly browned, and sounds hollow when tapped underneath. Transfer to a wire rack to cool. Serve in slices.

052 Pesto whirl bread

PREPARATION TIME *25 minutes, plus rising* **COOKING TIME** *25–30 minutes*
MAKES *2 loaves (each loaf serves 10–12)*

4½ cups strong white flour	¼ cup olive oil
2 teaspoons salt	About 1¾ cups warm water
1 teaspoon superfine sugar	6 tablespoons ready-made green
2 teaspoons easy-blend dried yeast	pesto sauce

1 Grease two 2lb loaf pans and set aside. Sift the flour and salt into a large bowl, then stir in the sugar and yeast. Make a well in the center, then add the oil and enough water, mixing to form a soft dough.

2 Turn the dough onto a lightly floured worktop and knead until smooth and elastic. Shape the dough into a round, then place it in a lightly oiled bowl, cover and let rise in a warm place until doubled in size.

3 Punch down the dough on a lightly floured worktop, then divide it in half. Roll or pat out each piece of dough to form a rectangle about 12 x 8 inches in size.

4 Spread some pesto sauce evenly over each rectangle of dough, then roll up each one fairly tightly like a jelly roll, starting from a short side. Reshape slightly if necessary and place in the loaf pans. Cover and let rise again until doubled in size.

5 Meanwhile, preheat the oven to 220°C/425°F/gas mark 7. Bake the loaves for 25–30 minutes, or until risen and golden brown. Turn out and cool on a wire rack. Serve in slices on its own or spread with butter.

VARIATION *Use ready-made red pesto sauce in place of traditional green pesto sauce.*

053 Spiced walnut bread

PREPARATION TIME *20 minutes, plus rising* **COOKING TIME** *30–35 minutes*
MAKES *1 loaf (serves 10–12)*

2⅓ cups strong white flour
1½ teaspoons salt
1½ cup strong wholewheat flour
1 sachet (¼oz) easy-blend dried yeast
1 teaspoon ground cinnamon

A pinch of ground cloves
About 1¼ cups warm water
1 cup walnut halves, roughly chopped
A little milk, for glazing

1   Grease or flour a cookie sheet and set aside. Sift the white flour and salt into a large bowl, then stir in the wholewheat flour, yeast, and ground spices. Make a well in the center, then add enough water, mixing to form a soft dough.
2   Turn the dough onto a lightly floured worktop and knead until smooth and elastic. Shape the dough into a round, then place it in a lightly oiled bowl, cover and let rise in a warm place until doubled in size.
3   Punch down the dough on a lightly floured worktop, then gently knead in 1 cup chopped walnuts until evenly distributed. Shape into a round or oval and place on the cookie sheet. Cover and let rise again for about 45 minutes, or until doubled in size.
4   Meanwhile, preheat the oven to 220°C/425°F/gas mark 7. Lightly brush the top of the loaf with milk, then scatter the remaining walnuts over the top.
5   Bake the loaf for 10 minutes, then reduce the oven temperature to 190°C/375°F/gas mark 5 and bake for a further 20–25 minutes, or until the bread is risen, lightly browned, and sounds hollow when tapped underneath. Transfer to a wire rack to cool. Serve in slices.

VARIATION *Use pecan nuts instead of walnuts.*

054 Coconut bread

PREPARATION TIME *20 minutes, plus rising* **COOKING TIME** *30 minutes* **MAKES** *1 loaf (serves 10–12)*

3 cups strong white flour
1 teaspoon salt
1 tablespoon butter, diced
1½ teaspoons easy-blend dried yeast

1 tablespoon superfine sugar
⅔ cup desiccated coconut
1 teaspoon vanilla extract
About 1¼ cups warm milk

1   Grease a 2lb loaf pan and set aside. Sift the flour and salt into a large bowl, then rub in the butter. Stir in the yeast, sugar, and coconut. Make a well in the center of the dry ingredients. Mix the vanilla extract with the milk, then add enough milk to the dry ingredients, mixing to form a soft dough.
2   Turn the dough onto a lightly floured worktop and knead until smooth and elastic. Shape the dough into a round, then place it in a lightly oiled bowl, cover and let rise in a warm place until doubled in size.
3   Punch down the dough on a lightly floured worktop and shape into an oblong. Press into the loaf pan, cover and let rise again for about 45 minutes, or until the dough reaches the top of the pan.
4   Meanwhile, preheat the oven to 200°C/400°F/gas mark 6. Bake the loaf for about 30 minutes, or until the bread is risen, golden brown, and sounds hollow when tapped underneath. Turn out and cool on a wire rack. Serve in slices.

TO MAKE IN BREADMAKER, *use quantities as listed in main recipe but amend following ingredients and use 1¼ cups milk, 1½ teaspoons salt, and use fast-action dried yeast. Add ingredients to breadmaker in order specified in your instruction book. Use Sweet or similar setting (or Basic White/Regular setting) for this recipe.*

055 Honey oatmeal bread

PREPARATION TIME *20 minutes, plus rising* **COOKING TIME** *30–35 minutes*
MAKES *1 loaf (serves 12–14)*

4 cups strong wholewheat flour
2 teaspoons salt
1 tablespoon butter, diced
1 cup packed rolled oats, plus extra
  for sprinkling

2 teaspoons easy-blend dried yeast
⅔ cup warm milk, plus extra for glazing
2 tablespoons thick set honey
About 1 cup warm water

1   Grease or flour a cookie sheet and set aside. Mix the flour and salt in a large bowl, then rub in the butter. Stir in the oats and yeast. Make a well in the center, then add the milk, honey, and enough water, mixing to form a soft dough.

2   Turn the dough onto a lightly floured worktop and knead until smooth and elastic. Shape the dough into a round, then place it in a lightly oiled bowl, cover and let rise in a warm place until doubled in size.

3   Punch down the dough on a floured worktop and shape into a round. Place on the cookie sheet, cover and let rise again for about 30 minutes, or until doubled in size.

4   Meanwhile, preheat the oven to 230°C/450°F/gas mark 8. Using a sharp knife, slash the top of the loaf down the center, brush with a little milk, and sprinkle with oats.

5   Bake the loaf for 10 minutes, then reduce the oven temperature to 200°C/400°F/gas mark 6 and bake for a further 20–25 minutes, or until the bread is risen, lightly browned, and sounds hollow when tapped underneath. Transfer to a wire rack to cool. Serve in slices.

056 Fruited breakfast braid

PREPARATION TIME *25 minutes, plus rising* **COOKING TIME** *30 minutes*
MAKES *1 large loaf (serves 10–12)*

1lb 2oz package white bread mix
3 tablespoons butter, diced
3 tablespoons superfine sugar
1 large egg, lightly beaten
About 1 cup warm water
⅓ cup ready-to-eat dried apricots,
   chopped

⅓ cup dried cranberries
⅓ cup dried cherries or golden raisins
1 cup confectioners' sugar, sifted
About 3–4 teaspoons orange juice
3 tablespoons toasted flaked almonds

1   Grease or flour a large cookie sheet and set aside. Place the bread mix in a large bowl and
   rub in the butter. Stir in the superfine sugar, then add the egg and enough water, mixing to
   form a soft dough.
2   Turn the dough onto a lightly floured worktop and knead until smooth and elastic. Knead
   the dried fruit evenly into the dough. Divide the dough into 3 equal pieces and roll each
   piece into a long sausage or rope shape, each about 12 inches long. Braid the dough ropes
   together, pressing the ends together to seal and place on the cookie sheet. Cover and let
   rise in a warm place for about 1 hour, or until doubled in size.
3   Meanwhile, preheat the oven to 190°C/375°F/gas mark 5. Bake the braid for about 30
   minutes, or until risen and golden brown, covering loosely with foil toward the end of the
   cooking time if the top is browning too quickly. Transfer the braid to a wire rack to cool.
4   Blend the confectioners' sugar with enough orange juice to make a thick, smooth frosting
   and spread this over the top of the braid. Sprinkle with toasted flaked almonds and serve
   in slices.

057 Cranberry and walnut loaf

PREPARATION TIME *35 minutes, plus rising* **COOKING TIME** *30–35 minutes*
MAKES *2 loaves (each loaf serves 10)*

2⅓ cups strong white flour
2⅓ cups strong wholewheat flour, plus
   extra for dusting
2 teaspoons salt
2 tablespoons butter, diced

⅔ cup dried cranberries
½ cup walnut halves, chopped
2 teaspoons easy-blend dried yeast
2 tablespoons malt extract
About 1½ cups warm water

1   Grease or flour 2 cookie sheets and set aside. Mix the flours and salt in a large bowl, then
   rub in the butter. Stir in the cranberries, walnuts, and yeast. Make a well in the center,
   then add the malt extract and enough water, mixing to form a soft dough.
2   Turn the dough onto a lightly floured worktop and knead until smooth and elastic. Shape
   the dough into a round, then place it in a lightly oiled bowl, cover and let rise in a warm
   place until doubled in size.
3   Punch down the dough on a lightly floured worktop, divide it in half and shape each half
   into a round or oval. Place on the cookie sheets, cover and let rise again for about 30
   minutes, or until doubled in size.
4   Meanwhile, preheat the oven to 220°C/425°F/gas mark 7. Dust each loaf with
   wholewheat flour, then, using a sharp knife, slash the tops of the loaves diagonally
   2 or 3 times.
5   Bake the loaves for 10 minutes, then reduce the oven temperature to 190°C/375°F/gas
   mark 5 and bake for a further 20–25 minutes, or until the bread is risen, lightly browned,
   and sounds hollow when tapped underneath. Transfer to a wire rack. Serve in slices.

058 Chocolate bread

PREPARATION TIME *30 minutes, plus rising* **COOKING TIME** *25 minutes* **MAKES** *1 loaf (serves 8–10)*

1½ cups strong white flour
1 tablespoon cocoa powder
½ teaspoon salt
2 tablespoons butter, diced
1½ teaspoons fast-action dried yeast
4 tablespoons superfine sugar

1 egg, lightly beaten
About ½ cup warm milk
4oz milk or semisweet chocolate,
  roughly chopped
Confectioners' sugar, for dusting

1   Grease a 1lb loaf pan or a deep 6-inch round cake pan and set aside. Sift the flour, cocoa powder, and salt into a large bowl, then rub in the butter. Stir in the yeast and superfine sugar. Make a well in the center, then add the egg and enough milk, mixing to form a soft dough.

2   Turn the dough onto a lightly floured worktop and knead until smooth and elastic. Knead the chocolate into the dough. Shape into an oblong or round, then place in the pan. Cover and let rise in a warm place until doubled in size (this may take 2–3 hours).

3   Meanwhile, preheat the oven to 200°C/400°F/gas mark 6. Using a sharp knife, slash the top of the loaf diagonally a couple of times, if desired.

4   Bake the loaf for about 25 minutes, or until the bread is cooked and sounds hollow when tapped underneath. Loosely cover the loaf with foil toward the end of the cooking time if the top is browning too quickly. Turn out and cool on a wire rack. Dust with sifted confectioners' sugar and serve in slices.

VARIATION *Use milk or semisweet chocolate chips in place of the chopped chocolate.*

059 ▣ Breakfast rolls

PREPARATION TIME *25 minutes, plus rising* **COOKING TIME** *15–20 minutes* **MAKES** *10–12 rolls*

**3 cups strong white flour, plus extra
   for dusting**
1 teaspoon salt
1½ teaspoons easy-blend dried yeast
Pinch of superfine sugar

2 tablespoons butter, diced
**⅔ cup warm milk, plus extra
   for glazing**
About ⅔ cup warm water

1 Grease or flour 2 cookie sheets and set aside. Sift the flour and salt into a large bowl, stir in the yeast and sugar, then rub in the butter. Make a well in the center, then add the milk and enough water, mixing to form a soft dough.

2 Turn the dough onto a lightly floured worktop and knead until smooth and elastic. Shape the dough into a round, then place it in a lightly oiled bowl, cover and let rise in a warm place until doubled in size.

3 Punch down the dough on a lightly floured worktop; divide it into 10 or 12 equal portions. Shape each portion into a round or oval and place on the cookie sheets, spacing them well apart. Cover and let rise again for about 30 minutes or until doubled in size.

4 Meanwhile, preheat the oven to 200°C/400°F/gas mark 6. Lightly brush the rolls with milk and dust with flour. Bake for 15–20 minutes, or until lightly browned. Transfer to a wire rack to cool. Serve warm or cold.

TO MAKE IN BREADMAKER, *use quantities as listed in main recipe but amend following ingredients and use ⅓ cup milk, ⅓ cup water, 1½ teaspoons salt, 1½ teaspoons fast-action dried yeast, and 2 teaspoons superfine sugar. Add ingredients to breadmaker in order specified in your instruction book. Use Dough setting for this recipe, then continue as above from Step 3 of main recipe.*

060 Plain crusty white rolls

PREPARATION TIME *25 minutes, plus rising* **COOKING TIME** *15–20 minutes* **MAKES** *10–12 rolls*

2⅓ cups strong white flour
1 teaspoon salt
½ teaspoon superfine sugar
1 teaspoon easy-blend dried yeast

1 tablespoon butter, diced
About 1 cup warm water
Lightly salted water, for glazing

1 Grease or flour 2 cookie sheets and set aside. Sift the flour and salt into a large bowl, stir in the sugar and yeast, then rub in the butter. Make a well in the center, then add enough warm water, mixing to form a soft dough.

2 Turn the dough onto a lightly floured worktop and knead until smooth and elastic. Shape the dough into a round, then place it in a lightly oiled bowl, cover and let rise in a warm place until doubled in size.

3 Punch down the dough on a lightly floured worktop; divide it into 10 or 12 equal portions. Roll each portion into a ball, press each one down on a floured worktop, then release.

4 Place the rolls on the cookie sheets, spacing them well apart, cover and let rise again for about 30 minutes, or until doubled in size.

5 Preheat the oven to 220°C/425°F/gas mark 7. Brush the tops of the rolls with lightly salted water. Bake for 15–20 minutes, or until the rolls are golden, crusty, and sound hollow when tapped underneath. Transfer to a wire rack to cool. Serve warm or cold.

061 🔲 Dinner rolls

PREPARATION TIME *25 minutes, plus rising* **COOKING TIME** *15–20 minutes* **MAKES** *12 rolls*

3 cups strong white flour
1½ teaspoons salt
½ teaspoon superfine sugar
1 sachet (¼oz) easy-blend dried yeast
2 tablespoons butter, diced

1 egg, beaten
About 1¼ cups warm milk
Poppy seeds or sesame seeds, for
sprinkling (optional)

1 Grease or flour 2 cookie sheets and set aside. Sift the flour and salt into a large bowl, stir in the sugar and yeast, then rub in the butter. Make a well in the center, then add the egg and enough milk, mixing to form a soft dough.

2 Turn the dough onto a lightly floured worktop and knead until smooth and elastic. Shape the dough into a round, then place it in a lightly oiled bowl, cover and let rise in a warm place until doubled in size.

3 Punch down the dough on a lightly floured worktop, then divide it into 12 equal portions. Roll each portion into a round, oval, or baton, or shape each portion into a long roll or rope and tie loosely in a single knot, pulling the ends through.

4 Place the rolls on the cookie sheets, spacing them well apart, cover and let rise again for about 30 minutes, or until doubled in size.

5 Meanwhile, preheat the oven to 220°C/425°F/gas mark 7. Lightly brush the tops of the rolls with a little water and sprinkle with poppy or sesame seeds, if desired. Bake the rolls for 15–20 minutes, or until risen and golden brown. Transfer to a wire rack to cool. Serve warm or cold.

TO MAKE IN BREADMAKER, *use quantities as listed in main recipe but amend following ingredients and use 1¼ cups milk, 2 teaspoons salt, 2 teaspoons superfine sugar, and use fast-action dried yeast. Add ingredients to breadmaker in order specified in your instruction book. Use Dough setting for this recipe, then continue as above from Step 3 of main recipe.*

062 Bridge rolls

PREPARATION TIME *25 minutes, plus rising* **COOKING TIME** *10–15 minutes* **MAKES** *24 small rolls*

3 cups strong white flour
2 teaspoons salt
1 teaspoon superfine sugar
1½ teaspoons easy-blend dried yeast

3 tablespoons butter, diced
1 egg, beaten
About 1¼ cups cold milk, plus extra
for glazing

1 Grease or flour 2 large cookie sheets and set aside. Sift the flour and salt into a large bowl, stir in the sugar and yeast, then rub in the butter. Make a well in the center, then add the egg and enough milk, mixing to form a soft dough.

2 Turn the dough onto a lightly floured worktop and knead until smooth and elastic. Shape the dough into a round, then place it in a lightly oiled bowl, cover and let rise in a warm place until doubled in size (the cold milk means the rise will take a little longer, but the resulting fine, light crumb, is worth the extra time).

3 Punch down the dough on a lightly floured worktop, then divide it into 24 equal portions. Shape each portion into an oval, tapered at each end.

4 Place the rolls on the cookie sheets, spacing them well apart, cover and let rise again for about 30 minutes or until doubled in size.

5 Meanwhile, preheat the oven to 230°C/450°F/gas mark 8. Lightly brush the tops of the rolls with a little milk. Bake for 5 minutes, then reduce the oven temperature to 200°C/400°F/gas mark 6, and bake for a further 5–10 minutes, or until the rolls are golden brown, and sound hollow when tapped underneath.

6 Transfer to a wire rack to cool and cover with a clean, dry dish towel to keep the crusts soft. Serve warm or cold.

063 Rustic wholewheat rolls

PREPARATION TIME *25 minutes, plus rising* **COOKING TIME** *15–20 minutes* **MAKES** *8–10 rolls*

2⅔ cups strong wholewheat flour, plus
    extra for dusting
1 teaspoon salt
1 tablespoon butter, diced

1½ teaspoons easy-blend dried yeast
1 teaspoon superfine sugar
About 1¼ cups warm water

1   Grease or flour 2 cookie sheets and set aside. Mix the flour and salt in a large bowl, then rub in the butter. Stir in the yeast and sugar. Make a well in the center, then add enough water, mixing to form a soft dough.

2   Turn the dough onto a lightly floured worktop and knead until smooth and elastic. Shape the dough into a round, then place it in a lightly oiled bowl, cover and let rise in a warm place until doubled in size.

3   Punch down the dough on a lightly floured worktop, then divide it into 8 or 10 equal portions. Roll and shape each piece of dough into a round or oval. Press down on each one slightly, then place the rolls on the cookie sheets, spacing them well apart. Cover and let rise again for about 30 minutes, or until doubled in size.

4   Meanwhile, preheat the oven to 220°C/425°F/gas mark 7. Dust the tops of the rolls with a little flour, then bake for 15–20 minutes, or until the rolls sound hollow when tapped underneath. Transfer to a wire rack to cool.

VARIATION *Shape the pieces of dough and place them in greased mini loaf pans before the second rise, if desired.*

064 Soft wholewheat rolls

PREPARATION TIME *25 minutes, plus rising* **COOKING TIME** *15–20 minutes* **MAKES** *8 rolls*

1½ cups strong wholewheat flour, plus
    extra for dusting
1 teaspoon salt
2 tablespoons butter, diced

1½ teaspoons easy-blend dried yeast
1 teaspoon superfine sugar
About ⅔ cup warm milk

1   Grease or flour 2 cookie sheets and set aside. Mix the flour and salt in a large bowl, then rub in the butter. Stir in the yeast and sugar. Make a well in the center, then add enough milk, mixing to form a soft dough.

2   Turn the dough onto a lightly floured worktop and knead until smooth and elastic. Shape the dough into a round, then place it in a lightly oiled bowl, cover and let rise in a warm place until doubled in size.

3   Punch down the dough on a lightly floured worktop, then divide it into 8 equal portions. Roll each portion of dough into a round or oval, press each one down firmly with the heel of your hand and release.

4   Place the rolls on the cookie sheets, spacing them well apart, cover and let rise again for 20–30 minutes, or until doubled in size.

5   Meanwhile, preheat the oven to 220°C/425°F/gas mark 7. Lightly dust the tops of the rolls with flour. Bake for 15–20 minutes, or until the rolls are lightly browned.

6   Transfer to a wire rack to cool and cover with a clean, dry dish towel to keep the crusts soft. Serve warm or cold.

065 ▣ Malted country rolls

PREPARATION TIME *25 minutes, plus rising* **COOKING TIME** *15–20 minutes* **MAKES** *10–12 rolls*

3 cups strong malted grain flour
1 teaspoon salt
1½ teaspoons easy-blend dried yeast
2 tablespoons butter, diced
1 tablespoon malt extract

⅔ cup warm milk, plus extra
   for glazing
About ⅔ cup warm water
Kibbled or cracked wheat,
   for sprinkling

1   Grease or flour 2 cookie sheets and set aside. Mix the flour and salt in a large bowl, stir in the yeast, then rub in the butter. Make a well in the center, then add the malt extract, milk, and enough water, mixing to form a soft dough.

2   Turn the dough onto a lightly floured worktop and knead until smooth and elastic. Shape the dough into a round, then place it in a lightly oiled bowl, cover and let rise in a warm place until doubled in size.

3   Punch down the dough on a lightly floured worktop and divide it into 10 or 12 equal portions. Shape each portion of dough into a round or oval and place on the cookie sheets, spacing them well apart. Gently press down on each roll to flatten them slightly. Cover and let rise again for about 30 minutes, or until doubled in size.

4   Meanwhile, preheat the oven to 200°C/400°F/gas mark 6. Lightly brush the rolls with milk and sprinkle with kibbled wheat. Bake the rolls for 15–20 minutes, or until lightly browned. Transfer to a wire rack to cool. Serve warm or cold.

TO MAKE IN BREADMAKER, *use quantities as listed in main recipe but amend following ingredients and use ⅔ cup milk, ½ cup water, 2 teaspoons salt, use fast-action dried yeast, and add 2 teaspoons light soft brown sugar. Add ingredients to breadmaker in order specified in your instruction book. Use Dough setting for this recipe, then continue as above from Step 3 of main recipe.*

066 Refrigerator rolls

PREPARATION TIME *35 minutes, plus rising* **COOKING TIME** *15 minutes* **MAKES** *20 small rolls*

4 cups strong white flour, plus extra
   for dusting
1 teaspoon salt
½ stick butter, diced
1 cup cold mashed potatoes

3 teaspoons easy-blend dried yeast
2 teaspoons superfine sugar
1 egg, beaten
½ cup warm milk
About ⅔ cup warm water

1   Grease or flour 2 cookie sheets and set aside. Sift the flour and salt into a large bowl, then rub in the butter. Add the mashed potatoes, rubbing them loosely into the flour, then stir in the yeast and sugar. Make a well in the center, then add the egg, milk, and enough water, mixing to form a soft dough.

2   Turn the dough onto a lightly floured worktop and knead until smooth and elastic. Shape the dough into a round, then place it in a lightly oiled bowl, cover with plastic wrap and leave in the refrigerator for 15 hours or more. After about 15 hours, the dough should have risen to the top of the bowl.

3   Punch down the dough and knead it on a lightly floured worktop, then return it to the bowl, cover and let rise in a warm place for 1½–2 hours, or until doubled in size.

4   Punch down the dough again on a lightly floured worktop, then divide it into 20 equal portions. Shape each portion of dough into a roll.

5   Place the rolls on the cookie sheets, spacing them well apart, dust with a little sifted flour, if desired, then cover and let rise again for about 30 minutes.

6   Meanwhile, preheat the oven to 220°C/425°F/gas mark 7. Bake the rolls for 15 minutes, or until risen and golden brown. Transfer to a wire rack to cool. Serve warm or cold.

067 Potato bread rolls

PREPARATION TIME *25 minutes, plus rising* COOKING TIME *15–20 minutes* MAKES *12 rolls*

1 large floury potato such as Yellow Finn
   or California long white, about 12oz
   in weight
3⅔ cups strong white or wholewheat
   flour, plus extra for dusting
1 sachet (¼oz) easy-blend dried yeast
2 teaspoons salt

½ cup gruyère or emmental cheese,
   finely grated
1½ teaspoons dried mixed herbs
A few turns of freshly ground black
   pepper
About ¾ cup warm water

1   Grease or flour 2 cookie sheets and set aside. Peel and dice the potato, then cook it in a
    saucepan of boiling water for 10–15 minutes, or until tender. Drain well, mash thoroughly,
    and set aside to cool slightly.
2   Mix the flour, yeast, salt, cheese, dried herbs, and black pepper in a large bowl. Add the
    mashed potatoes and work into the flour mixture using your fingers. Make a well in the
    center, then gradually add enough water, mixing to form a soft dough.
3   Turn the dough onto a lightly floured worktop and knead until smooth and elastic. Shape
    the dough into a round, then place it in a lightly oiled bowl, cover and let rise in a warm
    place until doubled in size.
4   Punch down the dough on a lightly floured worktop, then divide it into 12 equal portions.
    Roll each portion of dough into a round.
5   Place the rolls on the cookie sheets, spacing them well apart, and, using a sharp knife,
    score a cross in the top of each roll. Cover and let rise again until doubled in size.
6   Meanwhile, preheat the oven to 220°C/425°F/gas mark 7. Dust the rolls lightly with a
    little flour, then bake for 15–20 minutes, or until risen and golden brown. Transfer to a
    wire rack to cool. Serve warm or cold.

VARIATION *Use a mixture of warm water and warm milk in place of all water, if desired.*

068 Quickie bread rolls

PREPARATION TIME *15 minutes* COOKING TIME *15 minutes* MAKES *8 rolls*

1½ cups all-purpose flour
½ teaspoon salt
½ teaspoon baking soda
1 teaspoon cream of tartar

2 tablespoons butter, diced
About ⅔ cup milk
Beaten egg, to glaze
Poppy seeds, for sprinkling

1   Preheat the oven to 190°C/375°F/gas mark 5. Grease or flour a large cookie sheet and set
    aside. Sift the flour, salt, baking soda, and cream of tartar into a large bowl, then rub in
    the butter. Add enough milk, mixing to form a soft dough.
2   Turn the dough onto a lightly floured worktop and knead gently until smooth. Divide into 8
    equal portions and roll each portion of dough into an 8-inch rope or sausage, then tie each
    one loosely in a single knot.
3   Place the rolls on the cookie sheet, brush with beaten egg, and sprinkle with poppy seeds.
    Bake for 15 minutes, or until golden brown. Transfer to a wire rack to cool. Serve warm.

VARIATION *Add 1–1½ teaspoons dried mixed herbs with the flour, if desired.*

069 Butter rolls

PREPARATION TIME *25 minutes, plus rising* **COOKING TIME** *15 minutes* **MAKES** *12 rolls*

3⅔ cups strong white flour	¾ cup sour cream
1 teaspoon salt	1 egg, beaten
1 sachet (¼oz) fast-action dried yeast	About 5 tablespoons warm milk, plus
1 teaspoon superfine sugar	extra for glazing
½ stick butter, diced	Sesame seeds, for sprinkling

1. Grease or flour 2 cookie sheets and set aside. Sift the flour and salt into a large bowl, stir in the yeast and sugar, then rub in the butter. Make a well in the center, then add the sour cream, egg, and enough milk, mixing to form a soft dough.
2. Turn the dough onto a lightly floured worktop and knead until smooth and elastic. Divide the dough into 12 equal portions. Shape each portion of dough into a round or ball and place on the cookie sheets, spacing them well apart.
3. Using a sharp knife, score across the center of the top of each roll. Cover and let rise in a warm place until doubled in size.
4. Meanwhile, preheat the oven to 220°C/425°F/gas mark 7. Lightly brush the rolls with milk and sprinkle with sesame seeds. Bake the rolls for about 15 minutes, or until risen and golden brown. Transfer to a wire rack to cool. Serve warm or cold.

070 🏠 Panini rolls

PREPARATION TIME *25 minutes, plus rising* **COOKING TIME** *15 minutes* **MAKES** *12 rolls*

3 cups strong white flour	4 tablespoons extra-virgin olive oil, plus
2 teaspoons salt	extra for glazing
1 sachet (¼oz) easy-blend dried yeast	About 1¼ cups warm water

1. Grease or flour 2 cookie sheets and set aside. Sift the flour and salt into a large bowl, then stir in the yeast. Make a well in the center, then add the oil and enough water, mixing to form a soft dough.
2. Turn the dough onto a lightly floured worktop and knead until smooth and elastic. Shape the dough into a round, then place it in a lightly oiled bowl, cover and let rise in a warm place until doubled in size.
3. Punch down the dough on a lightly floured worktop and divide it into 12 equal portions. Shape each portion of dough into a ball and place on the cookie sheets, spacing them well apart. Brush with olive oil, cover and let rise in a warm place for 20–30 minutes, or until doubled in size.
4. Meanwhile, preheat the oven to 200°C/400°F/gas mark 6. Using a sharp knife, cut a cross in the top of each roll. Bake the rolls for about 15 minutes, or until golden brown. Transfer to a wire rack to cool. Serve warm or cold.

TO MAKE IN BREADMAKER, *use quantities as listed in main recipe but amend following ingredients and use 1¼ cups water, use fast-action dried yeast, and add 2 teaspoons superfine sugar. Add ingredients to breadmaker in order specified in your instruction book. Use Dough setting for this recipe, then continue as above from Step 3 of main recipe.*

071 Linseed rolls

PREPARATION TIME *25 minutes, plus rising* **COOKING TIME** *15–20 minutes* **MAKES** *12 rolls*

2 cups strong white flour
½ teaspoon salt
2 cups strong wholewheat flour
2 teaspoons fast-action dried yeast

1 tablespoon light soft brown sugar
2 tablespoons linseeds, plus extra for
sprinkling
About 1¼ cup warm water

1 Grease or flour 2 cookie sheets and set aside. Sift the white flour and salt into a large bowl, then stir in the wholewheat flour, yeast, sugar, and linseeds. Make a well in the center, then add enough water, mixing to form a soft dough.
2 Turn the dough onto a lightly floured worktop and knead until smooth and elastic. Divide the dough into 12 equal portions and shape each portion into an oval. Place on the cookie sheets, cover and let rise in a warm place until doubled in size.
3 Meanwhile, preheat the oven to 220°C/425°F/gas mark 7. Brush the rolls with a little water and sprinkle with linseeds. Bake the rolls for 15–20 minutes, or until risen and golden brown. Transfer to a wire rack to cool. Serve warm or cold.

072 🍞 Petit pains au lait

PREPARATION TIME *25 minutes, plus rising* **COOKING TIME** *15–20 minutes* **MAKES** *12 rolls*

3 cups strong white flour
1½ teaspoons salt
½ stick butter, diced
1 tablespoon superfine sugar

2 teaspoons easy-blend dried yeast
About 1¼ cups warm milk, plus extra
for glazing

1 Grease or flour 2 cookie sheets and set aside. Sift the flour and salt into a large bowl, then rub in the butter. Stir in the sugar and yeast. Make a well in the center, then add enough milk, mixing to form a soft dough.
2 Turn the dough onto a lightly floured worktop and knead until smooth and elastic. Shape the dough into a round, then place it in a lightly oiled bowl, cover and let rise in a warm place until doubled in size.
3 Punch down the dough on a lightly floured worktop and divide it into 12 equal portions. Shape each portion of dough into a 5-inch long roll, tapered at each end, and place on the cookie sheets, spacing them well apart. Cover and let rise in a warm place for 20–30 minutes, or until doubled in size.
4 Meanwhile, preheat the oven to 200°C/400°F/gas mark 6. Using a sharp knife, slash the top of each roll diagonally several times at regular intervals, then brush them with milk.
5 Bake the rolls for 15–20 minutes, or until golden brown. Transfer to a wire rack to cool. Serve warm or cold.

TO MAKE IN BREADMAKER, *use quantities as listed in main recipe but amend following ingredients and use 1¼ cups milk and fast-action dried yeast. Add ingredients to breadmaker in order specified in your instruction book. Use Dough setting for this recipe, then continue as above from Step 3 of main recipe.*

073 Golden cheddar twists

PREPARATION TIME *25 minutes, plus rising* **COOKING TIME** *15–20 minutes* **MAKES** *10 twists*

1lb 2oz package white bread mix
1 cup mature cheddar cheese,
  finely grated
1 teaspoon mustard powder

A few turns of freshly ground
  black pepper
About 1¼ cups warm water
Beaten egg or milk, to glaze

1 Grease or flour 2 cookie sheets and set aside. Place the bread mix in a bowl and stir in ¾ cup cheese, the mustard powder, and black pepper. Add enough water (according to package instructions), mixing to form a soft dough.

2 Turn the dough onto a lightly floured worktop and knead until smooth and elastic. Divide the dough into 10 equal portions. Roll each piece of dough into a long sausage or rope shape, then gently tie each one loosely in a single knot, pulling the ends through.

3 Place on the cookie sheets, spacing them well apart, brush with beaten egg or milk and sprinkle with the remaining grated cheese. Cover and let rise in a warm place for about 30 minutes, or until doubled in size.

4 Meanwhile, preheat the oven to 200°C/400°F/gas mark 6. Bake the twists for 15–20 minutes, or until risen and golden brown. Transfer to a wire rack. Serve warm or cold.

TO MAKE IN BREADMAKER, *use quantities as listed in main recipe but amend following ingredients and use 1½ cups water (or according to package mix). Use ¾ cup cheese in dough; use remaining cheese as instructed in Step 3 of main recipe. Add ingredients to breadmaker in order specified in your instruction book. Use Dough setting for this recipe, then continue as above from Step 2 of main recipe (punching down rather than kneading dough, then divide and shape dough and continue as directed).*

074 🍞 Scottish baps

PREPARATION TIME *25 minutes, plus rising* **COOKING TIME** *15–20 minutes* **MAKES** *10 baps*

3 cups strong white flour, plus extra
   for dusting
2 teaspoons salt
1½ teaspoons easy-blend dried yeast

Pinch of superfine sugar
⅔ cup warm milk, plus extra
   for glazing
About ⅔ cup warm water

1   Grease or flour 2 cookie sheets and set aside. Sift the flour and salt into a large bowl, then stir in the yeast and sugar. Make a well in the center, then add the milk and enough water, mixing to form a soft dough.

2   Turn the dough onto a lightly floured worktop and knead until smooth and elastic. Shape the dough into a round, then place it in a lightly oiled bowl, cover and let rise in a warm place until doubled in size.

3   Punch down the dough on a lightly floured worktop and divide it into 10 equal portions. Roll or pat each portion of dough into a round or oval about ½-inch thick. Place on the cookie sheets, spacing them well apart, then cover and let rise again for about 30 minutes, or until doubled in size.

4   Meanwhile, preheat the oven to 200°C/400°F/gas mark 6. Gently press the center of each bap to release any large air bubbles. Lightly brush the rolls with milk and dust with flour.

5   Bake the rolls for 15–20 minutes, or until lightly browned. Dust with a little more flour, then transfer to a wire rack to cool. Serve warm.

TO MAKE IN BREADMAKER, *use quantities as listed in main recipe but amend following ingredients and use ⅔ cup milk, ⅓ cup water, 1½ teaspoons salt, 2 teaspoons superfine sugar, and fast-action dried yeast. Add ingredients to breadmaker in order specified in your instruction book. Use Dough setting for this recipe, then continue as above from Step 3 of main recipe.*

075 🍞 Floury white baps

PREPARATION TIME *25 minutes, plus rising* **COOKING TIME** *15 minutes* **MAKES** *10 baps*

3 cups strong white flour, plus extra
   for dusting
1½ teaspoons salt
1½ teaspoons easy-blend dried yeast

½ teaspoon superfine sugar
1 cup warm milk, plus extra
   for glazing
About ½ cup warm water

1   Grease or flour 2 cookie sheets and set aside. Sift the flour and salt into a large bowl, then stir in the yeast and sugar. Make a well in the center, then add the milk and enough water, mixing to form a soft dough.

2   Turn the dough onto a lightly floured worktop and knead until smooth and elastic. Shape the dough into a round, then place it in a lightly oiled bowl, cover and let rise in a warm place until doubled in size.

3   Punch down the dough on a lightly floured worktop and divide it into 10 equal portions. Shape each portion of dough into a flat round, each about 3½ inches in diameter and place on the cookie sheets, spacing them well apart. Cover and let rise again for about 30 minutes, or until doubled in size.

4   Meanwhile, preheat the oven to 200°C/400°F/gas mark 6. Gently press the center of each bap to release any large air bubbles. Lightly brush the rolls with milk and dust with flour.

5   Bake the rolls for about 15 minutes, or until lightly browned. Dust with a little more flour, then transfer to a wire rack to cool. Serve warm or cold.

TO MAKE IN BREADMAKER, *use quantities as listed in main recipe but amend following ingredients and use 1 cup milk, ½ cup water, 2 teaspoons superfine sugar, and 1 teaspoon fast-action dried yeast. Add ingredients to breadmaker in order specified in your instruction book. Use Dough setting for this recipe, then continue as above from Step 3 of main recipe.*

076 Grissini

PREPARATION TIME *30 minutes, plus rising* COOKING TIME *15–20 minutes* MAKES *about 40*

1½ cups strong white flour
1½ teaspoons salt
1½ teaspoons easy-blend dried yeast

2 tablespoons olive oil
About ⅔ cup warm water

1   Grease or flour 2 cookie sheets and set aside. Sift the flour and salt into a large bowl, then stir in the yeast. Make a well in the center, then add the olive oil and enough water, mixing to form a soft dough.
2   Turn the dough onto a lightly floured worktop and knead until smooth and elastic. Shape the dough into a round, then place it in a lightly oiled bowl, cover and let rise in a warm place until doubled in size.
3   Meanwhile, preheat the oven to 200°C/400°F/gas mark 6. Punch down the dough on a lightly floured worktop, then roll it out to form a large square about 8 inches in diameter and about ¼ inch thick.
4   Using a sharp knife, cut the square in half to make 2 long, narrow rectangles, each about 8 x 4 inches. Cut each rectangle crosswise into strips about ½ inches wide. Roll and stretch each strip of dough until it is about 8 inches long. Place on the cookie sheets and let rise in a warm place for 10 minutes.
5   Bake the grissini for 15–20 minutes, or until golden brown and crisp, turning them over halfway through the cooking time. Transfer to a wire rack to cool. Serve cold. Store in an airtight container.

077 Sesame breadsticks

PREPARATION TIME *35 minutes, plus rising* COOKING TIME *15 minutes* MAKES *25–30 breadsticks*

2 cups white bread mix
2 tablespoons olive oil, plus extra for glazing

About ⅔ cup warm water
About ½ cup sesame seeds, for coating

1   Grease or flour 2 cookie sheets and set aside. Place the bread mix in a bowl, then add the oil and enough warm water, mixing to form a soft dough.
2   Turn the dough onto a lightly floured worktop and knead until smooth and elastic. Roll out to form a large rectangle about 17 x 8 inches in size and about ¼ inch thick.
3   Cut the rectangle in half lengthwise to make 2 long, narrow rectangles (each about 17 x 4 inches in size). Cut each rectangle crosswise into strips about 1 inch wide. Roll and stretch each strip of dough until it is about 10 inches long.
4   Spread the sesame seeds out on a chopping board. Lightly brush each dough stick with oil, then roll in the sesame seeds as each one is made. Place on the cookie sheets, then leave in a warm place for 10 minutes.
5   Meanwhile, preheat the oven to 200°C/400°F/gas mark 6. Bake the breadsticks for about 15 minutes, or until golden brown and crisp, turning them over halfway through the cooking time. Transfer to a wire rack to cool. Serve cold. Store in an airtight container.

VARIATION *Add 1–2 teaspoons dried Italian herb seasoning to the bread mix, before adding the oil and water. Shape and bake as above.*

078 Garlic bubble ring

PREPARATION TIME *25 minutes, plus rising* **COOKING TIME** *30–40 minutes* **SERVES** *12*

1lb 2oz package white bread mix	**¼ cup fresh Parmesan cheese, grated**
About 1¼ cups warm water	**2 cloves garlic, crushed**
1 stick butter, melted	**½ teaspoon salt**
1 egg, beaten	**1 teaspoon dried Italian herb seasoning**

1 Grease a 9-inch loose-bottomed springform pan fitted with a tube base, or a ring mold, and set aside. Place the bread mix in a large bowl and add enough water (according to package instructions), mixing to form a soft dough.

2 Turn the dough onto a lightly floured worktop and knead until smooth and elastic. Divide the dough into 12 equal portions and roll each piece into a ball.

3 Combine the melted butter, egg, Parmesan cheese, garlic, salt, and dried herbs in a small bowl, mixing well. Dip the dough balls into the butter mixture, coating them liberally all over, then arrange the dough balls in a single layer in the pan. Drizzle over any remaining butter mixture. Cover and let rise in a warm place until doubled in size.

4 Preheat the oven to 190°C/375°F/gas mark 5. Bake the ring for 30–40 minutes, or until risen and golden brown. Turn onto a wire rack. Pull the rolls apart to serve, warm or cold.

TO MAKE IN BREADMAKER, *use quantities as listed in main recipe but amend following ingredients and use 1¼ cups water (or according to package mix). Add ingredients to breadmaker in order specified in your instruction book. Use Dough setting, then continue as above from Step 2 of main recipe (punching down rather than kneading dough, then divide and shape dough and continue as directed).*

EVERYDAY BREADS AND ROLLS

68

079 Sesame ring breads

PREPARATION TIME *25 minutes, plus rising* COOKING TIME *10–15 minutes* MAKES *8 ring breads*

3⅔ cups strong white flour
1½ teaspoons salt
1 sachet (¼oz) easy-blend dried yeast
3 tablespoons unrefined or cold-pressed sesame oil

1 tablespoon clear honey
About 1 cup warm water
Beaten egg, to glaze
Sesame seeds, for sprinkling

1 Grease or flour 2 cookie sheets and set aside. Sift the flour and salt into a large bowl, then stir in the yeast. Make a well in the center, then add the sesame oil, honey, and enough water, mixing to form a soft dough.
2 Turn the dough onto a floured worktop and knead until smooth. Shape into a round, then place in a lightly oiled bowl, cover and let rise in a warm place until doubled in size.
3 Punch down the dough on a lightly floured worktop and divide into 8 equal portions. Roll each portion of dough into a sausage or rope shape about 12 inches long. Form each rope of dough into a ring and press the ends firmly together to seal.
4 Place on the cookie sheets, spacing them well apart. Cover and let rise again for about 30–45 minutes, or until doubled in size.
5 Meanwhile, preheat the oven to 200°C/400°F/gas mark 6. Lightly brush the rings with a little beaten egg and sprinkle with sesame seeds. Bake the rings for about 10–15 minutes, or until risen and golden brown. Transfer to a wire rack to cool. Serve warm.

TO MAKE IN BREADMAKER, *use quantities as listed in main recipe but amend following ingredients and use 3 cups strong white flour, 1 cup water, use fast-action dried yeast, and add 2 teaspoons superfine sugar. Add ingredients to breadmaker in order specified in your instruction book. Use Dough setting, then continue as above from Step 3 of main recipe.*

080 Sausage and salsa pasties

PREPARATION TIME *35 minutes, plus rising* COOKING TIME *15–20 minutes* MAKES *10 pasties*

1lb 2oz package white bread mix
½ cup mature cheddar cheese, finely grated
A good pinch of cayenne pepper
About 1¼ cups warm water

10 cold cooked, skinless thick sausages of your choice (pork, beef, herby, spicy, etc)
20 teaspoons tomato salsa (2 teaspoons per pastie)
Beaten egg, to glaze

1 Grease or flour 2 cookie sheets and set aside. Place the bread mix in a bowl and stir in the cheese and cayenne pepper. Add enough water (according to package instructions), mixing to form a soft dough.
2 Turn the dough onto a lightly floured worktop and knead until smooth and elastic. Roll out to form a 20 x 8-inch rectangle, then cut into ten 4-inch squares.
3 Place 1 sausage diagonally across 1 dough square, then spread 2 teaspoons salsa over the sausage. Fold the remaining two corners of the bread square over the sausage, pinching the edges together and pressing them down gently to seal (you will still be able to see both ends of the sausage).
4 Repeat with the remaining bread squares, sausages, and salsa, to make a total of 10 pasties. Place, seam-side up, on the cookie sheets, cover and let rise in a warm place for about 30 minutes, or until doubled in size.
5 Meanwhile, preheat the oven to 200°C/400°F/gas mark 6. Lightly brush the pasties with a little beaten egg, then bake for 15–20 minutes, or until risen and golden brown. Transfer to a wire rack to cool. Serve warm or cold.

TO MAKE IN BREADMAKER, *use quantities as listed in main recipe but use 1¼ cups water (or according to package mix). Add ingredients to breadmaker in order specified in your instruction book. Use Dough setting, then continue as above from Step 2 of main recipe (punching down rather than kneading dough, then roll out dough and continue as directed).*

081 Bagels

PREPARATION TIME *55 minutes, plus rising* **COOKING TIME** *15–20 minutes* **MAKES** *12 bagels*

1½ cups strong white flour	About 1½ cups warm water
1½ teaspoons salt	1 tablespoon granulated sugar
1½ cups strong wholewheat flour	Milk, for glazing
1 sachet (¼oz) easy-blend dried yeast	Poppy seeds, sesame seeds, or caraway
1 tablespoon superfine sugar	seeds, for sprinkling (optional)
2 tablespoons sunflower oil	

1   Grease 2 cookie sheets well and set aside. Sift the white flour and salt into a large bowl, then stir in the wholewheat flour, yeast, and superfine sugar. Make a well in the center, then add the oil and enough water, mixing to form a soft dough.
2   Turn the dough onto a lightly floured worktop and knead until smooth and elastic. Shape the dough into a round, then place it in a lightly oiled bowl, cover and let rise in a warm place until doubled in size.
3   Punch down the dough on a lightly floured worktop, then divide it into 12 equal portions. Shape each piece of dough into a ball, then, using the floured handle of a wooden spoon, make a hole through the center of each ball. Enlarge the holes by pulling the dough outward slightly to form rings, making sure the holes are big enough (bearing in mind that the holes will close slightly when the dough is risen and poached). Place on the cookie sheets, cover and let rise again for about 30 minutes, or until doubled in size.
4   Meanwhile, preheat the oven to 200°C/400°F/gas mark 6. Heat a large pan of water until it is simmering, then stir in the granulated sugar until dissolved. Carefully drop each bagel into the simmering water (3 or 4 at a time) and poach for about 3 minutes, turning once.
5   Remove the bagels from the water, drain well, then return the bagels to the cookie sheets. Brush each one with a little milk and sprinkle the tops with seeds, if desired.
6   Bake the bagels for 15–20 minutes, or until golden brown. Transfer to a wire rack to cool. Cut in half to serve, warm or cold.

082 🍞 Seeded knots

PREPARATION TIME *25 minutes, plus rising* **COOKING TIME** *15–20 minutes* **MAKES** *12 knots*

3⅔ cups strong white flour	2 tablespoons butter, diced
1 teaspoon salt	About 1¼ cups warm milk
1 sachet (¼oz) fast-action dried yeast	Caraway seeds, pumpkin seeds, and
1 teaspoon superfine sugar	poppy seeds, for sprinkling

1   Grease or flour 2 cookie sheets and set aside. Sift the flour and salt into a large bowl, stir in the yeast and sugar, then rub in the butter. Make a well in the center, then add enough milk, mixing to form a soft dough.
2   Turn the dough onto a lightly floured worktop and knead until smooth and elastic. Divide the dough into 12 equal portions. Roll each piece of dough into a long sausage or rope shape, then gently tie each one loosely in a single knot, pulling the ends through.
3   Place on the cookie sheets, spacing them well apart, then cover and let rise in a warm place for about 30 minutes, or until doubled in size.
4   Preheat the oven to 220°C/425°F/gas mark 7. Lightly brush the rolls with a little water and sprinkle 4 rolls with caraway seeds, 4 with pumpkin seeds, and 4 with poppy seeds.
5   Bake the rolls for 15–20 minutes or until risen and golden brown. Transfer to a wire rack to cool. Serve warm or cold.

TO MAKE IN BREADMAKER, *use quantities as listed in main recipe but amend following ingredients and use 1½ cups milk, 2 teaspoons salt, and 2 teaspoons superfine sugar. Add ingredients to breadmaker in order specified in your instruction book. Use Dough setting, then continue as above from Step 2 of main recipe (punching down rather than kneading dough, then divide and shape dough and continue as directed).*

EVERYDAY BREADS AND ROLLS

083 Poppyseed clover leaf rolls

PREPARATION TIME *25 minutes, plus rising* **COOKING TIME** *15–20 minutes* **MAKES** *10 rolls*

1lb 2oz package white bread mix
¾ cup gruyère or emmental cheese,
   finely grated
1 teaspoon mustard powder

A few turns of freshly ground black
   pepper
About 1¼ cups warm water
Beaten egg or milk, to glaze
Poppy seeds, for sprinkling

1 Grease or flour 2 cookie sheets and set aside. Place the bread mix in a bowl and stir in the cheese, mustard powder, and black pepper. Add enough water (according to package instructions), mixing to form a soft dough.

2 Turn the dough onto a floured worktop and knead until smooth and elastic. Divide the dough into 30 equal portions. Roll each piece into a small ball, then place them on the cookie sheets, in groups of 3, to make a clover-leaf shape. Make sure that each group of 3 balls are just touching each other so that they join together as they rise and cook.

3 Brush with beaten egg or milk and sprinkle with poppy seeds. Cover and let rise in a warm place for about 30 minutes or until doubled in size.

4 Meanwhile, preheat the oven to 200°C/400°F/gas mark 6. Bake the rolls for 15–20 minutes, or until risen and golden brown. Transfer to a wire. Serve warm or cold.

VARIATIONS *Use mature cheddar cheese in place of gruyère or emmental. Use sesame or caraway seeds in place of poppy seeds.*

084 Cherry and hazelnut twists

PREPARATION TIME *30 minutes, plus rising* **COOKING TIME** *15–20 minutes* **MAKES** *12 twists*

1½ cups strong white flour
½ teaspoon salt
2 tablespoons butter, diced
1½ teaspoons easy-blend dried yeast
2 tablespoons superfine sugar
½ cup dried cherries, halved

½ cup toasted hazelnuts,
   finely chopped
1½ teaspoons ground cinnamon
1 egg, lightly beaten
About ½ cup warm milk, plus extra
   for glazing
4 sugar cubes, coarsely crushed

1 Grease or flour 2 cookie sheets and set aside. Sift the flour and salt into a large bowl, then rub in the butter. Stir in the yeast, superfine sugar, cherries, hazelnuts, and cinnamon. Make a well in the center, then add the egg and enough milk, mixing to form a soft dough.

2 Turn the dough onto a lightly floured worktop and knead until smooth and elastic. Shape the dough into a round, then place it in a lightly oiled bowl, cover and let rise in a warm place until doubled in size.

3 Punch down the dough on a lightly floured worktop, then divide it into 12 equal pieces. Roll each piece of dough into a long sausage or rope shape, about 8 inches long, then gently tie each one into a single knot, pulling the ends through, and place on the cookie sheets. Cover and let rise again for about 45 minutes, or until doubled in size.

4 Meanwhile, preheat the oven to 190°C/375°F/gas mark 5. Brush the twists with a little milk and sprinkle with crushed sugar cubes. Bake the twists for 15–20 minutes, or until risen and golden brown. Transfer to a wire rack to cool. Serve warm or cold.

CHAPTER 2

Specialty and festive breads

Specialty breads are made from yeasted doughs which are enriched with a combination of other ingredients such as eggs, sugar, butter, dried fruit, or chocolate. Enriched breads, both sweet and savory, vary in texture from soft and airy loaves with a rich and buttery flavor, to deliciously light and flaky melt-in-the-mouth yeasted pastries, all of which are hard to resist.

Some specialty breads, such as Challah and Greek Easter Bread are traditionally baked to celebrate a particular festival, while others such as Stollen and Panettone are often made at customary times of the year, such as around Christmas.

We include a delicious selection of enriched, specialty breads from all over the world, including Brioche, Kugelhopf, or Pains au Chocolat, as well as tempting delights such as Croissants, Cinnamon Raisin Whirl, or Danish Pastries. We also include some simpler enriched dough recipes such as Devonshire Splits, Bath Buns, Chocolate Hazelnut Loaf, Chelsea Buns, or Teacakes.

085 Cherry kirsch savarin

PREPARATION TIME *40 minutes, plus rising* COOKING TIME *25–30 minutes* SERVES *10–12*

1½ cups strong white flour
½ teaspoon salt
2 tablespoons superfine sugar
1 sachet (¼oz) fast-action dried yeast
6 tablespoons warm milk
4 large eggs, lightly beaten
1 stick butter, melted
¾ cup granulated sugar

5 tablespoons Kirsch
3 tablespoons dry white wine
4½ tablespoons apricot jelly
1¼ cups heavy cream, whipped
½lb fresh or canned (drained) cherries, pitted
2 tablespoons pistachio nuts, chopped

1 Grease a 2-pint savarin mold and set aside. Sift the flour and salt into a large bowl, then stir in the superfine sugar and yeast. Make a well in the center, then add the milk, eggs, and melted butter and mix to form a smooth, very thick, batter-like dough.

2 Knead the dough in the bowl, beating it with your hand for 4–5 minutes, or until smooth, elastic and slightly stiffer, then pour the mixture evenly into the savarin mold. Cover and let rise in a warm place until the mixture almost reaches the top of the mold.

3 Preheat the oven to 200°C/400°F/gas mark 6. Bake the savarin for 25–30 minutes, or until golden. Turn onto a wire rack, then place the wire rack over a tray.

4 Place the granulated sugar in a saucepan with ¾ cup water. Heat gently, stirring until the sugar has dissolved, then bring to the boil and boil rapidly for 5 minutes. Remove the pan from the heat, then stir in the Kirsch and wine. Slowly pour the Kirsch mixture evenly over the savarin, catching the excess juices in the tray underneath. Repeat until all the syrup is absorbed—the savarin will swell and look shiny.

5 Place the savarin on a serving plate. Place the jelly in a saucepan with 1 tablespoon water and heat until melted. Brush the jelly all over the savarin and let cool.

6 Fill the center of the savarin with whipped cream and cherries. Decorate with a sprinkling of pistachio nuts. Serve in slices or wedges.

086 Brioche

PREPARATION TIME *30 minutes, plus rising* COOKING TIME *30–35 minutes* SERVES *10–12*

1½ cups strong white flour
¼ teaspoon salt
1½ teaspoons easy-blend dried yeast
2 tablespoons superfine sugar

½ stick butter, melted
2 large eggs, lightly beaten
1–2 tablespoons warm milk
Beaten egg, to glaze

1 Grease a 2-pint brioche mold and set aside. Sift the flour and salt into a large bowl, then stir in the yeast and sugar. Make a well in the center, then add the melted butter, eggs, and enough milk, mixing to form a soft dough.

2 Turn the dough onto a lightly floured worktop and knead until smooth and elastic. Shape the dough into a round, then place it in a lightly oiled bowl, cover and let rise in a warm place until doubled in size.

3 Punch down the dough on a lightly floured worktop, then cut a quarter from the dough and set aside. Knead the remaining large piece of dough and shape into a large round. Place it in the brioche mold. Shape the smaller piece of dough into a round, place it on top of the brioche and press down lightly. Cover and let rise again for about 30 minutes, or until the dough nearly reaches the top of the mold.

4 Meanwhile, preheat the oven to 230°C/450°F/gas mark 8. Lightly brush the brioche with beaten egg and bake for 10 minutes. Reduce the oven temperature to 190°C/375°F/gas mark 5 and bake for a further 20–25 minutes, or until the brioche is golden and sounds hollow when tapped underneath, covering it loosely with foil toward the end of the cooking time if the top is browning too quickly. Turn onto a wire rack to cool. Serve warm or cold.

087 Orange and cinnamon brioche

PREPARATION TIME *30 minutes, plus rising* **COOKING TIME** *40 minutes* **SERVES** *12–14*

3 cups strong white flour	1 teaspoon ground cinnamon
½ teaspoon salt	1½ sticks butter
1 sachet (¼oz) easy-blend dried yeast	3 large eggs, lightly beaten
4 tablespoons superfine sugar	About 3 tablespoons warm milk
1 tablespoon finely grated orange zest	Beaten egg yolk, to glaze

1 Grease a 3-pint brioche mold and set aside. Sift the flour and salt into a bowl, then stir in the yeast, sugar, orange zest, and cinnamon. Rub half the butter into the flour mixture, then make a well in the center. Melt the remaining butter, cool slightly, then add to the flour mixture together with the eggs and enough milk, mixing to form a soft dough.

2 Turn the dough onto a lightly floured worktop and knead until smooth and elastic. Shape the dough into a round, then place it in a lightly oiled bowl, cover and let rise in a warm place until doubled in size.

3 Punch down the dough on a lightly floured worktop, then cut a quarter from the dough and set aside. Knead the remaining large piece of dough, shape it into a large round ball and place it in the brioche mold. Shape the reserved piece of dough into a pear shape.

4 Make a hollow in the center of the large round of dough and place the thinner end of the pear-shaped piece of dough into the hollow. Cover and let rise again for about 30 minutes, or until the dough nearly reaches the top of the pan.

5 Meanwhile, preheat the oven to 200°C/400°F/gas mark 6. Brush the brioche with beaten egg yolk, then bake for about 40 minutes, or until risen and golden. Turn onto a wire rack to cool. Serve warm or cold in slices or wedges.

088 Rum babas

PREPARATION TIME *40 minutes, plus rising* COOKING TIME *15–20 minutes* MAKES *16 babas*

½ cup dried currants
8 tablespoons dark rum
2 tablespoons boiling water
1½ cups strong white flour
½ teaspoon salt
1 sachet (¼oz) easy-blend dried yeast

1 tablespoon superfine sugar
3 tablespoons warm milk
3 large eggs, lightly beaten
1 stick butter, softened
1¼ cups granulated sugar

1 Grease 16 small baba or dariole molds (each about 1/2-cup capacity) and set aside. Mix the currants, 4 tablespoons rum and the boiling water together in a small bowl and let soak. Sift the flour and salt into a large bowl, then stir in the yeast and superfine sugar. Make a well in the center, then add the milk and eggs and mix to form a smooth, very thick, batter-like dough.

2 Knead the dough in the bowl, beating it with your hand for 4–5 minutes, or until smooth, elastic and slightly stiffer. Cover and let rise in a warm place until doubled in size.

3 Punch down the dough in the bowl, then gradually work in the butter and soaked currants (without any remaining soaking liquid, which can be sprinkled over the babas just before serving), until a smooth, even, thick batter is formed. Spoon the mixture into the molds, filling each one about one-third full. Place on a cookie sheet, then cover and let rise again for about 30 minutes, or until the mixture almost reaches the top of the molds.

4 Meanwhile, preheat the oven to 200°C/400°F/gas mark 6. Bake the babas for 15–20 minutes, or until golden. Turn onto a wire rack to cool.

5 Place the granulated sugar and 2½ cups water in a pan and heat gently until the sugar has dissolved, then bring to the boil and boil rapidly for 5 minutes. Remove the pan from the heat, then add the babas to the hot syrup, one or two at a time, turning them over several times to ensure they absorb the syrup—the babas will swell and look shiny.

6 Lift the babas out of the syrup and place on a plate. Sprinkle the babas with the remaining rum just before serving. Combine any remaining syrup and soaking liquid and spoon over the babas to serve.

089 Fougasse

PREPARATION TIME *30 minutes, plus rising* COOKING TIME *25 minutes* MAKES *1 loaf (serves 10)*

2⅓ cups strong white flour
½ teaspoon salt
1½ teaspoons easy-blend dried yeast
1 tablespoon olive oil

About 1 cup warm water
¼ cup pitted black olives, chopped
½ cup walnuts, chopped
Olive oil, for brushing

1 Grease a cookie sheet and set aside. Sift the flour and salt into a large bowl, then stir in the yeast. Make a well in the center, then add the olive oil and enough water, mixing to form a soft dough.

2 Turn the dough onto a lightly floured worktop and knead until smooth and elastic. Shape the dough into a round, then place it in a lightly oiled bowl, cover and let rise in a warm place until doubled in size.

3 Punch down the dough on a lightly floured worktop, then flatten it slightly. Sprinkle the olives and walnuts evenly over the dough, then fold the dough over on itself two or three times to incorporate them. Shape the dough into a ball, then roll it out into an oblong about 10 inches long.

4 Make four parallel cuts diagonally through the dough leaving the edges intact. Gently stretch the dough to open the cuts, so that it resembles a ladder. Transfer to the cookie sheet, cover and let rise again for about 45 minutes, or until nearly doubled in size.

5 Preheat the oven to 220°C/425°F/gas mark 7. Brush the loaf with a little olive oil and bake for about 25 minutes, or until golden. Transfer to a wire rack to cool. Serve warm or cold.

090 Kugelhopf

PREPARATION TIME *25 minutes, plus rising* COOKING TIME *40 minutes* MAKES *1 loaf (serves 12)*

½ cup flaked almonds
2⅓ cups strong white flour
½ teaspoon salt
1½ teaspoons easy-blend dried yeast
⅔ cup golden raisins
1 teaspoon ground pudding spice

1 stick butter, softened
⅔ cup superfine sugar
2 large eggs, lightly beaten
½ cup warm milk, plus a little extra
   if necessary
Confectioners' sugar, to serve

1 Grease an 8-inch kugelhopf mold, sprinkle with the flaked almonds and set aside. Sift the flour and salt into a large bowl, then stir in the yeast, golden raisins, and pudding spice. Make a well in the center and set aside. In a separate bowl, cream together the butter and sugar, then gradually beat in the eggs and milk. Pour the creamed mixture into the well in the dry ingredients and mix well to form a very soft, silky dough, adding a little extra milk if necessary.

2 Turn the dough onto a lightly floured worktop and knead until smooth and elastic. Shape the dough into a round, then place it in a lightly oiled bowl, cover and let rise in a warm place until doubled in size.

3 Punch down the dough on a lightly floured worktop, then place it in the mold. Cover and let rise again for about 1 hour, or until it almost reaches the rim of the mold.

4 Meanwhile, preheat the oven to 200°C/400°F/gas mark 6. Bake the kugelhopf for about 40 minutes, or until golden and a skewer inserted in the center comes out clean. Turn onto a wire rack to cool. Dust with sifted confectioners' sugar just before serving.

091 Buchty

PREPARATION TIME *30 minutes, plus rising* COOKING TIME *30–35 minutes* MAKES *1 loaf (serves 16)*

3 cups strong white flour
1 teaspoon salt
1½ teaspoons easy-blend dried yeast
4 tablespoons superfine sugar

1¼ sticks butter
About ¼ cup milk, plus a little
   extra if necessary
3 large eggs, lightly beaten

1 Grease an 8-inch square loose-bottomed cake pan and set aside. Sift the flour and salt into a bowl, then stir in the yeast and sugar. Melt ½ stick butter in a small pan, then stir in the milk. Remove from the heat and leave until lukewarm.

2 Make a well in the center of the dry ingredients, add the butter mixture and eggs and mix to form a soft dough, adding a little extra milk, if necessary.

3 Turn the dough onto a lightly floured worktop and knead until smooth. Shape the dough into a round, place it in a lightly oiled bowl, then cover and let rise in a warm place until doubled in size.

4 Punch down the dough on a lightly floured worktop, then divide into 16 equal pieces and shape each piece into a ball. Melt the remaining butter, then roll the dough balls in the butter to coat them all over. Arrange the dough balls, so they are just touching each other, in the pan. Cover and let rise again for about 1 hour, or until doubled in size.

5 Meanwhile, preheat the oven to 190°C/375°F/gas mark 5. Brush any remaining melted butter over the top of the balls. Bake the buchty for 30–35 minutes, or until golden brown, covering it loosely with foil toward the end of the cooking time, if the top is browning too quickly. Turn onto a wire rack to cool. Pull the rolls apart to serve.

Stollen

PREPARATION TIME *30 minutes, plus rising* **COOKING TIME** *40 minutes* **MAKES** *1 loaf (serves 10–12)*

2⅓ cups strong white flour
½ teaspoon salt
1 teaspoon ground pudding spice
½ stick butter, diced
2 tablespoons superfine sugar
2 teaspoons easy-blend dried yeast
Finely grated zest of 1 lemon

1 cup luxury mixed dried fruit
½ cup blanched almonds, finely chopped
1 large egg, lightly beaten
About ½ cup warm milk
6oz ready-made marzipan
Confectioners' sugar and ground
   cinnamon, for dusting

1   Grease a cookie sheet and set aside. Sift the flour, salt and pudding spice into a large bowl, then rub in the butter. Stir in the superfine sugar, yeast, lemon zest, dried fruit, and almonds. Make a well in the center, then add the egg and enough milk, mixing to form a soft dough.

2   Turn the dough onto a lightly floured worktop and knead until smooth and elastic. Shape the dough into a round, place it in a lightly oiled bowl, cover and let rise in a warm place until doubled in size.

3   Punch down the dough on a lightly floured worktop, then shape into a rectangle about 8 x 4 inches in size and 1-inch thick. Roll the marzipan into a long sausage, just a little shorter than the length of the rectangle.

4   Place the marzipan log along the center of the dough, fold the dough over almost in half to enclose it, and press the edges together to seal. Transfer to the cookie sheet, cover and let rise again for 45–60 minutes.

5   Meanwhile, preheat the oven to 180°C/350°F/gas mark 4. Bake the stollen for about 40 minutes, or until it sounds hollow when tapped underneath. Transfer to a wire rack to cool. Dust with a mixture of sifted confectioners' sugar and ground cinnamon. Serve in slices.

VARIATION *Drizzle the baked stollen with a thin glacé icing in place of the dusting of confectioners' sugar and ground cinnamon.*

093 Christmas fruit bread

PREPARATION TIME *25 minutes, plus rising* **COOKING TIME** *30 minutes* **MAKES** *1 loaf (serves 10–12)*

2⅓ cups strong white flour
½ teaspoon salt
½ stick butter, diced
2 teaspoons easy-blend dried yeast
4 tablespoons superfine sugar
Finely grated zest of 1 small orange
⅓ cup mixed ready-to-eat dried apricots, chopped

⅓ cup golden raisins
⅓ cup candied cherries, chopped
⅓ cup flaked almonds
1 large egg, lightly beaten
Few drops of almond extract
About ½ cup warm milk
Confectioners' sugar, for dusting

1 Grease a 3-pint brioche mold or grease a cookie sheet and set aside. Sift the flour and salt into a large bowl, then lightly rub in the butter. Stir in the yeast, superfine sugar, orange zest, dried fruit, cherries, and almonds.
2 Make a well in the center, then add the egg, almond extract, and enough milk, mixing to form a soft dough.
3 Turn the dough onto a lightly floured worktop and knead until smooth and elastic. Shape the dough into a round, place it in a lightly oiled bowl, then cover and let rise in a warm place until doubled in size.
4 Punch down the dough on a lightly floured worktop, then shape into a round and place in the mold or on the cookie sheet. Cover and let rise again for about 1 hour.
5 Meanwhile, preheat the oven to 190°C/375°F/gas mark 5. Bake the bread for about 30 minutes, or until the loaf is deep golden brown and sounds hollow when tapped underneath. Turn onto a wire rack to cool. Serve dusted with sifted confectioners' sugar.

VARIATIONS *Use lemon zest in place of orange zest. Use dried cranberries or blueberries in place of golden raisins.*

094 Tsoureki

PREPARATION TIME *30 minutes, plus rising* **COOKING TIME** *45 minutes* **MAKES** *1 loaf (serves 10–12)*

2 cups strong white flour
½ teaspoon salt
¾ stick butter, diced
1½ teaspoons easy-blend dried yeast
4 tablespoons superfine sugar
Finely grated zest of 1 small lemon

2 large eggs, lightly beaten
4 tablespoons warm milk
3 eggs, hard-cooked, then colored with red food coloring paste and cooled
Beaten egg, to glaze

1 Grease a cookie sheet and set aside. Sift the flour and salt into a large bowl, then lightly rub in the butter. Stir in the yeast, sugar, and lemon zest. Make a well in the center, then add the beaten eggs and milk, mixing to form a soft dough.
2 Turn the dough onto a lightly floured worktop and knead until smooth and elastic. Shape the dough into a round, place it in a lightly oiled bowl, then cover and let rise in a warm place until doubled in size.
3 Punch down the dough on a lightly floured worktop, then divide it into 3 equal pieces. Roll each piece of dough into a long rope, about 14 inches in length, then braid the dough ropes together, pressing them together at both ends to seal. Place on the cookie sheet and push the dyed eggs into the loaf at regular intervals. Cover and let rise again for about 1 hour.
4 Meanwhile, preheat the oven to 180°C/350°F/gas mark 4. Brush the loaf with beaten egg to glaze, then bake for about 45 minutes, or until golden brown, covering the bread loosely with foil toward the end of the cooking time if the top is browning too quickly. Transfer to a wire rack to cool. Serve in slices.

095 🍞 Monkey bread

PREPARATION TIME *35 minutes, plus rising* COOKING TIME *40 minutes* MAKES *1 loaf (serves 16)*

⅔ cup golden raisins
4 tablespoons brandy
3 cups strong white flour
½ teaspoon salt
1 sachet (¼oz) easy-blend dried yeast
2 teaspoons superfine sugar
¾ cup warm milk

¼ cup warm water
1 large egg, lightly beaten
1 cup walnuts, finely chopped
1½ teaspoons ground pudding spice
⅔ cup light soft brown sugar
¾ stick butter melted

1 Place the golden raisins in a bowl, add the brandy and stir. let soak overnight. Grease a 9-inch loose-bottomed springform pan with a tube base, or a ring mold and set aside.

2 Sift the flour and salt into a large bowl, then stir in the yeast and superfine sugar. Make a well in the center, then add the milk, water and egg and mix to form a soft dough.

3 Turn the dough onto a floured worktop and knead until smooth and elastic. Shape into a round, then place in an oiled bowl, cover and let rise in a warm place until doubled in size. Mix the walnuts, pudding spice, and soft brown sugar in a bowl and set aside.

4 Punch down the dough on a lightly floured worktop, then divide into 32 pieces and roll into balls. Dip each ball into the butter, then roll in the walnut mixture, covering completely. Place half the balls in the pan, spacing them slightly apart. Spoon over the soaked golden raisins and any remaining walnut mixture. Top with the remaining dough balls and drizzle over any remaining butter. Cover and let rise for about 45 minutes, or until doubled in size.

5 Preheat the oven to 190°C/375°F/gas mark 5. Bake the loaf for about 40 minutes, or until risen and golden brown. Cool in the pan for 10 minutes, then invert onto a serving plate.

TO MAKE IN BREADMAKER, *use quantities as listed in main recipe but use fast-action dried yeast. Add ingredients to breadmaker in order specified in your instruction book. Use Dough setting for this recipe, then continue as above from end of Step 3 of main recipe. Serve warm or cold.*

096 🍞 Challah

PREPARATION TIME *45 minutes, plus rising* COOKING TIME *35–40 minutes* MAKES *1 loaf (serves 10)*

3⅔ cups strong white flour
1½ teaspoons salt
1 sachet (¼oz) easy-blend dried yeast
1 tablespoon superfine sugar
5 tablespoons olive oil

2 eggs, lightly beaten
About ½ cup warm water
Beaten egg, to glaze
Sesame or poppy seeds, for sprinkling

1 Sift the flour and salt into a bowl, then stir in the yeast and sugar. Make a well in the center, then add the oil, eggs, and enough warm water, mixing to form a soft dough.

2 Turn the dough onto a floured worktop and knead until smooth. Shape into a round, then place in a lightly oiled bowl, cover and let rise in a warm place until doubled in size.

3 Punch down the dough on a floured worktop, then divide into 4 equal portions. Roll each portion into a rope about 16 inches long. Braid the ropes together—place them next to each other and pinch the ends together at one end. Starting from the right, lift the first rope over the second and lift the third rope over the fourth, then place the fourth rope between the first and second ropes. Repeat and continue, to form a braid. Tuck the ends under; place braid on a greased cookie sheet. Cover and let rise until doubled in size.

4 Preheat the oven to 220°C/425°F/gas mark 7. Brush the dough with beaten egg and sprinkle with seeds. Bake the loaf for 15 minutes, then reduce the oven temperature to 190°C/375°F/gas mark 5 and bake for a further 20–25 minutes, or until risen and golden brown. Transfer to a wire rack to cool. Serve in slices or wedges.

TO MAKE IN BREADMAKER, *use quantities as listed in main recipe but amend following ingredients and use ⅔ cup water and use fast-action dried yeast. Add ingredients to breadmaker in order specified in your instruction book. Use Dough setting, then continue from Step 3 of main recipe.*

097 Festival fruit crown loaf

PREPARATION TIME *35 minutes, plus rising* **COOKING TIME** *45–50 minutes* **SERVES** *16*

1lb 2oz package white bread mix
½ stick butter, diced
2 tablespoons superfine sugar
Finely grated zest of 1 small orange
1 large egg, lightly beaten
About 1 cup warm water

1 cup golden raisins
4oz ready-made marzipan
1 cup confectioners' sugar
About 2–3 teaspoons orange juice
¼ cup toasted flaked almonds

1   Grease a deep 9-inch or 10-inch round cake pan and set aside. Place the bread mix in a large bowl and lightly rub in the butter. Stir in the superfine sugar and orange zest, then add the egg and enough water, mixing to form a soft dough.

2   Turn the dough onto a lightly floured worktop and knead until smooth and elastic. Knead the golden raisins into the dough. Divide the dough into 16 equal pieces and roll each piece into a ball. Divide the marzipan into 16 equal pieces and roll each one into a round.

3   Press a round of marzipan into the center of each roll of dough, then re-roll each one, enclosing the marzipan. Arrange 11 balls round the outside of the pan and fit the remaining 5 balls into the center. Cover and let rise in a warm place until doubled in size.

4   Preheat the oven to 190°C/375°F/gas mark 5. Bake the loaf for 45–50 minutes, or until risen and golden brown, covering it loosely with foil toward the end of the cooking time if the top is browning too quickly. Turn onto a wire rack to cool.

5   Blend the confectioners' sugar with enough orange juice to make a smooth frosting. Spread over the top of the loaf. Sprinkle with almonds. Pull the rolls apart to serve. Serve warm or cold.

098 🍞 Paradise braid

PREPARATION TIME *30 minutes, plus rising* **COOKING TIME** *45–50 minutes* **SERVES** *10*

3 cups strong white flour
½ teaspoon salt
½ stick butter, diced
1 sachet (¼oz) easy-blend dried yeast
4 tablespoons superfine sugar
2 large eggs, lightly beaten
About ⅔ cup warm milk

⅔ cup ready-to-eat dried pears, chopped
⅓ cup dried pineapple, chopped
½ cup blanched almonds, chopped
2 tablespoons butter, melted
Sifted confectioners' sugar, to decorate

1   Grease a cookie sheet and set aside. Sift the flour and salt into a large bowl, then lightly rub in the butter. Stir in the yeast and superfine sugar. Make a well in the center, then add the eggs and enough milk, mixing to form a soft dough.

2   Turn the dough onto a lightly floured worktop and knead until smooth and elastic. Knead the pears, pineapple, and almonds into the dough. Shape into a round, then place in a lightly oiled bowl, cover and let rise in a warm place until doubled in size.

3   Punch down the dough on a lightly floured worktop, then divide it into 3 equal pieces. Roll each piece into a long sausage or rope shape, about 12 inches long. Braid the dough ropes together, pressing them together at both ends to seal, then place on the cookie sheet. Cover and let rise again for about 45 minutes, or until almost doubled in size.

4   Meanwhile, preheat the oven to 190°C/375°F/gas mark 5. Bake the braid in the oven for about 45–50 minutes, or until risen and golden brown, covering it loosely with foil toward the end of the cooking time if the top is browning too quickly.

5   Transfer to a wire rack to cool slightly, then brush with melted butter and dust with sifted confectioners' sugar. Serve warm or cold in slices.

TO MAKE IN BREADMAKER, *use quantities as listed in main recipe but amend following ingredients and use ⅔ cup milk and use fast-action dried yeast. Add ingredients to breadmaker in order specified in your instruction book. Use Basic Raisin Dough or similar setting for this recipe (or use Dough setting) and add pears, pineapple, and almonds when machine makes a sound (beeps) to add extra ingredients during kneading cycle (or add extra ingredients 5 minutes before end of kneading cycle), then continue as above from Step 3 of main recipe.*

099 Greek easter bread

PREPARATION TIME *30 minutes, plus rising* COOKING TIME *35–40 minutes*
MAKES *1 loaf (serves 10–12)*

3⅔ cups strong white flour
½ teaspoon salt
1 sachet (¼oz) easy-blend dried yeast
½ cup superfine sugar
1 stick butter, melted

2 large eggs, lightly beaten
Few drops of almond extract
About ½ cup warm milk
Beaten egg, to glaze
Sifted confectioners' sugar, to serve

1 Grease a cookie sheet and set aside. Sift the flour and salt into a large bowl, then stir in the yeast and superfine sugar. Make a well in the center, then add the melted butter, eggs, almond extract, and enough milk, mixing to form a soft dough.

2 Turn the dough onto a lightly floured worktop and knead until smooth and elastic. Shape the dough into a round, place it in a lightly oiled bowl, then cover and let rise in a warm place until doubled in size.

3 Punch down the dough on a lightly floured worktop, then divide it into 3 equal pieces. Roll each piece into a long rope, then braid these ropes together. Shape the braid into a round or circle and press the ends together to seal. Place on the cookie sheet, cover and let rise again for about 45–60 minutes, or until doubled in size.

4 Meanwhile, preheat the oven to 190°C/375°F/gas mark 5. Brush the loaf with beaten egg to glaze, then bake for 35–40 minutes, or until golden brown, covering the bread loosely with foil toward the end of the cooking time if the top is browning too quickly. Transfer to a wire rack to cool. Dust with confectioners' sugar just before serving. Serve in slices.

100 Panettone

PREPARATION TIME *25 minutes, plus rising* COOKING TIME *45–50 minutes*
MAKES *1 loaf (serves 8–10)*

2¼ cups strong white flour
¼ teaspoon salt
1 sachet (¼oz) easy-blend dried yeast
4 tablespoons superfine sugar
⅔ cup golden raisins
⅓ cup chopped candied peel

Finely grated zest of 1 small lemon
3 large eggs, lightly beaten
4 tablespoons warm milk
1 stick butter, softened
1 tablespoon butter, melted

1 Grease and line a deep 7-inch round cake pan. Using string, tie a collar of a double layer of waxed paper around the outside of the pan, bringing the collar about 3 inches above the rim. Set aside.

2 Sift the flour and salt into a bowl, then stir in the yeast, sugar, golden raisins, candied peel, and lemon zest. Make a well in the center, then add the eggs, milk, and softened butter and beat the dough for 5 minutes or until it becomes elastic and leaves the sides of the bowl.

3 Turn the dough onto a floured worktop and knead until smooth, then shape into a round, place in a lightly oiled bowl, cover and let rise in a warm place until doubled in size.

4 Punch down the dough on a lightly floured worktop, then shape it into a ball. Place in the prepared pan and cut a cross in the top. Cover and let rise again for about 30 minutes, or until doubled in size.

5 Meanwhile, preheat the oven to 200°C/400°F/gas mark 6. Brush the top of the panettone liberally with melted butter. Bake for 15 minutes, then reduce the oven temperature to 180°C/350°F/gas mark 4 and bake for a further 30–35 minutes, or until the top is golden and crisp. Turn onto a wire rack to cool. Cut into wedges to serve.

101 Easter bread ring

PREPARATION TIME *30 minutes, plus rising* **COOKING TIME** *25 minutes* **MAKES** *1 loaf (serves 10–12)*

1½ cups strong white flour

½ teaspoon salt

½ stick butter, diced

1½ teaspoons easy-blend dried yeast

2 tablespoons superfine sugar

1 large egg, lightly beaten

About ½ cup warm milk,
  plus extra for glazing

⅓ cup golden raisins

⅓ cup ready-to-eat dried apricots,
  chopped

⅓ cup light soft brown sugar

1½ teaspoons ground pudding spice

1 cup confectioners' sugar, sifted

¼ cup toasted flaked almonds

1   Grease a cookie sheet and set aside. Sift the flour and salt into a large bowl, then lightly rub in 2 tablespoons of the butter. Stir in the yeast and superfine sugar. Make a well in the center, then add the egg and enough milk, mixing to form a soft dough.

2   Turn the dough onto a lightly floured worktop and knead until smooth and elastic. Shape the dough into a round, then place it in a lightly oiled bowl and let rise in a warm place until doubled in size.

3   Punch down the dough on a lightly floured worktop, then roll it out to form an 18 x 12-inch rectangle. Melt the remaining butter and brush it over the dough.

4   Combine the golden raisins, apricots, soft brown sugar, and pudding spice and sprinkle evenly over the dough. Starting from a long side, roll up the dough fairly tightly like a jelly roll. Make sure the seam is underneath, then shape the dough into a circle. Brush the ends with a little milk and press them together to seal. Place on the cookie sheet.

5   Using a sharp knife, cut two-thirds of the way through the dough at 1½-inch intervals. Twist the slices outward at an angle so they overlap slightly. Cover and let rise again for about 1 hour, or until doubled in size.

6   Meanwhile, preheat the oven to 200°C/400°F/gas mark 6. Bake the bread ring for about 25 minutes, or until it is risen and golden brown. Transfer to a wire rack to cool.

7   Mix the confectioners' sugar with about 4 teaspoons water to make a thin glacé frosting. Drizzle over the warm baked ring and sprinkle with flaked almonds. Serve warm or cold in slices.

102 Lemon fruit twist

PREPARATION TIME *35 minutes, plus rising* **COOKING TIME** *30–35 minutes* **SERVES** *12–14*

1lb 2oz package white bread mix
½ stick butter, diced
2 tablespoons superfine sugar
Finely grated zest of 1 lemon
1 large egg, lightly beaten
About 1 cup warm water

½ cup ready-to-eat dried apricots,
  chopped
½ cup golden raisins
1 cup confectioners' sugar, sifted
About 3–4 teaspoons lemon juice
¼ cup toasted flaked almonds

1 Grease a cookie sheet and set aside. Place the bread mix in a large bowl and lightly rub in the butter. Stir in the superfine sugar and lemon zest, then add the egg and enough warm water, mixing to form a soft dough.
2 Turn the dough onto a lightly floured worktop and knead until smooth and elastic. Knead the apricots and golden raisins into the dough.
3 Divide the dough into 3 equal pieces and roll each piece into a long sausage or rope shape, each about 12 inches in length. Braid the dough ropes together, pressing them together at both ends to seal, then place on the cookie sheet. Cover and let rise in a warm place until doubled in size.
4 Preheat the oven to 190°C/375°F/gas mark 5. Bake the braid for 30–35 minutes, or until risen and golden brown. Transfer to a wire rack to cool.
5 Blend the confectioners' sugar with enough lemon juice to make a thick, smooth frosting and spoon this over the top of the braid. Sprinkle with toasted flaked almonds and serve in slices.

103 ⬛ Apricot and almond ring

PREPARATION TIME *40 minutes, plus rising* **COOKING TIME** *25–30 minutes* **SERVES** *10*

3 cups strong white flour
1 teaspoon salt
1 sachet (¼oz) fast-action dried yeast
⅔ cup superfine sugar
2 large eggs, lightly beaten
About 1 cup warm milk

⅓ cup ready-to-eat dried apricots,
  chopped
⅔ cup blanched almonds, finely chopped
2 teaspoons ground cinnamon
½ stick butter, melted

1 Grease a 9-inch loose-bottomed springform pan with a tube base, or a ring mold. Set aside. Sift the flour and salt into a bowl, then stir in the yeast and 2 tablespoons sugar. Make a well in the center, then add the eggs and enough milk, mixing to form a soft dough.
2 Turn the dough onto a lightly floured worktop and knead until smooth and elastic. Knead in the apricots and ⅓ cup almonds. Divide the dough into 10 equal portions, then roll each portion into a ball.
3 Mix the remaining sugar, almonds, and cinnamon together. Roll each ball in the melted butter, then in the almond mixture, covering them completely. Arrange the balls in the pan.
4 Drizzle over any remaining melted butter, then sprinkle any remaining nut mixture over the top. Cover and let rise in a warm place until the dough reaches the top of the pan.
5 Meanwhile, preheat the oven to 200°C/400°F/gas mark 6. Bake the ring for 25–30 minutes, or until risen and golden brown. Let cool in the pan for a few minutes, then turn onto a wire rack and let cool completely. Serve warm or cold.

TO MAKE IN BREADMAKER, *use quantities as listed in main recipe but amend following ingredients and use 1 cup milk. Use 2 tablespoons superfine sugar in dough; add remaining sugar as instructed in Step 3 of main recipe. Add ingredients to breadmaker in order specified in your instruction book. Use Basic Raisin Dough or similar setting for this recipe (or use Dough setting) and add apricots and ⅓ cup almonds when machine makes a sound (beeps) to add extra ingredients during kneading cycle (or add extra ingredients 5 minutes before end of kneading cycle), then punch down dough and continue as above from end of Step 2 of main recipe.*

104 Chocolate hazelnut loaf

PREPARATION TIME *20 minutes, plus rising* **COOKING TIME** *30–35 minutes* **MAKES** *1 loaf (serves 8)*

1½ cups strong white flour	**2 tablespoons superfine sugar**
1 tablespoon cocoa powder	**½ cup ground hazelnuts**
½ teaspoon salt	**½ cup semisweet chocolate chips**
2 tablespoons butter, diced	**1 large egg, lightly beaten**
1½ teaspoons fast-action dried yeast	**About ½ cup warm milk**

1 Grease a 2lb loaf pan and set aside. Sift the flour, cocoa powder, and salt into a large bowl, then rub in the butter. Stir in the yeast, sugar, hazelnuts, and chocolate chips. Make a well in the center, then add the egg and enough milk, mixing to form a soft dough.

2 Turn the dough onto a lightly floured worktop and knead until smooth and elastic. Shape the dough into an oblong, then press it into the pan. Cover and let rise in a warm place until doubled in size.

3 Meanwhile, preheat the oven to 200°C/400°F/gas mark 6. Bake the loaf for 30–35 minutes, or until the bread is lightly browned and sounds hollow when tapped underneath. Turn onto a a wire rack to cool. Serve in slices.

VARIATION *Use milk or white chocolate chips in place of semisweet chocolate chips.*

105 Fruit braid

PREPARATION TIME *30 minutes, plus rising* **COOKING TIME** *30 minutes* **SERVES** *6–8*

1½ cups strong white flour	**⅔ cup raisins**
½ teaspoon salt	**⅓ cup raw brown sugar**
½ stick butter, diced	**1 teaspoon ground cinnamon**
1 sachet (¼oz) easy-blend dried yeast	**1 cooking apple, peeled, cored, and**
⅓ cup superfine sugar	**grated**
1 large egg, lightly beaten	**1 cup confectioners' sugar, sifted**
About ½ cup warm milk	**3–4 teaspoons lemon juice**

1 Grease a cookie sheet and set aside. Sift the flour and salt into a large bowl, then lightly rub in the butter. Stir in the yeast and superfine sugar. Make a well in the center, then add the egg and enough milk, mixing to form a soft dough.

2 Turn the dough onto a lightly floured worktop and knead until smooth and elastic. Shape the dough into a round, then place it in a lightly oiled bowl, cover and let rise in a warm place until doubled in size.

3 Punch down the dough on a lightly floured worktop, then roll it out to form a 12 x 8-inch rectangle. Combine the raisins, raw brown sugar, cinnamon, and grated apple and spoon this mixture evenly down the center third (lengthwise) of the dough (about 2½ inches wide).

4 On the longest sides of the dough, make diagonal cuts up to the filling at 1-inch intervals. Braid the strips of dough over the filling, pressing lightly to seal. Tuck the ends under to seal at the top and bottom of the braid. Place the braid on the cookie sheet, then cover and let rise again for about 30 minutes.

5 Meanwhile, preheat the oven to 180°C/350°F/gas mark 4. Bake the braid for about 30 minutes, or until risen and golden brown, covering it loosely with foil toward the end of the cooking time if the top is browning too quickly. Transfer to a wire rack to cool.

6 Blend the confectioners' sugar with a little lemon juice to make a thick, smooth glacé frosting. Spread the lemon frosting over the warm braid and serve warm or cold in slices.

VARIATIONS *Use golden raisins in place of raisins. Use ground pudding spice in place of cinnamon. Use light soft brown sugar in place of raw brown sugar.*

Drizzled danish apple braid

PREPARATION TIME *35 minutes, plus rising* COOKING TIME *25–30 minutes* SERVES *8*

1½ cups strong white flour
½ teaspoon salt
2 tablespoons butter, diced
1½ teaspoons easy-blend dried yeast
⅓ cup superfine sugar
1 large egg, lightly beaten
About ½ cup warm milk
5oz package ready-made almond paste,
   coarsely grated

1 large or 2 small cooking apples,
   peeled, cored, and thinly sliced
1 teaspoon ground cinnamon
Beaten egg, to glaze
¾ cup confectioners' sugar, sifted
1 tablespoon toasted flaked almonds, or
   chopped pistachio nuts, to decorate

1. Grease a cookie sheet and set aside. Sift the flour and salt into a large bowl, then lightly rub in the butter. Stir in the yeast and 2 tablespoons superfine sugar. Make a well in the center, then add the egg and enough milk, mixing to form a soft dough.
2. Turn the dough onto a lightly floured worktop and knead until smooth and elastic. Shape into a round, then place in a lightly oiled bowl and let rise in a warm place until doubled in size.
3. Punch down the dough on a lightly floured worktop, then roll it out to form a 12 x 8-inch rectangle. Place the almond paste evenly down the center third (lengthwise) of the dough (about 2½-inches wide). Toss the apple slices with the remaining superfine sugar and cinnamon, then spoon this mixture over the almond paste.
4. On the longest sides of the dough, make diagonal cuts up to the filling at 1-inch intervals. Braid the strips of dough over the filling, pressing lightly to seal. Tuck the ends under to seal at the top and bottom of the braid. Place the braid on the cookie sheet, then cover and let rise again until doubled in size.
5. Preheat the oven to 200°C/400°F/gas mark 6. Lightly brush the braid with beaten egg, then bake for 25–30 minutes, or until risen and golden. Transfer to a wire rack to cool.
6. Blend the confectioners' sugar with a little water to make a thin glacé frosting. Drizzle the frosting over the warm braid; sprinkle with almonds or pistachio nuts. Serve warm or cold in slices.

107 Cinnamon raisin whirl

PREPARATION TIME *30 minutes, plus rising* **COOKING TIME** *25–30 minutes*
MAKES *1 loaf (serves 10–12)*

1½ cups packed white bread mix
2 tablespoons superfine sugar
1 large egg, lightly beaten
About ½ cup warm water
⅓ cup light soft brown sugar

4 teaspoons ground cinnamon
Finely grated zest of 1 orange
⅔ cup raisins
1 tablespoon, melted

1 Grease a 2lb loaf pan and set aside. Mix the white bread mix and superfine sugar in a large bowl. Add the egg and enough warm water, mixing to form a soft dough.

2 Turn the dough onto a lightly floured worktop and knead until smooth and elastic. Roll out to form a rectangle about 12 x 8 inches in size. Mix together the soft brown sugar, cinnamon, orange zest, and raisins.

3 Brush the dough with melted butter to within ½ inch of the edges. Sprinkle the raisin mixture evenly over the buttered dough, then roll up the dough fairly tightly like a jelly roll, starting from a short side. Re-shape if necessary and place in the loaf pan. Cover and let rise in a warm place until doubled in size.

4 Meanwhile, preheat the oven to 200°C/400°F/gas mark 6. Bake the loaf for 25–30 minutes, or until golden brown. Turn onto a wire rack to cool. Serve in slices spread with a little butter, maple syrup, or honey.

108 Pecan scroll

PREPARATION TIME *35 minutes, plus rising* **COOKING TIME** *30–40 minutes*
MAKES *1 loaf (serves 10–12)*

3 cups strong white flour
1 teaspoon salt
1 sachet (¼oz) easy-blend dried yeast
1 cup superfine sugar
1 stick butter, melted
About ¾ cup warm milk

1 cup pecan nuts, ground or finely
   chopped
1 cup plain cake crumbs
1 large egg, lightly beaten
½ teaspoon ground cinnamon
¾ cup confectioners' sugar
Pecan nuts, to decorate

1 Grease a 2lb loaf pan and set aside. Sift the flour and salt into a large bowl, then stir in the yeast and ½ cup superfine sugar. Make a well in the center, then add ¾ stick melted butter and enough milk, mixing to form a soft dough.

2 Turn the dough onto a lightly floured worktop and knead until smooth and elastic. Shape the dough into a round, then place it in a lightly oiled bowl, cover and let rise in a warm place until doubled in size.

3 Punch down the dough on a lightly floured worktop, then roll it out to form a rectangle about 12 x 8 inches in size. Combine the remaining superfine sugar, ground or chopped pecan nuts, cake crumbs, and egg in a bowl, then spread this mixture over the dough.

4 Roll up the dough from each short edge to the center to make a scroll shape. Place in the loaf pan, scroll-side (crack-side) up, re-shaping it slightly to fit in the pan. Cover and let rise again for about 30 minutes, or until it just reaches the top of the pan.

5 Meanwhile, preheat the oven to 200°C/400°F/gas mark 6. Bake the scroll for 30–40 minutes, or until risen and golden brown. Turn, inverting onto a wire rack, so the scroll shape is uppermost. Brush the remaining melted butter all over the loaf, then sprinkle with cinnamon. Let cool.

6 Blend the confectioners' sugar with 2–3 teaspoons water to make a thin glacé frosting. Drizzle the frosting over the scroll, decorate with pecan nuts and let set. Serve in slices.

109 Mincemeat and apple ring

PREPARATION TIME *35 minutes, plus rising* COOKING TIME *20–25 minutes* SERVES *8*

1⅓ cups white bread mix
2 tablespoons butter, diced
2 tablespoons superfine sugar
1 large egg, lightly beaten
About ½ cup warm milk

8oz mincemeat
1 small cooking apple (about 4½oz),
   peeled, cored, and finely chopped
1 teaspoon ground pudding spice
Sifted confectioners' sugar, to decorate

1   Grease a cookie sheet and set aside. Place the bread mix in a large bowl and lightly rub in the butter. Stir in the superfine sugar, then add the egg and enough warm milk, mixing to form a soft dough.

2   Turn the dough onto a lightly floured worktop and knead until smooth and elastic. Roll out to form a 14 x 8-inch rectangle. Combine the mincemeat, chopped apple and pudding spice, then spread this mixture evenly over the dough, leaving a ½-inch border around the edges.

3   Starting from a long side, roll up the dough fairly tightly like a jelly roll. Make sure the seam is underneath, then shape the dough into a circle. Brush the ends with a little water and press together to seal. Place on the cookie sheet.

4   Using a sharp knife, cut two-thirds of the way through the dough at 1½-inch intervals. Twist the slices outward at an angle so they overlap slightly. Cover and let rise in a warm place for about 1 hour, or until doubled in size.

5   Meanwhile, preheat the oven to 200°C/400°F/gas mark 6. Bake the bread ring for 20–25 minutes, or until risen and golden brown. Transfer to a wire rack to cool. Dust with sifted confectioners' sugar and serve warm or cold in slices.

110 Cornish saffron bread

PREPARATION TIME *25 minutes, plus infusing, plus rising* COOKING TIME *25–30 minutes*
MAKES *2 loaves (each loaf serves 8–10)*

About 1 cup milk
1 teaspoon saffron strands
3 cups strong white flour
½ teaspoon salt
2 teaspoons easy-blend dried yeast
4 tablespoons superfine sugar

1 teaspoon ground pudding spice
½ stick butter, softened
⅓ cup golden raisins
⅓ cup raisins
1–2 tablespoons clear honey

1   Grease two 2lb loaf pans and set aside. Heat ½ cup milk in a saucepan until almost boiling. Place the saffron strands in a small heatproof bowl, pour over the milk and stir gently. Set aside to infuse for 30 minutes.

2   Heat the remaining milk in the pan until it is lukewarm, then set aside. Sift the flour and salt into a large bowl, then stir in the yeast, sugar, and pudding spice. Make a well in the center, then add the butter, strained saffron liquid, and enough warmed milk, mixing to form a soft dough.

3   Turn the dough onto a lightly floured worktop and knead until smooth and elastic. Knead the golden raisins and raisins evenly into the dough. Shape the dough into a round, then place it in a lightly oiled bowl, cover and let rise in a warm place until doubled in size.

4   Punch down the dough on a lightly floured worktop, then divide it in half and shape into 2 oblongs. Press into the loaf pans, cover and let rise again until the dough reaches the top of the pans.

5   Meanwhile, preheat the oven to 200°C/400°F/gas mark 6. Bake the loaves for 25–30 minutes, or until risen and golden brown. Remove from the oven and brush the top of the loaves with honey while still hot. Cool slightly in the pan, then turn onto a wire rack and let cool completely. Serve warm or cold in slices, spread with butter.

111 ⊡ Lemon frosted bun round

PREPARATION TIME *35 minutes, plus rising* **COOKING TIME** *25–30 minutes* **SERVES** *12*

1lb 2oz package white bread mix	2 large eggs, lightly beaten
4 tablespoons superfine sugar	About 1 cup warm milk
Finely grated zest and juice of 1 large	⅔ cup golden raisins
lemon	1 cup confectioners' sugar, sifted

1 Grease a 9-inch loose-bottomed springform pan with a tube base, or a ring mold. Set aside. Place the bread mix in a bowl, then stir in the superfine sugar and lemon zest. Make a well in the center, then add the eggs and enough milk, mixing to form a soft dough.

2 Turn the dough onto a lightly floured worktop and knead until smooth and elastic. Knead the golden raisins evenly into the dough. Divide the dough into 12 equal portions, then roll each portion into a ball. Arrange the balls in the pan, then cover and let rise in a warm place until the dough reaches the top of the pan.

3 Meanwhile, preheat the oven to 200°C/400°F/gas mark 6. Bake the ring for 25–30 minutes, or until risen and golden brown. Let cool in the pan for a few minutes, then turn onto a wire rack and let cool completely.

4 Blend the confectioners' sugar with enough lemon juice to make a thick, smooth frosting and spread this over the top of the ring before serving. Pull the buns apart to serve.

TO MAKE IN BREADMAKER, *use quantities as listed in main recipe but amend following ingredients and use 1 cup milk. Add ingredients to breadmaker in order specified in your instruction book. Use Basic Raisin Dough or similar setting for this recipe (or use Dough setting) and add golden raisins when machine makes a sound (beeps) to add extra ingredients during kneading cycle (or add them 5 minutes before end of kneading cycle), then continue as above from middle of Step 2 of main recipe (punching down dough, then dividing and shaping dough as directed, etc).*

112 ⊡ Devonshire splits

PREPARATION TIME *25 minutes, plus rising* **COOKING TIME** *15 minutes* **MAKES** *10 Devonshire splits*

2⅓ cups strong white flour	About 1 cup warm milk
½ teaspoon salt	Strawberry or raspberry jelly, and
3 tablespoons butter, diced	clotted cream, to serve
1½ teaspoons easy-blend dried yeast	Sifted confectioners' sugar, for dusting
3 tablespoons superfine sugar	

1 Grease 2 cookie sheets and set aside. Sift the flour and salt into a large bowl, then lightly rub in the butter. Stir in the yeast and superfine sugar. Make a well in the center, then add enough milk, mixing to form a soft dough.

2 Turn the dough onto a lightly floured worktop and knead until smooth and elastic. Shape the dough into a round, then place it in a lightly oiled bowl, cover and let rise in a warm place until doubled in size.

3 Punch down the dough on a lightly floured worktop, then divide into 10 equal portions and roll each portion into a ball. Place the dough balls on the cookie sheets and flatten them slightly. Cover and let rise again until doubled in size.

4 Meanwhile, preheat the oven to 220°C/425°F/gas mark 7. Bake the buns for about 15 minutes, or until they feel soft and sound hollow when tapped underneath. Transfer to a wire rack to cool.

5 Split each bun at an angle and fill with jelly and cream. Dust with sifted confectioners' sugar just before serving.

TO MAKE IN BREADMAKER, *use quantities as listed in main recipe but amend following ingredients and use 1 cup milk and use fast-action dried yeast. Add ingredients to breadmaker in order specified in your instruction book. Use Dough setting for this recipe, then continue as above from Step 3 of main recipe.*

113　Sticky fruit buns

PREPARATION TIME *25 minutes, plus rising* **COOKING TIME** *15–20 minutes* **MAKES** *16–18 buns*

1lb 2oz package white bread mix
1½ teaspoons ground pudding spice
½ stick butter, diced
2 tablespoons superfine sugar

⅔ cup golden raisins
1 large egg, lightly beaten
About 1 cup warm milk
2 tablespoons clear honey, to glaze

1　Grease 2 cookie sheets and set aside. Mix the bread mix and pudding spice in a large bowl, then lightly rub in the butter. Stir in the sugar and golden raisins, then add the egg and enough milk, mixing to form a soft dough.

2　Turn the dough onto a lightly floured worktop and knead until smooth and elastic. Divide the dough into about 16–18 equal pieces. Shape each piece into a ball and place on the cookie sheets. Flatten each ball slightly. Cover and let rise in a warm place until doubled in size.

3　Meanwhile, preheat the oven to 190°C/375°F/gas mark 5. Bake the buns for about 15–20 minutes, or until golden brown. Remove from the oven and brush the buns two times with honey while still hot. Transfer to a wire rack to cool. Serve warm or cold.

VARIATION *Use dried cranberries or chopped ready-to-eat dried apricots in place of golden raisins.*

114　🏠 Hot cross buns

PREPARATION TIME *35 minutes, plus rising* **COOKING TIME** *15–20 minutes* **MAKES** *12–14 buns*

3 cups strong white flour
1 teaspoon salt
1 teaspoon ground pudding spice
1 teaspoon ground cinnamon
1 teaspoon freshly grated nutmeg
½ stick butter, diced
1½ teaspoons easy-blend dried yeast
Finely grated zest of 1 lemon

2 tablespoons superfine sugar
½ cup golden raisins
2 tablespoons chopped candied peel
1 large egg, lightly beaten
About 1 cup warm milk
3oz ready-made shortcrust pastry
⅓ cup granulated sugar

1　Grease 2 cookie sheets. Sift the flour, salt, and spices into a large bowl, then rub in the butter. Stir in the yeast, lemon zest, superfine sugar, golden raisins, and candied peel. Make a well in the center, then add the egg and enough milk, mixing to form a soft dough.

2　Turn the dough onto a lightly floured worktop and knead until smooth and elastic. Shape the dough into a round, then place in a lightly oiled bowl, cover and let rise in a warm place until doubled in size.

3　Punch down the dough on a lightly floured worktop, then divide it into 12 or 14 equal pieces. Knead each piece into a ball and place on the cookie sheets. Flatten each ball slightly. Roll out the pastry on a lightly floured worktop and cut into narrow strips. Brush the buns with a little water and top each one with a pastry cross. Cover and let rise again for about 30 minutes, or until doubled in size.

4　Meanwhile, preheat the oven to 190°C/375°F/gas mark 5. Bake the buns for about 15–20 minutes, or until golden brown. Transfer to a wire rack.

5　Meanwhile, make the glaze. Place the granulated sugar in a saucepan with 3 tablespoons water. Heat gently, stirring until the sugar has dissolved, then bring to the boil and boil rapidly for 2 minutes. As soon as the buns come out of the oven, brush them two times with the sugar glaze. Let cool and serve warm or cold.

TO MAKE IN BREADMAKER, *use quantities as listed in main recipe but amend following ingredients and use 1 cup milk and use fast-action dried yeast. Add ingredients to breadmaker in order specified in your instruction book. Use Basic Raisin Dough or similar setting for this recipe (or use Dough setting) and add lemon zest, golden raisins, and candied peel when machine makes a sound (beeps) to add extra ingredients during kneading cycle (or add extra ingredients 5 minutes before end of kneading cycle), then continue as above from Step 3 of main recipe.*

🏠 Chelsea buns

PREPARATION TIME *30 minutes, plus rising* **COOKING TIME** *30 minutes* **MAKES** *12 buns*

1½ cups strong white flour
½ teaspoon salt
½ stick butter, diced
1½ teaspoons easy-blend dried yeast
2 tablespoons superfine sugar
1 large egg, lightly beaten

About ½ cup warm milk
½ cup mixed raisins and dried currants
⅓ cup golden raisins
⅓ cup light soft brown sugar
1½ teaspoons ground cinnamon
2 tablespoons clear honey, to glaze

1 Grease a 7-inch square cake pan and set aside. Sift the flour and salt into a large bowl, then lightly rub in 2 tablespoons butter. Stir in the yeast and superfine sugar. Make a well in the center, then add the egg and enough milk, mixing to form a soft dough.
2 Turn the dough onto a floured worktop and knead until smooth. Shape into a round, then place in a lightly oiled bowl, cover and let rise in a warm place until doubled in size.
3 Punch down the dough on a lightly floured worktop, then roll out to form a 12 x 9-inch rectangle. Melt the remaining butter and brush it over the dough.
4 Combine the dried fruit, brown sugar and cinnamon and sprinkle over the dough.
5 Follow Steps 4 and 5 of Spiced Apricot Chelsea Buns recipe (see page 92).
6 Remove from the oven and brush two times with honey while still hot. Cool slightly in the pan, then turn onto a wire rack. Serve warm or cold.

TO MAKE IN BREADMAKER, *use quantities as listed in main recipe but amend following ingredients and use ¼ cup milk and 1 teaspoon fast-action dried yeast. Use 2 tablespoons butter in dough; use remaining butter as instructed in Step 3 of main recipe. Add ingredients to breadmaker in order specified in your instruction book. Use Dough setting; continue from Step 3 of main recipe.*

116 Spiced apricot chelsea buns

PREPARATION TIME *25 minutes, plus rising* COOKING TIME *25–30 minutes* MAKES *12 buns*

1⅓ cups white bread mix
2 tablespoons superfine sugar
1 large egg, lightly beaten
About ½ cup warm milk
2 tablespoons butter, melted

⅔ cup ready-to-eat dried apricots,
  chopped
¼ cup dark soft brown sugar
Finely grated zest of 1 small orange
1 teaspoon ground pudding spice
4 tablespoons granulated sugar

1 Grease a 7-inch square cake pan and set aside. Mix the bread mix and superfine sugar in a large bowl, then add the egg and enough milk, mixing to form a soft dough.
2 Turn the dough onto a lightly floured worktop and knead until smooth and elastic. Roll out to form a 12 x 9-inch rectangle. Brush the melted butter over the dough.
3 Combine the apricots, soft brown sugar, orange zest, and pudding spice and sprinkle this mixture evenly over the dough, leaving a 1-inch border around the edges.
4 Starting from a long side, roll up the dough fairly tightly like a jelly roll. Cut into 12 even slices, then place the rolls, cut-side up, in the pan. Cover and let rise in a warm place until doubled in size.
5 Meanwhile, preheat the oven to 190°C/375°F/gas mark 5. Bake the buns for about 25–30 minutes, or until risen and golden brown.
6 Meanwhile, mix the granulated sugar with 4 tablespoons water in a pan. Heat gently until the sugar has dissolved, stirring, then bring to the boil and boil rapidly for 1–2 minutes without stirring, until syrupy. Brush the hot syrup over the warm buns. Cool slightly in the pan, then turn onto a wire rack and let cool completely. Serve warm or cold.

117 ⌂ Bath buns

PREPARATION TIME *30 minutes, plus rising* COOKING TIME *20 minutes* MAKES *about 16 buns*

3⅔ cups strong white flour
1 teaspoon salt
1 sachet (¼oz) easy-blend dried yeast
4 tablespoons superfine sugar
1 cup golden raisins
⅓ cup chopped candied peel

½ stick butter, melted
2 eggs, lightly beaten
About ⅔ cup warm milk
Beaten egg, to glaze
4 sugar cubes, coarsely crushed

1 Grease 2 cookie sheets and set aside. Sift the flour and salt into a large bowl, then stir in the yeast, superfine sugar, golden raisins, and candied peel. Make a well in the center, then add the melted butter, eggs, and enough milk, mixing to form a soft dough.
2 Turn the dough onto a lightly floured worktop and knead until smooth and elastic. Shape the dough into a round, then place it in a lightly oiled bowl, cover and let rise in a warm place until doubled in size.
3 Punch down the dough on a lightly floured worktop, then divide it into about 16 equal pieces. Knead each piece into a ball and place on the cookie sheets. Flatten each ball slightly. Cover and let rise again for about 30 minutes, or until doubled in size.
4 Meanwhile, preheat the oven to 190°C/375°F/gas mark 5. Brush the tops of the buns with beaten egg and sprinkle with the crushed sugar cubes. Bake the buns for about 20 minutes, or until risen and golden brown. Transfer to a wire rack to cool and serve warm or cold on their own or split and spread with butter.

TO MAKE IN BREADMAKER, *use quantities as listed in main recipe but amend following ingredients and use ⅔ cup milk and 2 teaspoons fast-action dried yeast. Add ingredients to breadmaker in order specified in your instruction book. Use Basic Raisin Dough or similar setting for this recipe (or use Dough setting) and add golden raisins and candied peel when machine makes a sound (beeps) to add extra ingredients during kneading cycle (or add extra ingredients 5 minutes before end of kneading cycle), then continue as above from Step 3 of main recipe.*

118 🍞 Croissants

PREPARATION TIME *45 minutes, plus rising* COOKING TIME *15–20 minutes* MAKES *12 croissants*

3⅔ cups strong white flour
½ teaspoon salt
2½ sticks butter, at room temperature
1 sachet (¼oz) easy-blend dried yeast

2 tablespoons superfine sugar
About 1¼ cups warm milk
Beaten egg, to glaze

1 Grease 2 cookie sheets and set aside. Sift the flour and salt into a large bowl, then lightly rub in ½ stick butter. Stir in the yeast and sugar. Make a well in the center, then add enough milk, mixing to form a soft dough.
2 Turn the dough onto a floured worktop and knead for 3–4 minutes. Shape into a round, then place in an oiled bowl, cover and let rise in a warm place until doubled in size.
3 Punch down the dough on a lightly floured worktop, then roll out to form a rectangle about 14 x 7 inches. Flatten the remaining butter into a block about ¾-inch thick. With a short side of the dough rectangle nearest to you, place the butter on top of the dough so that it covers the top two-thirds of the rectangle. Fold the bottom third of the dough over the middle third, then fold the top buttered third down over the top of the middle third to form a parcel. Seal the edges with a rolling pin.
4 Give the dough a quarter turn so the folded side is to the left. Roll into a rectangle as before, then fold the bottom third up and the top third down and seal the edges, as before. Wrap in waxed paper and chill in the refrigerator for 20 minutes. Repeat the rolling, folding and chilling two more times, turning the dough 90 degrees each time.
5 Roll out the dough on a lightly floured worktop to form a 21 x 14-inch rectangle and cut into 12 equal triangles. Roll each triangle into a sausage shape, starting from the long side and ending with the point of the triangle. Bend the ends of each croissant round to give a crescent or half-moon shape. Place on the cookie sheets. Cover and let rise again for about 30 minutes, or until almost doubled in size.
6 Preheat the oven to 220°C/425°F/gas mark 7. Lightly brush the croissants with beaten egg, then bake for 15–20 minutes, or until crisp and golden brown. Serve warm.

TO MAKE IN BREADMAKER, *use quantities as listed in main recipe but amend following ingredients and use 1¼ cups milk, 1 teaspoon salt and use fast-action dried yeast. Use ½ stick butter in dough; use remaining butter as instructed in Step 3 of main recipe. Add ingredients to breadmaker in order specified in your instruction book. Use Dough setting for this recipe, then continue as above from Step 3 of main recipe.*

119 🍞 Pains au chocolat

PREPARATION TIME *45 minutes, plus rising* COOKING TIME *15–20 minutes*
MAKES *12 pains au chocolat*

Ingredients for Croissants, with:

6oz semisweet or milk chocolate, finely chopped

1 Follow Steps 1, 2, 3 and 4 of Croissants recipe above.
2 Roll out the dough on a lightly floured worktop to form a 21 x 14-inch rectangle and cut into 12 equal rectangles. Divide the chopped chocolate among the rectangles. Roll up each rectangle to make flattish cylinder shapes, enclosing the chocolate completely. Place seam-side down on the cookie sheets. Cover and let rise again for about 30 minutes, or until almost doubled in size.
3 Preheat the oven to 200°C/400°F/gas mark 6. Lightly brush the pastries with beaten egg, then bake for 15–20 minutes, or until crisp and golden brown. Serve warm.

TO MAKE IN BREADMAKER, *use quantities as listed in main recipe but amend following ingredients and use 1¼ cups milk, 1 teaspoon salt and use fast-action dried yeast. Use ½ stick butter in dough; use remaining butter as instructed in Step 3 of Croissants recipe above. Add ingredients to breadmaker in order specified in your instruction book. Use Dough setting for this recipe, then continue as above from Step 3 of Croissants recipe above.*

Danish pastries

PREPARATION TIME *50 minutes, plus rising* **COOKING TIME** *15–20 minutes* **MAKES** *16 pastries*

3⅔ cups strong white flour
½ teaspoon salt
3 sticks butter, at room temperature
2 teaspoons easy-blend dried yeast
4 tablespoons superfine sugar
2 large eggs, lightly beaten

About 1 cup warm milk
6oz ready-made marzipan
16 apricot halves (canned or fresh)
Beaten egg, to glaze
1 cup confectioners' sugar, sifted

1   Grease 2 cookie sheets; set aside. Sift the flour and salt into a bowl; rub in ½ stick butter. Stir in the yeast and superfine sugar. Mix in the eggs and enough milk to form a soft dough.

2   Turn the dough onto a floured worktop and knead until smooth. Shape into a round, then place in a lightly oiled bowl, cover and let rise in a warm place until doubled in size.

3   Punch down the dough, then roll out to a rectangle about 14 x 8 inches in size. With a short side of the rectangle nearest to you, dot the top two-thirds of the dough with half of the remaining butter. Fold the bottom third of the dough up over the middle third, then fold the top third down over the top of the middle third to form a parcel. Seal the edges.

4   Give the dough a quarter turn so the folded side is to the left. Roll out to a rectangle, as before. Dot with the remaining butter and fold as before, then wrap in waxed paper and chill in the refrigerator for 15 minutes. Roll, fold and chill the dough two more times, turning the dough a quarter turn each time.

5   Divide the dough into 4 equal portions, then roll each one out on a floured worktop to form an 8-inch square. Cut each square into quarters. Place a round of almond paste in the middle of each square, then fold 2 opposite corners of each square into the middle and press to seal. Top the center of each with an apricot half, cut-side down. Place on the cookie sheets, cover and let rise for about 30 minutes, or until almost doubled in size.

6   Preheat the oven to 220°C/425°F/gas mark 7. Lightly brush the pastries with beaten egg, then bake for 15–20 minutes, or until crisp and golden brown. Transfer to a wire rack.

7   Blend the confectioners' sugar with 3–4 teaspoons water to make a thin glacé frosting. Drizzle a little frosting over each pastry while still warm. Let cool and serve warm or cold.

121 Cinnamon swirls

PREPARATION TIME *35 minutes, plus rising* **COOKING TIME** *20 minutes* **MAKES** *10 swirls*

3⅔ cups strong white flour
½ teaspoon salt
1 sachet (¼oz) fast-action dried yeast
1 cup superfine sugar
1 large egg, lightly beaten
2 tablespoons butter, melted

About 1¼ cups warm milk, plus extra
  for glazing
⅔ cup raisins
4–5 teaspoons ground cinnamon
1 cup confectioners' sugar, sifted

1   Grease 2 cookie sheets and set aside. Sift the flour and salt into a large bowl, then stir in the yeast and ⅔ cup superfine sugar. Make a well in the center, then add the egg, half the melted butter, and enough milk, mixing to form a soft dough.

2   Turn the dough onto a lightly floured worktop and knead until smooth and elastic. Knead the raisins and 2 teaspoons cinnamon evenly into the dough. Roll out to form a 12 x 9-inch rectangle. Lightly brush the remaining melted butter over the dough.

3   Combine the remaining superfine sugar and cinnamon and sprinkle evenly over the dough, leaving a ½-inch border around the edges. Starting from a long side, roll up the dough fairly tightly like a jelly roll. Cut into 10 even slices, then place the rolls, cut-side up, on the cookie sheets. Cover and let rise in a warm place until doubled in size.

4   Meanwhile, preheat the oven to 190°C/375°F/gas mark 5. Bake the swirls for about 20 minutes, or until risen and lightly browned. Transfer to a wire rack.

5   Meanwhile, blend the confectioners' sugar with 3–4 teaspoons water to make a thin glacé frosting. As soon as the swirls come out of the oven, brush them with the frosting. Let cool and serve warm or cold.

VARIATION *Use chopped ready-to-eat dried apricots or pears in place of raisins.*

122 Fruit and spice pinwheels

PREPARATION TIME *30 minutes, plus rising* **COOKING TIME** *20–25 minutes* **MAKES** *10 pinwheels*

3 cups strong white flour
½ teaspoon salt
1 sachet (¼oz) easy-blend dried yeast
2 tablespoons superfine sugar
1 large egg, lightly beaten
3 tablespoons butter, melted

About 1 cup warm milk
⅓ cup light soft brown sugar
⅔ cup golden raisins
⅓ cup dried currants
1 teaspoon ground pudding spice
Sifted confectioners' sugar, for dusting

1   Grease 2 cookie sheets and set aside. Sift the flour and salt into a bowl, then stir in the yeast and superfine sugar. Make a well in the center of the dry ingredients, then add the egg, 2 tablespoons melted butter, and enough milk, mixing to form a soft dough.

2   Turn the dough onto a lightly floured worktop and knead until smooth and elastic. Shape the dough into a round, then place it in a lightly oiled bowl, cover and let rise in a warm place until doubled in size.

3   Punch down the dough on a lightly floured worktop, then roll it out to form a 16 x 8-inch rectangle. Combine the soft brown sugar, golden raisins, dried currants, and pudding spice. Brush the remaining melted butter over the dough, then sprinkle the golden raisin mixture evenly over the dough, leaving a ½-inch border around the edges.

4   Starting from a long side, roll up the dough fairly tightly like a jelly roll. Cut into 10 even slices, each about 1½ inches thick, then place the pinwheels, cut-side up, on the cookie sheets. Cover and let rise again for 30–45 minutes, or until doubled in size.

5   Meanwhile, preheat the oven to 190°C/375°F/gas mark 5. Bake the pinwheels for 20–25 minutes, or until risen and lightly browned. Transfer to a wire rack to cool. Dust with sifted confectioners' sugar just before serving. Serve warm or cold.

123 Festive fruit snails

PREPARATION TIME *35 minutes, plus rising* **COOKING TIME** *20–25 minutes* **MAKES** *about 12 snails*

1lb 2oz package white bread mix	**½ cup mincemeat**
4 tablespoons superfine sugar	**⅓ cup ready-to-eat dried apricots,**
1 egg, lightly beaten	**finely chopped**
2 tablespoons butter, melted	**Beaten egg, to glaze**
About 1 cup warm milk	**2–3 tablespoons apricot jelly**

1 Grease 2 cookie sheets and set aside. Place the bread mix in a bowl and stir in the sugar. Make a well in the center, then add the egg, melted butter, and enough milk, mixing to form a soft dough.

2 Turn the dough onto a lightly floured worktop and knead until smooth and elastic. Divide the dough into about 12 equal pieces. Roll each piece into an 8-inch sausage or rope shape, then flatten. Combine the mincemeat and chopped apricots.

3 Spread the mincemeat mixture over the strips of dough, then roll up each one into a tight spiral or snail. Arrange the snails on the cookie sheets. Cover and let rise in a warm place until doubled in size.

4 Meanwhile, preheat the oven to 190°C/375°F/gas mark 5. Brush the snails with beaten egg, then bake for 20–25 minutes, or until risen and lightly browned. Transfer to a wire rack to cool.

5 Combine the jelly and 2–3 teaspoons water in a small pan and heat gently until the jelly has melted. Brush the apricot glaze over the snails and serve warm or cold.

VARIATION *Use dried cherries or cranberries in place of apricots.*

124 Spiced cranberry whirls

PREPARATION TIME *30 minutes, plus rising* **COOKING TIME** *20–25 minutes* **MAKES** *10–12 whirls*

1⅓ cups white bread mix	**½ cup dried cranberries**
⅓ cup superfine sugar	**⅓ cup golden raisins**
1 large egg, lightly beaten	**Finely grated zest of 1 small orange**
About ½ cup warm milk	**1 teaspoon ground pudding spice**
1 tablespoon, melted	**2 tablespoons clear honey, to glaze**

1 Grease an 8-inch square cake pan and set aside. Mix the bread mix and 2 tablespoons superfine sugar in a large bowl, then add the egg and enough milk, mixing to form a soft dough.

2 Turn the dough onto a lightly floured worktop and knead until smooth and elastic. Roll out to form a 14 x 8-inch rectangle. Brush the melted butter over the dough. Combine the remaining sugar, cranberries, golden raisins, orange zest, and pudding spice and sprinkle this mixture evenly over the dough, leaving a ½-inch border around the edges.

3 Starting from a long side, roll up the dough fairly tightly like a jelly roll. Cut into 10–12 even slices, then place the rolls, cut-side up, in the cake pan. Cover and let rise in a warm place until doubled in size.

4 Meanwhile, preheat the oven to 190°C/375°F/gas mark 5. Bake the whirls for 20–25 minutes, or until risen and golden brown.

5 Remove from the oven and brush the whirls two times with honey while still hot. Cool slightly in the pan, then turn onto a wire rack and let cool completely. Serve warm or cold.

VARIATIONS *Use dried cherries, cut in half, or dried blueberries in place of dried cranberries. Use lemon zest in place of orange zest.*

125 Sally lunn

PREPARATION TIME *25 minutes, plus rising* **COOKING TIME** *25 minutes* **MAKES** *1 loaf (serves 8)*

2⅓ cups strong white flour	**1 egg, lightly beaten**
½ teaspoon salt	**2 tablespoons butter, melted**
1½ teaspoons fast-action dried yeast	**About ⅔ cup warm milk, plus**
1 tablespoon superfine sugar	**1 tablespoon for the glaze**
Finely grated zest of ½ lemon	**1 tablespoon granulated sugar**

1   Grease a deep 8-inch round cake pan. Sift the flour and salt into a large bowl, then stir in the yeast, superfine sugar, and lemon zest. Make a well in the center, then add the egg, melted butter, and enough milk, mixing to form a soft dough.

2   Turn the dough onto a floured worktop and knead until smooth and elastic. Shape into a round and place in the pan. Cover and let rise in a warm place until doubled in size.

3   Meanwhile, preheat the oven to 220°C/425°F/gas mark 7. Bake the loaf for about 25 minutes, or until the bread is risen and golden brown.

4   Meanwhile, gently heat the remaining 1 tablespoon milk and the granulated sugar in a saucepan until the sugar has dissolved, then bring to the boil.

5   Remove the bread from the oven and brush with the glaze. Let cool in the pan for 10 minutes, then turn onto a wire rack and let cool completely. Slice into 2 or 3 layers horizontally, spread with heavy cream or butter, and re-assemble before serving.

126 🍞 Lardy cake

PREPARATION TIME *30 minutes, plus rising* **COOKING TIME** *30 minutes* **MAKES** *1 loaf (serves 10–12)*

3 cups strong white flour	**⅔ cup light soft brown sugar**
1 teaspoon salt	**½ cup dried currants**
⅔ cup pure pork fat	**½ cup golden raisins**
2 teaspoons easy-blend dried yeast	**⅓ cup chopped candied peel**
2 tablespoons superfine sugar,	**1 teaspoon ground pudding spice**
plus 1 tablespoon for glazing	**1 tablespoon boiling water**
About 1¼ cups warm water	

1   Grease a 10 x 8-inch shallow roasting pan and set aside. Sift the flour and salt into a large bowl, then rub in 1 tablespoon of the pork fat. Stir in the yeast and 2 tablespoons superfine sugar. Make a well in the center, then add enough water, mixing to form a soft dough.

2   Turn the dough onto a floured worktop and knead until smooth. Shape into a round, then place in a lightly oiled bowl, cover and let rise in a warm place until doubled in size.

3   Punch down the dough on a floured worktop, then roll out to form a rectangle about ¼-inch thick. With a short side of the rectangle nearest to you, dot the top two-thirds of the dough with flakes of one-third of the remaining pork fat. Sprinkle over one-third each of the sugar, dried fruits, candied peel, and pudding spice. Fold the bottom third of the dough up over the middle third, then fold the top third down over the middle third to form a parcel. Seal the edges with a rolling pin. Give the dough a quarter turn so the folded side is to the left.

4   Repeat this whole procedure, rolling, filling, and folding the dough, two more times, with the remaining pork fat, soft brown sugar, dried fruits, candied peel, and pudding spice. Fold, seal and turn as before. Roll out the dough to fit and place it in the pan. Cover and let rise again for about 1–1½ hours, or until almost doubled in size.

5   Preheat the oven to 200°C/400°F/gas mark 6. Score the top of the dough in a criss-cross pattern, then bake for about 30 minutes, or until risen and golden brown.

6   Dissolve the remaining 1 tablespoon superfine sugar in the boiling water, then brush this glaze over the top of the warm cake. Let cool in the pan for a few minutes, then unmold and serve warm or cold, cut into slices or squares.

TO MAKE IN BREADMAKER, *use quantities as listed in main recipe but amend following ingredients and use 1¼ cups water and 1½ teaspoons fast-action dried yeast. Use 1 tablespoon pork fat in dough; use remaining pork fat as instructed in main recipe. Add ingredients to breadmaker in order specified in your instruction book. Use Dough setting, then continue from Step 3 of main recipe.*

127 🏠 Doughnuts

PREPARATION TIME *35 minutes, plus rising* **COOKING TIME** *25 minutes* **MAKES** *16 doughnuts*

3⅔ cups strong white flour	2 large eggs, lightly beaten
½ teaspoon salt	About ¾ cup warm milk
2 tablespoons butter, diced	⅓ cup strawberry or raspberry jelly
2 teaspoons easy-blend dried yeast	Sunflower oil, for deep-frying
1 cup superfine sugar	1½ teaspoons ground cinnamon

1 Oil 2 cookie sheets and set aside. Sift the flour and salt into a large bowl, then lightly rub in the butter. Stir in the yeast and ½ cup sugar. Make a well in the center, then stir in the eggs and enough milk, mixing to form a soft dough.
2 Turn the dough onto a floured worktop and knead until smooth. Shape into a round, then place in a lightly oiled bowl, cover and let rise in a warm place until doubled in size.
3 Punch down the dough on a lightly floured worktop, then divide into 16 equal pieces. Shape each piece of dough into a ball, then flatten each one into a disc about ½-inch thick.
4 Place 1 heaped teaspoon of jelly into the middle of each piece of dough, gather the edges of the dough up and over the jelly, enclosing it completely, then pinch the edges firmly together to seal, and roll into a ball. Place the doughnuts on the cookie sheets, cover and let rise again for about 30 minutes, or until almost doubled in size.
5 Heat some oil in a deep-fat fryer to 170°C/325°F and cook the doughnuts in batches in the hot oil for about 6 minutes, or until golden all over, turning once.
6 Remove the doughnuts from the fryer using a slotted spoon and drain on paper towels.
7 Combine the remaining sugar and cinnamon in a bowl and toss the doughnuts in the sugar mixture, coating them all over. Serve immediately.

TO MAKE IN BREADMAKER, *use quantities as listed in main recipe but amend following ingredients and use ¾ cup milk, 1 teaspoon salt, and 1½ teaspoons fast-action dried yeast. Use ½ cup superfine sugar in dough; use remaining sugar as instructed in Step 7 of main recipe. Add ingredients to breadmaker in order specified in your instruction book. Use Dough setting for this recipe, then continue as above from Step 3 of main recipe.*

128 🏠 Teacakes

PREPARATION TIME *25 minutes, plus rising* **COOKING TIME** *20–25 minutes* **MAKES** *8 teacakes*

3 cups strong white flour	2 tablespoons superfine sugar
1 teaspoon salt	⅔ cup dried currants
2 tablespoons butter, diced	About 1 cup warm milk,
1½ teaspoons easy-blend dried yeast	plus extra for glazing

1 Grease 2 cookie sheets and set aside. Sift the flour and salt into a large bowl, then lightly rub in the butter. Stir in the yeast, sugar, and dried currants. Make a well in the center, then stir in enough milk, mixing to form a soft dough.
2 Turn the dough onto a floured worktop and knead until smooth. Shape into a round, then place in a lightly oiled bowl, cover and let rise in a warm place until doubled in size.
3 Punch down the dough on a floured worktop, then divide into 8 equal pieces. Roll and shape each piece into a round teacake and prick each one two times on top with a fork. Place on the cookie sheets, cover and let rise for about 30 minutes, or until doubled in size.
4 Preheat the oven to 200°C/400°F/gas mark 6. Brush the teacakes with a little milk, then bake for 20–25 minutes, or until risen and golden brown. Transfer to a wire rack to cool. To serve, split each teacake in half, toast lightly and spread with butter or jelly.

TO MAKE IN BREADMAKER, *use quantities as listed in main recipe but amend following ingredients and use 1¼ cups milk, 1¼ teaspoons salt and use fast-action dried yeast. Add ingredients to breadmaker in order specified in your instruction book. Use Basic Raisin Dough or similar setting for this recipe (or use Dough setting) and add dried currants when machine makes a sound (beeps) to add extra ingredients during kneading cycle (or add currants 5 minutes before end of kneading cycle), then continue as above from Step 3 of main recipe.*

129 Teacake fingers

PREPARATION TIME *25 minutes, plus rising* **COOKING TIME** *20 minutes* **MAKES** *12 teacake fingers*

1lb 2oz package white bread mix
½ stick butter, diced
2 tablespoons superfine sugar
⅔ cup golden raisins

⅓ cup chopped candied peel
⅔ cup warm milk
About ⅔ cup warm water
Beaten egg, to glaze

1   Grease 2 cookie sheets and set aside. Place the bread mix in a large bowl, then lightly rub in the butter. Stir in the sugar, golden raisins, and candied peel, then add the milk and enough water, mixing to form a soft dough.

2   Turn the dough onto a lightly floured worktop and knead until smooth and elastic. Divide the dough into 12 equal pieces. Roll and shape each piece of dough into a long roll or finger shape and place on the cookie sheets. Cover and let rise in a warm place until doubled in size.

3   Meanwhile, preheat the oven to 190°C/375°F/gas mark 5. Brush the rolls with beaten egg, then bake them for about 20 minutes, or until risen and golden brown. Transfer to a wire rack to cool. Serve split, lightly toasted and spread with butter.

VARIATIONS *Add 1–2 teaspoons ground pudding spice to the bread mix, for extra flavor, if desired. Use dried currants or raisins in place of candied peel.*

130 Fruit and spice swizzle sticks

PREPARATION TIME *35 minutes, plus rising* COOKING TIME *20 minutes* MAKES *12 swizzle sticks*

1½ cups strong white flour
½ teaspoon salt
2 tablespoons butter, diced
1½ teaspoons easy-blend dried yeast
2 tablespoons superfine sugar
½ cup ready-to-eat dried pears, finely
    chopped

⅓ cup ready-to-eat dried pineapple,
    finely chopped
1½ teaspoons ground cinnamon
1 egg, lightly beaten
About ½ cup warm milk, plus extra
    for glazing
4 sugar cubes, coarsely crushed

1   Grease 2 cookie sheets and set aside. Sift the flour and salt into a large bowl, then lightly
    rub in the butter. Stir in the yeast, superfine sugar, dried fruit, and cinnamon. Make a well
    in the center, then add the egg and enough milk, mixing to form a soft dough.
2   Turn the dough onto a lightly floured worktop and knead until smooth and elastic. Shape
    the dough into a round, then place it in a lightly oiled bowl, cover and let rise in a warm
    place until doubled in size.
3   Punch down the dough on a lightly floured worktop, then divide into 12 equal pieces. Roll
    each piece into a long sausage or rope shape, then twist each one several times and
    place firmly in position on the cookie sheets. Cover and let rise again for about 30
    minutes, or until doubled in size.
4   Preheat the oven to 190°C/375°F/gas mark 5. Brush the twists with a little milk and
    sprinkle with crushed sugar cubes. Bake the twists for about 20 minutes, or until risen and
    golden brown. Transfer to a wire rack to cool. Serve warm or cold.

VARIATION *Use ready-to-eat dried apricots in place of pineapple.*

131 Cranberry and orange spirals

PREPARATION TIME *30 minutes, plus rising* COOKING TIME *25–30 minutes* MAKES *12 spirals*

1⅓ cups white bread mix
2 tablespoons superfine sugar
1 egg, lightly beaten
About ½ cup warm milk
2 tablespoons butter, melted

1 cup dried cranberries
⅓ cup dark soft brown sugar
Finely grated zest of 1 small orange
1 teaspoon ground cinnamon
2 tablespoons clear honey, to glaze

1   Grease a 7-inch square cake pan and set aside. Mix the bread mix and superfine sugar in
    a large bowl, then add the egg and enough milk, mixing to form a soft dough.
2   Turn the dough onto a lightly floured worktop and knead until smooth and elastic. Roll out
    to form a 12 x 9-inch rectangle. Brush the melted butter over the dough. Combine the
    cranberries, soft brown sugar, orange zest, and cinnamon and sprinkle this mixture evenly
    over the dough, leaving a 1-inch border around the edges.
3   Starting from a long side, roll up the dough fairly tightly like a jelly roll. Cut into 12 even
    slices, then place the spirals, cut-side up, in the cake pan. Cover and let rise in a warm
    place until doubled in size.
4   Meanwhile, preheat the oven to 190°C/375°F/gas mark 5. Bake the spirals for 25–30
    minutes, or until risen and golden brown. Remove from the oven and brush the spirals two
    times with honey while still hot. Cool slightly in the pan, then turn onto a wire rack. Serve
    warm or cold.

VARIATION *Use raisins in place of cranberries.*

132 Cherry and cranberry swirls

PREPARATION TIME *30 minutes, plus rising* **COOKING TIME** *15–20 minutes* **MAKES** *12 swirls*

1lb 2oz package white bread mix
4 tablespoons superfine sugar
2 eggs, lightly beaten
About 1 cup warm milk
2 tablespoons butter, melted
½ cup dried cherries, halved

½ cup dried cranberries
⅓ cup light soft brown sugar
Finely grated zest of 1 small orange or lemon
1 teaspoon ground pudding spice
2–3 tablespoons clear honey, to glaze

1 Grease a 9-inch square cake pan and set aside. Mix the bread mix and superfine sugar in a large bowl, then add the eggs and enough milk, mixing to form a soft dough.

2 Turn the dough onto a lightly floured worktop and knead until smooth and elastic. Roll out to form a 12-inch square. Brush the melted butter over the dough.

3 Combine the cherries, cranberries, brown sugar, orange or lemon zest, and pudding spice and sprinkle this mixture evenly over the dough, leaving a ½-inch border along one edge.

4 Starting at the opposite covered edge, roll up the dough fairly tightly and press the edges together to seal. Cut into 12 even slices, then place the swirls, cut-side up, in the cake pan. Cover and let rise in a warm place for 30–40 minutes, or until doubled in size.

5 Meanwhile, preheat the oven to 200°C/400°F/gas mark 6. Bake the swirls for 15–20 minutes, or until risen and golden brown.

6 Remove from the oven and brush the swirls two times with honey while still hot. Cool slightly in the pan, then turn onto a wire rack and let cool. Serve warm or cold.

133 🍞 Apple and cinnamon pull-apart

PREPARATION TIME *40 minutes, plus rising* **COOKING TIME** *25–30 minutes* **SERVES** *12*

3 cups strong white flour
1 teaspoon salt
2 teaspoons fast-action dried yeast
2 tablespoons superfine sugar
1 large egg, lightly beaten
⅔ cup warm milk
About ½ cup warm water

1 cup light soft brown sugar
1½ teaspoons ground cinnamon
3 dessert apples, peeled, cored, and thinly sliced
4 tablespoons heavy cream
2 tablespoons butter, diced
¼ cup hazelnuts, finely chopped

1 Grease a 9-inch loose-bottomed springform pan fitted with a tube base, or a ring mold, and set aside. Sift the flour and salt into a large bowl, then stir in the yeast and superfine sugar. Add the egg, milk, and enough water, mixing to form a soft dough.

2 Turn the dough onto a lightly floured worktop and knead until smooth and elastic. Roll out to form a 16 x 8-inch rectangle. Combine ⅓ cup soft brown sugar and the cinnamon, then add the apple slices and toss to mix well.

3 Spoon the apple mixture evenly over the dough, leaving a ½-inch border around the edges. Starting from a long side, roll up the dough fairly tightly. Cut into 12 even slices, then place the slices upright but at an angle (so they rest on each other) in the pan. Cover and let rise in a warm place for about 1½–2 hours, or until doubled in size.

4 Preheat the oven to 190°C/375°F/gas mark 5. Bake the loaf for 25–30 minutes, or until risen and golden brown. Cool slightly in the pan, then turn onto a wire rack.

5 Meanwhile, place the remaining soft brown sugar, the cream, and butter in a small pan and heat gently, stirring until the sugar has dissolved. Bring gently to the boil, then simmer, uncovered, for about 4 minutes, or until the mixture thickens slightly.

6 Brush the hot pull-apart with the caramel mixture, then sprinkle with the hazelnuts. Pull the rolls apart to serve. Serve warm or cold.

TO MAKE IN BREADMAKER, *use quantities as listed in main recipe but amend following ingredients and use ⅔ cup milk and ½ cup water. Add ingredients to breadmaker in order specified in your instruction book. Use Dough setting for this recipe, then continue as above from Step 2 of main recipe (punching down rather than kneading dough, then shape dough and continue as directed).*

134 Scots black bun (Scotch bun)

PREPARATION TIME *30 minutes, plus rising* **COOKING TIME** *50–60 minutes*
MAKES *1 loaf (serves 16–18)*

3 cups strong white flour
1 teaspoon salt
1 teaspoon ground allspice
1 teaspoon ground ginger
1 teaspoon freshly grated nutmeg
1¼ sticks butter, diced
2 teaspoons easy-blend dried yeast

2 teaspoons superfine sugar
About 1 cup warm water
1⅓ cups raisins
1⅓ cups golden raisins
⅓ cup chopped candied peel
½ cup flaked almonds

1   Grease a deep 8-inch round cake pan and set aside. Sift the flour, salt, and ground spices into a large bowl, lightly rub in the butter, then stir in the yeast and sugar. Make a well in the center, then add enough water, mixing to form a soft dough.

2   Turn the dough onto a lightly floured worktop and knead until smooth and elastic. Shape the dough into a round, then place it in a lightly oiled bowl, cover and let rise in a warm place until doubled in size.

3   Punch down the dough on a lightly floured worktop, then cut off one third of the dough and reserve it. Combine the dried fruits, candied peel, and almonds; gradually knead this mixture evenly into the larger piece of dough. The dough will gradually darken in color.

4   Shape the fruit dough into a ball, then roll out the reserved piece of dough to form a large square. Place the fruit dough in the center of the square and bring the sides of the plain dough to the center, pinching them together to seal, enclosing the fruit dough completely.

5   Turn the loaf over, so that the smooth surface is on top, then place it in the cake pan, gently pressing it down. Prick the loaf all over with a fork, going right through to the fruit dough. Cover and let rise again for 45–60 minutes.

6   Meanwhile, preheat the oven to 180°C/350°F/gas mark 4. Bake the loaf for 50–60 minutes, or until the bread is golden brown and sounds hollow when tapped underneath. Turn onto a wire rack to cool. Serve in slices on its own or buttered.

135 Selkirk bannock

PREPARATION TIME *30 minutes, plus rising* **COOKING TIME** *1 hour* **MAKES** *1 loaf (serves 8)*

2⅓ cups strong white flour
½ teaspoon salt
2 teaspoons easy-blend dried yeast
2 tablespoons superfine sugar

½ stick butter, melted
About ¾ cup warm milk
1⅓ cups golden raisins
1 egg yolk

1   Grease a cookie sheet and set aside. Sift the flour and salt into a large bowl, then stir in the yeast and sugar. Make a well in the center, then add the melted butter and enough milk, mixing to form a soft dough.

2   Turn the dough onto a lightly floured worktop and knead until smooth and elastic. Shape the dough into a round, then place it in a lightly oiled bowl, cover and let rise in a warm place until doubled in size.

3   Punch down the dough on a lightly floured worktop, then knead the golden raisins evenly into the dough. Shape into a large round and place on the cookie sheet. Cover and let rise again until doubled in size.

4   Meanwhile, preheat the oven to 190°C/375°F/gas mark 5. Combine the egg yolk with 1 tablespoon water, then brush this mixture over the risen loaf.

5   Bake the loaf for about 1 hour, or until it is golden brown and sounds hollow when tapped underneath, covering it loosely with foil toward the end of the cooking time if the top is browning too quickly. Turn onto a wire rack to cool. Serve in slices.

136 Irish barm brack

PREPARATION TIME *25 minutes, plus rising* **COOKING TIME** *45 minutes* **MAKES** *1 loaf (serves 8–10)*

3 cups strong white flour
½ teaspoon salt
2 teaspoons easy-blend dried yeast
4 tablespoons superfine sugar
⅔ cup golden raisins
⅔ cup dried currants

1½ teaspoons ground cinnamon
½ stick butter, softened
1 egg, lightly beaten
About ¾ cup warm milk
1 tablespoon granulated sugar
2 tablespoons boiling water

1 Grease a deep 8-inch round cake pan and set aside. Sift the flour and salt into a large bowl, then stir in the yeast, superfine sugar, dried fruit, and cinnamon. Make a well in the center, then add the butter, egg and enough milk, mixing to form a soft dough.

2 Turn the dough onto a lightly floured worktop and knead until smooth and elastic. Shape the dough into a round, then place it in a lightly oiled bowl, cover and let rise in a warm place until doubled in size.

3 Punch down the dough on a lightly floured worktop, then shape into a round and place in the cake pan. Cover and let rise again until doubled in size.

4 Meanwhile, preheat the oven to 200°C/400°F/gas mark 6. Bake the loaf for about 45 minutes, or until it is golden brown and sounds hollow when tapped underneath, covering it loosely with foil toward the end of the cooking time if the top is browning too quickly.

5 Meanwhile, dissolve the granulated sugar in the boiling water. When the loaf is baked, brush with the sugar glaze, then return it to the oven for a further 1–2 minutes. Turn onto a wire rack to cool. Serve in slices on its own or buttered.

VARIATIONS *Replace ⅓ cup golden raisins with chopped candied peel, if desired. Use raisins in place of dried currants.*

137 Welsh bara brith

PREPARATION TIME *25 minutes, plus overnight soaking, plus rising* **COOKING TIME** *30–35 minutes* **MAKES** *1 loaf (serves 10–12)*

1⅔ cups mixed dried fruit
1½ cups hot tea, strained
3 cups strong white flour
1 teaspoon salt
1 teaspoon ground pudding spice

½ stick butter, diced
2 teaspoons easy-blend dried yeast
⅓ cup light soft brown sugar
About ¼ cup warm milk

1 Grease a 2lb loaf pan and set aside. Place the dried fruit in a large bowl, pour over the hot tea, stir well, then cover and let soak overnight. The next day, sift the flour, salt and pudding spice into a large bowl, then lightly rub in the butter. Stir in the yeast and sugar. Make a well in the center, stir in the fruit mixture and juices, then add enough milk, mixing to form a soft dough.

2 Turn the dough onto a lightly floured worktop and knead until smooth and elastic. Shape the dough into a round, then place it in a lightly oiled bowl, cover and let rise in a warm place until doubled in size.

3 Punch down the dough on a lightly floured worktop, then shape into an oblong and place in the loaf pan. Cover and let rise again for 45 minutes, or until almost doubled in size.

4 Meanwhile, preheat the oven to 200°C/400°F/gas mark 6. Bake the loaf for 30–35 minutes, or until it sounds hollow when tapped underneath. Turn onto a wire rack to cool. Serve in slices spread with butter.

VARIATION *Brush the baked loaf two times with clear honey while still warm, if desired.*

138 🍞 Pesto parmesan pull-apart

PREPARATION TIME *30 minutes, plus rising* **COOKING TIME** *30–35 minutes* **SERVES** *16*

3 cups strong white flour
1 teaspoon salt
1½ teaspoons easy-blend dried yeast
1 teaspoon superfine sugar

About 1¼ cups warm water
3 tablespoons green pesto sauce
⅓ cup fresh Parmesan cheese, grated
Beaten egg, to glaze

1   Grease a deep 9-inch round cake pan and set aside. Sift the flour and salt into a bowl, then stir in the yeast and sugar. Mix in enough water to form a soft dough.

2   Turn the dough onto a floured worktop and knead until smooth. Shape into a round, then place in an oiled bowl, cover and let rise in a warm place until doubled in size.

3   Punch down the dough on a floured worktop, then roll out to form a 16 x 11-inch rectangle. Spread the pesto sauce over the dough, then sprinkle with Parmesan cheese.

4   Starting from a long side, roll up the dough fairly tightly like a jelly roll. Cut into 16 even slices, then place the rolls, cut-side up, in a circular pattern in the cake pan. Cover and let rise again for about 30 minutes, or until doubled in size.

5   Preheat the oven to 200°C/400°F/gas mark 6. Brush the spirals with beaten egg, then bake for 30–35 minutes, or until deep golden brown. Cool slightly in the pan, then turn onto a wire rack to cool completely. Pull the rolls apart to serve. Serve warm or cold.

TO MAKE IN BREADMAKER, *use quantities as listed in main recipe but amend following ingredients and use 1¼ cups water, 1¼ teaspoons salt, 1½ teaspoons superfine sugar and use fast-action dried yeast. Add ingredients to breadmaker in order specified in your instruction book. Use Dough setting for this recipe, then continue as above from Step 3 of main recipe.*

139 ▣Cheese and herb tear 'n' share

PREPARATION TIME *25 minutes, plus rising* **COOKING TIME** *40 minutes* **SERVES** *12*

1lb 2oz package white bread mix
About 1⅓ cups water warm water
½ stick butter, melted
1 large egg, lightly beaten
¼ cup fresh Parmesan cheese, grated

2 cloves garlic, crushed
½ teaspoon salt
¼ teaspoon freshly ground black pepper
2 teaspoons dried herbes de Provence

1 Grease a deep 8-inch round cake pan and set aside. Place the bread mix in a bowl and add enough water (according to package instructions), mixing to form a soft dough.
2 Turn the dough onto a lightly floured worktop and knead until smooth and elastic. Divide the dough into 12 equal portions, then roll each portion into a ball. Combine the melted butter, egg, Parmesan cheese, garlic, salt, black pepper, and herbs in a small bowl.
3 Dip the dough balls into the butter mixture, coating them liberally all over, then arrange the balls in a single layer in the cake pan. Drizzle over any remaining butter mixture. Cover and let rise in a warm place for about 45 minutes, or until doubled in size.
4 Meanwhile, preheat the oven to 190°C/375°F/gas mark 5. Bake the loaf for about 40 minutes, or until golden brown. Turn onto a wire rack to cool. Pull the rolls apart to serve. Serve warm or cold.

TO MAKE IN BREADMAKER, *use quantities as listed in main recipe but amend following ingredients and use 1¼ cups water (or according to package mix). Add ingredients to breadmaker in order specified in your instruction book. Use Dough setting for this recipe, then continue as above from Step 2 of main recipe (punching down rather than kneading dough, then divide and shape dough and continue as directed).*

140 Fruit and nut snack bread

PREPARATION TIME *35 minutes, plus rising* **COOKING TIME** *35 minutes* **SERVES** *12*

3 cups strong white flour
½ teaspoon salt
3 tablespoons butter, diced
2 teaspoons fast-action dried yeast
2 tablespoons superfine sugar
Finely grated zest of 1 lemon
1 egg, lightly beaten

About 1 cup warm water
⅔ cup ready-to-eat dried apricots
⅓ cup dried cranberries
1 cup confectioners' sugar, sifted
About 3–4 teaspoons lemon juice
¼ cup toasted flaked almonds

1 Grease a deep 9-inch loose-bottomed round cake pan and set aside. Sift the flour and salt into a large bowl, then lightly rub in the butter. Stir in the yeast, superfine sugar, and lemon zest, then add the egg and enough water, mixing to form a soft dough.
2 Turn the dough onto a lightly floured worktop and knead until smooth and elastic. Knead the apricots and cranberries evenly into the dough. Roll out to form a 16 x 8-inch rectangle.
3 Starting from a long side, roll up the dough fairly tightly like a jelly roll. Cut into 12 even slices. Place 11 slices upright (seam-side down) around the edges of the pan and place the remaining slice in the center, cut-side up, to make a flower-type shape. Cover and let rise in a warm place until doubled in size.
4 Meanwhile, preheat the oven to 190°C/375°F/gas mark 5. Bake the bread for about 35 minutes, or until golden brown, covering it loosely with foil toward the end of the cooking time if the top is browning too quickly. Let stand for a few minutes, then turn onto a wire rack to cool.
5 Blend the confectioners' sugar with enough lemon juice to make a fairly thin glacé frosting and drizzle this over the top of the bread. Sprinkle with flaked almonds and pull the rolls apart to serve. Serve warm or cold.

CHAPTER 3

Flat breads

Some of the flat breads in this chapter, such as traditional Chapatis, Parathas, and Puris, are made from unleavened doughs, while others such as Naan, Calzone, and Focaccia contain yeast to give the dough a rise and lift. Alternate recipes such as Roti and Wheat Tortillas use baking powder as a leavening agent.

Flat breads, whether leavened or unleavened, vary in texture, flavor, and shape. They may be crisp or chewy, plain or rich, and most of them are quick and easy to prepare and cook.

Many flat breads provide an ideal accompaniment to numerous dishes, and some are great for dipping or mopping up sauces, while others such as Pitta Bread and Wheat Tortillas are great for filling or wrapping to create a quick and easy supper or snack.

We include a whole variety of tempting flat bread recipes from across the world, ranging from flavorful Spiced Naan Bread, Lavash, Pizzas, and Moroccan Flat Breads, to delicious Drop Scones, English Muffins, Potato Cakes, Bannocks, and Pretzels.

141 ⌂ Naan bread

PREPARATION TIME *20 minutes, plus rising* **COOKING TIME** *10–12 minutes*
MAKES *4 good-sized naan bread*

2 cups strong white flour
1 teaspoon salt
1½ teaspoons easy-blend dried yeast
4 tablespoons plain yogurt (at room
  temperature)

1 tablespoon sunflower oil
About ½ cup warm milk
About 3 tablespoons melted ghee or
  butter, for brushing

1 Sift the flour and salt into a large bowl, then stir in the yeast. Make a well in the center,
   then add the yogurt, oil, and enough milk, mixing to form a soft dough.
2 Turn the dough onto a floured worktop and knead until smooth. Shape into a round, then
   place in a lightly oiled bowl, cover and let rise in a warm place until doubled in size.
3 Punch down the dough on a lightly floured worktop, then divide into 4 equal portions. Roll
   out each piece of dough to form a flat oval or teardrop shape, about ¼-inch thick and
   9 inches long. Cover and leave for 15 minutes.
4 Preheat the oven to 230°C/450°F/gas mark 8. Put 2 cookie sheets in the oven to heat.
   Place the naan breads on the hot cookie sheets and brush with melted ghee or butter.
5 Bake for 10–12 minutes, or until puffed up. Wrap in a clean dish towel and serve warm.

TO MAKE IN BREADMAKER, *use quantities as listed in main recipe but amend following ingredients
and use ½ cup milk and 1 teaspoon fast-action dried yeast, and add 1½ teaspoons superfine sugar.
Add ingredients to breadmaker in order specified in your instruction book. Use Basic Dough or
Pizza Dough setting for this recipe, then continue as above from Step 3 of main recipe.*

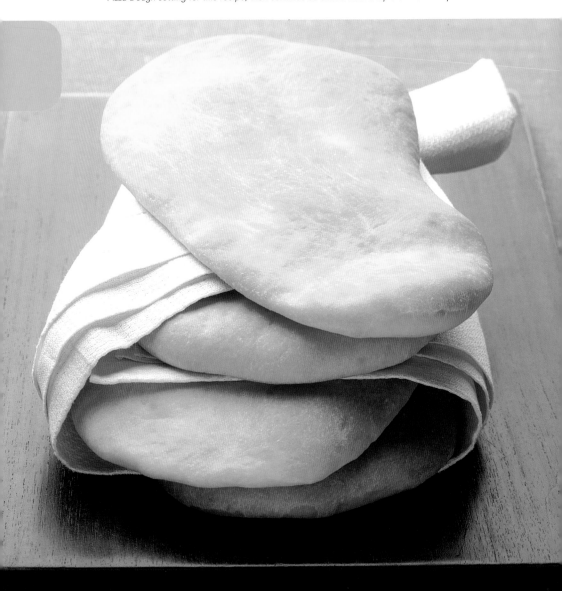

142 ▣ Spiced naan bread

PREPARATION TIME *20 minutes, plus rising* **COOKING TIME** *10–12 minutes* **MAKES** *4*

Ingredients for Naan Bread, with:
1½ teaspoons ground cilantro

1 teaspoon ground cumin
1 teaspoon hot chili powder

1   Sift the flour and salt into a large bowl, then stir in the yeast and ground spices. Make a well in the center, then add the yogurt, oil, and enough milk, mixing to form a soft dough.
2   Follow Steps 2, 3, 4, and 5 of Naan Bread recipe opposite.

TO MAKE IN BREADMAKER, *follow instructions given for Naan Bread recipe opposite.*

143 ▣ Garlic and cilantro naan

PREPARATION TIME *20 minutes, plus rising* **COOKING TIME** *10–12 minutes* **MAKES** *4*

Ingredients for Naan Bread, with:
1½ teaspoons ground cilantro
1 large clove garlic, crushed

1–2 teaspoons black onion seeds
1–2 tablespoons chopped fresh cilantro

1   Sift the flour and salt into a bowl, then stir in the yeast, ground cilantro, and garlic. Make a well in the center; stir in the yogurt, oil, and enough milk, mixing to form a soft dough.
2   Follow Steps 2, 3, 4, and 5 of Naan bread recipe opposite, sprinkling with the onion seeds and chopped cilantro just before baking.

TO MAKE IN BREADMAKER, *use quantities as listed in main recipe but amend following ingredients and use ½ cup milk and 1 teaspoon fast-action dried yeast, and add 1½ teaspoons superfine sugar. Add ingredients to breadmaker in order specified in your instruction book. Use Basic Dough or Pizza Dough setting, then continue as directed from Step 3 of Naan Bread recipe opposite.*

144 Chapatis

PREPARATION TIME *20 minutes* **COOKING TIME** *15–20 minutes* **MAKES** *6 chapatis*

1½ cups all-purpose wholewheat flour or chapati flour
½ teaspoon salt

About ¾ cup warm water
Melted butter or ghee, for brushing

1   Mix the flour and salt in a bowl, then add enough water, mixing to form a soft dough. Turn the dough onto a lightly floured worktop and knead for about 5 minutes, or until the dough feels soft and elastic. Place the dough in a bowl, cover and let rest for 10 minutes.
2   Divide the dough into 6 equal portions and shape into small balls. On a lightly floured worktop, roll each ball into a round about ⅛-inch thick.
3   Heat a griddle or large, heavy-based skillet until very hot, then cook a chapati on the griddle for about 1–2 minutes, or until small bubbles appear on the surface.
4   Using a palette knife, turn the chapati over and cook the other side for about 1–2 minutes. Use a clean dish towel to press down the edges so they cook as it rises and puffs up.
5   Remove from the pan, place on a clean dish towel and brush with a little melted butter or ghee. Cover and keep warm while cooking the remaining chapatis. Stack the cooked hot chapatis on top of each other and serve immediately.

145 Parathas

PREPARATION TIME *30 minutes, plus resting* **COOKING TIME** *15–20 minutes* **MAKES** *8 parathas*

1½ cups all-purpose wholewheat flour or chapati flour	About ⅔ cup warm water
½ teaspoon salt	Melted ghee or vegetable oil, for brushing

1. Mix the flour and salt in a bowl, then gradually add enough warm water, mixing to form a soft dough. Turn the dough onto a lightly floured worktop and knead for 2–3 minutes, or until the dough is smooth and pliable, then place it in a clean bowl, cover and let rest for 30 minutes.
2. Divide the dough into 8 equal portions. On a lightly floured worktop, roll each portion of dough into a round about 4–5 inches in diameter. Brush a little ghee or oil over a round of dough. Fold it in half, then brush a little ghee or oil over the top and fold it in half again to form a triangle. Repeat with the remaining rounds of dough.
3. Roll out one triangle of dough on a lightly floured worktop to form a larger round about 5–7 inches in diameter. Brush a griddle or a large, heavy-based skillet with a little ghee or oil and heat until hot.
4. Cook a paratha on the griddle for about 1 minute, or until bubbles start to appear on the surface. Brush the top with a little more ghee or oil and turn over to cook the other side. Cook the second side for about 1 minute, or until crisp and both sides are speckled with brown patches. As the paratha cooks, press the edges down with a wooden spatula or clean dish towel to ensure even cooking.
5. Place the cooked paratha on a warm plate, cover and keep warm. Repeat with the remaining triangles of dough, rolling out and cooking each one individually. Stack the cooked hot parathas on top of each other, then serve warm as they are or folded.

146 Puris (Pooris)

PREPARATION TIME *20 minutes, plus resting* **COOKING TIME** *20–25 minutes* **MAKES** *20 puris*

1 cup all-purpose flour	2 tablespoons vegetable oil, plus extra for deep-frying
1 teaspoon salt	
1 cup all-purpose wholewheat flour	About ½ cup warm water

1. Sift the white flour and salt into a bowl, then stir in the wholewheat flour. Make a well in the center, then add the 2 tablespoons oil, and enough water, mixing with your hands to form quite a stiff dough.
2. Turn the dough onto a lightly floured worktop and knead for about 5 minutes, or until smooth and elastic. Shape the dough into a round, then place it in a clean bowl, cover with a damp cloth and let rest for 1 hour.
3. Divide the dough into about 20 equal portions. On a lightly floured worktop, roll each portion of dough into a thin round about 4–4½ inches in diameter and 1/16–1/8-inch thick.
4. Heat some oil (a depth of about 3¼ inches) in a deep, heavy-based pan until hot. Add one round of dough to the oil and deep-fry for about 30 seconds, or until the puri puffs up and is golden brown underneath. Using a wooden spoon or spatula, turn the puri over and deep-fry for about 30 seconds, or until golden brown all over.
5. Remove from the oil using a slotted spoon or spatula, drain on paper towels and keep warm. Repeat with the remaining rounds of dough. Serve hot.

VARIATION *Use buckwheat, rye or chapati flour (found in most Indian grocers) in place of wholewheat flour.*

147 Roti (West Indian)

PREPARATION TIME *30 minutes, plus resting* **COOKING TIME** *15–20 minutes* **MAKES** *8 roti*

3 cups fine all-purpose wholewheat
   flour or chapati flour
1 teaspoon baking powder
1 teaspoon salt

About 1¼ cups water
About ⅔ cup melted ghee or
   vegetable oil

1. Mix the flour, baking powder, and salt in a bowl, then gradually add enough water, mixing to form a firm dough. Turn the dough onto a lightly floured worktop and knead for 2–3 minutes, or until the dough is smooth and pliable, then place it in a clean bowl, cover and let rest for 30 minutes.
2. Divide the dough into 8 equal portions. On a lightly floured worktop, roll each portion into a round about 7 inches in diameter. Brush a little ghee or oil over a round of dough. Fold it in half, then brush a little ghee or oil over the top and fold it in half again to form a triangle. Repeat with the remaining rounds of dough. Cover and set aside for 10 minutes.
3. Roll out one triangle of dough on a lightly floured worktop to form a round about 8–9 inches in diameter. Brush both sides of the round with a little ghee or vegetable oil.
4. Heat a griddle or a large, heavy-based skillet until hot, then cook a roti on the griddle for about 1 minute. Brush the top with a little more ghee or oil and turn over to cook the other side. Cook the second side for about 2 minutes, then turn over again and cook for about 1 minute, or until it is lightly browned all over.
5. Place the cooked roti on a warm plate, cover and keep warm. Repeat with the remaining triangles of dough, rolling out and cooking each one individually. Stack the cooked roti on top of each other, then serve warm as they are or folded.

148 Lavash

PREPARATION TIME *30 minutes, plus rising and resting* **COOKING TIME** *25 minutes*
MAKES *12–15 lavash*

2⅓ cups strong white flour
1 teaspoon salt
1 cup fine plain wholewheat flour

1 sachet (¼oz) easy-blend dried yeast
About 1¼ cups warm water

1. Sift the white flour and salt into a large bowl, then stir in the wholewheat flour and yeast. Make a well in the center, then add enough water, mixing to form a soft dough.
2. Turn the dough onto a lightly floured worktop and knead until smooth and elastic. Shape the dough into a round, then place it in a lightly oiled bowl, cover and let rise in a warm place until doubled in size.
3. Punch down the dough on a lightly floured worktop, then divide into 12–15 portions. Shape each portion into a round, cover and let rest for 30 minutes.
4. Take one ball of dough at a time and roll it out on a lightly floured worktop as thinly as possible to make a large, almost translucent round about 5–6 inches in diameter. Dust off any excess flour.
5. Heat a griddle or heavy-based skillet until very hot. Cook the dough round on the hot griddle for about 1 minute, then flip it over and briefly cook the other side for about 30 seconds, or until the bread is lightly browned.
6. Remove with a palette knife to a wire rack to cool. Repeat with the remaining balls of dough, rolling out and cooking each one individually. Serve warm or cold.

VARIATION *Cook the lavash in the oven rather than on a griddle, if you prefer. Simply preheat the oven to 230°C/450°F/gas mark 8. Place 3 cookie sheets in the oven to heat. Roll out the dough balls as directed and stack them, one on top of another, with waxed paper between each one. Place 1 lavash on each cookie sheet and bake in the oven for 6–8 minutes, or until they are starting to brown. Transfer to a wire rack to cool and cook the remaining lavash. Serve as above.*

149 Seeded flat bread

PREPARATION TIME *20 minutes, plus rising and resting* **COOKING TIME** *30–40 minutes*
MAKES *1 flat bread (serves 6–8)*

2 cups strong white flour
1 teaspoon salt
2 cups strong wholewheat flour
2 teaspoons easy-blend dried yeast
1 teaspoon superfine sugar

3 tablespoons olive oil
⅔ cup buttermilk
About ⅔ cup warm water
Caraway seeds, fennel seeds, and
   coarse sea salt, for sprinkling

1 Grease or flour a cookie sheet and set aside. Sift the white flour and salt into a large bowl, then stir in the wholewheat flour, yeast, and sugar. Make a well in the center, then add the oil, buttermilk, and enough water, mixing to form a soft dough.

2 Turn the dough onto a lightly floured worktop and knead until smooth and elastic. Shape the dough into a round, then place it in a lightly oiled bowl, cover and let rise in a warm place until doubled in size.

3 Punch down the dough on a lightly floured worktop, then roll it out to form a flat round about ¾-inch thick. Place on the cookie sheet, then flute or decoratively pinch around the edges of the dough. Cover and let rest for 20 minutes.

4 Preheat the oven to 190°C/375°F/gas mark 5. Brush the top of the dough with a little water and sprinkle with a mixture of caraway seeds, fennel seeds, and coarse sea salt.

5 Bake for 30–40 minutes, or until the bread is risen and golden brown. Transfer to a wire rack to cool. Serve warm or cold cut into wedges.

150 ▣ North African flat breads

PREPARATION TIME *20 minutes* **COOKING TIME** *15–20 minutes* **MAKES** *8 flat breads*

2⅔ cups strong white flour, plus extra for
   dusting
2 teaspoons salt
1 sachet (¼oz) fast-action dried yeast

5 tablespoons olive oil, plus extra
   for glazing
About 1¼ cups warm water

1 Grease or flour 2 cookie sheets and set aside. Sift the flour and salt into a large bowl, then stir in the yeast. Make a well in the center, then add the oil and enough water, mixing to form a soft dough.

2 Turn the dough onto a lightly floured worktop and knead until smooth and elastic. Divide the dough into 8 equal portions. Roll out each portion to make a flat round about 4 inches in diameter.

3 Place on the cookie sheets, then cover and let rise in a warm place for about 1 hour, or until slightly risen.

4 Meanwhile, preheat the oven to 230°C/450°F/gas mark 8. Brush a little oil over the top of each flat bread and dust with a little flour.

5 Bake for 15–20 minutes, or until the flat breads are risen and golden brown. Serve warm.

TO MAKE IN BREADMAKER, *use ingredient quantities as listed in main recipe but amend following ingredients and use 1 cup water and 1½ teaspoons fast-action dried yeast, and add 1½ teaspoons superfine sugar. Add ingredients to breadmaker in order specified in your instruction book. Use Basic Dough or Pizza Dough setting for this recipe, then continue as above from Step 2 of main recipe (punching down rather than kneading dough, then divide and shape dough and continue as directed).*

151 🍞 Moroccan flat breads

PREPARATION TIME *25 minutes, plus rising* **COOKING TIME** *15–20 minutes*
MAKES *4 flat breads (each flat bread serves 1)*

2 cups strong white flour
¼ teaspoon salt
1 teaspoon fennel seeds
1 teaspoon easy-blend dried yeast

2 teaspoons clear honey
About ¾ cup warm milk
Beaten egg, to glaze

1   Grease or flour 2 cookie sheets and set aside. Sift the flour and salt into a large bowl, then stir in the fennel seeds and yeast. Make a well in the center, then add the honey and enough milk, mixing to form a soft dough.
2   Turn the dough onto a lightly floured worktop and knead until smooth and elastic. Shape the dough into a round, then place it in a lightly oiled bowl, cover and let rise in a warm place until doubled in size.
3   Punch down the dough on a lightly floured worktop and divide it into 4 equal portions. Roll each portion into a round about 3½ inches in diameter, and about ¾-inch thick.
4   Place on the cookie sheets, then using a sharp knife or scissors, cut twelve ½-inch deep slashes all around the edge of each dough round at regular intervals. Cover and set aside in a warm place for 20 minutes.
5   Preheat the oven to 220°C/425°F/gas mark 7. Brush the tops of the dough rounds with beaten egg, then bake for 15–20 minutes, or until the breads are risen slightly and golden brown. Transfer to a wire rack to cool. Serve whole or cut into quarters.

TO MAKE IN BREADMAKER, *use quantities as listed in main recipe but amend following ingredients and use ¾ cup milk, 1 teaspoon salt and use fast-action dried yeast. Add ingredients to breadmaker in order specified in your instruction book. Use Basic Dough or Pizza Dough setting for this recipe, then continue as above from Step 3 of main recipe.*

152 🍞 Pitta bread

PREPARATION TIME *25 minutes, plus rising* **COOKING TIME** *10 minutes* **MAKES** *8 pitta bread*

2⅓ cups strong white flour
1 teaspoon salt
1½ teaspoons easy-blend dried yeast

1 teaspoon superfine sugar
1 tablespoon olive oil
About 1 cup warm water

1   Sift the flour and salt into a large bowl, then stir in the yeast and sugar. Make a well in the center, then add the oil and enough water, mixing to form a soft dough.
2   Turn the dough onto a lightly floured worktop and knead until smooth and elastic. Shape the dough into a round, then place it in a lightly oiled bowl, cover and let rise in a warm place until doubled in size.
3   Punch down the dough on a lightly floured worktop, then divide it into 8 equal portions. Roll out each piece of dough to form a flat oval, about ⅛–¼-inch thick and about 5½–6 inches in length. Lay the dough ovals on a floured dish towel, cover and let rise at normal room temperature for about 30 minutes.
4   Meanwhile, preheat the oven to 230°C/450°F/gas mark 8. Put 3 cookie sheets in the oven to heat. Place the pitta breads on the hot cookie sheets and bake for about 10 minutes, or until puffed up and golden brown.
5   Serve warm or wrap in a clean dish towel and let cool on a wire rack, then re-heat under a broiler when required. To serve, split open and stuff with your favorite filling.

TO MAKE IN BREADMAKER, *use ingredient quantities as listed in main recipe but amend following ingredients and use 1 cup water, 1½ teaspoons salt, and 1 teaspoon fast-action dried yeast. Add ingredients to breadmaker in order specified in your instruction book. Use Basic Dough or Pizza Dough setting for this recipe, then continue as above from Step 3 of main recipe.*

153 Onion, olive, and oregano calzone

PREPARATION TIME *1¼–1½ hours, plus rising* **COOKING TIME** *25 minutes*
MAKES *4 calzones (each calzone serves 2)*

For the pizza dough
3 cups strong white flour
1 teaspoon salt
1½ teaspoons easy-blend dried yeast
2 tablespoons olive oil
About 1 cup warm milk

Beaten egg, to glaze

For the filling
4 tablespoons olive oil
4 red onions, thinly sliced
2 cloves garlic, crushed
½lb mushrooms, sliced
1 cup pitted black olives, sliced
2–4 tablespoons chopped fresh oregano
Sea salt and freshly ground black pepper
**2 cups fresh Parmesan or cheddar
   cheese, finely grated**

1 Grease or flour 2 cookie sheets and set aside. Make the dough. Sift the flour and salt into a large bowl, then stir in the yeast. Make a well in the center, then add the oil and enough milk, mixing to form a soft dough.
2 Turn the dough onto a floured worktop and knead until smooth. Shape into a round, then place in a lightly oiled bowl, cover and let rise in a warm place until doubled in size.
3 Prepare the filling. Heat the oil in a skillet, add the onions and garlic and sauté for about 8 minutes, or until just softened. Add the mushrooms and sauté for 3–4 minutes. Remove the pan from the heat and stir in the olives, oregano, and seasoning. Set aside.
4 Punch down the dough on a lightly floured worktop, then divide into 4 equal portions. Roll out each portion to form an 8-inch round, which is about ¼ inch thick.
5 Cover half of each round with some filling and top with Parmesan, leaving a small border around the edge. Brush the edges with water and fold the plain half over the filling, pressing the edges together. Brush with beaten egg and place on the cookie sheets.
6 Meanwhile, preheat the oven to 200°C/400°F/gas mark 6. Bake the calzones for 25 minutes, or until risen and golden brown. Serve warm.

154 Blue cheese and bacon quiche

PREPARATION TIME *1 hour, 10 minutes, plus rising* **COOKING TIME** *35 minutes*
MAKES *2 quiches (each quiche serves 6–8)*

For the dough
3⅔ cups strong white flour
1 teaspoon salt
3 teaspoons fast-action dried yeast
3 tablespoons olive oil
2 eggs, beaten
About 1 cup warm milk
Fresh herb sprigs, to garnish

For the filling
½ stick butter
1lb bacon, diced
4 onions, thinly sliced
**2½ cups blue cheese, such as Stilton
   or Roquefort, crumbled**
6 eggs
1½ cups light cream
Sea salt and freshly ground black pepper

1 Make the dough. Sift the flour and salt into a large bowl, then stir in the yeast. Make a well in the center, then add the oil, eggs, and enough milk, mixing to form a soft dough.
2 Turn the dough onto a lightly floured worktop and knead until smooth and elastic. Divide in half, then roll out each piece and use each to line a 11-inch fluted tart pan. Cover and let rise in a warm place for 30 minutes.
3 Gently press back the risen dough in the pans to re-shape it, if necessary. Meanwhile, preheat the oven to 190°C/375°F/gas mark 5 and prepare the filling. Melt the butter in a skillet, add the bacon and sauté for 5 minutes, or until just cooked. Remove to a plate and keep warm. Add the onions to the pan and sauté for 8 minutes, or until softened.
4 Place half the bacon in the flan cases and top with the onions, cheese, and remaining bacon. Beat the eggs, cream, and seasoning together, then pour over the bacon and cheese.
5 Bake each quiche (one at a time) in the oven for about 35 minutes, or until the case is cooked and the filling is lightly set and golden. Garnish with herb sprigs. Serve warm.

155 Pancetta, pepper, & olive pizza

PREPARATION TIME *45 minutes, plus rising* **COOKING TIME** *20–25 minutes*
MAKES *2 pizzas (each pizza serves 4–6)*

For the pizza dough
3 cups strong white flour
1 teaspoon salt
1½ teaspoons easy-blend dried yeast
2 tablespoons olive oil
About 1¼ cups warm water

For the topping
2 tablespoons olive oil

2 cloves garlic, crushed
1 cup smoked pancetta, diced
2 large red bell peppers, cored and sliced
14oz can chopped tomatoes with herbs,
  drained
2 tablespoons tomato paste
Sea salt and freshly ground black pepper
1 cup whole black olives
1 cup Parmesan cheese, grated

1   Follow Steps 1 and 2 of the Calzone recipe opposite, using the warm water instead of milk.
2   Prepare the topping. Heat the oil in a skillet, add the garlic and sauté for 30 seconds. Add the pancetta and stir-fry over a high heat until it releases its fat and browns lightly. Remove from the pan and set aside. Add the bell peppers to the pan and sauté for 7 minutes, or until just softened. Remove the pan from the heat and add the pancetta to the bell peppers.
3   Punch down the dough on a lightly floured worktop, then divide it in half. Roll out each piece thinly to form a 12-inch round. Transfer each round to a cookie sheet. Mix together the chopped tomatoes, tomato paste, and seasoning. Spread this mixture over the bases to within ½ inch of the edge. Spoon the bell pepper and pancetta mixture evenly over the tomatoes, then scatter the olives over the top. Sprinkle with the Parmesan.
4   Meanwhile, preheat the oven to 220°C/425°F/gas mark 7. Bake each pizza (one at a time) for 20–25 minutes, or until the base is crisp and the topping is golden. Serve warm.

TO MAKE IN BREADMAKER, *use quantities as listed in main recipe but amend following ingredients and use 1¼ cups water, use fast-action dried yeast, and add 2 teaspoons superfine sugar. Add ingredients to breadmaker in order specified in your instruction book. Use Basic Dough or Pizza Dough setting for this recipe, then continue as above from Step 3 of main recipe.*

156 Wheat tortillas

PREPARATION TIME *30 minutes, plus resting* **COOKING TIME** *30–35 minutes* **MAKES** *12 tortillas*

1½ cups all-purpose flour
1 teaspoon salt
1 teaspoon baking powder

3 tablespoons shortening
About ⅔ cup warm water

1   Sift the flour, salt, and baking powder into a large bowl, then lightly rub in the shortening. Make a well in the center, then add enough water, mixing to form a soft dough. Knead the dough lightly in the bowl, then cover and let rest for 10 minutes.
2   Divide the dough into 12 equal portions. Roll out each portion on a lightly floured worktop to form a 6–7-inch round. Cover to keep moist.
3   Heat a griddle or large, heavy-based skillet until hot, then add one tortilla and cook for 1½–2 minutes, or until the surface starts to bubble and the underside is speckled brown. Turn the tortilla over and brown the other side—it should stay flexible.
4   Remove the tortilla from the pan and wrap in a clean dish towel to keep warm. Repeat with the remaining tortillas, stacking the cooked tortillas as you go. Serve warm.

TIP *To re-heat tortillas, wrap them in foil and place in a preheated oven at 180°C/350°F/ gas mark 4 for about 5 minutes, or until warm.*

157 ⊡ Focaccia breads

PREPARATION TIME *25 minutes, plus rising* **COOKING TIME** *20–25 minutes* **MAKES** *8 focaccia breads*

3 cups strong white flour
1 teaspoon salt
2 teaspoons easy-blend dried yeast

3 tablespoons olive oil, plus extra for
**   drizzling**
About 1 cup warm water
Coarse sea salt, for sprinkling

1   Grease or flour 2 cookie sheets and set aside. Sift the flour and salt into a large bowl, then stir in the yeast. Make a well in the center, then add the 3 tablespoons oil and enough water, mixing to form a soft dough.
2   Turn the dough onto a lightly floured worktop and knead until smooth and elastic. Shape the dough into a round, then place it in a lightly oiled bowl, cover and let rise in a warm place until doubled in size.
3   Punch down the dough on a lightly floured worktop and divide it into 8 equal portions. Roll each portion of dough into a ball, then flatten each ball into a round about 4 inches in diameter, making the edges slightly thicker than the centers.
4   Place on the cookie sheets, cover and let rise again for about 30–45 minutes, or until slightly risen.
5   Meanwhile, preheat the oven to 200°C/400°F/gas mark 6. Drizzle a little olive oil over each focaccia, sprinkle with sea salt and spray with a little water.
6   Bake for 20–25 minutes, or until the focaccia are risen and golden brown, spraying them with a little water again after the first 5 minutes of the cooking time. Transfer to a wire rack to cool. Serve warm or cold, whole or cut into quarters.

TO MAKE IN BREADMAKER, *use quantities as listed in main recipe but amend following ingredients and use 1 cup water and 1½ teaspoons fast-action dried yeast, and add 1½ teaspoons granulated sugar. Add ingredients to breadmaker in order specified in your instruction book. Use Basic Dough or Pizza Dough setting for this recipe, then continue as above from Step 3 of main recipe.*

158 Sun-dried tomato & olive focaccia

PREPARATION TIME *30 minutes, plus rising* **COOKING TIME** *20–25 minutes* **MAKES** *1 loaf (serves 6)*

3 cups strong white flour
1 teaspoon salt
2 teaspoons easy-blend dried yeast
½ cup sun-dried tomatoes in oil, drained
and chopped

¼ cup pitted black olives, chopped
3 tablespoons olive oil, plus extra for
drizzling
About 1 cup warm water
Coarse sea salt, for sprinkling

1 Grease or flour a cookie sheet and set aside. Sift the flour and salt into a large bowl, then
stir in the yeast. Stir in the tomatoes and olives. Make a well in the center, then add the 3
tablespoons oil and enough water, mixing to form a soft dough.
2 Turn the dough onto a lightly floured worktop and knead until smooth and elastic. Shape
the dough into a round, then place it in a lightly oiled bowl, cover and let rise in a warm
place until doubled in size.
3 Punch down the dough on a lightly floured worktop, then roll out to form a flat oval about
1 inch thick. Place the dough on the cookie sheet, cover and let rise again until doubled in
size.
4 Meanwhile, preheat the oven to 200°C/400°F/gas mark 6. Using your fingertips, make
deep dimples all over the surface of the dough. Drizzle with oil and sprinkle with sea salt.
Bake for 20–25 minutes, or until cooked and golden. Transfer to a wire rack to cool. Serve
warm or cold in chunks or slices.

159 ▣ English muffins

PREPARATION TIME *25 minutes, plus rising* COOKING TIME *35 minutes* MAKES *8–10 muffins*

3⅔ cups strong white flour
1½ teaspoons salt
1½ teaspoons easy-blend dried yeast
1 teaspoon superfine sugar

½ stick butter, melted
⅔ cup warm milk
About ⅔ cup warm water
Sunflower oil, for greasing

1   Generously flour a large cookie sheet and set aside. Sift the flour and salt into a large bowl, then stir in the yeast and sugar. Make a well in the center, then add the melted butter, milk, and enough water, mixing to form a soft dough.

2   Turn the dough onto a lightly floured worktop and knead until smooth and elastic. Shape the dough into a round, then place it in a lightly oiled bowl, cover and let rise in a warm place until doubled in size.

3   Punch down the dough on a lightly floured worktop and divide it into 8–10 equal portions. Shape each portion into a round with straight sides, each about ½–¾ inches thick. Place on the cookie sheet, cover and let rise again for about 30–40 minutes, or until springy to the touch.

4   Brush a griddle or large, heavy-based skillet with a little oil and heat until warm. Carefully transfer 3–4 muffins onto the griddle and cook in batches over a moderate heat for 8–10 minutes, or until golden brown underneath. Turn them over and cook the other side for about 8 minutes, or until golden brown.

5   Remove the muffins from the pan and wrap them in a clean dish towel, if serving warm. Otherwise transfer them to a wire rack to cool. Cook the remaining muffins.

6   To serve, split the muffins open and serve with butter. If serving from cold, broil the muffins on both sides under a broiler, then split and spread with butter.

TO MAKE IN BREADMAKER, *use quantities as listed in main recipe but amend following ingredients and use 3 cups strong white flour, ½ cup milk, ½ cup water, and use fast-action dried yeast. Add ingredients to breadmaker in order specified in your instruction book. Use Dough setting for this recipe, then continue as above from Step 3 of main recipe.*

160 Pikelets

PREPARATION TIME *25 minutes, plus rising* COOKING TIME *40 minutes* MAKES *about 24 pikelets*

1 cup strong white flour
1 cup all-purpose flour
1 teaspoon salt
½ teaspoon baking soda
1 teaspoon easy-blend dried yeast

1 teaspoon superfine sugar
1 tablespoon sunflower oil, plus extra
  for greasing
⅔ cup warm milk
1¼ cups warm water

1   Sift the flours, salt, and baking soda into a large bowl, then stir in the yeast and sugar. Make a well in the center, then add the 1 tablespoon oil, the milk, and water. Stir to make a batter, then beat vigorously for about 5 minutes, or until smooth and thick. Cover and set aside in a warm place for about 1–1½ hours, or until sponge-like in texture (the top will be full of small bubbles).

2   Beat the batter for a further 2–3 minutes. Heat a greased griddle or large, heavy-based skillet until hot. Drop 1–2 tablespoons batter at a time in circles onto the griddle. Cook for 2–3 minutes on each side until golden brown, turning over once using a palette knife.

3   Transfer to a wire rack to cool. Repeat with the remaining batter, until all the batter is used up, greasing the griddle for each batch.

4   To serve, eat the pikelets warm and freshly cooked, or broil them under a preheated broiler on both sides and spread with butter.

161 Crumpets

PREPARATION TIME *25 minutes, plus rising* COOKING TIME *30 minutes* MAKES *12–14 crumpets*

1 cup strong white flour
1 cup plain white flour
1 teaspoon salt
½ teaspoon baking soda
1 teaspoon easy-blend dried yeast

1 teaspoon superfine sugar
1 tablespoon sunflower oil, plus extra
** for cooking**
⅔ cup warm milk
1¼ cups warm water

1. Sift the flours, salt, and baking soda into a large bowl, then stir in the yeast and sugar. Make a well in the center, then add the 1 tablespoon oil, the milk, and water. Stir to make a batter, then beat vigorously for about 5 minutes, or until smooth and thick. Cover and set aside in a warm place for about 1–1½ hours, or until sponge-like in texture (the top will be full of small bubbles).
2. Beat the batter for a further 2–3 minutes, then transfer it to a jug. Heat a little oil on a griddle or in a large, non-stick skillet. Grease the insides of four or six 3–3½-inch crumpet rings or plain metal cookie cutters.
3. Place the rings onto the hot griddle and leave for a couple of minutes until very hot. Pour about ½ inch batter into each ring and cook for 5–6 minutes, or until the top is set and full of tiny bubbles.
4. Loosen around the edge of each crumpet using a knife, carefully remove each ring (using an oven glove), flip the crumpets over and cook the other side for 1–2 minutes, or until pale golden.
5. Transfer to a wire rack. Repeat with the remaining batter, until all the batter is used up, wiping, greasing, and heating the rings for each batch. To serve, toast the crumpets under a preheated broiler on both sides, and spread with butter.

162 Griddle scones

PREPARATION TIME *15 minutes* COOKING TIME *25 minutes* MAKES *8–10 scones*

1½ cups self-rising white flour
A pinch of salt
½ teaspoon freshly grated nutmeg
½ stick butter, diced
4 tablespoons superfine sugar

½ cup dried currants
1 egg, beaten
About 3–4 tablespoons milk
Sunflower oil, for greasing

1. Sift the flour, salt, and nutmeg into a bowl, then lightly rub in the butter until the mixture resembles fine bread crumbs. Stir in the sugar and dried currants, then make a well in the center. Add the egg and enough milk, mixing to form a firm, pliable dough.
2. Roll out the dough on a lightly floured worktop to about ¾ inch thick. Cut into triangles or 2½-inch rounds.
3. Heat a lightly greased griddle or large, heavy-based skillet over a medium heat until moderately hot. Cook the scones in batches on the griddle for about 5 minutes on each side, turning once, until the scones are well risen, browned, and cooked through.
4. Transfer to a wire rack to cool for a few minutes, then split and serve spread with butter or jelly.

VARIATIONS *Use ground cinnamon in place of nutmeg. Use golden raisins or dried cranberries in place of dried currants.*

163 Drop scones

PREPARATION TIME *10 minutes* COOKING TIME *20 minutes* MAKES *10–12 drop scones*

1 cup self-rising white flour
2 tablespoons superfine sugar
1 egg, beaten

⅔ cup milk
Sunflower oil, for greasing

1   Sift the flour into a bowl, then stir in the sugar. Make a well in the center and stir in the egg, then gradually stir in the milk, mixing to make a smooth, thick, creamy batter.
2   Grease a griddle or large, heavy-based skillet until hot. Cook the mixture in batches and drop spoonfuls of the mixture onto the hot griddle. Cook over a moderate heat for 2–3 minutes until the top of the scones is covered with bubbles and the underside is golden. Turn over using a palette knife and cook for a further 2–3 minutes until golden on the other side.
3   Remove from the griddle and wrap in a warm, clean dish towel. Repeat with the remaining batter, until all the batter is used up. Serve the drop scones warm, spread with butter, jelly, or honey.

VARIATION *Once the underside of the scones is just set and almost cooked, sprinkle each one with a few dried currants, then turn them over and cook the other side.*

164 Singin' hinnie

PREPARATION TIME *15 minutes* **COOKING TIME** *20 minutes* **SERVES** *8*

2⅓ cups all-purpose flour
1 teaspoon salt
1 teaspoon cream of tartar
½ teaspoon baking soda
1½ teaspoons ground cinnamon
¾ stick butter, diced

¾ cup dried currants
1 cup milk
Sunflower oil, for greasing
Softened butter, to serve
1 tablespoon superfine sugar,
   for sprinkling

1   Sift the flour, salt, cream of tartar, baking soda, and cinnamon into a bowl, then lightly rub in the diced butter. Stir in the currants, then make a well in the center and add the milk, mixing to make a very soft dough.
2   Turn the dough onto a lightly floured worktop and knead gently. Roll out the dough to form a round about 10 inches in diameter and about ¾ inch thick.
3   Lightly grease a griddle or large, heavy-based skillet and heat over a low heat. Place the dough round on the griddle and cook for about 20 minutes, or until golden brown on both sides and cooked through, carefully turning over once using two spatulas, halfway through cooking.
4   Serve hot, split in half crosswise and spread with softened butter. Sprinkle with superfine sugar and cut into wedges to serve.

165 Blini with smoked salmon

PREPARATION TIME *30 minutes, plus rising* **COOKING TIME** *30 minutes*
MAKES *about 24 blini (serves 6–8)*

1 cup all-purpose flour
½ teaspoon salt
1 cup buckwheat flour
½ teaspoon fast-action dried yeast
2 cups warm milk
1 egg, separated

Sunflower oil, for greasing
½lb thinly sliced smoked salmon
1 cup crème fraîche
Lemon wedges and chopped fresh
   chives or dill, to garnish

1   Sift the all-purpose flour and salt into a large bowl, then stir in the buckwheat flour and yeast. Make a well in the center, then gradually beat in the milk to make a smooth batter. Cover and set aside in a warm place for 45–60 minutes, or until the mixture is frothy and has doubled in volume.
2   Beat the egg yolk into the batter. In a separate bowl, whisk the egg white until stiff, then fold the whisked egg white into the batter.
3   Brush a griddle or large, non-stick skillet with oil and heat until hot. Spoon about 2 tablespoons batter onto the griddle for each blini; you should be able to cook 3 or 4 blini at a time.
4   Cook the blini over a moderate heat for 2–3 minutes, or until the top is bubbly and has set. Turn the blini over using a palette knife and cook for a further 2–3 minutes, or until lightly browned.
5   Wrap the cooked blini in a clean dish towel and keep warm. Cook the remaining blini in batches until all the batter is used up, greasing the pan for each batch.
6   To serve, arrange the blini on serving plates, with the smoked salmon slices and a dollop of crème fraîche alongside. Garnish with lemon wedges and fresh chives or dill and serve.

VARIATIONS *Use plain wholewheat flour in place of buckwheat flour. Use smoked trout fillets in place of smoked salmon.*

166 Potato cakes

PREPARATION TIME *15 minutes* COOKING TIME *15 minutes* MAKES *about 14 potato cakes*

**2 cups cooked mashed potatoes,
cooled slightly (until cool enough
to handle)**
½ teaspoon salt

2 tablespoons butter, softened
1 cup all-purpose flour
Sunflower oil, for greasing

1 Place the mashed potatoes in a bowl, add the salt and softened butter and mix well. Gradually knead in the flour, adding only enough to bind the mixture and make a soft, but not sticky dough. Cover and chill in the refrigerator for 30 minutes.
2 Turn the dough onto a lightly floured worktop and roll out until it is about ¼ inch thick. Cut the dough into about 14 even triangles or squares.
3 Heat a griddle or large, heavy-based skillet over a medium-high heat and add a little oil to grease the pan.
4 Cook the potato cakes in batches, for about 2 minutes on each side, until browned all over, turning one time. Keep warm while cooking the remaining potato cakes. Serve warm.

TIP *1lb 10oz whole (unpeeled) potatoes will yield about 2 cups mashed potatoes.*

167 Bannocks

PREPARATION TIME *15 minutes* COOKING TIME *40 minutes* MAKES *about 18 bannocks*

1 cup medium oatmeal
⅔ cup plain wholewheat flour
2 teaspoons baking powder
1 teaspoon salt

2 tablespoons butter, diced
About ⅔ cup milk
Sunflower oil, for greasing

1 Combine the oatmeal, flour, baking powder, and salt in a bowl, then lightly rub in the butter. Make a well in the center, then add enough milk, mixing to form a soft dough.
2 Roll out the dough on a lightly floured worktop to about ¼ inch thick, then using a cookie cutter, cut the dough into 2-inch rounds.
3 Lightly grease a griddle or large, heavy-based skillet with a little oil and heat over a medium-low heat. Cook the bannocks in batches on the griddle, for about 10 minutes on each side, or until they are just beginning to brown, turning once.
4 Keep warm while cooking the remaining bannocks. Serve warm.

168 Oatcakes

PREPARATION TIME *10 minutes* COOKING TIME *20–25 minutes* MAKES *8 oatcakes*

⅔ cup medium oatmeal
¼ teaspoon salt
1 tablespoon butter, melted

3–4 tablespoons boiling water
Sunflower oil, for greasing

1 Mix the oatmeal and salt in a bowl. Using a round-bladed knife, stir in the melted butter and enough boiling water to bind the mixture—it should be firm, but not sticky or crumbly. Gently knead the dough to bring it together, then divide it in half.
2 On a very lightly floured worktop, roll out each piece of dough to form a round about 6 inches in diameter and about ¼ inch thick. Cut each round into 4 quarters or triangles.
3 Heat a very lightly greased griddle or large, heavy-based skillet over a medium heat until warm. Using a palette knife or spatula, place 4 oatcakes on the griddle and cook over a low heat for 5–6 minutes, or until the edges start to curl upward. Turn them over using the palette knife and cook the second side for about 5 minutes, or until firm.
4 Transfer to a wire rack to cool. Repeat with the remaining oatcakes. Serve cold.

169 Rye crispbreads

PREPARATION TIME *25 minutes, plus rising* **COOKING TIME** *20 minutes*
MAKES *about 20 crispbreads*

2⅓ cups strong white flour	2 teaspoons easy-blend dried yeast
2 teaspoons salt	1 tablespoon fennel seeds
1 cup (packed) rye flour	1 tablespoon molasses
2 tablespoons butter, diced	About 1¼ cups warm water

1 Grease 3 cookie sheets and set aside. Sift the white flour and salt into a bowl, then stir in the rye flour. Rub in the butter, then stir in the yeast and fennel seeds. Make a well in the center, then add the molasses and enough water, mixing to form a firm dough.
2 Turn the dough onto a lightly floured worktop and knead until smooth, firm and elastic. Shape the dough into a round, then place it in a lightly oiled bowl, cover and let rise in a warm place until doubled in size.
3 Punch down the dough on a lightly floured worktop, then divide into 20 equal portions. Roll each portion into a small round about 4 inches in diameter and about ⅛ inch thick.
4 Using a fork, prick each round of dough all over, then place them on the cookie sheets. Cover and let rise again for about 30–45 minutes, or until slightly risen.
5 Meanwhile, preheat the oven to 190°C/375°F/gas mark 5. Bake the crispbreads for about 20 minutes, or until slightly risen, lightly browned and crisp. Transfer to a wire rack to cool. Serve cold.

170 Pretzels

PREPARATION TIME *30 minutes, plus rising* **COOKING TIME** *20 minutes* **MAKES** *about 16 pretzels*

3 cups strong white flour	½ cup warm milk
1 teaspoon fine salt	About ½ cup warm water
1 teaspoon superfine sugar	Beaten egg, to glaze
1½ teaspoons easy-blend dried yeast	Coarse sea salt or caraway seeds,
1 tablespoon butter, melted	for sprinkling

1 Grease or flour 2 cookie sheets and set aside. Sift the flour and fine salt into a large bowl, then stir in the sugar and yeast. Make a well in the center, then add the melted butter, milk, and enough water, mixing to form a soft dough.
2 Turn the dough onto a lightly floured worktop and knead until smooth and elastic. Shape the dough into a round, then place it in a lightly oiled bowl, cover and let rise in a warm place until doubled in size.
3 Punch down the dough on a lightly floured worktop, then divide it into 16 equal portions. Roll each piece of dough into a long thin rope, about 10–12 inches in length. Bend each rope into a horseshoe shape, then lift up the ends and cross them over. Press the ends lightly onto the curve of the horseshoe to give a knotted effect.
4 Place on the cookie sheets, cover and let rise again for about 20 minutes, or until they are just beginning to rise.
5 Meanwhile, preheat the oven to 200°C/400°F/gas mark 6. Brush the pretzels with beaten egg, then sprinkle them with coarse sea salt or caraway seeds.
6 Bake the pretzels for about 20 minutes, or until they are slightly risen and golden brown—they will be slightly crispy on the outside and soft and doughy on the inside. Transfer to a wire rack to cool. Serve cold.

VARIATIONS *Replace 1 cup of the white flour with rye flour. Sprinkle the pretzels with sesame seeds in place of coarse salt or caraway seeds.*

CHAPTER 4

Quick breads

Quick breads are quick and relatively easy to make compared to many other types of bread: ingredients are simply mixed together and baked, without the need for prolonged kneading or rising periods, creating a wide range of delicious sweet and savory breads.

Some quick breads, such as those that have been enriched with butter, eggs, or fruit, should keep well for several days if wrapped in foil or kept in an airtight container. Other quick breads, such as scones and muffins, are best served freshly baked and warm from the oven.

We include a wide range of versatile and tasty quick breads to tempt you. Choose from traditional recipes such as Soda Bread, Wheaten Bread, or Damper Bread; classic scone recipes such as Rich Fruit Scones or Fresh Strawberry Scones; or more creative recipes such as Bacon and Stilton Pull-Apart or Blueberry Wedges.

171 Soda bread

PREPARATION TIME *15 minutes* COOKING TIME *30–35 minutes* MAKES *1 loaf (serves 8)*

3 cups all-purpose flour, plus extra
for dusting
1 teaspoon salt

2 teaspoons baking soda
2 tablespoons butter, diced
About 1¼ cups buttermilk

1 Preheat the oven to 200°C/400°F/gas mark 6. Lightly flour a cookie sheet and set aside.
Sift the flour, salt, and baking soda into a large bowl, then lightly rub in the butter.
Gradually add enough buttermilk, mixing to form a soft dough.

2 Turn the dough onto a lightly floured worktop and knead gently for 1–2 minutes. Shape
the dough into a large round and place on the cookie sheet. Using a sharp knife, cut a
deep cross in the top of the dough and sprinkle with a little flour.

3 Bake the loaf for 30–35 minutes, or until risen and lightly browned. The bread should
sound hollow when tapped underneath. Transfer to a wire rack to cool. Serve warm or
cold in slices or wedges.

172 Home-style soda bread

PREPARATION TIME *15 minutes* COOKING TIME *30–35 minutes* MAKES *1 loaf (serves 8)*

1⅓ cups all-purpose flour
1 teaspoon salt
2 teaspoons baking soda

1⅓ cups all-purpose wholewheat flour,
plus extra for dusting
⅔ cup rolled oats
About 1¼ cups buttermilk

1 Preheat the oven to 200°C/400°F/gas mark 6. Lightly flour a cookie sheet and set aside.
Sift the white flour, salt, and baking soda into a large bowl, then stir in the wholewheat
flour and oats. Gradually add enough buttermilk, mixing to form a soft, but not sticky
dough.

2 Gather the dough together using your hands, then turn it onto a lightly floured worktop
and knead gently for 1–2 minutes. Shape the dough into an oval loaf and place on the
cookie sheet. Using a sharp knife, cut 2–3 crosses in the top of the dough and sprinkle
with a little wholewheat flour.

3 Bake the loaf for 30–35 minutes, or until slightly risen and lightly browned. The bread
should sound hollow when tapped underneath. Transfer to a wire rack to cool. Serve warm
or cold in slices.

173 Wholewheat soda round

PREPARATION TIME *15 minutes* COOKING TIME *30–35 minutes* MAKES *1 loaf (serves 8)*

3 cups plain wholewheat flour,
plus extra for dusting
1 teaspoon salt
2 teaspoons baking soda

A few turns of freshly ground
black pepper
2 tablespoons butter, diced
1¼ cups buttermilk
A little milk, to mix

1 Preheat the oven to 200°C/400°F/gas mark 6. Lightly flour a cookie sheet and set aside.
Mix the flour, salt, baking soda, and black pepper in a large bowl, then lightly rub in the
butter. Gradually add the buttermilk, and enough milk, mixing to form a soft, but not
sticky dough.

2 Gather the dough together using your hands, then turn it onto a lightly floured worktop
and knead gently for 1–2 minutes. Shape the dough into an 8-inch round and place on the
cookie sheet. Using a sharp knife, cut a deep cross in the top of the dough and sprinkle
with a little flour.

3 Bake the loaf for 30–35 minutes, or until risen and lightly browned. It should sound hollow
when tapped underneath. Transfer to a wire rack to cool. Serve in slices or wedges.

174 Tomato and olive soda bread

PREPARATION TIME *20 minutes* **COOKING TIME** *30–40 minutes* **MAKES** *1 loaf (serves 8)*

3 cups all-purpose flour
1½ teaspoons baking soda
1½ teaspoons cream of tartar
1 teaspoon salt
A few turns of freshly ground
   black pepper
2 teaspoons dried herbes de Provence

½ stick butter, diced
¾ cup sun-dried tomatoes in oil, drained,
   patted dry, and finely chopped
⅓ cup pitted black olives, drained and
   finely chopped
About 1¼ cups buttermilk

1 Preheat the oven to 200°C/400°F/gas mark 6. Grease or flour a cookie sheet and
   set aside. Sift the flour, baking soda, and cream of tartar into a large bowl, then stir in
   the salt, pepper, and dried herbs. Lightly rub in the butter until the mixture resembles
   bread crumbs.
2 Stir in the chopped tomatoes and olives, mixing well. Make a well in the center, then
   gradually add enough buttermilk, mixing to form a soft dough.
3 Turn the dough onto a floured worktop and knead lightly, then shape into an 8-inch round.
   Place on the cookie sheet and, using a sharp knife, mark the round into 8 even wedges.
4 Bake the loaf for 30–40 minutes, or until risen and golden brown. Transfer to a wire rack
   to cool. Serve warm or cold cut into wedges.

175 Wheaten bread

PREPARATION TIME *20 minutes* **COOKING TIME** *50–60 minutes* **MAKES** *1 large loaf (serves 14–16)*

1½ cups all-purpose flour

2 teaspoons salt

3 cups all-purpose wholewheat flour

1 tablespoon superfine sugar

2 teaspoons baking soda

2 tablespoons butter, diced

About 2½ cups buttermilk

1 Preheat the oven to 190°C/375°F/gas mark 5. Grease a deep 8-inch round loose-bottomed cake pan or a cookie sheet and set aside.

2 Sift the white flour and salt into a bowl, then stir in the wholewheat flour, sugar, and baking soda. Lightly rub the butter into the flour mixture, then stir in enough buttermilk, mixing to form a soft dough.

3 Shape the dough into a round, then place it in the pan or on the cookie sheet.

4 Bake the loaf for 50–60 minutes, or until it is risen, deep golden brown and crusty on top, and sounds hollow when tapped underneath. Turn onto a wire rack to cool. Serve warm or cold in slices.

176 Honey wheat bread

PREPARATION TIME *15 minutes* **COOKING TIME** *25–30 minutes* **MAKES** *1 loaf (serves 8–10)*

3 cups plain wholewheat flour
2 teaspoons baking soda
1 teaspoon salt
1 teaspoon ground cinnamon

2 tablespoons butter, diced
4 tablespoons clear honey
About 1 cup milk

1 Preheat the oven to 200°C/400°F/gas mark 6. Grease or flour a cookie sheet and set aside. Mix the flour, baking soda, salt, and cinnamon in a large bowl, then lightly rub in the butter. Add the honey and enough milk, mixing to form a soft dough.
2 Turn the dough onto a lightly floured worktop and knead gently. Shape the dough into an 8-inch round and place on the cookie sheet. Using a sharp knife, cut 3 diagonal slashes across the top of the loaf, about ½ inch deep.
3 Bake the loaf for 25–30 minutes, or until risen and lightly browned. Transfer to a wire rack to cool. Serve warm or cold in slices or wedges.

177 Rustic cheesy herb bread

PREPARATION TIME *20 minutes* **COOKING TIME** *30–40 minutes* **MAKES** *1 loaf (serves 8)*

2⅓ cups plain wholewheat flour
½ cup fine or pinhead oatmeal
2 teaspoons baking soda
2 teaspoons cream of tartar
½ teaspoon salt
1 cup mature cheddar cheese,
  finely grated

3–4 tablespoons chopped fresh
  mixed herbs
½ teaspoon mustard powder
1¼ cups buttermilk
A little milk, for mixing and glazing
1 tablespoon medium oatmeal, for
  sprinkling

1 Preheat the oven to 200°C/400°F/gas mark 6. Grease or flour a cookie sheet and set aside. Put the flour, fine oatmeal, baking soda, cream of tartar, salt, cheese, chopped herbs, and mustard powder in a large bowl and mix well. Stir in the buttermilk, and a little milk, if necessary, mixing to form a soft dough.
2 Lightly knead the dough, then shape into an 8-inch round. Place the round on the cookie sheet, brush the top with a little milk and sprinkle with medium oatmeal. Using a sharp knife, mark the round into 8 even wedges, cutting quite deeply into the dough.
3 Bake the loaf for 30–40 minutes, or until well-risen, firm to the touch, and golden brown. Transfer to a wire rack to cool. Break into wedges to serve. Serve warm or cold.

178 Cheddar, herb, and onion bread

PREPARATION TIME *25 minutes* **COOKING TIME** *1–1¼ hours* **MAKES** *1 loaf (serves 10–12)*

1 tablespoon olive oil
1 large onion, finely chopped
1½ cups self-rising white flour
1½ cups self-rising wholewheat flour
2 teaspoons salt
Freshly ground black pepper
2 teaspoons mustard powder

½ stick butter, diced
1¼ cups mature cheddar cheese,
  finely grated
3–4 tablespoons chopped fresh
  mixed herbs
2 eggs, beaten
1¼ cups milk

1 Preheat the oven to 190°C/375°F/gas mark 5. Grease a 2lb loaf pan and set aside. Heat the oil in a skillet, add the onion and sauté for about 5 minutes, or until softened.
2 Mix the flours, salt, a few turns of black pepper, and the mustard powder in a large bowl. Lightly rub in the butter until the mixture resembles bread crumbs. Stir in the cheese, chopped herbs, and sautéed onion. Add the eggs and milk and stir to mix well.
3 Turn the mixture into the pan and level the top. Bake for 1–1¼ hours, or until risen and golden brown. Turn onto a wire rack to cool. Serve warm or cold in slices.

179 ▣ Cheese and date bread

PREPARATION TIME *20 minutes* **COOKING TIME** *45 minutes* **MAKES** *1 loaf (serves 8–10)*

1½ cups self-rising white flour
A pinch of salt
½ stick butter, diced
¾ cup mature cheddar cheese,
   finely grated

⅔ cup pitted dried dates,
   finely chopped
2 eggs
⅔ cup milk

1. Preheat the oven to 190°C/375°F/gas mark 5. Grease a 2lb loaf pan and set aside. Sift the flour and salt into a bowl, then lightly rub in the butter until the mixture resembles bread crumbs. Stir in three-quarters of the cheese, and the dates.
2. Beat the eggs and milk together, then add to the date mixture and mix well to combine.
3. Turn the mixture into the pan and level the top. Sprinkle with the remaining cheese.
4. Bake the loaf for about 45 minutes, or until risen and golden brown. Turn onto a wire rack to cool. Serve warm or cold in slices.

TO MAKE IN BREADMAKER, *remove kneading blade from bread pan; grease and line base and sides of pan. Follow main recipe as above, then transfer mixture to prepared pan; level surface. Select Bake Only setting and bake for 45–50 minutes or until bread is cooked. Remove bread pan from machine; let stand for 5 minutes. Turn loaf onto wire rack to cool.*

180 Beer bread

PREPARATION TIME *15 minutes* **COOKING TIME** *40 minutes* **MAKES** *2 loaves (each loaf serves 10–12)*

6 cups all-purpose wholewheat flour
2 tablespoons baking powder
1 teaspoon salt

1 tablespoon clear honey
3 cups full-flavored beer

1. Preheat the oven to 180°C/350°F/gas mark 4. Grease two 2lb loaf pans and set aside. Mix the flour, baking powder, and salt together in a large bowl, then add the honey and beer, stirring to form a soft, wet dough.
2. Divide the mixture between the two loaf pans and level the top. Bake the loaves for about 40 minutes, or until risen and golden brown—a cake tester inserted in the center should come out clean
3. Cool the loaves slightly in the pans, then turn onto a wire rack and let cool completely. Serve warm or cold in slices.

181 Damper bread

PREPARATION TIME *15 minutes* **COOKING TIME** *30–40 minutes* **MAKES** *1 loaf (serves 10–12)*

2⅔ cups self-rising white flour, plus
   extra for dusting
1 teaspoon salt
3 tablespoons butter, diced

2 teaspoons superfine sugar
1 cup milk, plus extra for glazing
About ½ cup water

1. Preheat the oven to 200°C/400°F/gas mark 6. Grease or flour a cookie sheet and set aside. Sift the flour and salt into a large bowl, then lightly rub in the butter. Stir in the sugar, then add the milk and enough water, mixing to form a soft dough.
2. Turn the dough onto a lightly floured worktop and knead gently. Shape the dough into a 7-inch round and place on the cookie sheet. Cut a cross in the top of the dough about ½ inch deep. Brush the loaf with milk and dust with a little sifted flour.
3. Bake the loaf for 30–40 minutes, or until risen and deep golden brown. Cover loosely with foil toward the end of the cooking time if the top is browning too quickly. Transfer to a wire rack to cool. Serve warm or cold in slices or wedges.

182 Country-style corn bread

PREPARATION TIME *20 minutes* **COOKING TIME** *45 minutes* **MAKES** *1 loaf (serves 10–12)*

1 stick butter
1½ cups cornmeal, plus extra
   for dusting
1½ cups self-rising white flour
¼ teaspoon salt

2 eggs
1¼ cup milk
1 cup canned corn kernels
   (drained weight)

1 Preheat the oven to 190°C/375°F/gas mark 5. Grease a 2lb loaf pan and set aside. Melt the butter in a pan over a gentle heat, then remove from the heat and set aside.

2 Mix the cornmeal, flour, and salt in a large bowl. Separate the eggs and add the egg yolks to the cornmeal mixture, together with the melted butter and milk, and mix to form quite a soft and sticky dough.

3 In a separate bowl, whisk the egg whites until stiff. Fold the whisked egg whites and corn kernels into the cornmeal mixture until evenly mixed.

4 Transfer the mixture to the loaf pan and level the top. Sprinkle the top of the loaf with a little cornmeal.

5 Bake the loaf for about 45 minutes, or until slightly risen and golden brown. Turn onto a wire rack to cool. Serve warm or cold in slices.

VARIATIONS *Use plain wholewheat flour or medium or fine oatmeal in place of cornmeal. Add 1–2 teaspoons dried mixed herbs with the flour, if desired.*

183 Onion, olive, and chive bread

PREPARATION TIME *25 minutes* **COOKING TIME** *35–40 minutes* **MAKES** *1 loaf (Serves 8–10)*

2 tablespoons olive oil
2 onions, finely chopped
2⅔ cups self-rising white flour
1 teaspoon salt
A pinch of hot chili powder

3–4 tablespoons chopped fresh chives
⅓ cup pitted green olives (drained
   weight), finely chopped
2 eggs
About ⅔ cup milk

1 Preheat the oven to 200°C/400°F/gas mark 6. Grease or flour a cookie sheet and set aside. Heat the oil in a skillet, add the onions, and sauté over a medium heat for about 10 minutes, or until softened. Remove the pan from the heat and set aside.

2 Sift the flour and salt into a large bowl, then stir in the chili powder, chives, olives, and onions. Add the eggs, then stir in enough milk, mixing to form a soft, but not sticky dough.

3 Gather the dough together using your hands, then turn it onto a lightly floured worktop and knead gently for 1–2 minutes. Shape the dough into an oval or round and place on the cookie sheet. Using a sharp knife, score the top of the dough with several diagonal slashes, if desired.

4 Bake the loaf for 35–40 minutes, or until risen and lightly browned. Transfer to a wire rack to cool. Serve warm or cold in slices.

VARIATION *Use red onions in place of regular onions.*

184 Quick cheese and herb bread

PREPARATION TIME *25 minutes* **COOKING TIME** *45 minutes* **MAKES** *1 loaf (serves 8)*

1 cup self-rising white flour
1 teaspoon salt
1 cup self-rising wholewheat flour
½ stick butter, diced
¾ 1 cup mature cheddar cheese, grated
1 teaspoon mustard powder

1 small clove garlic, crushed
1½ tablespoons chopped fresh parsley
1½ tablespoons chopped fresh chives
1 egg, beaten
About ⅔ cup milk

1 Preheat the oven to 190°C/375°F/gas mark 5. Grease or flour a cookie sheet and set aside. Sift the white flour and salt into a large bowl, then stir in the wholewheat flour. Lightly rub in the butter until the mixture resembles bread crumbs.
2 Stir in the cheese, mustard powder, garlic, and chopped herbs and mix well. Add the egg and enough milk, mixing to form a soft, but not sticky dough.
3 Knead the dough gently on a lightly floured worktop, then form it into a 7-inch round.
4 Place on the cookie sheet, then bake for about 45 minutes, or until risen and golden brown. Transfer to a wire rack to cool. Serve warm or cold in slices or wedges.

185 Cheese and celery loaf

PREPARATION TIME *20 minutes* **COOKING TIME** *45 minutes* **MAKES** *1 loaf (serves 8–10)*

1½ cups self-rising white flour
A pinch of salt
2 tablespoons butter, diced
1 large stick of celery, finely chopped
1 clove garlic, crushed

1 cup mature cheddar cheese, grated
1 teaspoon caraway seeds
1 egg, beaten
About ⅔ cup milk, plus extra
    for glazing

1 Preheat the oven to 190°C/375°F/gas mark 5. Grease a 1lb loaf pan and set aside. Sift the flour and salt into a bowl, then rub in the butter until the mixture resembles bread crumbs. Stir in the celery, garlic, ¾ cup of the cheese, and the caraway seeds. Make a well in the center, then add the egg and enough milk, mixing to form a soft dough.
2 Knead the dough gently and quickly on a lightly floured worktop, then shape it into an oblong and place in the loaf pan. Brush the top of the loaf with milk and sprinkle with the remaining cheese.
3 Bake the loaf for about 45 minutes, or until risen and lightly browned. Turn onto a wire rack to cool. Serve warm or cold in slices, spread with butter.

VARIATIONS *Use self-rising wholewheat flour in place of the white flour. Use emmental cheese in place of cheddar.*

186 ⌂Celery and walnut loaf

PREPARATION TIME *25 minutes* **COOKING TIME** *45–60 minutes* **MAKES** *1 loaf (serves 8–10)*

1½ cups self-rising white flour
1 teaspoon baking powder
½ stick butter, diced
2 sticks celery, finely chopped
½ cup walnuts, finely chopped

¾ cup mature cheddar cheese,
 finely grated
Sea salt and freshly ground black pepper
1 egg, beaten
About 4 tablespoons milk

1   Preheat the oven to 190°C/375°F/gas mark 5. Grease a 1lb loaf pan or a cookie sheet and set aside. Sift the flour and baking powder into a bowl, then lightly rub in the butter until the mixture resembles bread crumbs.

2   Stir in the celery, walnuts, cheese, and seasoning and mix well. Add the egg and enough milk, mixing to form a soft, but not sticky dough. Turn the dough onto a lightly floured worktop and knead gently until smooth.

3   Shape the dough into an oblong and place it in the pan, or shape the dough into a round and place it on the cookie sheet.

4   Bake the loaf for 45–60 minutes, or until risen and golden brown. Turn onto a wire rack to cool. Serve warm or cold in slices, spread with butter.

TO MAKE IN BREADMAKER, *remove kneading blade from bread pan; grease and line base and sides of pan. Follow main recipe as above, then transfer mixture to prepared pan; level surface. Select Bake Only setting and bake for 45–50 minutes or until loaf is cooked. Remove bread pan from machine; let stand for 5 minutes. Turn loaf onto wire rack to cool.*

187 Parmesan herb twist

PREPARATION TIME *20 minutes* COOKING TIME *25–30 minutes* MAKES *1 loaf (serves 10–12)*

3 cups all-purpose flour, plus extra
  for dusting
2 teaspoons baking soda
1 teaspoon salt
2 tablespoons butter, diced

¾ cup fresh Parmesan cheese,
  finely grated
2 teaspoons superfine sugar
1 garlic clove, crushed
1 tablespoon dried herbes de Provence
About ¾ cup buttermilk

1 Preheat the oven to 200°C/400°F/gas mark 6. Grease or flour a cookie sheet and set aside. Sift the flour, baking soda, and salt into a large bowl, then lightly rub in the butter. Stir in the Parmesan cheese, sugar, garlic, and dried herbs, then gradually add enough buttermilk, mixing to form a soft dough.

2 Turn the dough onto a lightly floured worktop and knead gently. Divide the dough in half and roll each portion of dough into a rope about 12-inches long. Lay the ropes side by side on the worktop and press the top ends together to seal. Carefully twist the ropes of dough around each other, tucking the bottom ends under to seal.

3 Transfer the twisted loaf onto the cookie sheet and dust with a little sifted flour. Bake for 25–30 minutes, or until risen and golden brown. Transfer to a wire rack to cool. Serve warm or cold in slices.

188 Gruyère cheese twists

PREPARATION TIME *15 minutes* COOKING TIME *12–15 minutes* MAKES *about 32 twists*

⅔ cup all-purpose flour
3 tablespoons butter, diced
½ cup gruyère cheese, finely grated

½ teaspoon mustard powder
1 egg, beaten

1 Preheat the oven to 180°C/350°F/gas mark 4. Grease 2 cookie sheets and set aside. Sift the flour into a bowl and lightly rub in the butter until the mixture resembles bread crumbs. Stir in the cheese and mustard powder, then add enough beaten egg to form a soft dough.

2 Knead the dough gently until smooth. Roll out the dough on a lightly floured worktop to form a rectangle about 16 x 5 inches. Lightly brush the dough all over with the remaining beaten egg.

3 Cut the dough crosswise into thin rectangular strips about ½ inch wide, then twist the pastry strips and place them firmly in position on the cookie sheets, leaving a little space between each one.

4 Bake the cheese twists for 12–15 minutes, or until golden brown. Carefully transfer the twists to a wire rack to cool. Serve warm or cold.

VARIATIONS *For extra flavor and crunch, sprinkle the unbaked glazed twists with sesame seeds or poppy seeds. Use mature cheddar cheese in place of gruyère.*

189 Parmesan sesame swizzle sticks

PREPARATION TIME *25 minutes* **COOKING TIME** *15–20 minutes* **MAKES** *about 36 swizzle sticks*

1 cup self-rising white flour
¼ teaspoon salt
1 teaspoon mustard powder
1 cup self-rising wholewheat flour
3 tablespoons butter, diced
½ cup fresh Parmesan cheese,

finely grated
1 egg, beaten
About ⅓ cup milk, plus extra for glazing
1½ tablespoons sesame seeds

1   Preheat the oven to 180°C/350°F/gas mark 4. Grease 2 cookie sheets and set aside. Sift the white flour, salt, and mustard powder into a bowl, then stir in the wholewheat flour. Lightly rub the butter into the flour. Stir in the Parmesan cheese, then add the egg and enough milk, mixing to form a soft dough.
2   Turn the dough onto a lightly floured worktop and knead gently. Roll out to form a 9-inch square. Trim the edges so they are straight, then lightly brush the dough with milk and sprinkle the sesame seeds evenly over the dough.
3   Cut the square of dough evenly in half, then cut each half crosswise into strips that are about ½-inch wide. Twist the strips and place them on the cookie sheets, leaving a little space between each one. Press down lightly on the ends of each stick so they do not lose their shape during baking.
4   Bake the sticks for 15–20 minutes, or until lightly browned and crisp. Cool on the cookie sheets for a few minutes, then transfer to a wire rack. Serve warm or cold. Store in an airtight container.

VARIATIONS *Use mature cheddar cheese in place of Parmesan. Use poppy seeds in place of sesame seeds.*

190 Smoked ham and mustard twists

PREPARATION TIME *25 minutes* **COOKING TIME** *15–20 minutes* **MAKES** *about 36 twists*

1½ cups self-rising white flour
¼ teaspoon salt
3 tablespoons butter, diced
⅓ cup lean smoked ham,
    finely chopped

4 teaspoons wholegrain mustard
1 egg, beaten
About ⅓ cup milk, plus extra
    for glazing

1   Preheat the oven to 180°C/350°F/gas mark 4. Grease 2 cookie sheets and set aside. Sift the flour and salt into a bowl, then lightly rub in the butter. Stir in the chopped ham and mustard, then add the egg and enough milk, mixing to form a soft dough.
2   Turn the dough onto a lightly floured worktop and knead gently. Roll out the dough to form a 9-inch square. Trim the edges so they are straight, then lightly brush the dough with milk to glaze.
3   Cut the square of dough evenly in half, then cut each half crosswise into strips that are about ½-inch wide. Twist the strips and place them on the cookie sheets, leaving a little space between each one. Press down lightly on the ends of each twist so they do not lose their shape during baking.
4   Bake the twists for 15–20 minutes, or until lightly browned and crisp. Cool on the cookie sheet for a few minutes, then transfer to a wire rack. Serve warm or cold.

191 Ham and spinach pinwheels

PREPARATION TIME *20 minutes* **COOKING TIME** *10–15 minutes* **MAKES** *about 14 pinwheels*

1½ cups self-rising white flour
1 teaspoon baking powder
A pinch of salt
½ stick butter, diced
About ⅔ cup milk
1 tablespoon Dijon mustard

⅓ cup cooked lean ham slices
 (smoked or unsmoked), diced
Small handful fresh baby spinach
 leaves, shredded
¾ cup gruyère cheese, grated

1 Preheat the oven to 220°C/425°F/gas mark 7. Grease 2 cookie sheets and set aside. Sift the flour, baking powder, and salt into a bowl, then lightly rub in the butter until the mixture resembles bread crumbs. Make a well in the center, then stir in enough milk, mixing to form a soft dough.

2 Turn the dough onto a lightly floured worktop and knead gently. Roll out to form a rectangle about 12 x 9 inches. Spread the mustard evenly over the dough.

3 Combine the ham, spinach, and cheese and sprinkle this mixture evenly over the dough. Starting on a long side, roll up the dough fairly tightly like a jelly roll. Trim the edges off each end of the roll and discard the trimmings, then cut the roll into about 14 even slices.

4 Place the slices on the cookie sheets, leaving a little space between each one. Bake for 10–15 minutes, or until risen and golden brown. Transfer to a wire rack to cool and serve warm or cold.

VARIATIONS *Use ready-made green or red pesto sauce in place of mustard. Use fresh Parmesan cheese in place of gruyère.*

192 Hot cheese triangles

PREPARATION TIME *20 minutes* **COOKING TIME** *10 minutes* **MAKES** *8–10 triangles*

1 cup self-rising white flour
A pinch of salt
1 teaspoon baking powder
1 cup self-rising wholewheat flour
1 teaspoon mustard powder

2 tablespoons butter, diced
1 cup emmental cheese, finely grated
About ⅔ cup milk, plus extra for glazing

1　Preheat the oven to 220°C/425°F/gas mark 7. Grease or flour a large cookie sheet and set aside. Sift the white flour, salt, and baking powder into a bowl, then stir in the wholewheat flour and mustard powder.
2　Lightly rub in the butter until the mixture resembles bread crumbs, then stir in ¾ cup cheese. Make a well in the center, then stir in enough milk, mixing to form a soft dough.
3　Turn the dough onto a lightly floured worktop, knead gently, then roll or pat out to about 1-inch thickness. Cut into even triangles. Place the triangles on the cookie sheet, leaving a little space between each one. Brush the tops with milk, then sprinkle over the remaining cheese.
4　Bake the scone triangles for about 10 minutes, or until well-risen and golden brown. Transfer to a wire rack to cool. Serve hot, warm or cold.

VARIATION *Use cheddar cheese in place of emmental.*

193 Pesto whirls

PREPARATION TIME *20 minutes* **COOKING TIME** *12–15 minutes* **MAKES** *about 20 whirls*

1½ cups self-rising white flour
1 teaspoon baking powder
1 teaspoon mustard powder
A pinch of salt
A few turns of freshly ground black
　pepper
½ stick butter, diced

1 egg, beaten
3–4 tablespoons milk
5 tablespoons ready-made green pesto
　sauce
¾ cup fresh Parmesan cheese, finely
　grated

1　Preheat the oven to 200°C/400°F/gas mark 6. Grease 2 cookie sheets and set aside. Sift the flour, baking powder, and mustard powder into a bowl. Stir in the salt and pepper, then lightly rub in the butter until the mixture resembles bread crumbs.
2　Make a well in the center, then add the egg and enough milk, mixing to form a soft dough. Turn the dough onto a lightly floured worktop and knead gently.
3　Roll out the dough to form a rectangle about 14 x 10 inches. Spread the pesto sauce evenly over the dough, almost to the edges, then sprinkle the Parmesan cheese evenly over the top. From a long side, roll up the dough fairly tightly like a jelly roll, then cut into ⅜-inch slices using a sharp knife.
4　Place the whirls on the cookie sheets, leaving a little space between each one. Bake for 12–15 minutes, or until golden brown. Transfer to a wire rack to cool. Serve warm or cold.

VARIATION *Once cut and placed on the cookie sheets, sprinkle the whirls with extra grated cheese or sesame seeds before baking, if desired.*

194 Cheese and pineapple squares

PREPARATION TIME *20 minutes* **COOKING TIME** *10 minutes* **MAKES** *about 10–12 squares*

1½ cups self-rising wholewheat flour
1 teaspoon baking powder
A pinch of salt
3 tablespoons butter, diced
1 teaspoon mustard powder

¾ cup mature cheddar cheese, finely grated
¼ cup ready-to-eat dried pineapple, finely chopped
About ⅔ cup milk, plus extra for glazing

1   Preheat the oven to 220°C/425°F/gas mark 7. Grease or flour a large cookie sheet and set aside. Mix the flour, baking powder, and salt in a bowl, then lightly rub in the butter until the mixture resembles bread crumbs. Stir in the mustard powder, cheese, and dried pineapple, then add enough milk, mixing to form a soft dough.
2   Turn the dough onto a lightly floured worktop and knead gently. Lightly roll out the dough until about ¾ inch thick. Using a sharp knife, cut the dough into 2-inch squares and place them on the cookie sheet, leaving a little space between each one.
3   Brush the tops with milk, then bake for about 10 minutes, or until well risen and golden brown. Transfer to a wire rack to cool. Serve warm or cold.

VARIATIONS *Use chopped ready-to-eat dried pears or apricots in place of pineapple. Use 1 beaten egg in place of some of the milk, if desired.*

195 Tomato and basil tear 'n' share

PREPARATION TIME *20 minutes* **COOKING TIME** *20 minutes* **SERVES** *8*

1½ cups self-rising white flour
A pinch of salt
1 teaspoon baking powder
3 tablespoons butter, diced
½ cup sun-dried tomatoes in oil,

well-drained, patted dry, and finely chopped
2 tablespoons chopped fresh basil
About ½ cup milk
1 egg, beaten

1   Preheat the oven to 200°C/400°F/gas mark 6. Grease a deep 7-inch round loose-bottomed cake pan and set aside. Sift the flour, salt, and baking powder into a bowl, then lightly rub in the butter. Stir in the chopped tomatoes and basil, then add enough milk, mixing to form a soft dough.
2   Turn the dough onto a lightly floured worktop and knead gently. Divide the dough into 8 equal portions and roll each piece into a ball. Break the egg into a small bowl and beat with a fork.
3   Roll the dough balls in the beaten egg to lightly coat them all over, then arrange the balls in a single layer in the pan, flattening each one slightly.
4   Bake for about 20 minutes, or until risen and golden brown. Let cool in the pan for a few minutes, then turn onto a wire rack. To serve, tear off the individual rolls. Serve warm or cold.

VARIATIONS *Use chopped pitted black olives in place of sun-dried tomatoes. Use chopped fresh mixed herbs in place of basil.*

196 Bacon and stilton pull-apart

PREPARATION TIME *25 minutes* **COOKING TIME** *25–30 minutes* **SERVES** *16*

3 cups self-rising white flour
¼ teaspoon salt
2 teaspoons baking powder
¾ stick butter, diced
1 egg, beaten
About 1 cup milk

1 tablespoon butter, melted
½ cup cooked cold lean bacon, finely
chopped
1½ cups stilton cheese, crumbled
Beaten egg, to glaze

1 Preheat the oven to 200°C/400°F/gas mark 6. Grease a deep 10-inch round cake pan and set aside. Sift the flour, salt, and baking powder into a large bowl, then lightly rub in the diced butter. Add the egg and enough milk, mixing to form a soft dough.

2 Turn the dough onto a lightly floured worktop and knead gently, then roll out to form a 16 x 11-inch rectangle. Lightly brush the melted butter evenly over the dough. Scatter the chopped bacon evenly over the dough, then sprinkle the crumbled stilton cheese over the top.

3 Starting from a long side, roll up the dough fairly tightly like a jelly roll. Cut into 16 even slices, then place the rolls, cut-side up, in a circular pattern in the pan, so the slices are touching each other.

4 Brush the tops of the spirals with beaten egg, then bake for 25–30 minutes, or until risen and golden brown. Cool slightly in the pan, then turn onto a wire rack. Serve warm or cold.

VARIATIONS *Use lean smoked ham, or cooked chorizo, or pancetta in place of bacon. Use other blue cheeses such as danish blue or dolcelatte in place of stilton.*

197 Plain oven scones

PREPARATION TIME *15 minutes* **COOKING TIME** *10 minutes* **MAKES** *about 8 scones*

1½ cups self-rising white flour
A pinch of salt
1 teaspoon baking powder

3 tablespoons butter, diced
About ⅔ cup milk
Beaten egg or milk, to glaze

1 Preheat the oven to 220°C/425°F/gas mark 7. Grease or flour a large cookie sheet and set aside. Sift the flour, salt, and baking powder into a bowl, then lightly rub in the butter until the mixture resembles fine bread crumbs. Stir in enough milk, mixing to form a soft dough.

2 Turn the dough onto a lightly floured worktop and knead gently, then roll out until about ¾ inch thick. Using a plain or fluted 2½-inch cutter, cut the dough into rounds. Place on the cookie sheet, leaving a little space between each one.

3 Brush the tops with beaten egg or milk, then bake for about 10 minutes, or until well risen and golden brown. Transfer to a wire rack to cool. Serve warm or cold.

VARIATIONS *Add 2 tablespoons superfine sugar and the finely grated zest of 1 lemon with the flour, if desired. Replace half the white flour with self-rising wholewheat flour.*

198 Mini Parmesan scones

PREPARATION TIME *20 minutes* **COOKING TIME** *8–10 minutes* **MAKES** *about 32 mini scones*

1½ cups self-rising white flour
A pinch of salt
2 tablespoons butter, diced
1 cup fresh Parmesan cheese,
   finely grated

1 egg, beaten
About ½ cup milk, plus extra
   for glazing
1 tablespoon sesame seeds
   (optional)

1 Preheat the oven to 220°C/425°F/gas mark 7. Grease or flour 2 cookie sheets and set aside. Sift the flour and salt into a bowl, then lightly rub in the butter until the mixture resembles bread crumbs. Stir in ¾ cup cheese, then add the egg and enough milk, mixing to form a soft dough.

2 Turn the dough onto a lightly floured worktop, knead gently, then roll or pat out lightly until about ½ inch thick. Cut into rounds or squares using a 1-inch cutter or sharp knife. Place on the cookie sheets, leaving a little space between each one.

3 Brush the tops with milk, then mix together the remaining cheese and sesame seeds, if using, and sprinkle over the top.

4 Bake the scones for 8–10 minutes, or until well risen and golden brown. Transfer to a wire rack to cool. Serve warm or cold.

199 Buttermilk scones

PREPARATION TIME *15 minutes* **COOKING TIME** *10 minutes* **MAKES** *about 8 scones*

1½ cups self-rising white flour
A pinch of salt
1 teaspoon baking powder

2 tablespoons butter, diced
About ⅔ cup buttermilk
Beaten egg or milk, to glaze

1 Preheat the oven to 220°C/425°F/gas mark 7. Grease or flour a large cookie sheet and set aside. Sift the flour, salt, and baking powder into a bowl; lightly rub in the butter until the mixture resembles bread crumbs. Stir in enough buttermilk, mixing to form a soft dough.

2 Turn the dough onto a lightly floured worktop and knead gently, then roll out until about ¾ inch thick. Using a plain or fluted 2½-inch cutter, cut the dough into rounds. Place on the cookie sheet, leaving a little space between each one.

3 Brush the tops with beaten egg or milk, then bake for about 10 minutes, or until well risen and golden brown. Transfer to a wire rack to cool. Serve warm or cold.

200 Cheesy pear scones

Preparation time: 20 minutes **COOKING TIME** *10 minutes* **MAKES** *about 12–14 scones*

1¼ cups plain wholewheat flour
2 cups wheatmeal
A pinch of salt
2 teaspoons baking powder
3 tablespoons butter, diced

1 cup mature cheddar cheese,
   finely grated
1 cup ready-to-eat dried pears,
   finely chopped
About ⅔ cup milk, plus extra for glazing

1 Preheat the oven to 220°C/425°F/gas mark 7. Grease or flour a large cookie sheet and set aside. Mix the flour, wheatmeal, salt, and baking powder in a bowl, then lightly rub in the butter until the mixture resembles bread crumbs. Stir in ¾ cup cheese and the dried pears, then add enough milk, mixing to form a soft dough.

2 Turn the dough onto a lightly floured worktop and knead gently. Roll or pat out the dough until about ¾ inch thick. Using a 2-inch plain cutter, cut the dough into rounds and place them on the cookie sheet, leaving a little space between each one.

3 Brush the tops with milk and sprinkle with the remaining cheese. Bake for 10 minutes, or until risen and golden brown. Transfer to a wire rack to cool. Serve warm or cold.

201 Wholewheat cheese scones

PREPARATION TIME *20 minutes* **COOKING TIME** *15–20 minutes* **MAKES** *6–8 scones*

1½ cups all-purpose wholewheat flour
1 tablespoon baking powder
Pinch of salt
A good pinch of cayenne pepper

3 tablespoons butter, diced
1¼ cups mature cheddar cheese,
  finely grated
About ⅔ cup milk, plus extra for glazing

1 Preheat the oven to 200°C/400°F/gas mark 6. Grease a cookie sheet and set aside. Mix the flour, baking powder, salt, and cayenne pepper in a bowl, then lightly rub in the butter until the mixture resembles bread crumbs. Stir in 1 cup of the cheese, then add enough milk, mixing to form a soft dough.

2 Knead the dough gently, then roll or pat out on a lightly floured worktop until about ¾–1 inch thick. Cut out 2½–3-inch rounds using a plain or fluted cutter. Place the scones on the cookie sheet, leaving a little space between each one.

3 Brush the tops with milk and sprinkle with the remaining cheese. Bake for 15–20 minutes, or until risen and golden brown. Transfer to a wire rack to cool. Serve warm or cold.

202 Rich fruit scones

PREPARATION TIME *20 minutes* **COOKING TIME** *8–10 minutes* **MAKES** *about 10 scones*

1½ cups all-purpose flour
4 teaspoons baking powder
A pinch of salt
½ stick butter, diced

2 tablespoons superfine sugar
⅓ cup golden raisins
1 egg, beaten
About ⅓ cup milk, plus extra for glazing

1 Preheat the oven to 220°C/425°F/gas mark 7. Grease or flour a large cookie sheet and set aside. Sift the flour, baking powder, and salt into a bowl, then lightly rub in the butter until the mixture resembles bread crumbs. Stir in the sugar and golden raisins, then add the egg and enough milk, mixing to form a soft dough.
2 Turn the dough onto a lightly floured worktop and knead gently, then roll out until about ¾ inch thick. Cut into rounds using a plain or fluted 2-inch cutter. Place the scones on the cookie sheet, leaving a little space between each one, then brush the tops with milk.
3 Bake the scones for 8–10 minutes, or until well risen and golden brown. Transfer to a wire rack to cool. Serve warm or cold.

VARIATION *Add 1 teaspoon ground cinnamon with the flour, if desired.*

203 Wholewheat fruit scones

PREPARATION TIME *20 minutes* **COOKING TIME** *10 minutes* **MAKES** *about 10 scones*

1 cup self-rising white flour
A pinch of salt
1 teaspoon baking powder
1 cup self-rising wholewheat flour
½ stick butter, diced

2 tablespoons superfine sugar
⅓ cup raisins
About ⅔ cup milk, plus extra for glazing

1 Preheat the oven to 220°C/425°F/gas mark 7. Grease or flour a large cookie sheet and set aside. Sift the white flour, salt, and baking powder into a bowl, then stir in the wholewheat flour. Lightly rub in the butter until the mixture resembles bread crumbs, then stir in the sugar and raisins. Add enough milk, mixing to form a soft dough.
2 Turn the dough onto a lightly floured worktop and knead gently, then roll out until about ¾ inch thick. Cut the dough into rounds using a plain or fluted 2-inch cutter. Place the scones on the cookie sheet, leaving a little space between each one, then brush the tops with milk.
3 Bake the scones for about 10 minutes, or until risen and golden brown. Transfer to a wire rack to cool. Serve warm or cold.

VARIATIONS *Use golden raisins or chopped ready-to-eat dried apricots in place of raisins. Use buttermilk in place of regular milk.*

204 Apple and cinnamon scone round

PREPARATION TIME *20 minutes* **COOKING TIME** *25–30 minutes* **SERVES** *8*

1 cup self-rising white flour
A pinch of salt
1 teaspoon baking powder
1 cup self-rising wholewheat flour
3 tablespoons butter, diced
⅓ cup light soft brown sugar
1 teaspoon ground cinnamon

1 medium–large cooking apple (about
   10oz in weight), peeled, cored, and
   coarsely grated
3–4 tablespoons milk, plus extra
   for glazing
1 tablespoon raw brown sugar

1 Preheat the oven to 200°C/400°F/gas mark 6. Grease or flour a cookie sheet and set aside. Sift the white flour, salt, and baking powder into a bowl, then stir in the wholewheat flour. Lightly rub in the butter until the mixture resembles bread crumbs.
2 Stir in the soft brown sugar and cinnamon, then add the grated apple and mix well. Stir in enough milk to form a soft, but not sticky dough.
3 Turn the dough onto a floured worktop, knead lightly, then shape into an 7-inch round.
4 Place the scone round on the cookie sheet, brush the top with milk and sprinkle with the raw brown sugar. Using a sharp knife, mark the top of the scone round into 8 even wedges, cutting deeply into the dough.
5 Bake the scone round for 25–30 minutes, or until risen and golden brown. Transfer to a wire rack to cool. Break into wedges and serve warm or cold.

VARIATION *Use ground ginger in place of cinnamon.*

205 Festive cheese and fruit scone ring

PREPARATION TIME *25 minutes* **COOKING TIME** *15–20 minutes* **SERVES** *12*

1½ cups self-rising white flour
2 tablespoons butter, diced
2 tablespoons superfine sugar
About ⅔ cup milk

½ cup golden raisins
1 cup mature cheddar cheese,
   crumbled

1 Preheat the oven to 200°C/400°F/gas mark 6. Flour a cookie sheet and set aside. Sift the flour into a bowl, then lightly rub in the butter until the mixture resembles bread crumbs. Stir in the sugar, then add enough milk, mixing to form a soft dough.
2 Turn the dough onto a lightly floured worktop and roll out to form a rectangle about 12 x 8 inches in size. Sprinkle the golden raisins and ¾ cup cheese evenly over the dough. Starting from a long side, roll up the dough fairly tightly like a jelly roll.
3 Transfer the dough roll to the cookie sheet and form into a ring, pressing the ends together to seal. Using a sharp knife, cut through the dough at about 1-inch intervals, not quite cutting through to the center. Twist the slices so that the cut sides face upward, then sprinkle with the remaining cheese.
4 Bake the scone ring for 15–20 minutes, or until risen and golden brown. Transfer to a wire rack to cool. Serve warm or cold.

VARIATION *Use chopped ready-to-eat dried apricots or pears in place of golden raisins.*

206 Apple and apricot scone wedges

PREPARATION TIME *20 minutes* COOKING TIME *25–30 minutes* SERVES *8*

1½ cups all-purpose wholewheat flour
A pinch of salt
2 teaspoons baking powder
1 teaspoon ground cinnamon
½ stick butter, diced
2 tablespoons light soft brown sugar
½ cup ready-to-eat dried apricots,
    finely chopped

1 medium–large cooking apple, about
    10oz) in weight, peeled, cored, and
    coarsely grated
3–4 tablespoons milk, plus extra
    for glazing
1 tablespoon granulated sugar

1   Preheat the oven to 200°C/400°F/gas mark 6. Grease or flour a cookie sheet and set
    aside. Mix the flour, salt, baking powder, and cinnamon in a bowl, then lightly rub in the
    butter until the mixture resembles bread crumbs. Stir in the soft brown sugar, apricots,
    and apple, then add enough milk, mixing to form a soft dough.
2   Turn the dough onto a lightly floured worktop and knead gently, then shape into a 7-inch
    round. Place on the cookie sheet, brush with milk, and sprinkle with the granulated sugar.
    Using a sharp knife, mark the top of the scone round into 8 even wedges, cutting deeply
    into the dough.
3   Bake the scone round for 25–30 minutes, or until risen and golden brown. Transfer to a
    wire rack to cool. Break into wedges and serve warm or cold.

VARIATIONS *Use half wholewheat and half all-purpose flour in place of all wholewheat flour. Use
ground ginger in place of cinnamon. Use dried cranberries in place of apricots.*

207 Fresh strawberry scones

PREPARATION TIME *15 minutes* COOKING TIME *8–10 minutes* MAKES *12 scones*

1½ cups self-rising wholewheat flour
1 teaspoon baking powder
A pinch of salt
½ stick butter, diced
2 tablespoons superfine sugar

¾ cup fresh strawberries, chopped
About ½ cup milk, plus extra for glazing
Strawberry jelly and whipped cream or
    crème fraîche, to serve

1   Preheat the oven to 220°C/425°F/gas mark 7. Grease or flour a cookie sheet and set
    aside. Put the flour, baking powder, and salt in a large bowl and stir to mix, then lightly
    rub in the butter until the mixture resembles bread crumbs. Stir in the sugar and
    strawberries, then add enough milk, mixing to form a soft dough.
2   Turn the dough onto a lightly floured worktop, knead gently, then lightly roll or pat out
    until about ¾ inch thick. Cut out 12 rounds using a 2-inch cutter, and place on the cookie
    sheet, leaving a little space between each one. Brush the tops with milk to glaze.
3   Bake the scones for 8–10 minutes, or until well risen and golden brown. Transfer to a wire
    rack to cool. Split in half to serve, spread with butter, if desired, and top with jelly and
    cream or crème fraîche. Serve warm or cold.

VARIATIONS *Replace half the wholewheat flour with self-rising white flour, if desired. To give these
scones a warm, spicy flavor, add 1 teaspoon ground cinnamon with the flour at the start of the
recipe.*

208 Mini apricot scones

PREPARATION TIME *20 minutes* **COOKING TIME** *8–10 minutes* **MAKES** *about 32 mini scones*

1½ cups self-rising white flour
1 teaspoon baking powder
A pinch of salt
½ stick butter, diced

½ cup ready-to-eat dried apricots,
 finely chopped
About ⅔ cup milk

1 Preheat the oven to 220°C/425°F/gas mark 7. Grease or flour 2 cookie sheets and set aside. Sift the flour, baking powder, and salt into a bowl, then lightly rub in the butter until the mixture resembles fine bread crumbs. Stir in the apricots. Make a well in the center, then add enough milk, mixing to form a soft dough.
2 Turn the dough onto a lightly floured worktop, knead gently, then roll or pat out lightly until about ½ inch thick. Cut into rounds or shapes using a 1-inch cutter or sharp knife and place on the cookie sheets, leaving a little space between each one.
3 Bake the scones for 8–10 minutes, or until well-risen and golden brown. Transfer to a wire rack to cool. Serve warm or cold.

209 Orchard scone wedges

PREPARATION TIME *20 minutes* **COOKING TIME** *25–30 minutes* **SERVES** *8*

1½ cups self-rising white flour
1 teaspoon baking powder
A pinch of salt
½ stick butter, diced
2 tablespoons superfine sugar

⅓ cup golden raisins
⅓ cup ready-to-eat dried pears,
 finely chopped
About ⅔ cup milk

1 Preheat the oven to 200°C/400°F/gas mark 6. Grease or flour a cookie sheet and set aside. Sift the flour, baking powder, and salt into a bowl, then lightly rub in the butter until the mixture resembles bread crumbs. Stir in the sugar, golden raisins, and pears, then add enough milk, mixing to form a soft dough.
2 Turn the dough onto a lightly floured worktop and knead gently, then shape into a 7-inch round. Place the scone round on the cookie sheet. Using a sharp knife, mark the top of the round into 8 even wedges, cutting deeply into the dough.
3 Bake the scone round for 25–30 minutes, or until risen and golden brown. Transfer to a wire rack to cool. Break into wedges and serve warm or cold.

210 Cherry coconut scones

PREPARATION TIME *15 minutes* **COOKING TIME** *8–10 minutes* **MAKES** *10–12 scones*

1 cup self-rising white flour
A pinch of salt
1 teaspoon baking powder
1 cup self-rising wholewheat flour
2 tablespoons butter, diced

2 tablespoons light soft brown sugar
⅓ cup candied cherries, finely chopped
⅔ cup shredded unsweetened coconut
About ⅔ cup milk, plus extra for glazing

1 Preheat the oven to 220°C/425°F/gas mark 7. Grease or flour a cookie sheet and set aside. Sift the white flour, salt, and baking powder into a bowl, then stir in the wholewheat flour. Lightly rub in the butter until the mixture resembles bread crumbs, then stir in the sugar, cherries, and coconut. Make a well in the center, then add enough milk, mixing to form a soft dough.
2 Turn the dough onto a lightly floured worktop and knead gently, then roll out until about ¾ inch thick. Cut into rounds using a 2-inch plain or fluted cutter. Place on the cookie sheet, leaving a little space between each one, then brush the tops with milk.
3 Bake the scones for 8–10 minutes, or until well-risen and golden brown. Transfer to a wire rack to cool. Serve warm or cold.

211 Blueberry wedges

PREPARATION TIME *15 minutes* **COOKING TIME** *20–25 minutes* **SERVES** *8*

1½ cups self-rising wholewheat flour	⅓ cup superfine sugar
A pinch of salt	1 cup fresh blueberries, washed and
1 teaspoon baking powder	dried
1 teaspoon ground cinnamon	4 tablespoons sour cream
½ stick butter, diced	About ½ cup milk

1   Preheat the oven to 200°C/400°F/gas mark 6. Grease a cookie sheet and set aside. Mix the flour, salt, baking powder, and cinnamon in a bowl, then lightly rub in the butter until the mixture resembles bread crumbs. Stir in the sugar and blueberries, then add the sour cream and enough milk, mixing to form a fairly soft dough.

2   Knead the dough briefly on a lightly floured worktop, then shape the dough into an 8-inch round. Place the scone round on the cookie sheet. Using a sharp knife, mark the top of the scone round into 8 even wedges, cutting fairly deeply into the dough.

3   Bake the scone round for 20–25 minutes, or until risen and lightly browned. Transfer to a wire rack to cool. Cut or break the scone round into wedges and serve warm or cold.

VARIATION *Use ground pudding spice in place of cinnamon.*

212 Fruitburst twists

PREPARATION TIME *25 minutes* COOKING TIME *15–20 minutes* MAKES *about 36 twists*

1½ cups self-rising white flour
¼ teaspoon salt
3 tablespoons butter, diced
2 tablespoons superfine sugar
1 teaspoon ground cinnamon

⅔ cup mixed ready-to-eat dried tropical fruit (such as pineapple, papaya and mango), finely chopped
1 egg, beaten
About ⅓ cup milk, plus extra for glazing

1 Preheat the oven to 180°C/350°F/gas mark 4. Grease 2 cookie sheets and set aside. Sift the flour and salt into a bowl, then rub in the butter. Stir in the sugar, cinnamon, and dried fruit, then add the egg and enough milk, mixing to form a soft dough.
2 Turn the dough onto a lightly floured worktop and knead gently. Roll out to form a 9-inch square. Trim the edges so they are straight, then brush the dough with milk to glaze.
3 Cut the square of dough evenly in half, then cut each half crosswise into strips that are about ½ inch wide. Twist the strips and place them on the cookie sheets, leaving a little space between each one. Press down lightly on the ends of each twist so they do not lose their shape during baking.
4 Bake for 15–20 minutes, or until lightly browned and crisp. Cool on the cookie sheets for a few minutes, then transfer to a wire rack. Serve warm or cold.

VARIATIONS *Use mixed chopped ready-to-eat dried pears, peaches and apricots in place of the tropical fruit. For a slightly more pronounced spice flavor, add an extra ½ teaspoon ground cinnamon, if desired.*

213 Fruit and nut swirls

PREPARATION TIME *20 minutes* COOKING TIME *10–15 minutes* MAKES *about 12 swirls*

1½ cups self-rising white flour
A pinch of salt
1 teaspoon baking powder
½ stick butter, diced
2 tablespoons superfine sugar

About ½ cup milk, plus extra for glazing
⅔ cup luxury mixed dried fruit
½ cup chopped and toasted mixed nuts
1 teaspoon ground pudding spice

1 Preheat the oven to 220°C/425°F/gas mark 7. Grease 2 cookie sheets and set aside. Sift the flour, salt, and baking powder into a bowl, then lightly rub in the butter. Stir in the sugar, then add enough milk, mixing to form a soft dough.
2 Turn the dough onto a lightly floured worktop and knead lightly, then roll out to form a 12 x 9-inch rectangle. Combine the dried fruit, nuts, and pudding spice, then sprinkle this mixture evenly over the dough, lightly pressing it into the dough.
3 Starting from a long side, roll up the dough fairly tightly like a jelly roll. Cut into about 12 even slices, then place the slices, cut-side up, on the cookie sheets, leaving a little space between each one.
4 Brush the tops of the swirls with a little milk, then bake for 10–15 minutes, or until risen and golden brown. Transfer to a wire rack to cool. Serve warm or cold.

214 Lemon and golden raisin whirls

PREPARATION TIME *20 minutes* COOKING TIME *10–15 minutes* MAKES *about 12 whirls*

1½ cups self-rising white flour
A pinch of salt
1 teaspoon baking powder
½ stick butter, diced
3 tablespoons superfine sugar

About ½ cup milk, plus extra for glazing
⅔ cup cup golden raisins
⅓ cup candied cherries, washed, dried,
   and chopped
Finely grated zest of 1 lemon

1   Preheat the oven to 220°C/425°F/gas mark 7. Grease 2 cookie sheets and set aside. Sift the flour, salt, and baking powder into a bowl, then lightly rub in the butter. Stir in the sugar, then add enough milk, mixing to form a soft dough.
2   Turn the dough onto a lightly floured worktop and knead lightly, then roll out to form a 12 x 9-inch rectangle. Combine the golden raisins, cherries, and lemon zest, then sprinkle this mixture evenly over the dough, lightly pressing it into the dough.
3   Starting from a long side, roll up the dough fairly tightly like a jelly roll. Cut into about 12 even slices, then place the slices, cut-side up, on the cookie sheets, leaving a little space between each one.
4   Brush the tops of the whirls with a little milk, then bake for 10–15 minutes, or until risen and golden brown. Transfer to a wire rack to cool. Serve warm or cold.

VARIATIONS *Use chopped ready-to-eat pitted dried dates or dried pineapple in place of golden raisins. Use dried cranberries or cherries in place of candied cherries. Use the finely grated zest of 1 small orange in place of lemon zest.*

215 Fruited bran loaf

PREPARATION TIME *10 minutes, plus 1 hour soaking* COOKING TIME *45–60 minutes*
MAKES *1 loaf (serves 8)*

1⅔ cups wheat bran sticks
   (All Bran-type breakfast cereal)
½ cup light soft brown sugar
⅓ cup golden raisins

⅓ cup raisins
1¼ cups milk
1 cup self-rising wholewheat flour
1 teaspoon ground cinnamon

1   Place the bran sticks, sugar, dried fruit, and milk in a bowl and stir to mix. Let soak for 1 hour.
2   Meanwhile, preheat the oven to 180°C/350°F/gas mark 4. Grease and line a 1lb loaf pan and set aside. Add the flour and cinnamon to the fruit mixture and fold in until well mixed.
3   Transfer the mixture to the loaf pan and level the top. Bake for 45–60 minutes, or until slightly risen and firm to the touch, and until a cake tester inserted in the center comes out clean.
4   Remove the loaf from the oven and let cool in the pan for a few minutes, then turn onto a wire rack. Serve warm or cold in slices.

VARIATIONS *Use chopped ready-to-eat dried apricots in place of the raisins. Use ground ginger in place of the cinnamon.*

216 ◧ Golden gingerbread

PREPARATION TIME *20 minutes, plus cooling* **COOKING TIME** *1–1¼ hours*
MAKES *1 loaf (serves 8–10)*

⅔ cup light soft brown sugar
¾ stick butter
½ cup light corn syrup
1½ cups all-purpose flour
A pinch of salt

1 teaspoon baking powder
2 teaspoons ground ginger
1 egg, beaten
⅔ cup milk

1 Preheat the oven to 170°C/325°F/gas mark 3. Grease and line a 2lb loaf pan and set aside. Place the sugar, butter, and syrup in a saucepan and heat gently until melted and blended, stirring. Remove the pan from the heat and cool slightly.

2 Sift the flour, salt, baking powder, and ginger into a bowl and make a well in the center. Mix together the egg and milk and pour into the center of the dry ingredients together with the melted mixture. Beat together using a wooden spoon until smooth and thoroughly mixed. Pour the mixture into the loaf pan.

3 Bake the gingerbread for 1–1¼ hours, or until risen and lightly browned and a cake tester inserted in the center comes out clean.

4 Remove from the oven and let cool in the pan for a few minutes, then turn onto a wire rack. Serve warm or cold in slices.

TO MAKE IN BREADMAKER, *remove kneading blade from bread pan; grease and line base and sides of pan. Follow main recipe as above, then transfer mixture to prepared pan; level surface. Select Bake Only setting and bake for 60–70 minutes or until gingerbread is cooked. Remove bread pan from machine; let stand for 5 minutes. Turn gingerbread onto wire rack to cool.*

217 Spiced apple quick bread

PREPARATION TIME *25 minutes* **COOKING TIME** *1¼–1½ hours* **MAKES** *1 loaf (serves 10–12)*

1½ cups all-purpose flour
2 teaspoons baking powder
½ teaspoon ground nutmeg
½ teaspoon ground cinnamon
½ teaspoon ground pudding spice
1 stick butter, softened
1 cup light soft brown sugar
2 eggs, beaten

⅔ cup golden raisins
1 medium cooking apple, peeled, cored, and finely chopped
1–2 dessert apples, peeled, cored, and thinly sliced
2 tablespoons butter, melted
2 tablespoons raw brown sugar

1 Preheat the oven to 180°C/350°F/gas mark 4. Grease and line a 2lb loaf pan and set aside. Sift the flour, baking powder, and ground spices into a bowl and set aside. Cream the softened butter and soft brown sugar together in a separate bowl until light and fluffy, then gradually beat in the eggs. Fold in the flour mixture, golden raisins, and chopped cooking apple until well mixed.

2 Transfer the mixture to the loaf pan and level the top. Arrange overlapping slices of dessert apples over the top of the mixture, covering it completely, then brush the apple slices with melted butter and sprinkle the raw brown sugar evenly over the top.

3 Bake the bread for 1¼–1½ hours, or until firm to the touch and a cake tester inserted in the center comes out clean. Cover loosely with foil toward the end of the cooking time if the top is browning too quickly.

4 Remove the bread from the oven and let cool in the pan for 10 minutes, then turn onto a wire rack. Serve warm or cold in slices.

VARIATION *Use chopped ready-to-eat dried apricots, pears, or peaches in place of golden raisins.*

218 🏠 Date and walnut loaf

PREPARATION TIME *20 minutes, plus 15 minutes standing* **COOKING TIME** *45–60 minutes*
MAKES *1 loaf (serves 10–12)*

1⅓ cups pitted dried dates, chopped
⅔ cup boiling water
¾ stick butter, softened
½ cup (packed) light soft brown sugar

1 egg, beaten
1½ cups self-rising white flour
1 teaspoon baking powder
½ cup walnuts, chopped

1   Preheat the oven to 180°C/350°F/gas mark 4. Grease and line a 2lb loaf pan and set
    aside. Place the dates in a bowl and pour over the boiling water. Stir to mix, then
    set aside for 15 minutes.
2   Cream the butter and sugar together in a separate bowl until pale and fluffy, then
    gradually beat in the egg. Fold in the flour, baking powder, walnuts, and date mixture,
    stirring until well mixed. Turn the mixture into the loaf pan and level the top.
3   Bake the loaf for 45–60 minutes, or until firm to the touch and a cake tester inserted in
    the center comes out clean. Turn onto a wire rack to cool. Serve warm or cold in slices.

TO MAKE IN BREADMAKER, *remove kneading blade from bread pan; grease and line base and sides
of pan. Follow main recipe as above, then transfer mixture to prepared pan; level surface. Select
Bake Only setting and bake for 45–55 minutes, or until loaf is cooked. Remove bread pan from
machine; let stand for 5 minutes. Turn loaf out of bread pan onto wire rack to cool.*

219 🏠 Banana and honey quick bread

PREPARATION TIME *20 minutes* **COOKING TIME** *1–1¼ hours* **MAKES** *1 loaf (serves 8–10)*

1 stick butter, softened
⅔ cup light soft brown sugar
⅓ cup thick set honey
2 eggs, beaten

1½ cups self-rising white or wholewheat
  flour
½ teaspoon ground nutmeg or cinnamon
2 large bananas
A squeeze of lemon juice

1   Preheat the oven to 180°C/350°F/gas mark 4. Grease and line a 2lb loaf pan and set
    aside. Place the butter, sugar, and honey in a bowl and beat together until light and fluffy.
    Gradually beat in the eggs, then fold in the flour and nutmeg or cinnamon.
2   Peel the bananas and mash the flesh with a little lemon juice. Fold the mashed bananas
    into the bread mixture until well mixed, then spoon the mixture into the loaf pan and level
    the top.
3   Bake the loaf for 1–1¼ hours, or until risen, golden brown and firm to the touch. Cover
    loosely with foil toward the end of the cooking time if the top is browning too quickly.
4   Remove the bread from the oven and let cool in the pan for a few minutes, then turn onto
    a wire rack to cool. Serve warm or cold in slices.

TO MAKE IN BREADMAKER, *remove kneading blade from bread pan; grease and line base and sides
of pan. Follow main recipe as above, then transfer mixture to prepared pan; level top. Select Bake
Only setting and bake for 60–70 minutes, or until bread is cooked. Remove bread pan from
machine; let stand for 5 minutes. Turn bread out of bread pan onto wire rack to cool.*

220 Malted fruit loaf

PREPARATION TIME *20 minutes* **COOKING TIME** *40 minutes* **MAKES** *1 loaf (serves 10–12)*

1½ cups self-rising white flour
1 teaspoon baking soda
1 teaspoon ground pudding spice
3 tablespoons malt extract
2 tablespoons light corn syrup

½ cup milk
1 egg, beaten
1 cup golden raisins
2 tablespoons clear honey, to glaze

1 Preheat the oven to 180°C/350°F/gas mark 4. Grease and line a 2lb loaf pan and set aside. Sift the flour, baking soda, and pudding spice into a bowl. Set aside.
2 Place the malt extract, syrup, and milk in a saucepan and heat gently until melted and blended, stirring occasionally. Remove the pan from the heat and cool slightly, then mix in the egg.
3 Make a well in the center of the dry ingredients, then add the melted mixture, mixing well with a wooden spoon. Fold in the golden raisins. Transfer to the loaf pan and level the top.
4 Bake the loaf for about 40 minutes, or until risen and browned. Cover loosely with foil toward the end of the cooking time if the top is browning too quickly.
5 Cool slightly in the pan, then turn onto a wire rack. While the loaf is still warm, brush it two times with honey to glaze. Let cool and serve warm or cold in slices.

221 Apricot and date breakfast loaf

PREPARATION TIME *20 minutes, plus 4 hours soaking (or soaking overnight)*
COOKING TIME *1 hour* **MAKES** *1 loaf (serves 12)*

1 cup ready-to-eat dried apricots, chopped
1 cup pitted dried dates, chopped
⅔ cup golden raisins
½ cup light soft brown sugar
⅔ cup cold brewed tea, strained
2 eggs, beaten
1½ cups self-rising wholewheat flour
2 teaspoons ground cinnamon

1 Place the dried fruit and sugar in a large bowl and stir to mix, then add the tea and mix well. Cover and let soak for at least 4 hours or overnight, until most of the tea has been absorbed and the fruit is plumped up.
2 Meanwhile, preheat the oven to 180°C/350°F/gas mark 4. Grease and line a 2lb loaf pan and set aside. Stir the eggs into the fruit mixture, then add the flour and cinnamon and mix thoroughly.
3 Turn the batter into the loaf pan and level the top. Bake for about 1 hour, or until firm to the touch.
4 Remove the loaf from the oven and let cool in the pan for a few minutes, then turn onto a wire rack. Serve warm or cold in slices.

VARIATIONS *Use dried blueberries in place of golden raisins. Use ground ginger in place of ground cinnamon.*

222 Gingered banana bread

PREPARATION TIME *20 minutes* **COOKING TIME** *1–1¼ hours* **MAKES** *1 loaf (serves 12)*

1 stick butter, softened
½ cup cup light soft brown sugar
2 eggs, beaten
1½ cups self-rising white flour
½ teaspoon baking soda
A pinch of salt
2 teaspoons ground ginger
3 bananas
A squeeze of lemon juice
⅔ cup preserved stem ginger, drained and finely chopped

1 Preheat the oven to 180°C/350°F/gas mark 4. Grease and line a 2lb loaf pan and set aside. Cream the butter and sugar together in a bowl until light and fluffy. Gradually add the eggs, beating well after each addition. Sift the flour, baking soda, salt, and ginger together, then fold into the creamed mixture.
2 Peel the bananas and mash the flesh with the lemon juice. Add the mashed bananas to the toasted mixture and beat until well mixed. Stir in the stem ginger and mix well.
3 Turn the mixture into the loaf pan and level the top. Bake for 1–1¼ hours, or until well risen, golden brown and just firm to the touch.
4 Remove the loaf from the oven and let cool in the pan for a few minutes, then turn onto a wire rack. Serve warm or cold in slices.

223 Dutch gingerbread

PREPARATION TIME *15 minutes* **COOKING TIME** *1¼ hours* **MAKES** *1 loaf (serves 12–14)*

3 cups all-purpose flour
2½ teaspoons baking powder
3 teaspoons ground ginger
1 teaspoon ground pudding spice

½ cup light soft brown sugar
1¼ cups light corn syrup
½ cup milk

1   Preheat the oven to 170°C/325°F/gas mark 3. Grease a 2lb loaf pan and set aside. Sift the flour, baking powder, and ground spices into a large bowl, then stir in the sugar.
2   Make a well in the center and add the corn syrup. Using a wooden spoon, start beating the syrup into the flour, then gradually add the milk, a little at a time, beating well, to form a soft, dropping consistency.
3   Transfer the mixture to the loaf pan and level the top. Bake the loaf for 50 minutes, then reduce the oven temperature to 150°C/300°F/gas mark 2 and bake for a further 20–25 minutes, or until the loaf is risen and deep golden brown, and a cake tester inserted in the center comes out clean.
4   Remove the gingerbread from the oven and let cool in the pan for a few minutes, then turn onto a wire rack. Serve warm or cold in slices.

224 Banana and date quick bread

PREPARATION TIME *20 minutes* **COOKING TIME** *1–1¼ hours* **MAKES** *1 loaf (serves 10)*

1½ cups all-purpose wholewheat flour
2 teaspoons baking powder
1 teaspoon ground pudding spice or
   nutmeg
1 stick butter, diced
⅔ cup light soft brown sugar

⅓ cup thick-set honey
2 eggs, beaten
2 large bananas, peeled and mashed
   with a squeeze of lemon juice
⅔ cup pitted dried dates, finely chopped

1   Preheat the oven to 180°C/350°F/gas mark 4. Grease and line a 2lb loaf pan and set aside. Put the flour, baking powder, and spice in a bowl, then lightly rub in the butter until the mixture resembles bread crumbs. Add the sugar, honey, eggs, bananas, and dates and beat together until well mixed.
2   Turn the mixture into the loaf pan and level the top. Bake for 1–1¼ hours, or until well risen and firm to the touch.
3   Remove the bread from the oven and let cool in the pan for a few minutes, then turn onto a wire rack. Serve warm or cold in slices.

225 Apricot and golden raisin loaf

PREPARATION TIME *20 minutes* **COOKING TIME** *1 hour* **MAKES** *1 loaf (serves 10–12)*

1 cup self-rising white flour
1 cup self-rising wholewheat flour
2 teaspoons ground cinnamon
⅔ cup light soft brown sugar
1⅓ cups ready-to-eat dried apricots,

   chopped
1⅓ cups golden raisins
2 eggs, beaten
⅔ cup milk

1   Preheat the oven to 180°C/350°F/gas mark 4. Grease and line a 2lb loaf pan and set aside. Mix the flours, cinnamon, and sugar in a bowl, then add the apricots and golden raisins and mix well.
2   Add the eggs and milk and beat well until thoroughly mixed. Turn the mixture into the loaf pan and level the top.
3   Bake the loaf for about 1 hour, or until golden brown and firm to the touch. Turn onto a wire rack to cool. Serve warm or cold in slices.

226 Sugared lemon loaf

PREPARATION TIME *20 minutes* **COOKING TIME** *40–45 minutes* **MAKES** *1 loaf (serves 10–12)*

1½ sticks butter, softened
1 cup light soft brown sugar
2 eggs, beaten
1 cup self-rising white flour
1 teaspoon baking powder

Finely grated zest of 2 lemons
½ cup golden raisins
About 1–2 tablespoons milk
8 sugar cubes, coarsely crushed

1 Preheat the oven to 180°C/350°F/gas mark 4. Grease and line a 2lb loaf pan and set aside. Cream the butter and soft brown sugar together in a bowl until light and fluffy, then gradually beat in the eggs.
2 Sift the flour and baking powder into the creamed mixture, then fold in with the lemon zest until well mixed. Fold in the golden raisins, then add enough milk, mixing to form a soft, dropping consistency.
3 Turn the mixture into the loaf pan and level the top. Sprinkle the crushed sugar cubes evenly over the top. Bake for 40–45 minutes, or until well-risen and golden brown.
4 Remove the loaf from the oven and let cool in the pan for 5 minutes, then turn onto a wire rack. Serve warm or cold in slices.

VARIATIONS *Use superfine sugar in place of soft brown sugar. Use the finely grated zest of 2 small oranges in place of lemon zest.*

227 Date and muesli quick bread

PREPARATION TIME *15 minutes, plus 30 minutes soaking* **COOKING TIME** *1 hour*
MAKES *1 loaf (serves 10–12)*

1½ cups pitted dried dates, roughly
  chopped
⅔ cup strong hot tea, strained
¾ stick butter, softened
½ cup light soft brown sugar

1 egg, beaten
1½ cups self-rising white flour
1 teaspoon baking powder
3oz muesli (of your choice)

1 Place the dates in a bowl, pour over the tea and let soak for 30 minutes.
2 Meanwhile, preheat the oven to 180°C/350°F/gas mark 4. Grease and line a 2lb loaf pan and set aside. Cream the butter and sugar together in a bowl until pale and fluffy, then beat in the egg.
3 Sift the flour and baking powder into the bowl and fold into the creamed mixture. Add the muesli, dates, and soaking liquid and stir to mix well.
4 Transfer the mixture to the loaf pan and level the top. Bake for about 1 hour, or until risen and firm to the touch—a cake tester inserted in the center should come out clean.
5 Remove the quick bread from the oven and let cool in the pan for a few minutes, then turn onto a wire rack. Serve warm or cold in slices.

228 ☐ Fruit and spice quick bread

PREPARATION TIME *20 minutes* **COOKING TIME** *1 hour* **MAKES** *1 loaf (serves 10–12)*

1½ cups self-rising white flour
½ teaspoon baking soda
1 tablespoon ground pudding spice
⅔ cup light soft brown sugar
⅔ cup golden raisins
⅔ cup raisins

⅔ cup dried currants
⅔ cup ready-to-eat dried apricots,
  finely chopped
2 eggs
⅔ cup milk

1   Preheat the oven to 180°C/350°F/gas mark 4. Grease a 2lb loaf pan and set aside. Sift the
    flour, baking soda, and pudding spice into a bowl.
2   Add the sugar and dried fruit and mix well. Beat the eggs and milk together and add to
    the fruit mixture. Beat until thoroughly mixed. Turn the mixture into the loaf pan and
    level the top.
3   Bake the bread for about 1 hour, or until risen, golden brown, and firm to the touch.
4   Remove the bread from the oven and let cool in the pan for a few minutes, then turn onto
    a wire rack. Serve warm or cold in slices.

TO MAKE IN BREADMAKER, *remove kneading blade from bread pan; grease and line base and sides
of pan. Follow main recipe as above, then transfer mixture to prepared pan; level surface. Select
Bake Only setting and bake for 60–70 minutes or until bread is cooked. Remove bread pan from
machine; let stand for 5 minutes. Turn bread onto wire rack to cool.*

229 Prune and hazelnut quick bread

PREPARATION TIME *20 minutes, plus 4 hours soaking* **COOKING TIME** *1–1¼ hours*
MAKES *1 loaf (serves 10–12)*

1⅔ cups ready-to-eat pitted dried prunes, chopped
1 cup light soft brown sugar
1¼ cups cold brewed tea, strained
1 egg, beaten

½ cup hazelnuts, chopped
½ cup walnuts, chopped
1½ cups self-rising wholewheat flour
1 cup bran

1   Put the prunes, sugar, and tea in a large bowl and mix together. Cover and let soak for about 4 hours, or until most of the tea has been absorbed by the fruit.
2   Preheat the oven to 180°C/350°F/gas mark 4. Grease and line a 2lb loaf pan and set aside. Add the egg, nuts, flour, and bran to the prune mixture and mix thoroughly.
3   Turn the mixture into the loaf pan and level the top. Bake in the oven for 1–1¼ hours, or until a cake tester inserted in the center comes out clean.
4   Remove the bread from the oven and let cool in the pan for a few minutes, then turn onto a wire rack. Serve warm or cold in slices.

VARIATIONS *Use pitted dried dates in place of prunes. Use almonds in place of hazelnuts.*

230 Banana raisin bran loaf

PREPARATION TIME *20 minutes* **COOKING TIME** *1–1¼ hours* **MAKES** *1 loaf (serves 10–12)*

1 stick butter, softened
⅔ cup light soft brown sugar
3 eggs, beaten
1¼ cups self-rising wholewheat flour
1 cup bran
1 teaspoon baking powder

A pinch of salt
2 teaspoons ground ginger or cinnamon
3 bananas, peeled and mashed with a squeeze of lemon juice
1 cup raisins

1   Preheat the oven to 180°C/350°F/gas mark 4. Grease and line a 2lb loaf pan and set aside. Put the butter, sugar, eggs, flour, bran, baking powder, salt, and ginger or cinnamon in a large bowl and beat together until thoroughly mixed.
2   Add the mashed bananas to the batter and beat until well mixed. Fold in the raisins. Spoon the mixture into the loaf pan and level the top.
3   Bake the loaf for 1–1¼ hours, or until well risen, golden brown, and firm to the touch.
4   Remove the loaf from the oven and let cool in the pan for a few minutes, then turn onto a wire rack. Serve warm or cold in slices.

VARIATIONS *Use self-rising white flour in place of wholewheat flour. Use chopped pitted dried dates or pecan nuts in place of raisins.*

231 ⊡ Fruity hazelnut quick bread

PREPARATION TIME *20 minutes, plus 30 minutes soaking* **COOKING TIME** *1–1¼ hours*
MAKES *1 loaf (serves 10–12)*

½ cup golden raisins
½ cup ready-to-eat dried apricots,
   roughly chopped
1½ cups bran
1¼ cups milk
1 cup self-rising white flour
A pinch of salt

1 cup self-rising wholewheat flour
½ stick butter, diced
1 cup hazelnuts, chopped
⅔ cup raw brown sugar
1 teaspoon ground pudding spice
2 eggs, beaten

1   Place the golden raisins, apricots, and bran in a bowl, add the milk and stir to mix well. Cover and let soak for 30 minutes.
2   Meanwhile, preheat the oven to 180°C/350°F/gas mark 4. Grease and line a 2lb loaf pan and set aside. Sift the white flour and salt into a bowl, stir in the wholewheat flour, then lightly rub in the butter until the mixture resembles bread crumbs. Add the bran mixture, hazelnuts, sugar, spice, and eggs and mix thoroughly.
3   Turn the mixture into the loaf pan and level the top. Bake the loaf for 1–1¼ hours, or until golden brown and firm to the touch. Cover loosely with foil after about 1 hour if the top is browning too quickly. Turn onto a wire rack to cool. Serve warm or cold in slices.

TO MAKE IN BREADMAKER, *remove kneading blade from bread pan; grease and line base and sides of pan. Follow main recipe as above, then transfer mixture to prepared pan; level surface. Select Bake Only setting and bake for 60–70 minutes or until bread is cooked. Remove bread pan from machine; let stand for 5 minutes. Turn bread onto wire rack to cool.*

232 Chocolate banana bread

PREPARATION TIME *20 minutes* **COOKING TIME** *1–1¼ hours* **MAKES** *1 loaf (serves 10–12)*

1 stick butter, softened
⅔ cup light soft brown sugar
⅓ cup thick set honey
2 eggs, beaten
1½ cups self-rising white flour
½ teaspoon baking powder

¼ cup cocoa powder
2 ripe bananas, peeled and mashed with
   a little lemon juice (total weight of
   bananas including skins = about 10oz)
About 1 tablespoon milk
Sifted confectioners' sugar, for dusting

1   Preheat the oven to 180°C/350°F/gas mark 4. Grease and line a 2lb loaf pan and set aside. Cream the butter, soft brown sugar, and honey together in a bowl until light and fluffy. Gradually beat in the eggs. Sift the flour, baking powder, and cocoa powder into the bowl, then fold into the creamed mixture, mixing well.
2   Fold in the mashed bananas and enough milk, mixing to form a fairly soft consistency. Transfer the mixture to the loaf pan and level the top.
3   Bake in the oven for 1–1¼ hours, or until risen and firm to the touch and a cake tester inserted in the center comes out clean. Cover loosely with foil for the last 30 minutes or so of the cooking time if the top is browning too quickly.
4   Remove the loaf from the oven and let cool in the pan for a few minutes, then turn onto a wire rack. Dust with sifted confectioners' sugar and serve warm or cold in slices.

233 Frosted raisin loaf

PREPARATION TIME *20 minutes, plus soaking overnight* **COOKING TIME** *1¼ hours*
MAKES *1 loaf (serves 10–12)*

1⅓ cups raisins
⅔ cup golden raisins
1¼ cups strong hot tea, strained
1⅓ cups light soft brown sugar
2 cups self-rising white flour

1½ teaspoons ground pudding spice
1 egg, beaten
1½ cups confectioners' sugar, sifted
About 5–6 teaspoons orange juice

1   Place the raisins and golden raisins in a large bowl, pour over the hot tea and stir to mix.
    Cover and let soak overnight.
2   The next day, preheat the oven to 170°C/325°F/gas mark 3. Grease and line a 2lb loaf pan
    and set aside. Stir the brown sugar into the dried fruit mixture, then sift in the flour and
    pudding spice. Add the egg and stir with a wooden spoon until thoroughly mixed.
3   Turn the mixture into the loaf pan and level the top. Bake for about 1¼ hours, or until risen
    and firm to the touch—a cake tester inserted in the center should come out clean.
4   Remove the loaf from the oven and let cool in the pan for a few minutes, then turn onto a
    wire rack and let cool completely.
5   Combine the confectioners' sugar with enough orange juice to make a thick frosting.
    Spread this frosting evenly over the top of the cake. Let set. Serve in slices.

234 Raisin and orange muffins

PREPARATION TIME *20 minutes* **COOKING TIME** *15–20 minutes*
MAKES *9 large or 12 medium-sized muffins*

1 cup all-purpose wholewheat flour	**¼ cup superfine sugar**
⅔ cup all-purpose flour	**1 egg, beaten**
1 tablespoon baking powder	**1 cup milk**
A pinch of salt	**Finely grated zest of 1 orange**
½ stick butter, melted	**⅔ cup raisins**

1   Preheat the oven to 200°C/400°F/gas mark 6. Grease 9 or 12 cups of a 12-cup muffin pan or line each cup with a paper muffin case and set aside. Reserve 2 tablespoons wholewheat flour and set aside. Put the remaining wholewheat flour in a bowl, then sift the all-purpose flour, baking powder, and salt into the bowl and stir to mix.
2   Mix together the melted butter, sugar, egg, milk, and orange zest. Pour the egg mixture over the dry ingredients, then fold the ingredients gently together—just enough to combine the ingredients. The mixture should look quite lumpy; over-mixing will result in heavy muffins. Toss the raisins in the remaining flour, then fold gently into the muffin mixture.
3   Spoon the mixture into the muffin cups, dividing it evenly between each one.
4   Bake the muffins for 15–20 minutes, or until well risen and golden brown. Transfer to a wire rack to cool. Serve warm or cold.

VARIATIONS *Use lemon zest in place of orange zest. Use golden raisins or dried blueberries in place of raisins.*

235 Spiced apple muffins

PREPARATION TIME *20 minutes* **COOKING TIME** *20 minutes* **MAKES** *9 muffins*

1⅓ cups all-purpose wholewheat flour	**1 cup milk**
1 tablespoon baking powder	**½ stick butter, melted**
1½ teaspoons ground pudding spice	**1 medium cooking apple, peeled, cored,**
A pinch of salt	**and chopped**
⅓ cup light soft brown sugar	**Sifted confectioners' sugar, to decorate**
1 egg, beaten	

1   Preheat the oven to 200°C/400°F/gas mark 6. Grease 9 cups of a 12-cup muffin pan or line 9 cups with paper muffin cases and set aside. Place the flour, baking powder, pudding spice, salt, and soft brown sugar in a bowl and mix well.
2   In a separate large bowl, mix together the egg, milk, and melted butter, then gently fold into the flour mixture—just enough to combine the ingredients. The mixture should look quite lumpy; over-mixing will result in heavy muffins. Gently fold in the chopped apple. Divide the mixture evenly between the muffin cups.
3   Bake the muffins for about 20 minutes, or until well risen and golden brown. Transfer to a wire rack to cool. Serve the muffins warm or cold, dusted with a little sifted confectioners' sugar.

VARIATIONS *Use all-purpose flour or a mixture of wholewheat and white flour in place of all wholewheat flour. Use ground cinnamon in place of pudding spice. Use 1 large chopped dessert pear in place of cooking apple.*

236 Fresh blueberry muffins

PREPARATION TIME *20 minutes* **COOKING TIME** *15–20 minutes* **MAKES** *12 muffins*

1½ cups self-rising white flour
1 teaspoon baking powder
⅓ cup superfine sugar
½ teaspoon freshly grated nutmeg
1¼ cups fresh blueberries

3 tablespoons sunflower seeds
½ stick butter, melted
1 egg, beaten
1 cup milk

1   Preheat the oven to 200°C/400°F/gas mark 6. Grease each cup of a 12-cup muffin pan or line each cup with a paper muffin case and set aside. Sift the flour and baking powder into a bowl, then stir in the sugar, nutmeg, blueberries, and 2 tablespoons sunflower seeds.

2   In a separate small bowl, mix together the melted butter, egg, and milk, then add this to the flour mixture. Gently fold the ingredients together—just enough to combine the ingredients. The mixture should look quite lumpy; over-mixing will result in heavy muffins.

3   Spoon the mixture into the muffin cups, dividing it evenly between each one. Sprinkle the remaining sunflower seeds over the top.

4   Bake the muffins for 15–20 minutes, or until risen and golden brown. Transfer to a wire rack to cool. Serve warm or cold.

237 Poppyseed muffins

PREPARATION TIME *20 minutes* **COOKING TIME** *20 minutes* **MAKES** *9 muffins*

1⅓ cups all-purpose flour
1 tablespoon baking powder
A pinch of salt
Finely grated zest of 1 lemon
2 tablespoons poppy seeds

½ stick butter, melted
⅓ cup superfine sugar
1 egg, beaten
1 cup milk

1   Preheat the oven to 200°C/400°F/gas mark 6. Grease 9 cups of a 12-cup muffin pan or line 9 cups with paper muffin cases and set aside. Sift the flour, baking powder, and salt into a large bowl, then stir in the lemon zest and poppy seeds.

2   In a separate small bowl, mix together the melted butter, sugar, egg, and milk, then add this to the flour mixture. Gently fold the ingredients together—just enough to combine the ingredients. The mixture should look quite lumpy; over-mixing will result in heavy muffins.

3   Divide the mixture evenly between the muffin cups, filling each case about two-thirds full.

4   Bake the muffins for about 20 minutes, or until risen and golden brown. Transfer to a wire rack to cool. Serve warm or cold.

VARIATIONS *Use sesame or sunflower seeds in place of poppy seeds. Use the finely grated zest of 1 small orange in place of lemon zest.*

238 Apple bran muffins

PREPARATION TIME *20 minutes* **COOKING TIME** *15–20 minutes* **MAKES** *12 muffins*

1 cup all-purpose flour	**⅓ cup light soft brown sugar**
1 tablespoon baking powder	**1 egg, beaten**
A pinch of salt	**1 cup milk**
1 cup bran	**1 small cooking apple, peeled, cored,**
½ stick butter	**and chopped**

1   Preheat the oven to 200°C/400°F/gas mark 6. Grease each cup of a 12-cup muffin pan or line each cup with a paper muffin case and set aside. Reserve 3 tablespoons flour. Sift the remaining flour into a bowl with the baking powder and salt. Stir in the bran.

2   Place the butter in a small pan and heat gently until melted. Remove the pan from the heat and cool slightly, then mix the melted butter with the sugar, egg, and milk.

3   Pour the egg mixture over the dry ingredients, then fold the ingredients gently together—just enough to combine the ingredients. The mixture should look quite lumpy; over-mixing will result in heavy muffins.

4   Toss the chopped apple in the remaining flour, then fold gently into the muffin mixture. Spoon the mixture into the muffin cups, dividing it evenly between each one.

5   Bake the muffins for 15–20 minutes, or until well risen and golden brown. Transfer to a wire rack to cool. Serve warm or cold.

VARIATION *Add the finely grated zest of 1 lemon or 1 small orange with the egg mixture, if desired.*

239 Pear and golden raisin muffins

PREPARATION TIME *20 minutes* **COOKING TIME** *15–20 minutes* **MAKES** *12 muffins*

⅓ cup all-purpose flour	**½ stick butter**
1 tablespoon baking powder	**1 egg, beaten**
⅔ cup all-purpose wholewheat flour	**1 cup milk**
1 cup bran	**⅓ cup ready-to-eat dried pears, chopped**
A pinch of salt	**⅓ cup golden raisins**
⅓ cup light soft brown sugar	

1   Preheat the oven to 200°C/400°F/gas mark 6. Grease each cup of a 12-cup muffin pan or line each cup with a paper muffin case and set aside. Sift the white flour and baking powder into a bowl, then stir in the wholewheat flour, bran, salt, and sugar.

2   Place the butter in a small pan and heat gently until melted. Remove the pan from the heat and cool slightly, then mix the melted butter with the egg and milk.

3   Pour the egg mixture over the dry ingredients, then fold the ingredients gently together—just enough to combine them. The mixture should look quite lumpy; over-mixing will result in heavy muffins.

4   Gently fold in the pears and golden raisins. Spoon the mixture into the muffin cups, dividing it evenly between each one.

5   Bake the muffins for 15–20 minutes, or until well risen and golden brown. Transfer to a wire rack to cool. Serve warm or cold.

VARIATIONS *Add 1–1½ teaspoons ground cinnamon with the bran, if desired. Use dried cranberries or chopped ready-to-eat dried apricots in place of pears.*

240 Fruity breakfast muffins

PREPARATION TIME *20 minutes* **COOKING TIME** *20 minutes* **MAKES** *9 muffins*

1⅓ cups all-purpose wholewheat flour
1 tablespoon baking powder
A pinch of salt
1 cup small fresh raspberries or
  blackberries

½ stick butter, melted
⅓ cup light soft brown sugar
1 egg, beaten
1 cup milk

1 Preheat the oven to 200°C/400°F/gas mark 6. Grease 9 cups of a 12-cup muffin pan or line 9 cups with paper muffin cases and set aside. Place the flour, baking powder, and salt in a large bowl and mix well, then gently stir in the raspberries.
2 In a separate small bowl, mix together the melted butter, sugar, egg, and milk, then add this to the flour mixture. Gently fold the ingredients together—just enough to combine them. The mixture should look quite lumpy; over-mixing will result in heavy muffins.
3 Divide the mixture evenly between the muffin cups, filling each case about two-thirds full.
4 Bake the muffins for about 20 minutes, or until risen and golden brown. Transfer to a wire rack to cool. Serve warm or cold.

VARIATIONS *Use fresh blueberries in place of raspberries or blackberries. Add 1–1½ teaspoons ground cinnamon with the flour, if desired.*

241 Banana pecan muffins

PREPARATION TIME *20 minutes* **COOKING TIME** *20 minutes* **MAKES** *9 muffins*

1 cup all-purpose wholewheat flour
⅓ cup fine or pinhead oatmeal
1 tablespoon baking powder
A pinch of salt
½ cup pecan nuts, chopped
½ stick butter, melted

⅓ cup light soft brown sugar
1 egg, beaten
1 cup milk
1 large banana, peeled and mashed with
  a little lemon juice

1 Preheat the oven to 200°C/400°F/gas mark 6. Grease 9 cups of a 12-cup muffin pan or line 9 cups with paper muffin cases and set aside. Place the flour, oatmeal, baking powder, and salt in a large bowl and mix well, then stir in the pecan nuts.
2 In a separate small bowl, mix together the melted butter, sugar, egg, and milk, then add this to the flour mixture. Gently fold the ingredients together—just enough to combine them. The mixture should look quite lumpy; over-mixing will result in heavy muffins.
3 Gently fold in the mashed banana. Divide the mixture evenly between the muffin cups, filling each case about two-thirds full.
4 Bake the muffins for about 20 minutes, or until well risen and golden brown. Transfer to a wire rack to cool. Serve warm or cold.

VARIATION *Use walnuts in place of pecan nuts.*

242 Double chocolate-chip muffins

PREPARATION TIME *25 minutes* **COOKING TIME** *20 minutes* **MAKES** *12 muffins*

1½ cups self-rising white flour
2 teaspoons baking powder
A pinch of salt
⅓ cup cocoa powder, sifted
⅔ cup light soft brown sugar
1 cup milk

½ cup natural yoghurt
1 egg, lightly beaten
1 teaspoon vanilla extract
½ stick butter, melted
6oz milk or semisweet chocolate,
    roughly chopped into small chunks

1   Preheat the oven to 200°C/400°F/gas mark 6. Grease each cup of a 12-cup muffin pan or line each cup with a paper muffin case. Set aside. Sift the flour, baking powder, salt, and cocoa powder into a large bowl, then stir in the sugar.
2   Combine the milk, yoghurt, egg, and vanilla extract, then stir this into the flour mixture together with the melted butter, mixing well. Fold in the chopped chocolate. Divide the mixture evenly between the muffin cups, filling each one about three-quarters full.
3   Bake the muffins for about 20 minutes, or until risen and firm to the touch. Transfer to a wire rack to cool. Serve warm or cold.

VARIATION *Use milk, semisweet, or white chocolate chips in place of chopped chocolate.*

243 Raspberry wholewheat muffins

PREPARATION TIME *20 minutes* COOKING TIME *15–20 minutes* MAKES *12 muffins*

1 cup plain wholewheat flour
⅔ cup all-purpose flour
1 tablespoon baking powder
A pinch of salt
½ stick butter, melted

¼ cup superfine sugar
1 egg, beaten
1 cup milk
1 cup frozen raspberries
Sifted confectioners' sugar, to decorate

1 Preheat the oven to 200°C/400°F/gas mark 6. Grease each cup of a 12-cup muffin pan or line each cup with a paper muffin case and set aside. Reserve 3 tablespoons wholewheat flour and set aside. Put the remaining wholewheat flour in a bowl, then sift the white flour, baking powder, and salt into the bowl and stir to mix.

2 Mix together the melted butter, superfine sugar, egg, and milk. Pour the egg mixture over the dry ingredients, then fold the ingredients gently together—just enough to combine the ingredients. The mixture should look quite lumpy; over-mixing will result in heavy muffins.

3 Toss the raspberries in the remaining flour, then fold gently into the muffin mixture. Spoon the mixture into the muffin cups, dividing it evenly between each one.

4 Bake the muffins for 15–20 minutes, or until well risen and golden brown. Transfer to a wire rack to cool. Serve warm or cold, dusted with a little sifted confectioners' sugar.

VARIATIONS *Use fresh blueberries or chopped (peeled and cored) cooking apple in place of raspberries. Add the finely grated zest of 1 small orange with the egg mixture, if desired.*

244 Glazed fruit and orange muffins

PREPARATION TIME *30 minutes* COOKING TIME *15–20 minutes*
MAKES *9 large or 12 medium-sized muffins*

1⅓ cups all-purpose flour
1 tablespoon baking powder
A pinch of salt
½ stick butter
⅓ cup granulated sugar
1 egg, beaten

1 cup milk
Finely grated zest of 1 orange
⅔ cup golden raisins
3 tablespoons apricot jelly
Thinly pared zest of 1 small orange

1 Preheat the oven to 200°C/400°F/gas mark 6. Grease 9 or 12 cups of a 12-cup muffin pan or line each cup with a paper muffin case and set aside. Sift the flour, baking powder, and salt into a bowl.

2 Place the butter in a small pan and heat gently until melted. Remove the pan from the heat and cool slightly, then mix the melted butter with the sugar, egg, milk, and finely grated orange zest.

3 Pour the egg mixture over the dry ingredients, then fold the ingredients gently together— just enough to combine the ingredients. The mixture should look quite lumpy; over-mixing will result in heavy muffins.

4 Gently fold in the golden raisins. Spoon the mixture into the muffin cups, dividing it evenly between each one. Bake the muffins for 15–20 minutes, or until well risen and golden brown. Transfer to a wire rack to cool.

5 To prepare the apricot glaze, put the jelly and 3 tablespoons water in a small pan and stir over a moderate heat until dissolved and blended. Sieve the glaze and return to the pan, then add the pared orange zest and simmer for 1 minute. Brush the apricot and orange glaze over the cool muffins. Serve.

VARIATIONS *Use lemon zest in place of orange zest. Top the muffins with a little orange or lemon glacé or buttercream frosting in place of the apricot glaze, if desired.*

245 Wholewheat banana muffins

PREPARATION TIME *20 minutes* **COOKING TIME** *20 minutes*
MAKES *9 large or 12 medium-size muffins*

1⅓ cups all-purpose wholewheat flour
1 tablespoon baking powder
A pinch of salt
½ teaspoon ground nutmeg
⅓ cup raisins
½ stick butter, melted

⅓ cup light soft brown sugar
1 egg, beaten
1 cup milk
2 medium bananas, peeled and mashed
   with a little lemon juice

1   Preheat the oven to 200°C/400°F/gas mark 6. Grease 9 or 12 cups of a 12-cup muffin pan
    or line each cup with a paper muffin case and set aside. Mix the flour, baking powder,
    salt, nutmeg, and raisins in a bowl.
2   In a separate small bowl, mix together the melted butter, sugar, egg, and milk. Pour the
    egg mixture over the dry ingredients, then fold the ingredients gently together—just
    enough to combine them. The mixture should look quite lumpy; over-mixing will result in
    heavy muffins.
3   Gently fold in the mashed bananas. Spoon the mixture into the muffin cups, dividing it
    evenly between each one.
4   Bake the muffins for about 20 minutes, or until risen and evenly browned. Transfer to a
    wire rack to cool. Serve warm or cold.

246 Apricot and lemon muffins

PREPARATION TIME *20 minutes* **COOKING TIME** *20 minutes* **MAKES** *9 muffins*

⅔ cup all-purpose flour
1 tablespoon baking powder
A pinch of salt
1 cup all-purpose wholewheat flour
½ stick butter
⅓ cup golden granulated sugar

1 egg, beaten
1 cup milk
Finely grated zest of 1 lemon
⅔ cup ready-to-eat dried apricots,
   chopped
Sifted confectioners' sugar, to decorate

1   Preheat the oven to 200°C/400°F/gas mark 6. Grease 9 cups of a 12-cup muffin pan or line
    9 cups with paper muffin cases and set aside. Sift the white flour, baking powder, and salt
    into a large bowl, then stir in the wholewheat flour.
2   Place the butter in a small pan and heat gently until melted. Remove from the heat and
    cool slightly, then mix the butter with the granulated sugar, egg, milk, and lemon zest.
3   Add this to the flour mixture, then gently fold the ingredients together—just enough to
    combine them. The mixture should look quite lumpy; over-mixing will result in heavy
    muffins.
4   Gently fold in the apricots. Divide the mixture evenly between the muffin cups.
5   Bake the muffins for about 20 minutes, or until well risen and golden brown. Transfer to
    a wire rack to cool. Dust the muffins with sifted confectioners' sugar and serve warm
    or cold.

VARIATION *Top these tasty muffins with a lemon glacé or buttercream frosting instead of dusting
with confectioners' sugar, if desired.*

247 Mini maple pecan muffins

PREPARATION TIME *30 minutes* **COOKING TIME** *10 minutes* **MAKES** *about 48 mini muffins*

1½ cups all-purpose flour
1 tablespoon baking powder
A pinch of salt
⅓ cup light soft brown sugar
½ stick butter, melted

3 tablespoons maple syrup
⅔ cup milk
2 eggs, beaten
1 cup pecan nuts, finely chopped
Sifted confectioners' sugar, to decorate

1   Preheat the oven to 200°C/400°F/gas mark 6. Line two 24-cup mini muffin pans with
    paper cases or lay out about 48 paper mini muffin cases on 2 cookie sheets. Set aside.
    Sift the flour, baking powder, and salt into a bowl, then stir in the soft brown sugar.
2   Combine the melted butter, maple syrup, milk, and eggs in a separate bowl. Make a well
    in the center of the dry ingredients and pour in the egg mixture. Gently fold the
    ingredients together, just enough to combine them. The mixture should look quite lumpy;
    over-mixing will result in heavy muffins.
3   Gently fold in the pecan nuts, then spoon the mixture into the muffin cases, filling each
    one about two-thirds full.
4   Bake the muffins for about 10 minutes, or until well risen and golden brown. Transfer to
    a wire rack to cool. Dust with sifted confectioners' sugar just before serving, if desired.
    Serve warm or cold.

VARIATIONS *Use chopped walnuts in place of pecan nuts. Use light corn syrup or clear honey in
place of maple syrup.*

248 Mini orange and date muffins

PREPARATION TIME *30 minutes* **COOKING TIME** *10 minutes* **MAKES** *about 40 mini muffins*

1 cup all-purpose flour
1 tablespoon baking powder
A pinch of salt
1 cup bran
⅓ cup light soft brown sugar
½ stick butter, melted

1 egg, beaten
1 cup milk
Finely grated zest of 1 orange
⅔ cup pitted dried dates, finely chopped
Sifted confectioners' sugar, to decorate

1 Preheat the oven to 200°C/400°F/gas mark 6. Line about 40 cups of two 24-cup mini muffin pans with paper cases or lay out about 40 paper mini muffin cases on 2 cookie sheets. Set aside. Sift the flour, baking powder, and salt into a bowl, then stir in the bran and soft brown sugar.
2 Combine the melted butter, egg, milk, and orange zest in a separate bowl. Make a well in the center of the dry ingredients and pour in the egg mixture. Gently fold the ingredients together, just enough to combine them. The mixture should look quite lumpy; over-mixing will result in heavy muffins.
3 Gently fold in the chopped dates, then spoon the mixture into the muffin cases, filling each one about two-thirds full.
4 Bake the muffins for about 10 minutes, or until well risen and golden brown. Transfer to a wire rack to cool. Dust with confectioners' sugar just before serving. Serve warm or cold.

VARIATIONS *Use pitted dried prunes in place of dates. Use lemon zest in place of orange zest.*

249 Cherry and walnut muffins

PREPARATION TIME *20 minutes* **COOKING TIME** *20 minutes* **MAKES** *10 muffins*

1½ cups self-rising white flour
1 teaspoon baking powder
A pinch of salt
½ cup superfine sugar
¼ cup walnuts, chopped

⅔ cup cup candied cherries, chopped
½ stick butter
1 large egg, beaten
⅔ cup milk

1 Preheat the oven to 200°C/400°F/gas mark 6. Grease 10 cups of a 12-cup muffin pan or line 10 cups with paper muffin cases and set aside. Sift the flour, baking powder, and salt into a large bowl, then stir in the sugar, walnuts and cherries.
2 Place the butter in a small pan and heat gently until melted. Remove the pan from the heat and cool slightly, then mix the melted butter with the egg and milk.
3 Add the egg mixture to the dry ingredients, then gently fold the ingredients together—just enough to combine them. The mixture should look quite lumpy; over-mixing will result in heavy muffins. Divide the mixture evenly between the muffin cups.
4 Bake the muffins for about 20 minutes, or until well risen and golden brown. Transfer to a wire rack to cool and serve warm or cold.

VARIATIONS *Use chopped pecan nuts or hazelnuts in place of walnuts. Use chopped dried cherries in place of candied cherries.*

250 Pineapple oatmeal muffins

PREPARATION TIME *20 minutes* **COOKING TIME** *15–20 minutes*
MAKES *9 large or 12 medium-sized muffins*

1 cup all-purpose wholewheat flour
⅓ cup fine or pinhead oatmeal
1 tablespoon baking powder
A pinch of salt
1½ teaspoons ground cinnamon
½ stick butter, melted

¼ cup light soft brown sugar
1 egg, beaten
1 cup milk
⅓ cup ready-to-eat dried pineapple,
    finely chopped
Sifted confectioners' sugar, to decorate

1   Preheat the oven to 200°C/400°F/gas mark 6. Grease 9 or 12 cups of a 12-cup muffin pan
    or line each cup with a paper muffin case and set aside. Reserve 3 tablespoons flour and
    set aside. Put the remaining flour in a bowl, then stir in the oatmeal, baking powder, salt,
    and cinnamon.
2   Mix together the melted butter, soft brown sugar, egg, and milk. Pour the egg mixture over
    the dry ingredients, then fold the ingredients gently together—just enough to combine
    them. The mixture should look quite lumpy; over-mixing will result in heavy muffins.
3   Toss the chopped pineapple in the reserved flour, then fold gently into the muffin mixture.
    Spoon the mixture into the muffin cups, dividing it evenly between each one.
4   Bake the muffins for 15–20 minutes, or until well risen and golden brown. Transfer to a
    wire rack to cool. Serve warm or cold, dusted with a little sifted confectioners' sugar.

VARIATIONS *Use bran in place of oatmeal. Use chopped ready-to-eat dried apricots or peaches in
place of pineapple.*

251 Blackberry streusel muffins

PREPARATION TIME *20 minutes* **COOKING TIME** *20 minutes* **MAKES** *10–12 muffins*

For the muffins
1⅔ cups plain white flour
1 tablespoon baking powder
A pinch of salt
½ cup light soft brown sugar
1 cup milk
1 egg, beaten
1 teaspoon vanilla extract

½ stick butter, melted
1½ cups fresh blackberries

For the streusel topping
⅓ cup plain white flour
2 tablespoons light soft brown sugar
1 teaspoon ground pudding spice
2 tablespoons butter, diced

1   Preheat the oven to 200°C/400°F/gas mark 6. Grease 10 or 12 cups of a 12-cup muffin pan
    or line each cup with a paper muffin case and set aside. Make the streusel topping.
    Combine the flour, sugar, and spice in a bowl, then lightly rub in the diced butter, until the
    mixture resembles coarse bread crumbs. Set aside.
2   Make the muffins. Sift the flour, baking powder, and salt into a bowl, then stir in the sugar.
3   Combine the milk, egg, and vanilla extract, then gently stir this into the flour mixture
    together with the melted butter. Fold in the blackberries—just enough to combine them.
    The mixture should look quite lumpy; over-mixing will result in heavy muffins.
4   Divide the muffin mixture evenly between the muffin cups. Sprinkle some streusel mixture
    over each muffin.
5   Bake the muffins for about 20 minutes, or until well risen and firm to the touch. Transfer
    to a wire rack to cool. Serve warm or cold.

VARIATION *Use fresh blueberries or raspberries in place of blackberries.*

252 Mini chocolate-chip muffins

PREPARATION TIME *30 minutes* **COOKING TIME** *10 minutes* **MAKES** *about 40 mini muffins*

1⅓ cups all-purpose flour
1 tablespoon baking powder
A pinch of salt
½ stick butter, melted
⅓ cup superfine sugar

1 egg, beaten
1 cup milk
4oz semisweet chocolate chips
  (or a mixture of semisweet and
  white chocolate chips)

1   Preheat the oven to 200°C/400°F/gas mark 6. Line about 40 cups of two 24-cup mini muffin pans with paper cases or lay out about 40 paper mini muffin cases on 2 cookie sheets. Set aside. Sift the flour, baking powder, and salt into a bowl.
2   Combine the melted butter, sugar, egg, and milk in a separate bowl. Make a well in the center of the dry ingredients and pour in the egg mixture. Gently fold the ingredients together, only enough to combine them. The mixture should look quite lumpy; over-mixing will result in heavy muffins.
3   Gently fold in the chocolate chips, then spoon the mixture into the muffin cases, filling each one about two-thirds full.
4   Bake the muffins for about 10 minutes, or until well risen and golden brown. Transfer to a wire rack to cool. Serve warm or cold.

VARIATIONS *Use chopped toasted hazelnuts in place of 2oz chocolate chips. Use the mixture to make 9 large or 12 medium-sized regular muffins—grease the cups of a regular muffin pan or line them with paper cases. Make the muffin mixture as directed above, then spoon the mixture into the muffin cups, dividing it evenly between each one. Bake the muffins for 15–20 minutes.*

253 Cheesy bacon muffins

PREPARATION TIME *20 minutes* **COOKING TIME** *20 minutes* **MAKES** *12 muffins*

2 cups self-rising white flour
½ teaspoon baking powder
1 teaspoon paprika
A pinch of salt
¾ stick butter, diced

6 slices cold cooked lean bacon,
  chopped
1½ cups medium or mature cheddar
  cheese, grated
1 egg, beaten
1¼ cups milk

1   Preheat the oven to 200°C/400°F/gas mark 6. Grease each cup of a 12-cup muffin pan or line each cup with a paper muffin case. Set aside. Sift the flour, baking powder, paprika, and salt into a large bowl, then lightly rub in the butter.
2   Stir in the bacon and cheese, then add the egg and milk, stirring gently to mix well.
3   Spoon the mixture into the muffin cups, dividing it evenly between each one.
4   Bake the muffins for about 20 minutes, or until well risen, golden brown, and firm to the touch. Transfer to a wire rack to cool. Serve warm or cold.

VARIATIONS *Just before baking, sprinkle each muffin with a little extra grated cheese, if desired. Use emmental or gruyère cheese in place of cheddar.*

CHAPTER 5
Breadmaker recipes

Breadmakers take the hard work out of breadmaking and allow you to be creative and produce a wide range of delicious sweet and savory breads with very little effort. Breadmakers also enable you to create shaped breads and rolls, such as braids and knots, enriched doughs such as lardy cake and croissants, and specialty loaves such as baguettes, by using the Dough Only setting and then baking them in an oven in the conventional way.

There are many different breadmakers available today, and all vary in the features they have to offer, so it's worth doing a little research to ensure you buy a breadmaker that will meet your requirements.

Among the tempting recipes included in this chapter are basic breads such as White or Wholewheat Bread, as well as flavored breads such as Caraway Seed Bread or Herby Polenta Bread. Or choose from delights such as Sesame Bagels, Poppyseed Knots, or Marbled Chocolate Quick Bread.

254 🍞 Basic white bread

PREPARATION TIME *10 minutes* **COOKING TIME** *varies according to breadmaker*
MAKES *1 medium loaf (serves 10)*

1½ cups water
3⅔ cups strong white flour
1 tablespoon skim milk powder
1½ teaspoons salt

2 teaspoons granulated sugar
2 tablespoons butter, diced
1 teaspoon fast-action dried yeast

1 Please note, bread machines vary, so add the ingredients to the bread pan in the order specified in your instruction booklet (if this differs from the instructions given here).
2 Pour the water into the bread machine pan. Sprinkle over the flour, covering the water completely. Sprinkle the milk powder over the flour. Add the salt, sugar, and butter, placing them in separate corners of the bread pan. Make a small indent in the center of the flour and add the yeast.
3 Close the lid, set the machine to the program recommended in the manual (usually Basic White/Normal setting), select size of loaf and type of crust, and press Start.
4 Once the baking cycle has finished, remove the bread pan from the machine and turn the loaf onto a wire rack to cool. Serve in slices.

255 🏠 Basic wholewheat bread

PREPARATION TIME *10 minutes* **COOKING TIME** *varies according to breadmaker*
MAKES *1 medium loaf (serves 10)*

1½ cups water
1⅔ cups strong wholewheat flour
1⅔ cups strong white flour
1 tablespoon skim milk powder

1½ teaspoons salt
2 teaspoons granulated sugar
2 tablespoons butter, diced
1 teaspoon fast-action dried yeast

1   Please note, bread machines vary, so add the ingredients to the bread pan in the order specified in your instruction booklet (if this differs from the instructions given here).
2   Pour the water into the bread machine pan. Sprinkle over each type of flour in turn, ensuring that the water is completely covered. Sprinkle the milk powder over the flour. Add the salt, sugar, and butter, placing them in separate corners of the bread pan. Make a small indent in the center of the flour and add the yeast.
3   Close the lid, set the machine to the program recommended in the manual (usually Basic White/Normal or Wholewheat setting), select size of loaf and type of crust, and press Start.
4   Once the baking cycle has finished, remove the bread pan from the machine and turn the loaf onto a wire rack to cool. Serve in slices.

256 🏠 Home-style wholewheat bread

PREPARATION TIME *10 minutes* **COOKING TIME** *varies according to breadmaker*
MAKES *1 medium loaf (serves 10)*

1½ cups water
3 cups strong wholewheat flour
⅔ cup strong white flour
1½ teaspoons salt

2 teaspoons granulated sugar
2 tablespoons butter, diced
1 teaspoon fast-action dried yeast

1   Please note, bread machines vary, so add the ingredients to the bread pan in the order specified in your instruction booklet (if this differs from the instructions given here).
2   Pour the water into the bread machine pan. Sprinkle over each type of flour in turn, ensuring that the water is completely covered. Add the salt, sugar, and butter, placing them in separate corners of the bread pan. Make a small indent in the center of the flour and add the yeast.
3   Close the lid, set the machine to the program recommended in the manual (usually Wholewheat or Multigrain setting), select size of loaf and type of crust, and press Start.
4   Once the baking cycle has finished, remove the bread pan from the machine and turn the loaf onto a wire rack to cool. Serve in slices.

257 🏠 Malted wheat bread

PREPARATION TIME *10 minutes* **COOKING TIME** *varies according to breadmaker*
MAKES *1 medium loaf (serves 10)*

1¼ cups water
2 tablespoons malt extract
3 cups strong malted grain flour
1 tablespoon skim milk powder

1½ teaspoons salt
2 teaspoons granulated sugar
2 tablespoons butter, diced
1 teaspoon fast-action dried yeast

1   Please note, bread machines vary, so add the ingredients to the bread pan in the order specified in your instruction booklet (if this differs from the instructions given here).
2   Pour the water into the bread machine pan, then add the malt extract. Sprinkle over the flour, covering the water completely. Sprinkle the milk powder over the flour. Add the salt, sugar, and butter, placing them in separate corners of the bread pan. Make a small indent in the center of the flour and add the yeast.
3   Close the lid, set the machine to the program recommended in the manual (usually Wholewheat or Multigrain setting), select size of loaf and type of crust, and press Start.
4   Once the baking cycle has finished, remove the bread pan from the machine and turn the loaf onto a wire rack to cool. Serve in slices.

258 🏠 Farmhouse loaf

PREPARATION TIME *10 minutes* **COOKING TIME** *varies according to breadmaker*
MAKES *1 medium loaf (serves 10)*

1½ cups water
3 cups strong white flour, plus extra for
    dusting
1 cup strong wholewheat flour
1 tablespoon skim milk powder

1½ teaspoons salt
2 teaspoons light soft brown sugar
2 tablespoons butter, diced
1½ teaspoons fast-action dried yeast

1   Please note, bread machines vary, so add the ingredients to the bread pan in the order specified in your instruction booklet (if this differs from the instructions given here).
2   Pour the water into the bread machine pan. Sprinkle over each of the flours in turn, covering the water completely. Sprinkle the milk powder over the flour. Add the salt, sugar, and butter, placing them in separate corners of the bread pan. Make a small indent in the center of the flour and add the yeast.
3   Close the lid, set the machine to the program recommended in the manual (usually Basic White/Normal setting), select size of loaf and type of crust, and press Start. If possible, 10 minutes before the baking cycle starts, brush the top of the loaf with water and dust with a little flour. Using a sharp knife, cut a slash, about ½ inch deep, along the length of the loaf.
4   Once the baking cycle has finished, remove the bread pan from the machine and turn the loaf onto a wire rack to cool. Serve in slices.

259 ▣Cottage loaf

PREPARATION TIME *20 minutes, plus mixing and kneading in breadmaker, plus rising*
COOKING TIME *30–35 minutes* **MAKES** *1 loaf (serves 10–12)*

Warm water, to mix (according to bread mix package instructions)
1lb 2oz package white bread mix

1 teaspoon salt
Strong white flour, for dusting

1 Please note, bread machines vary, so add the ingredients to the bread pan in the order specified in your instruction booklet (if this differs from the instructions given here).
2 Pour the correct amount of water (according to bread mix package instructions) into the bread machine pan. (To ensure a good-shaped cottage loaf, the bread dough for this recipe needs to be firm enough so that the bottom round of dough can support the weight of the top piece of dough without sagging, so you may not need to add all the water as directed. However, if you do end up with a slightly misshapen loaf, don't worry, it will still taste delicious!) Sprinkle over the bread mix, covering the water completely. Close the lid, set the machine to the Dough setting, and press Start.
3 Meanwhile, grease or flour 2 cookie sheets and set aside. When the dough cycle has finished, remove the dough from the machine, punch it down on a lightly floured worktop, then cut off one third of the dough. Shape both pieces of dough into plump balls and place each one on a cookie sheet. Cover and let rise in a warm place until doubled in size.
4 Preheat the oven to 220°C/425°F/gas mark 7. Gently flatten each ball of dough and very carefully place the smaller ball on top of the larger one. Gently push the floured handle of a wooden spoon down through the center of the dough to join both pieces together, then slightly enlarge the hole with your fingers. Let rest for 5–10 minutes.
5 Mix the salt with 1 tablespoon hot water until dissolved, then lightly brush all over the loaf and dust with a little flour. Using a very sharp knife, make slashes at regular intervals around the top of the bread and around the base. Bake the loaf in the oven for about 30–35 minutes, or until the bread is golden brown and sounds hollow when tapped underneath. Transfer to a wire rack to cool. Serve in slices.

260 ▣Milk loaf

PREPARATION TIME *10 minutes* **COOKING TIME** *varies according to breadmaker*
MAKES *1 medium loaf (serves 10)*

1 cup milk, at room temperature
½ cup water
3 cups strong white flour
1½ teaspoons salt

2 teaspoons granulated sugar
2 tablespoons butter, diced
1 teaspoon fast-action dried yeast

1 Please note, bread machines vary, so add the ingredients to the bread pan in the order specified in your instruction booklet (if this differs from the instructions given here).
2 Pour the milk and water into the bread machine pan. Sprinkle over the flour, ensuring that the water is completely covered. Add the salt, sugar, and butter, placing them in separate corners of the bread pan. Make a small indent in the center of the flour and add the yeast.
3 Close the lid, set the machine to the program recommended in the manual (usually Basic White/Normal setting), select size of loaf and type of crust, and press Start.
4 Once the baking cycle has finished, remove the bread pan from the machine and turn the loaf onto a wire rack to cool. Serve in slices.

261 🍞 Caraway seed bread

PREPARATION TIME *10 minutes* **COOKING TIME** *varies according to breadmaker*
MAKES *1 medium loaf (serves 10)*

1½ cups water
2 tablespoons clear honey
3 cups strong wholewheat flour
1 cup strong white flour
2 tablespoons caraway seeds

2 tablespoons skim milk powder
1½ teaspoons salt
2 tablespoons butter, diced
1 teaspoon fast-action dried yeast

1 Please note, bread machines vary, so add the ingredients to the bread pan in the order specified in your instruction booklet (if this differs from the instructions given here).
2 Pour the water into the bread machine pan, then add the honey. Sprinkle over each flour in turn, covering the water completely. Sprinkle the seeds over the flour, then sprinkle the milk powder over the seeds. Add the salt and butter, placing them in separate corners of the bread pan. Make a small indent in the center of the flour and add the yeast.
3 Close the lid, set the machine to the program recommended in the manual (usually Multigrain or Wholewheat setting), select size of loaf and type of crust, and press Start.
4 Once the baking cycle has finished, remove the bread pan from the machine and turn the loaf onto a wire rack to cool. Serve in slices.

VARIATIONS *Use cumin or fennel seeds in place of caraway seeds. Use maple syrup in place of honey.*

262 🍞 Seeded rye bread

PREPARATION TIME *10 minutes* **COOKING TIME** *varies according to breadmaker*
MAKES *1 medium loaf (serves 10)*

1½ cups water
1 tablespoon clear honey
3 cups strong white flour
1 cup rye flour
2 tablespoons caraway seeds

2 tablespoons skim milk powder
1½ teaspoons salt
2 tablespoons butter, diced
1 teaspoon fast-action dried yeast

1 Please note, bread machines vary, so add the ingredients to the bread pan in the order specified in your instruction booklet (if this differs from the instructions given here).
2 Pour the water into the bread machine pan, then add the honey. Sprinkle over each flour in turn, covering the water completely. Sprinkle the seeds over the flour, then sprinkle the milk powder over the seeds. Add the salt and butter, placing them in separate corners of the bread pan. Make a small indent in the center of the flour and add the yeast.
3 Close the lid, set the machine to the program recommended in the manual (usually Basic White/Normal setting), select size of loaf and type of crust, and press Start.
4 Once the baking cycle has finished, remove the bread pan from the machine and turn the loaf onto a wire rack to cool. Serve in slices.

VARIATION *Use strong wholewheat flour in place of rye flour.*

263 ▣Sunflower seed loaf

PREPARATION TIME *10 minutes* **COOKING TIME** *varies according to breadmaker*
MAKES *1 medium loaf (serves 10)*

1¼ cups water
2 tablespoons sunflower oil
1½ cups strong white flour
1½ cups strong malted grain flour
1 tablespoon skim milk powder

1½ teaspoons salt
2 teaspoons granulated sugar
1 teaspoon fast-action dried yeast
5 tablespoons sunflower seeds

1   Please note, bread machines vary, so add the ingredients to the bread pan in the order specified in your instruction booklet (if this differs from the instructions given here).
2   Pour the water into the bread machine pan, then add the oil. Sprinkle over each type of flour in turn, covering the water completely. Sprinkle the milk powder over the flours. Add the salt and sugar, placing them in separate corners of the bread pan. Make a small indent in the center of the flour and add the yeast.
3   Close the lid, set the machine to the program recommended in the manual (usually Basic White/Normal setting, with Raisin setting or similar, if available), select size of loaf and type of crust, and press Start.
4   Add the sunflower seeds when the machine makes a sound (beeps) to add extra ingredients during the kneading cycle (or 5 minutes before the end of the kneading cycle).
5   Once the baking cycle has finished, remove the bread pan from the machine and turn the loaf onto a wire rack to cool. Serve in slices.

264 ▣Six-seed bread

PREPARATION TIME *10 minutes* **COOKING TIME** *varies according to breadmaker*
MAKES *1 medium loaf (serves 10)*

1¼ cups water
2 tablespoons sunflower oil
1½ cups strong white flour
1½ cups strong malted grain flour
1 tablespoon skim milk powder
1½ teaspoons salt
2 teaspoons granulated sugar

1 teaspoon fast-action dried yeast
2 tablespoons sunflower seeds
1 tablespoon pumpkin seeds
2 teaspoons EACH of sesame seeds and
   poppy seeds
1 teaspoon EACH of caraway seeds and
   cumin *or* fennel seeds

1   Please note, bread machines vary, so add the ingredients to the bread pan in the order specified in your instruction booklet (if this differs from the instructions given here).
2   Pour the water into the bread machine pan, then add the oil. Sprinkle over each type of flour in turn, covering the water completely. Sprinkle the milk powder over the flours. Add the salt and sugar, placing them in separate corners of the bread pan. Make a small indent in the center of the flour and add the yeast.
3   Close the lid, set the machine to the program recommended in the manual (usually Basic White/Normal setting, with Raisin setting or similar, if available), select size of loaf and type of crust, and press Start. Combine the seeds. Add the mixed seeds when the machine makes a sound (beeps) to add extra ingredients during the kneading cycle (or 5 minutes before the end of the kneading cycle).
4   Once the baking cycle has finished, remove the bread pan from the machine and turn the loaf onto a wire rack to cool. Serve in slices.

VARIATION *Packages of prepared mixed seeds suitable for breadmaking are available. Use 5 tablespoons ready-mixed seeds in place of seeds listed above.*

265 🍞Sun-dried tomato rolls

PREPARATION TIME *20 minutes, plus mixing and kneading time in breadmaker, plus rising*
COOKING TIME *20 minutes* **MAKES** *about 10 good-size rolls*

1½ cups water
2 tablespoons oil from a jar of sun-dried
   tomatoes
3⅔ cups strong white flour, plus extra
   for dusting
1 teaspoon salt

1 teaspoon granulated sugar
1 teaspoon fast-action dried yeast
1 cup sun-dried tomatoes in oil (drained
   weight), patted dry and chopped
Milk, for glazing

1. Please note, bread machines vary, so add the ingredients to the bread pan in the order specified in your instruction booklet (if this differs from the instructions given here).
2. Pour the water into the bread machine pan, then add the oil. Sprinkle over the flour, covering the water completely. Add the salt and sugar, placing them in separate corners of the bread pan. Make a small indent in the center of the flour and add the yeast. Close the lid, set the machine to the Dough setting, and press Start.
3. Meanwhile, grease or flour 2 cookie sheets and set aside. When the dough cycle has finished, remove the dough from the machine, punch it down on a lightly floured worktop, then knead the chopped sun-dried tomatoes evenly into the dough.
4. Divide the dough into about 10 equal portions. Roll and shape each piece into a round or oval, then flatten slightly. Place on the cookie sheets, spacing them well apart. Cover and let rise in a warm place for about 30 minutes, or until doubled in size.
5. Preheat the oven to 200°C/400°F/gas mark 6. Brush the tops of the rolls with milk and dust with flour. Bake in the oven for about 20 minutes, or until they are golden brown and sound hollow when tapped underneath. Transfer to a wire rack to cool. Serve warm.

266 🍞French bread

PREPARATION TIME *15 minutes, plus mixing and kneading time in breadmaker, plus rising*
COOKING TIME *15–20 minutes* **MAKES** *2 French sticks (each loaf serves 4–6)*

1¼ cups water
3 cups strong white flour
⅓ cup all-purpose flour

1½ teaspoons salt
1 teaspoon granulated sugar
1 teaspoon fast-action dried yeast

1. Please note, bread machines vary, so add the ingredients to the bread pan in the order specified in your instruction booklet (if this differs from the instructions given here).
2. Pour the water into the bread machine pan. Sprinkle over each type of flour in turn, covering the water completely. Add the salt and sugar, placing them in separate corners of the bread pan. Make a small indent in the center of the flour and add the yeast. Close the lid, set the machine to the French Dough setting or similar, and press Start.
3. Meanwhile, flour a cookie sheet; set aside. When the dough cycle has finished, remove the dough from the machine and punch it down on a floured worktop. Divide the dough in half. Roll out each portion of dough to make a rectangle about 8 x 3 inches.
4. Starting from a long edge, gently roll up each rectangle of dough like a jelly roll. Gently roll and stretch each piece of dough to make a loaf about 11–13 inches long. Place between the folds of a pleated dish towel for support, cover and let rise in a warm place until doubled in size.
5. Preheat the oven to 220°C/425°F/gas mark 7. Roll the loaves onto the cookie sheet. Using a sharp knife, cut several diagonal slashes in the top of each loaf at regular intervals. Spray the inside of the hot oven with water, then immediately bake the loaves for 15–20 minutes, or until crisp and golden. Transfer to a wire rack. Serve warm or cold.

267 Rosemary ciabatta rolls

PREPARATION TIME *20 minutes, plus mixing and kneading time in breadmaker, plus rising*
COOKING TIME *20 minutes* **MAKES** *about 10 good-size rolls*

1½ cups water
2 tablespoons olive oil
3⅔ cups strong white flour,
  plus extra for dusting
1 teaspoon salt

1 teaspoon granulated sugar
1 teaspoon fast-action dried yeast
1 tablespoon finely chopped fresh
  rosemary
Milk, for glazing

1. Please note, bread machines vary, so add the ingredients to the bread pan in the order specified in your instruction booklet (if this differs from the instructions given here).
2. Pour the water into the bread machine pan, then add the oil. Sprinkle over the flour, covering the water completely. Add the salt and sugar, placing them in separate corners of the bread pan. Make a small indent in the center of the flour and add the yeast. Close the lid, set the machine to the Dough setting, and press Start.
3. Meanwhile, grease or flour 2 cookie sheets and set aside. When the dough cycle has finished, remove the dough from the machine, punch it down on a lightly floured worktop, then knead the chopped rosemary evenly into the dough.
4. Divide the dough into about 10 equal portions. Roll and shape each piece into a round or oval, then flatten slightly. Place on the cookie sheets, spacing them well apart. Cover and let rise in a warm place for about 30 minute, or until doubled in size.
5. Preheat the oven to 200°C/400°F/gas mark 6. Brush the tops of the rolls with milk and dust with flour. Bake in the oven for about 20 minutes, or until they are golden brown and sound hollow when tapped underneath. Transfer to a wire rack to cool. Serve warm.

Sun-dried tomato bread

PREPARATION TIME *10 minutes* **COOKING TIME** *varies according to breadmaker*
MAKES *1 medium loaf (serves 8–10)*

1¼ cups water
1 tablespoon oil from a jar of sun-dried
  tomatoes
3 cups strong white flour
½ cup fresh Parmesan cheese, finely
  grated

1½ teaspoons salt
2 teaspoons superfine sugar
1 teaspoon fast-action dried yeast
½ cup sun-dried tomatoes in oil (drained
  weight), patted dry and chopped

1   Please note, bread machines vary, so add the ingredients to the bread pan in the order
    specified in your instruction booklet (if this differs from the instructions given here).
2   Pour the water into the bread machine pan, then add the oil. Sprinkle over the flour,
    ensuring that the water is completely covered. Sprinkle over the Parmesan cheese. Add
    the salt and sugar, placing them in separate corners of the bread pan. Make a small
    indent in the center of the flour and add the yeast.
3   Close the lid, set the machine to the program recommended in the manual (usually Basic
    White/Normal setting, with Raisin setting or similar, if available), select size of loaf and
    type of crust, and press Start.
4   Add the sun-dried tomatoes when the machine makes a sound (beeps) to add extra
    ingredients during the kneading cycle (or 5 minutes before the end of the kneading cycle).
5   Once the baking cycle has finished, remove the bread pan from the machine and turn the
    loaf onto a wire rack to cool. Serve in slices.

269 ▢Tomato focaccia

PREPARATION TIME *20 minutes, plus mixing and kneading time in breadmaker, plus rising*
COOKING TIME *25 minutes* **MAKES** *2 loaves (each loaf serves 6)*

1⅓ cups water
3 tablespoons oil from a jar of sun-dried
   tomatoes
3⅔ cups strong white flour
1 teaspoon salt

1 teaspoon granulated sugar
1 teaspoon fast-action dried yeast
1 cup sun-dried tomatoes in oil (drained
   weight), patted dry, and chopped
1 tablespoon olive oil, for glazing

1   Please note, bread machines vary, so add the ingredients to the bread pan in the order
    specified in your instruction booklet (if this differs from the instructions given here).
2   Pour the water into the bread machine pan, then add the sun-dried tomato oil. Sprinkle
    over the flour, covering the water completely. Add the salt and sugar, placing them in
    separate corners of the bread pan. Make a small indent in the center of the flour and add
    the yeast. Close the lid, set the machine to the Dough setting, and press Start.
3   Meanwhile, grease or flour 2 cookie sheets and set aside. When the dough cycle has
    finished, remove the dough from the machine, punch it down on a lightly floured worktop,
    then knead the chopped tomatoes evenly into the dough.
4   Divide the dough in half. Shape each portion into a round flat bread, about 1 inch thick
    and about 6 inches in diameter. Place on the cookie sheets, cover and let rise in a warm
    place until doubled in size.
5   Preheat the oven to 200°C/400°F/gas mark 6. Using your fingertips, make deep indents
    over the entire surface of each dough round, then brush the dough with a little olive oil.
    Bake in the oven for about 25 minutes, or until cooked and golden brown. Transfer to a
    wire rack to cool. Serve warm in slices or chunks.

270 ▢Mediterranean olive bread rolls

PREPARATION TIME *20 minutes, plus mixing and kneading time in breadmaker, plus rising*
COOKING TIME *20 minutes* **MAKES** *about 10 good-size rolls*

1½ cups water
2 tablespoons extra-virgin olive oil,
   plus extra for glazing
3⅔ cups strong white flour
1 teaspoon salt

1 teaspoon granulated sugar
1 teaspoon fast-action dried yeast
½ cup pitted black olives (drained
   weight), chopped

1   Please note, bread machines vary, so add the ingredients to the bread pan in the order
    specified in your instruction booklet (if this differs from the instructions given here).
2   Pour the water into the bread machine pan, then add the oil. Sprinkle over the flour,
    covering the water completely. Add the salt and sugar, placing them in separate corners of
    the bread pan. Make a small indent in the center of the flour and add the yeast. Close the
    lid, set the machine to the Dough setting, and press Start.
3   Meanwhile, grease or flour 2 cookie sheets and set aside. When the dough cycle has
    finished, remove the dough from the machine, punch it down on a lightly floured worktop,
    then knead the chopped olives evenly into the dough.
4   Divide the dough into about 10 equal portions. Roll and shape each piece into a round or
    oval, then flatten slightly. Place on the cookie sheets, spacing them well apart. Cover and
    let rise in a warm place for about 30 minutes, or until doubled in size.
5   Preheat the oven to 200°C/400°F/gas mark 6. Brush the tops of the rolls with olive oil.
    Bake in the oven for about 20 minutes, or until they are golden brown and sound hollow
    when tapped underneath. Transfer to a wire rack to cool. Serve warm.

VARIATION *Knead 1–2 tablespoons chopped fresh mixed herbs into the dough with the olives.*

271 ▣ Herby polenta bread

PREPARATION TIME *10 minutes* **COOKING TIME** *varies according to breadmaker*
MAKES *1 medium loaf (serves 10)*

1¼ cups water
3 tablespoons clear honey
3 tablespoons chopped fresh mixed
   herbs such as flat-leaf parsley, chives
   and basil
½ cup polenta

2⅓ cups strong wholewheat flour
1 cup strong white flour
1½ teaspoons salt
2 tablespoons butter, diced
1½ teaspoons fast-action dried yeast

1. Please note, bread machines vary, so add the ingredients to the bread pan in the order specified in your instruction booklet (if this differs from the instructions given here).
2. Pour the water into the bread machine pan, then add the honey. Sprinkle over the chopped herbs and polenta, then sprinkle over each of the flours in turn, covering the water completely. Add the salt and butter, placing them in separate corners of the bread pan. Make a small indent in the center of the flour and add the yeast.
3. Close the lid, set the machine to the program recommended in the manual (usually Wholewheat setting), select size of loaf and type of crust, and press Start.
4. Once the baking cycle has finished, remove the bread pan from the machine and turn the loaf onto a wire rack to cool. Serve in slices.

VARIATION *Use maple syrup in place of honey.*

272 ▣ Cheese and bacon bread

PREPARATION TIME *20 minutes* **COOKING TIME** *varies according to breadmaker*
MAKES *1 medium loaf (serves 10)*

1½ cups water
3⅔ cups strong wholewheat flour
1½ tablespoons skim milk powder
1½ teaspoons salt

1 tablespoon granulated sugar
1 teaspoon fast-action dried yeast
⅓ cup cold cooked lean bacon, chopped
¾ cup mature cheddar cheese, grated

1. Please note, bread machines vary, so add the ingredients to the bread pan in the order specified in your instruction booklet (if this differs from the instructions given here).
2. Pour the water into the bread machine pan. Sprinkle over the flour, covering the water completely. Sprinkle the milk powder over the flour. Add the salt and sugar, placing them in separate corners of the bread pan. Make a small indent in the center of the flour and add the yeast.
3. Close the lid, set the machine to the program recommended in the manual (usually Basic White/Normal setting, with Raisin setting or similar, if available), select size of loaf and type of crust, and press Start.
4. Combine the bacon and cheese. Add the bacon and cheese mixture when the machine makes a sound (beeps) to add extra ingredients during the kneading cycle (or 5 minutes before the end of the kneading cycle).
5. Once the baking cycle has finished, remove the bread pan from the machine and turn the loaf onto a wire rack to cool. Serve in slices.

VARIATIONS *Use chopped lean smoked cooked ham in place of bacon. Use emmental cheese in place of cheddar.*

273 ▣Cheese and olive bread

PREPARATION TIME *10 minutes* **COOKING TIME** *varies according to breadmaker*
MAKES *1 medium loaf (serves 8–10)*

1¼ cups water
1 tablespoon extra-virgin olive oil
3 cups strong white flour
⅔ cup fresh Parmesan cheese,
    finely grated
2 teaspoons dried Italian herb seasoning

1½ teaspoons salt
2 teaspoons superfine sugar
1 teaspoon fast-action dried yeast
¼ cup mixed pitted black and green
    olives, chopped

1   Please note, bread machines vary, so add the ingredients to the bread pan in the order specified in your instruction booklet (if this differs from the instructions given here).
2   Pour the water into the bread machine pan, then add the oil. Sprinkle over the flour, ensuring that the water is completely covered. Sprinkle over the Parmesan cheese and dried herbs. Add the salt and sugar, placing them in separate corners of the bread pan. Make a small indent in the center of the flour and add the yeast.
3   Close the lid, set the machine to the program recommended in the manual (usually Basic White/Normal setting, with Raisin setting or similar, if available), select size of loaf and type of crust, and press Start.
4   Add the mixed olives when the machine makes a sound (beeps) to add extra ingredients during the kneading cycle (or 5 minutes before the end of the kneading cycle).
5   Once the baking cycle has finished, remove the bread pan from the machine and turn the loaf onto a wire rack to cool. Serve in slices.

274 ▣Sesame bagels

PREPARATION TIME *10 minutes, plus mixing and kneading time in breadmaker, plus 10 minutes to shape bagels, plus rising* **COOKING TIME** *20 minutes* **MAKES** *12 bagels*

1¼ cups water
2 tablespoons sunflower oil
3 cups strong white flour
1½ teaspoons salt
1 tablespoon superfine sugar

1 sachet (¼oz) fast-action dried yeast
1 tablespoon malt extract
Milk or water, for glazing
About 2 tablespoons sesame seeds,
    for sprinkling

1   Please note, bread machines vary, so add the ingredients to the bread pan in the order specified in your instruction booklet (if this differs from the instructions given here).
2   Pour the water into the bread machine pan, then add the oil. Sprinkle over the flour, covering the water completely. Add the salt and sugar, placing them in separate corners of the bread pan. Make a small indent in the center of the flour and add the yeast. Close the lid, set the machine to the Dough setting, and press Start.
3   Meanwhile, grease 2 cookie sheets and set aside. When the dough cycle has finished, remove the dough from the machine, punch it down on a lightly floured worktop, then divide it into 12 equal portions.
4   Shape each piece of dough into a ball, then, using the floured handle of a wooden spoon, make a hole through the center of each ball. Enlarge the holes by pulling the dough outwards slightly to form rings, making sure the holes are big enough (bearing in mind they will close slightly when the dough is risen and poached). Place on the cookie sheets, cover and let rise in a warm place for about 30 minutes, or until doubled in size.
5   Meanwhile, preheat the oven to 200°C/400°F/gas mark 6. Heat a large pan of water until it is simmering, then stir in the malt extract until dissolved. Carefully drop each bagel into the simmering water (three or four at a time) and poach for about 3 minutes, turning once. Remove the bagels from the water using a slotted spoon, drain well, then return the bagels to the cookie sheets.
6   Brush each one with a little milk or water and sprinkle the tops with sesame seeds. Bake the bagels in the oven for about 20 minutes, or until cooked and golden brown. Transfer to a wire rack to cool. Cut in half to serve.

275 🍞English wholewheat muffins

PREPARATION TIME *20 minutes, plus mixing and kneading in breadmaker, plus rising*
COOKING TIME *25 minutes* **MAKES** *8–10 muffins*

1½ cups milk (at room temperature)
1½ cups strong white flour
1½ cups strong wholewheat flour
1½ teaspoons salt

1 teaspoon superfine sugar
1 tablespoon butter, diced
1½ teaspoons fast-action dried yeast
Sunflower oil, for greasing

1   Please note, bread machines vary, so add the ingredients to the bread pan in the order
    specified in your instruction booklet (if this differs from the instructions given here).
2   Pour the milk into the bread machine pan. Sprinkle over each flour in turn, ensuring that
    the milk is completely covered. Add the salt, sugar, and butter, placing them in separate
    corners of the bread pan. Make a small indent in the center of the flour and add the yeast.
    Close the lid, set the machine to the Dough setting, and press Start.
3   Meanwhile, generously flour a large cookie sheet and set aside. When the dough cycle
    has finished, remove the dough from the machine, punch it down on a lightly floured
    worktop, then divide it into 8–10 equal portions.
4   Shape each portion of dough into a round with straight sides, about ½–¾ inch thick.
    Place on the cookie sheet, cover and let rise for about 30 minutes, or until almost doubled
    in size.
5   Brush a griddle or large, heavy-based skillet with a little oil and heat until warm. Carefully
    transfer 3–4 muffins onto the griddle and cook in batches over a moderate heat for 7–10
    minutes, or until golden brown underneath. Turn them over and cook the other side for
    about 7 minutes, or until lightly browned.
6   Remove the muffins from the pan and wrap them in a clean dish towel, if serving warm.
    Otherwise transfer them to a wire rack to cool. Cook the remaining muffins in batches.
7   To serve, split the muffins open and serve with butter. If serving from cold, broil the
    muffins on both sides, then split and spread with butter.

VARIATION *Use rice flour to flour the cookie sheet, if desired.*

276 🍞Garden herb bread

PREPARATION TIME *10 minutes* **COOKING TIME** *varies according to breadmaker*
MAKES *1 medium loaf (serves 10)*

1½ cups water
3⅔ cups strong white flour
1 tablespoon skim milk powder
2 tablespoons chopped fresh parsley
2 tablespoons chopped fresh chives

2 teaspoons chopped fresh thyme
1½ teaspoons salt
2 teaspoons granulated sugar
2 tablespoons butter, diced
1 teaspoon fast-action dried yeast

1   Please note, bread machines vary, so add the ingredients to the bread pan in the order
    specified in your instruction booklet (if this differs from the instructions given here).
2   Pour the water into the bread machine pan. Sprinkle over the flour, covering the water
    completely. Sprinkle the milk powder over the flour. Mix the herbs, then sprinkle them
    over the milk powder. Add the salt, sugar, and butter, placing them in separate corners of
    the bread pan. Make a small indent in the center of the flour and add the yeast.
3   Close the lid, set the machine to the program recommended in the manual (usually Basic
    White/Normal setting), select size of loaf and type of crust, and press Start.
4   Once the baking cycle has finished, remove the bread pan from the machine and turn the
    loaf onto a wire rack to cool. Serve in slices.

VARIATION *Use 2 tablespoons chopped fresh cilantro or basil in place of the thyme.*

277 Poppyseed knots

PREPARATION TIME *20 minutes, plus mixing and kneading in breadmaker, plus rising*
COOKING TIME *15–20 minutes* **MAKES** *10 knots*

Warm water, to mix (according to bread mix package instructions)
1lb 2oz package white bread mix

Beaten egg or milk, to glaze
Poppy seeds, for sprinkling

1 Please note, bread machines vary, so add the ingredients to the bread pan in the order specified in your instruction booklet (if this differs from the instructions given here).
2 Pour the correct amount of water (according to bread mix package instructions) into the bread machine pan. Sprinkle over the bread mix, covering the water completely. Close the lid, set the machine to the Dough setting, and press Start.
3 Meanwhile, grease or flour 2 cookie sheets and set aside. When the dough cycle has finished, remove the dough from the machine, punch it down on a lightly floured worktop, then divide it into 10 equal portions. Roll each piece of dough into a long sausage or rope shape, then gently tie each one loosely in a single knot, pulling the ends through.
4 Place on the cookie sheets, spacing them well apart, brush with beaten egg or milk, and sprinkle with poppy seeds. Cover and let rise in a warm place for about 30 minutes, or until doubled in size.
5 Meanwhile, preheat the oven to 200°C/400°F/gas mark 6. Bake the knots in the oven for 15–20 minutes, or until risen and golden brown. Transfer to a wire rack to cool. Serve warm or cold.

278 ▣ Malted golden raisin loaf

PREPARATION TIME *10 minutes* COOKING TIME *varies according to breadmaker*
MAKES *1 medium loaf (serves 10)*

1½ cups water
3 tablespoons malt extract
3⅔ cups strong white flour
1 tablespoon skim milk powder
1½ teaspoons salt

2 teaspoons superfine sugar
2 tablespoons butter, diced
1 teaspoon fast-action dried yeast
⅔ cup golden raisins

1 Please note, bread machines vary, so add the ingredients to the bread pan in the order specified in your instruction booklet (if this differs from the instructions given here).
2 Pour the water into the bread machine pan, then add the malt extract. Sprinkle over the flour, covering the water completely, then sprinkle the milk powder over the flour. Add the salt, sugar, and butter, placing them in separate corners of the bread pan. Make a small indent in the center of the flour and add the yeast.
3 Close the lid, set the machine to the program recommended in the manual (usually Basic White/Normal setting, with Raisin setting or similar, if available), select size of loaf and type of crust, and press Start.
4 Add the golden raisins when the machine makes a sound (beeps) to add extra ingredients during the kneading cycle (or 5 minutes before the end of the kneading cycle).
5 Once the baking cycle has finished, remove the bread pan from the machine and turn the loaf onto a wire rack to cool. Serve in slices.

VARIATION *Use raisins, dried cranberries, or chopped ready-to-eat dried apricots or pears in place of golden raisins.*

279 ▣ Banana-chip muesli loaf

PREPARATION TIME *15 minutes* COOKING TIME *1–1¼ hours* MAKES *1 loaf (serves 10)*

1½ sticks butter, softened
1 cup light soft brown sugar
3 eggs, beaten
1 cup self-rising white flour

2oz muesli (of your choice), such as
  Swiss-style muesli
½ cup banana chips
Sifted confectioners' sugar, for
  decorating (optional)

1 Remove the kneading blade from the bread pan and grease and line the base and sides of the pan. Cream the butter and soft brown sugar together in a bowl until light and fluffy, then gradually beat in the eggs. Sift the flour into the bowl, then fold the flour into the creamed mixture together with the muesli and banana chips, mixing well.
2 Spoon the mixture into the pan and level the top. Place the bread pan in position in the machine and close the lid. Select the Bake Only setting and enter 60 minutes on the timer. Press Start.
3 After baking, a cake tester inserted in the center of the loaf should come out clean. If the loaf requires further baking, select the same program as before and enter a further 10–15 minutes on the timer, or until the loaf is risen and cooked.
4 Remove the bread pan from the machine using oven gloves, then let stand for 10 minutes, before turning the loaf onto a wire rack to cool. Dust with sifted confectioners' sugar, if desired, and serve warm or cold in slices.

280 ▣ Frosted orange quick bread

PREPARATION TIME *15 minutes* **COOKING TIME** *1 hour* **MAKES** *1 loaf (serves 10)*

For the quick bread
1 stick butter, softened
⅓ cup light soft brown sugar
2 eggs, beaten
1 cup self-rising white flour, sifted
1 cup self-rising wholewheat flour
1½ teaspoons ground ginger
8 tablespoons orange marmalade
About 1 tablespoon milk

For the frosting
¾ stick butter, softened
1 teaspoon finely grated orange zest
1½ cups confectioners' sugar, sifted
2 teaspoons orange juice

1   Make the quick bread. Remove the kneading blade from the bread pan and grease and line the base and sides of the pan. Cream the butter and soft brown sugar together in a bowl until light and fluffy, then gradually beat in the eggs.
2   Add the flours and ginger to the bowl and fold into the creamed mixture, mixing well. Fold in the marmalade and enough milk, mixing to make a fairly soft consistency. Spoon the mixture into the pan and level the top.
3   Place the bread pan in position in the machine and close the lid. Select the Bake Only setting and enter 60 minutes on the timer. Press Start. After baking, a cake tester inserted in the center of the bread should come out clean. If the bread requires further baking, select the same program as before and enter a further 5–10 minutes on the timer, or until the bread is risen and cooked. If the mixture is just very slightly sticky on the top, this should cook through during the standing period.
4   Remove the bread pan from the machine using oven gloves, then let stand for 10 minutes, before turning the bread onto a wire rack to cool.
5   Make the frosting. Cream the butter in a bowl until it is pale and fluffy, then beat in the orange zest. Gradually stir in the confectioners' sugar and orange juice, mixing to make a soft frosting. Spread the frosting over the top of the cooled quick bread. Serve in slices.

281 ▣ Lemon blueberry loaf

PREPARATION TIME *15 minutes* **COOKING TIME** *1–1¼ hours* **MAKES** *1 loaf (serves 10)*

1½ cups self-rising white flour
1 stick butter, diced
⅔ cup superfine sugar
⅓ cup ground almonds or ground
    hazelnuts
Finely grated zest and juice of 1 lemon

2 eggs, beaten
4 tablespoons milk
1¾ cups fresh blueberries, rinsed
    and dried
½ cup confectioners' sugar, sifted

1   Remove the kneading blade from the bread pan and grease and line the base and sides of the pan. Sift the flour into a bowl, then lightly rub in the butter. Stir in the superfine sugar, nuts, and lemon zest, then beat in the eggs and milk, mixing well. Fold in the blueberries.
2   Spoon the mixture into the pan and level the top. Place the bread pan in position in the machine and close the lid. Select the Bake Only setting and enter 60 minutes on the timer. Press Start.
3   After baking, a cake tester inserted in the center of the loaf should come out clean. If the loaf requires further baking, select the same program as before and enter a further 10–15 minutes on the timer, or until the loaf is risen and cooked.
4   Remove the bread pan from the machine using oven gloves, then let stand for 10 minutes, before turning the loaf onto a wire rack to cool.
5   Combine the confectioners' sugar with 1–2 teaspoons lemon juice to give a fairly thin glacé frosting. Drizzle the frosting over the cold loaf. Serve in slices.

VARIATION *Spread the top of the cold cooked loaf with lemon buttercream frosting in place of glacé frosting, if preferred.*

282 ▣ Marbled chocolate quick bread

PREPARATION TIME *25 minutes* **COOKING TIME** *1 hour* **MAKES** *1 loaf (serves 10)*

1½ sticks butter, softened
1 cup light soft brown sugar
3 eggs, beaten
1½ cups all-purpose flour
2½ teaspoons baking powder
2 ripe bananas, peeled and mashed with
   a little lemon juice (total weight of

bananas including skins = about 10oz)
¼ cup cocoa powder
2 teaspoons milk
½ teaspoon ground ginger
Sifted confectioners' sugar and cocoa
   powder, for dusting

1 Remove the kneading blade from the bread pan and grease and line the base and sides of
the pan. Cream the butter and brown sugar together in a bowl. Gradually beat in the eggs.
Sift the flour and baking powder into the bowl; fold in, mixing well. Fold in the bananas.

2 Place half the bread mixture in a separate bowl and sift the cocoa powder into this bowl.
Add the milk and fold the ingredients together. Stir the ground ginger into the plain
banana mixture in the other bowl.

3 Place alternate spoonfuls of each bread mixture into the pan, then gently swirl a sharp
knife or skewer through the mixture to create a marbled effect.

4 Place the bread pan in position in the machine and close the lid. Select the Bake Only
setting and enter 55 minutes on the timer. Press Start. After baking, a cake tester inserted
in the center of the bread should come out clean. If the bread requires further baking,
select the same program as before and enter a further 5–10 minutes on the timer, or until
the bread is cooked.

5 Remove the bread pan from the machine using oven gloves, then let stand for 10 minutes,
before turning the bread onto a wire rack. Dust with sifted confectioners' sugar and cocoa
powder and serve warm or cold in slices.

283 🍞Hawaiian fruit bread

PREPARATION TIME *15 minutes, plus soaking overnight* **COOKING TIME** *1–1¼ hours*
MAKES *1 loaf (serves 10)*

1¾ cups mixed ready-to-eat dried
   tropical fruit (such as pineapple,
   mango, pears, cranberries, cherries,
   melon, etc), chopped
¾ cup strong hot tea, strained
1½ cups all-purpose wholewheat flour
3 teaspoons baking powder

1½ teaspoons ground pudding spice
1 cup light soft brown sugar
Finely grated zest of 1 orange
⅓ cup shredded unsweetened coconut
1 egg, beaten
4 tablespoons milk
Sifted confectioners' sugar, to decorate

1 Remove the kneading blade from the bread pan and grease and line the base and sides of the pan. Put the mixed fruits in a large bowl, pour over the hot tea, stir to mix, then let soak overnight.
2 The next day, combine the flour, baking powder, pudding spice, soft brown sugar, orange zest, and coconut in a bowl, then add to the soaked fruits, together with the egg and milk, and mix thoroughly. Spoon the mixture into the pan and level the top.
3 Place the bread pan in position in the machine and close the lid. Select the Bake Only setting and enter 60 minutes on the timer. Press Start. After baking, a cake tester inserted in the center of the bread should come out clean. If the bread requires further baking, select the same program as before and enter a further 10–15 minutes on the timer, or until the bread is cooked.
4 Remove the bread pan from the machine using oven gloves, then let stand for 5 minutes, before turning the bread onto a wire rack to cool. Dust with sifted confectioners' sugar and serve warm or cold in slices.

VARIATION *Use pre-mixed luxury mixed dried fruits in place of the tropical fruit.*

284 🍞Apricot and walnut quick bread

PREPARATION TIME *20 minutes* **COOKING TIME** *1–1¼ hours* **MAKES** *1 loaf (serves 10)*

2 cups all-purpose flour
2½ teaspoons baking powder
1½ teaspoons ground pudding spice
¾ stick butter, diced
½ cup soft brown sugar

1 cup ready-to-eat dried apricots,
   chopped
⅔ cup golden raisins
¾ cup walnuts, chopped
1 cup milk
1 egg, beaten

1 Remove the kneading blade from the bread pan and grease and line the base and sides of the pan. Sift the flour, baking powder, and pudding spice into a bowl, then lightly rub in the butter. Stir in the sugar, apricots, golden raisins, and walnuts. Gradually beat in the milk and egg until well mixed. Spoon the mixture into the pan and level the top.
2 Place the bread pan in position in the machine and close the lid. Select the Bake Only setting and enter 60 minutes on the timer. Press Start. After baking, a cake tester inserted in the center of the bread should come out clean. If the bread requires further baking, select the same program as before and enter a further 10–15 minutes on the timer, or until the bread is cooked.
3 Remove the bread pan from the machine using oven gloves, then let stand for 5 minutes, before turning the bread onto a wire rack to cool. Serve warm or cold in slices.

VARIATIONS *Use raisins or dried blueberries in place of golden raisins. Use hazelnuts or pecans in place of walnuts.*

CHAPTER 6
Gluten-free breads

For those with a sensitivity to gluten, this chapter will be an invaluable source of creative and tasty recipes for you to enjoy. It includes a tempting range of both hand-made gluten-free recipes, as well as a selection of tasty gluten-free breads made using a breadmaker.

Gluten-free breads, by the very nature of the ingredients used to create them, tend to be slightly different in texture and flavor to ordinary breads, but are just as appealing and delicious. They have a slightly more crumbly, closer, but light texture, and many are enjoyed at their best when served warm and freshly baked.

There is a delicious selection of gluten-free recipes in this chapter, including Basic White and Basic Brown Bread, Cheesy Onion Cornbread, Soy Bread, Fresh Herb Bread, or Italian Tomato Bread, as well as tasty sweet recipes such as Seeded Fruit and Nut Quick Bread, Apricot and Cranberry Loaf, Lemon Drizzle Loaf, or Fruit and Spice Scones.

285 Cheesy onion cornbread

PREPARATION TIME *35 minutes* **COOKING TIME** *30 minutes* **MAKES** *1 loaf (serves 8–10)*

1 tablespoon sunflower oil
1 onion, thinly sliced
1½ cups gluten-free cornmeal
¾ cup rice flour
¼ cup soy flour
1 tablespoon gluten-free baking powder
1 teaspoon superfine sugar

1 teaspoon salt
1 cup mature cheddar cheese,
  coarsely grated
1 cup warm milk
2 eggs, lightly beaten
3 tablespoons butter, melted

1   Preheat the oven to 190°C/375°F/gas mark 5. Grease a 2lb loaf pan and set aside. Heat the oil in a skillet, add the onion, and cook gently for 10–15 minutes, or until softened, stirring occasionally. Remove the pan from the heat and set aside to cool.

2   Place the cornmeal, rice flour, soy flour, baking powder, sugar, and salt in a bowl and mix well. Stir in the cheese. In a small bowl, beat together the milk, eggs, and melted butter, then add to the flour mixture, stirring to mix well.

3   Reserve about 1 tablespoon of the cooled, cooked onions. Stir the remaining onions into the bread mixture. Transfer the mixture to the loaf pan and level the top. Sprinkle the reserved onions evenly over the top.

4   Bake for about 30 minutes, or until the loaf is risen and golden brown. Turn onto a wire rack to cool. Serve warm or cold in slices.

VARIATIONS *Use 4–6 shallots in place of onion. Use gruyère or emmental cheese in place of cheddar.*

286 Chili cornbread

PREPARATION TIME *30 minutes* **COOKING TIME** *30 minutes* **MAKES** *1 loaf (serves 10)*

1 tablespoon sunflower oil
6 scallions, finely chopped
2 large fresh red or green chilies,
  seeded and finely chopped
1½ cups gluten-free cornmeal
⅓ cup rice flour
½ cup gram (garbanzo) flour
1 tablespoon gluten-free baking powder

1 teaspoon light soft brown sugar
1 teaspoon salt
¾ cup fresh Parmesan cheese, finely
  grated
1 cup warm milk
2 eggs, lightly beaten
3 tablespoons butter, melted

1   Preheat the oven to 190°C/375°F/gas mark 5. Grease a 2lb loaf pan and set aside. Heat the oil in a skillet, add the scallions and chilies, and sauté for about 5 minutes, or until softened. Remove the pan from the heat and set aside to cool.

2   Place the cornmeal, rice flour, gram flour, baking powder, sugar, and salt in a bowl and mix well. Stir in the Parmesan cheese. In a small bowl, beat together the milk, eggs, and melted butter, then add to the flour mixture, stirring to mix well. Stir in the cooled, cooked scallions and chilies.

3   Transfer the mixture to the loaf pan and level the top. Bake for about 30 minutes, or until the loaf is risen and golden brown.

4   Remove the loaf from the oven and let cool in the pan for a few minutes, then turn onto a wire rack. Serve warm or cold in slices.

VARIATIONS *Use 2–3 shallots in place of scallions. Use mature cheddar or gruyère cheese in place of Parmesan.*

287 Buckwheat and rice bread

PREPARATION TIME *20 minutes, plus rising* **COOKING TIME** *30 minutes* **MAKES** *1 loaf (serves 8–10)*

2 cups brown rice flour
½ cup buckwheat flour or soy flour
½ cup gluten-free cornmeal
1 teaspoon salt
3 tablespoons butter, diced

1 sachet (¼oz) fast-action dried yeast
1 teaspoon superfine sugar
1 egg, beaten
1 cup warm milk
1 cup warm water

1 Grease a 2lb loaf pan and set aside. Place the rice flour, buckwheat or soy flour, cornmeal, and salt in a bowl and stir to mix. Lightly rub in the butter, then stir in the yeast and sugar.

2 Make a well in the center, then add the egg, milk, and water and beat together until thoroughly mixed to form a smooth, thick consistency.

3 Transfer the mixture to the loaf pan and level the top. Cover and set aside in a warm place until the mixture has risen to the top of the pan.

4 Meanwhile, preheat the oven to 200°C/400°F/gas mark 6. Bake the loaf for about 30 minutes, or until lightly browned. Remove from the oven and turn onto a wire rack to cool. Serve warm or cold in slices.

VARIATION *For extra flavor and crunch, brush the top of the bread with a little beaten egg and sprinkle with sesame or poppy seeds before baking.*

288 Soy bread

PREPARATION TIME *20 minutes, plus rising* **COOKING TIME** *25–30 minutes*
MAKES *1 loaf (serves 12–14)*

2 cups brown rice flour
½ cup soy flour
1 teaspoon salt
½ stick butter, diced
½ cup mature cheddar cheese, grated

1 sachet (¼oz) fast-action dried yeast
1 teaspoon light soft brown sugar
1 egg, beaten
1¼ cups warm milk
⅔ cup warm water

1 Grease a 2½lb loaf pan and set aside. Place the rice flour, soy flour, and salt in a bowl and stir to mix. Lightly rub in the butter, then stir in the cheese, yeast, and sugar. Make a well in the center, then add the egg, milk, and water and beat together until thoroughly mixed to form a smooth, thick consistency.

2 Transfer the mixture to the loaf pan and level the top. Cover and set aside in a warm place for about 45 minutes, or until the mixture has risen to the top of the pan.

3 Meanwhile, preheat the oven to 200°C/400°F/gas mark 6. Bake the loaf for 25–30 minutes, or until lightly browned. Remove from the oven, and turn onto a wire rack to cool. Serve warm or cold in slices.

289 Parmesan herb bread

PREPARATION TIME *15 minutes* **COOKING TIME** *30–40 minutes* **MAKES** *1 loaf (serves 12–14)*

1lb package gluten-free bread mix
¾ cup fresh Parmesan cheese,
finely grated
2 teaspoons dried herbes de Provence

2 cups milk (at room
temperature)
3 tablespoons sunflower oil

1 Preheat the oven to 180°C/350°F/gas mark 4. Grease and line a 2½lb loaf pan and set aside. Place the bread mix in a bowl, add the cheese and herbs and stir to mix.

2 Add the milk and oil and beat the ingredients together using a wooden spoon until smooth and well mixed. Continue mixing for a further 2–3 minutes.

3 Transfer the mixture to the loaf pan and level the top. Cover and let stand for 15–20 minutes, or until the dough has risen above the top of the pan.

4 Bake the loaf for 30–40 minutes, or until risen and golden brown. Turn onto a wire rack to cool. Serve warm or cold in slices.

VARIATIONS *Use mature cheddar or gruyère cheese in place of Parmesan. Use 2–3 tablespoons of chopped fresh mixed herbs in place of the dried herbs.*

290 Red onion and rosemary pizza

PREPARATION TIME *25 minutes* **COOKING TIME** *25–30 minutes* **MAKES** *1 pizza (serves 4–6)*

2 tablespoons olive oil
2 red onions, thinly sliced
1 clove garlic, thinly sliced
1 red or yellow bell pepper, seeded and sliced
1 cup gluten-free cornmeal
⅓ cup potato flour
½ cup soy flour
1 teaspoon gluten-free baking powder

½ teaspoon salt
½ stick butter, diced
About 7 tablespoons milk
4 plum tomatoes, skinned, seeded, and chopped
2–3 teaspoons chopped fresh rosemary
Sea salt and freshly ground black pepper
1¼ cups mozzarella cheese, grated
Fresh rosemary sprigs, to garnish

1   Heat 1½ tablespoons oil in a skillet, add the onions, garlic, and bell pepper, and sauté for about 10 minutes, or until softened. Remove the pan from the heat and set aside.

2   Preheat the oven to 200°C/400°F/gas mark 6. Place the cornmeal, potato flour, soy flour, baking powder, and salt in a bowl and stir to mix. Lightly rub in the butter until the mixture resembles bread crumbs, then add enough milk, mixing to make a soft dough.

3   Place the dough on a sheet of non-stick baking paper, then roll or press out to form a 10-inch round, making the edges slightly thicker than the center. Brush the pizza dough with the remaining oil.

4   Combine the chopped tomatoes, chopped rosemary, and seasoning and spread this mixture over the dough. Spoon the onion mixture over the tomatoes and top with the cheese.

5   Bake for 25–30 minutes, or until the pizza base is crisp and golden brown. Garnish with rosemary sprigs and serve immediately, cut into slices, with a mixed green salad.

291 Cheese and seed bread

PREPARATION TIME *15 minutes* **COOKING TIME** *30–40 minutes* **MAKES** *1 loaf (serves 12–14)*

1lb package gluten-free bread mix
1 cup mature cheddar cheese, grated
⅔ cup sunflower seeds

2 cups milk (at room temperature)
3 tablespoons sunflower oil

1   Preheat the oven to 180°C/350°F/gas mark 4. Grease and line a 2½lb loaf pan and set aside. Put the bread mix in a bowl, add the cheese and sunflower seeds, and stir to mix.

2   Add the milk and oil and beat the ingredients together using a wooden spoon until smooth and well mixed. Continue mixing for a further 2–3 minutes.

3   Transfer the mixture to the loaf pan and level the top. Cover and let stand for 15–20 minutes, or until the dough has risen above the top of the pan.

4   Bake the loaf for 30–40 minutes, or until risen and golden brown. Turn onto a wire rack to cool. Serve warm or cold in slices.

VARIATIONS *Use gruyère, emmental, or fresh Parmesan cheese in place of cheddar. Just before baking, sprinkle the top of the loaf with extra sunflower seeds, if desired.*

292 Ginger quick bread

PREPARATION TIME *20 minutes, plus cooling* **COOKING TIME** *1–1¼ hours*
MAKES *1 loaf (serves 8–10)*

⅔ cup light soft brown sugar
¾ stick butter
¼ cup light corn syrup
¼ cup molasses
7 tablespoons milk
1 egg, beaten
1¼ cups gluten-free all-purpose flour

½ cup gram (garbanzo) flour
1½ teaspoons gluten-free baking powder
A pinch of salt
2 teaspoons ground ginger
1 teaspoon ground cinnamon or
    pudding spice

1   Preheat the oven to 170°C/325°F/gas mark 3. Grease and line a 2lb loaf pan and set
    aside. Place the sugar, butter, syrup, and molasses in a saucepan and heat gently until
    melted and blended, stirring occasionally. Remove the pan from the heat and cool slightly,
    then stir in the milk and egg.
2   Place the flours, baking powder, salt, and ground spices in a bowl and stir to mix. Make a
    well in the center, pour in the syrup mixture, and beat together until thoroughly mixed.
    Pour the mixture into the loaf pan.
3   Bake the loaf for 1–1¼ hours, or until firm to the touch—a cake tester inserted in the
    center should come out clean. Remove the bread from the oven and let cool in the pan for
    a few minutes, then turn onto a wire rack. Store in an airtight container or wrapped in foil.
    Serve warm or cold in slices.

VARIATIONS *Fold ¼ cup finely chopped, preserved stem ginger into the raw bread mixture, if
desired. Add 1–2 extra teaspoons of ground ginger for a more pronounced gingery flavor.*

293 Seeded fruit and nut quick bread

PREPARATION TIME *20 minutes* **COOKING TIME** *1 hour* **MAKES** *1 loaf (serves 8–10)*

⅔ cup pitted dried dates, chopped
⅔ cup pitted ready-to-eat dried apricots,
  chopped
⅔ cup pitted golden raisins or raisins
⅔ cup light soft brown sugar
1½ cups gluten-free self-rising flour
1 teaspoon gluten-free baking powder

2 teaspoons ground pudding spice
¾ cup chopped mixed nuts, such as
  pecans and hazelnuts
⅔ cup mixed seeds, such as millet,
  sunflower, and sesame seeds
2 eggs, beaten
⅔ cup milk

1   Preheat the oven to 180°C/350°F/gas mark 4. Grease a 2lb loaf pan and set aside. Place
    the dates, apricots, golden raisins, and sugar in a bowl and stir to mix. Place the flour,
    baking powder, spice, mixed nuts, and seeds in a separate bowl and mix well.
2   Stir the eggs and milk into the fruit, then add the flour mixture and beat together until
    thoroughly mixed. Spoon the mixture into the loaf pan and level the top.
3   Bake the loaf for about 1 hour, or until firm to the touch and lightly browned.
4   Remove the bread from the oven and let cool in the pan for a few minutes, then turn onto
    a wire rack. Serve warm or cold in slices.

VARIATIONS *If you can't find gluten-free self-rising flour, simply use 1½ cups gluten-free all-purpose
flour with a total of 2 teaspoons of gluten-free baking powder. Use ready-to-eat dried figs, pitted
prunes, or peaches in place of the apricots. Use walnuts in place of pecans.*

294 Tropical quick bread

PREPARATION TIME *20 minutes* **COOKING TIME** *1 hour* **MAKES** *1 loaf (serves 8–10)*

1½ cups gluten-free all-purpose flour
2 teaspoons gluten-free baking powder
1 stick butter, diced
⅔ cup light soft brown sugar
2 teaspoons ground pudding spice
1 teaspoon ground cinnamon

2⅓ cups mixed ready-to-eat dried
  tropical fruit (such as pitted dates,
  apricots, mango, pineapple,
  and papaya), chopped
2 eggs, beaten
⅔ cup milk

1   Preheat the oven to 180°C/350°F/gas mark 4. Grease a 2lb loaf pan and set aside. Sift the
    flour and baking powder into a bowl, then lightly rub in the butter. Stir in the sugar, spices,
    and dried fruit.
2   Add the eggs and milk and mix together until thoroughly combined. Spoon the mixture into
    the loaf pan and level the top.
3   Bake the loaf for about 1 hour, or until firm to the touch and lightly browned—a cake
    tester inserted in the center should come out clean. Cover the bread loosely with foil
    toward the end of the cooking time if the top is browning too quickly.
4   Remove the bread from the oven and let cool in the pan for a few minutes, then turn onto
    a wire rack. Serve warm or cold in thick slices.

VARIATION *Use a mixture of other dried fruits such as dried cranberries, cherries or blueberries, and
golden raisins or raisins in place of the tropical fruits.*

295 Lemon drizzle loaf

PREPARATION TIME *20 minutes* **COOKING TIME** *40–45 minutes* **MAKES** *1 loaf (serves 8–10)*

1½ sticks butter, softened
1 cup light soft brown sugar
3 eggs, beaten
Finely grated zest and juice of 1 lemon

1¼ cups gluten-free all-purpose flour
1 teaspoon gluten-free baking powder
¼ cup granulated sugar

1 Preheat the oven to 180°C/350°F/gas mark 4. Grease a 2lb loaf pan and set aside. Cream the butter and soft brown sugar together in a bowl until pale and fluffy. Gradually beat in the eggs, then beat in the lemon zest.
2 Sift the flour and baking powder into the bowl, then fold into the creamed mixture until well mixed. Transfer the mixture to the loaf pan and level the top.
3 Bake the loaf for 40–45 minutes, or until risen and golden brown—a cake tester inserted in the center should come out clean.
4 Meanwhile, mix together the lemon juice and granulated sugar in a small bowl.
5 Remove the loaf from the oven and place on a wire rack. Pour the lemon mixture evenly over the top of the hot loaf. Let the loaf cool completely in the pan. Once cool, turn and serve in slices.

VARIATION *Use the finely grated zest and juice of 1 small orange in place of the lemon.*

296 Banana bread

PREPARATION TIME *20 minutes* **COOKING TIME** *1–1¼ hours* **MAKES** *1 loaf (serves 10)*

1 stick butter, softened
½ cup light soft brown sugar
⅓ cup thick-set honey
2 eggs, beaten
1½ cups gluten-free all-purpose flour
1½ teaspoons gluten-free baking powder

1 teaspoon ground cinnamon
2 large bananas (total weight of bananas
   with skin = about 1lb)
A squeeze of lemon juice
½ cup walnuts, chopped

1 Preheat the oven to 180°C/350°F/gas mark 4. Grease and line a 2lb loaf pan and set aside. Place the butter, sugar, and honey in a bowl and beat together until light and fluffy. Gradually beat in the eggs, then fold in the flour, baking powder, and cinnamon.
2 Peel the bananas and mash the flesh with a little lemon juice. Fold the mashed bananas and walnuts into the bread mixture until well mixed, then spoon the mixture into the loaf pan and level the top.
3 Bake for 1–1¼ hours, or until risen, golden brown, and firm to touch. Cover loosely with foil toward the end of the cooking time if the top is browning too quickly.
4 Remove the bread from the oven and let cool in the pan for a few minutes, then turn onto a wire rack. Serve warm or cold in slices.

VARIATION *Use pecans, raisins, or chopped pitted dried dates in place of walnuts.*

297 Cinnamon golden raisin loaf

PREPARATION TIME *20 minutes* **COOKING TIME** *1 hour* **MAKES** *1 loaf (serves 8–10)*

1½ cups gluten-free all-purpose flour
2 teaspoons gluten-free baking powder
1 stick butter, diced
⅔ cup light soft brown sugar
1 tablespoon ground cinnamon

1⅓ cup golden raisins
1 cup ready-to-eat dried apricots, chopped
2 eggs, beaten
⅔ cup milk

1 Preheat the oven to 180°C/350°F/gas mark 4. Grease a 2lb loaf pan and set aside. Sift the flour and baking powder into a bowl, then lightly rub in the butter. Stir in the sugar, cinnamon, and dried fruit.

2 Add the eggs and milk and mix together until thoroughly combined. Spoon the mixture into the loaf pan and level the top.

3 Bake the loaf for about 1 hour, or until firm to the touch, and lightly browned—a cake tester inserted in the center should come out clean. Cover the loaf loosely with foil toward the end of the cooking time if the top is browning too quickly.

4 Remove the loaf from the oven and let cool in the pan for a few minutes, then turn onto a wire rack. Serve warm or cold in thick slices.

VARIATIONS *Use raisins in place of golden raisins, and dried cranberries or blueberries in place of apricots. Use ground pudding spice or ginger in place of cinnamon.*

298 Fruit and spice scones

PREPARATION TIME *15 minutes* **COOKING TIME** *10 minutes* **MAKES** *about 8 scones*

1½ cups gluten-free all-purpose flour
A pinch of salt
2 teaspoons gluten-free baking powder
½ stick butter, diced
2 tablespoons superfine sugar

½ cup golden raisins
1 teaspoon ground cinnamon
About ⅔ cup milk, plus extra for glazing

1 Preheat the oven to 220°C/425°F/gas mark 7. Grease or flour a cookie sheet and set aside. Sift the flour, salt, and baking powder into a bowl, then lightly rub in the butter until the mixture resembles bread crumbs. Stir in the sugar, golden raisins, and cinnamon, then stir in enough milk, mixing to form a fairly soft dough.

2 Turn the dough onto a lightly floured worktop and knead lightly. Roll out the dough to a ¾ inch thickness and cut into rounds using a 2½-inch fluted or plain cutter. Place the scones on the cookie sheet, leaving a little space between each one, then brush the tops with milk.

3 Bake the scones for about 10 minutes, or until risen and golden brown. Transfer to a wire rack to cool. Serve warm.

VARIATION *Use chopped ready-to-eat dried apricots in place of golden raisins.*

299 Spiced apple scone round

PREPARATION TIME *20 minutes* **COOKING TIME** *25–30 minutes* **SERVES** *8*

1½ cups gluten-free all-purpose flour
A pinch of salt
2 teaspoons baking powder
½ stick butter, diced
⅔ cup light soft brown sugar
1½ teaspoons ground cinnamon

1 large cooking apple (about 12oz in weight), peeled, cored, and coarsely grated
1 egg, beaten
Milk, for glazing
1 tablespoon raw brown sugar

1 Preheat the oven to 200°C/400°F/gas mark 6. Grease or flour a cookie sheet and set aside. Sift the flour, salt, and baking powder into a bowl, then lightly rub in the butter until the mixture resembles bread crumbs.
2 Stir in the soft brown sugar and cinnamon, then add the grated apple and mix well. Stir in enough egg to form a soft but not sticky dough.
3 Turn the dough onto a lightly floured worktop, knead lightly, then shape into a 7-inch round.
4 Place the scone round on the cookie sheet, brush the top with milk, and sprinkle over the raw brown sugar. Using a sharp knife, mark the top of the scone round into 8 even wedges, cutting fairly deeply into the dough.
5 Bake the scone round for 25–30 minutes, or until risen and golden brown. Transfer to a wire rack to cool. Break into wedges and serve warm.

300 Zesty apricot muffins

PREPARATION TIME *20 minutes* **COOKING TIME** *15–20 minutes*
MAKES *8 large or 12 medium-sized muffins*

1 cup gluten-free cornmeal
¾ cup rice flour
1 tablespoon gluten-free baking powder
A pinch of salt
½ stick butter, melted
⅓ cup superfine sugar

1 egg, beaten
1 cup milk
Finely grated zest of 1 orange
⅔ cup ready-to-eat dried apricots, chopped

1 Preheat the oven to 200°C/400°F/gas mark 6. Grease 8 or 12 cups of a 12-cup muffin pan or line each cup with a paper muffin case and set aside. Place the cornmeal, rice flour, baking powder, and salt in a bowl and stir to mix.
2 Mix together the melted butter, sugar, egg, milk, and orange zest and pour over the dry ingredients. Fold the ingredients together gently—just enough to combine them. The mixture will look quite lumpy, which is correct as over-mixing will result in heavy muffins.
3 Fold in the apricots, then spoon the mixture into the prepared muffin cups, dividing it evenly between each one.
4 Bake the muffins for 15–20 minutes, or until risen and golden brown. Transfer to a wire rack to cool. Serve warm or cold.

VARIATIONS *Use raisins or dried cranberries in place of the apricots. Use the finely grated zest of 1 lemon in place of orange zest. Use light soft brown sugar in place of superfine sugar.*

301 Apple ginger muffins

PREPARATION TIME *20 minutes* **COOKING TIME** *15–20 minutes*
MAKES *8 large or 12 medium-sized muffins*

1 cup gluten-free cornmeal	**⅓ cup light soft brown sugar**
¾ cup rice flour	**1 egg, beaten**
1 tablespoon gluten-free baking powder	**1 cup milk**
A pinch of salt	**1 small cooking apple (peeled and cored**
1½ teaspoons ground ginger	**weight), chopped**
½ stick butter, melted	

1   Preheat the oven to 200°C/400°F/gas mark 6. Grease 8 or 12 cups of a 12-cup muffin pan or line each cup with a paper muffin case and set aside. Place the cornmeal, rice flour, baking powder, salt, and ginger in a bowl and stir to mix.
2   Mix together the melted butter, sugar, egg, and milk and pour over the dry ingredients. Fold the ingredients together gently—just enough to combine them. The mixture will look quite lumpy, which is correct as over-mixing will result in heavy muffins.
3   Fold in the chopped apple, then spoon the mixture into the prepared muffin cups, dividing it evenly between each one.
4   Bake the muffins for 15–20 minutes, or until risen and golden brown. Transfer to a wire rack to cool. Serve warm or cold.

VARIATIONS *Use fresh raspberries or blackberries in place of chopped apple. Use ground cinnamon or pudding spice in place of ginger.*

302 Blueberry and lemon muffins

PREPARATION TIME *20 minutes* **COOKING TIME** *15–20 minutes*
MAKES *8 large or 12 medium-sized muffins*

1 cup gluten-free cornmeal	**1 egg, beaten**
¾ cup rice flour	**1 cup milk**
1 tablespoon gluten-free baking powder	**Finely grated zest of 1 lemon**
A pinch of salt	**⅓ cup dried blueberries**
½ stick butter, melted	**⅓ cup dried cranberries**
⅔ cup light soft brown sugar	

1   Preheat the oven to 200°C/400°F/gas mark 6. Grease 8 or 12 cups of a 12-cup muffin pan or line each cup with a paper muffin case and set aside. Place the cornmeal, rice flour, baking powder, and salt in a bowl and stir to mix.
2   Mix together the melted butter, sugar, egg, milk, and lemon zest and pour over the dry ingredients. Fold the ingredients together gently—just enough to combine them. The mixture will look quite lumpy, which is correct as over-mixing will result in heavy muffins.
3   Fold in the blueberries and cranberries, then spoon the mixture into the prepared muffin cups, dividing it evenly between each one.
4   Bake the muffins for 15–20 minutes, or until risen and golden brown. Transfer to a wire rack to cool. Serve warm or cold.

VARIATIONS *Use dried cherries, halved, or chopped ready-to-eat dried apricots in place of cranberries. Use the finely grated zest of 1 small orange or 1½ teaspoons ground cinnamon in place of lemon zest.*

303 🍞 Basic gluten-free white loaf

PREPARATION TIME *10 minutes* **COOKING TIME** *varies according to breadmaker*
MAKES *1 medium loaf (serves 10–12)*

1¼ cups milk (at room temperature)
4 tablespoons sunflower oil
2 eggs, lightly beaten
3 cups gluten-free white bread flour

2 tablespoons superfine sugar
1 teaspoon salt
1 sachet (¼oz) fast-action dried yeast

1   Please note, breadmakers vary, so add the ingredients to the bread pan in the order specified in your instruction booklet (if this differs from the instructions given here). Place the milk in a bowl, add the oil and eggs, and whisk together until well mixed.

2   Pour the milk mixture into the breadmaker pan. Sprinkle over the flour, covering the liquid completely. Sprinkle the sugar evenly over the flour, then add the salt. Make a small indent in the center of the flour and add the yeast.

3   Close the lid, set the machine to the program recommended in the manual (usually Rapid Bake setting gives the best results), select size of loaf and type of crust, and press Start. A couple of minutes after mixing has begun, lift the lid of the machine briefly and scrape down the sides of the pan with a plastic spatula to ensure even mixing. Close the lid once again.

4   Once the baking cycle has finished, remove the bread pan from the machine and turn the loaf onto a wire rack to cool. Serve in slices.

304 🍞 Gluten-free wholewheat bread

PREPARATION TIME *10 minutes* **COOKING TIME** *varies according to breadmaker*
MAKES *1 medium loaf (serves 10–12)*

1¼ cups milk (at room temperature)
4 tablespoons sunflower oil
2 eggs, lightly beaten
3 cups gluten-free wholewheat

bread flour
2 tablespoons superfine sugar
1 teaspoon salt
1 sachet (¼oz) fast-action dried yeast

1   Please note, breadmakers vary, so add the ingredients to the bread pan in the order specified in your instruction booklet (if this differs from the instructions given here). Place the milk in a bowl, add the oil and eggs, and whisk together until well mixed.

2   Pour the milk mixture into the breadmaker pan. Sprinkle over the flour, covering the liquid completely. Sprinkle the sugar evenly over the flour, then add the salt. Make a small indent in the center of the flour and add the yeast.

3   Close the lid, set the machine to the program recommended in the manual (usually Rapid Bake setting gives the best results), select size of loaf and type of crust, and press Start. A couple of minutes after mixing has begun, lift the lid of the machine briefly and scrape down the sides of the pan with a plastic spatula to ensure even mixing. Close the lid once again.

4   Once the baking cycle has finished, remove the bread pan from the machine and turn the loaf onto a wire rack to cool. Serve in slices.

TIPS *If the cooked loaf looks pale in color, brush the top with a little melted butter or oil and broil for a few minutes until lightly browned. Alternately, brush the top of the hot loaf with a little beaten egg white, then sprinkle with seeds (such as sesame or poppy seeds) for savory bread, and crushed sugar lumps, raw brown sugar, or toasted shredded unsweetened coconut for sweet breads.*

305 ◉ Fresh herb bread

PREPARATION TIME *15 minutes*   **COOKING TIME** *varies according to breadmaker*
MAKES *1 medium loaf (serves 10–12)*

3 cups gluten-free white bread flour
½ cup gram (garbanzo) flour
⅓ cup water
2 eggs, beaten
4 tablespoons olive oil
4 tablespoons chopped fresh mixed herbs (parsley, basil, oregano, and chives)
½ cup fresh Parmesan cheese, finely grated
1 tablespoon superfine sugar
1½ teaspoons salt
2½ teaspoons fast-action dried yeast

1. Please note, breadmakers vary, so add the ingredients to the bread pan in the order specified in your instruction booklet (if this differs from the instructions given here). Mix the flours together and set aside. Place the water in a bowl, add the eggs, oil, and chopped herbs, and whisk together until well mixed.
2. Pour the water mixture into the breadmaker pan. Sprinkle over the Parmesan cheese, then the flours, covering the liquid completely. Sprinkle the sugar evenly over the flour, then add the salt. Make a small indent in the center of the flour and add the yeast.
3. Close the lid, set the machine to the program recommended in the manual (usually Rapid Bake setting gives the best results), select size of loaf and type of crust, and press Start. A couple of minutes after mixing has begun, lift the lid of the machine and scrape down the sides of the pan with a plastic spatula to ensure even mixing. Close the lid once again.
4. Once the baking cycle has finished, remove the bread pan from the machine and turn the loaf onto a wire rack to cool. Serve in slices.

306 ▣ Herbed olive bread

PREPARATION TIME *15 minutes* **COOKING TIME** *varies according to breadmaker*
MAKES *1 medium loaf (serves 10–12)*

1⅓ cups milk (at room temperature)
4 tablespoons olive oil
2 eggs, lightly beaten
2 teaspoons dried Italian
   herb seasoning
¾ cup fresh Parmesan cheese,
   finely grated

½ cup pitted black olives (drained
   weight), chopped
3 cups gluten-free wholewheat
   bread flour
2 tablespoons superfine sugar
1 teaspoon salt
1 sachet (¼oz) fast-action dried yeast

1 Please note, breadmakers vary, so add the ingredients to the bread pan in the order specified in your instruction booklet (if this differs from the instructions given here). Place the milk in a bowl, add the oil, eggs, and dried herbs, and whisk together until well mixed.

2 Pour the milk mixture into the breadmaker pan. Sprinkle the Parmesan cheese over the milk, followed by the olives. Sprinkle over the flour, covering the liquid, cheese, and olives completely. Sprinkle the sugar evenly over the flour, then add the salt. Make a small indent in the center of the flour and add the yeast.

3 Close the lid, set the machine to the program recommended in the manual (usually Rapid Bake setting gives the best results), select size of loaf and type of crust, and press Start. A couple of minutes after mixing has begun, lift the lid of the machine briefly and scrape down the sides of the pan with a plastic spatula to ensure even mixing. Close the lid once again.

4 Once the baking cycle has finished, remove the bread pan from the machine and turn the loaf onto a wire rack to cool. Serve in slices.

307 ▣ Mixed seed loaf

PREPARATION TIME *10 minutes* **COOKING TIME** *varies according to breadmaker*
MAKES *1 medium loaf (serves 10–12)*

1⅓ cups milk (at room temperature)
4 tablespoons sunflower oil
2 eggs, lightly beaten
3 cups gluten-free white
   bread flour

5 tablespoons mixed seeds such as
   sunflower, pumpkin, caraway, poppy
   seeds, and linseeds
2 tablespoons superfine sugar
1 teaspoon salt
1 sachet (¼oz) fast-action dried yeast

1 Please note, breadmakers vary, so add the ingredients to the bread pan in the order specified in your instruction booklet (if this differs from the instructions given here). Place the milk in a bowl, add the oil and eggs, and whisk together until well mixed.

2 Pour the milk mixture into the breadmaker pan. Sprinkle over the flour, covering the liquid completely. Sprinkle the mixed seeds evenly over the flour, then add the sugar and salt. Make a small indent in the center of the flour and add the yeast.

3 Close the lid, set the machine to the program recommended in the manual (usually Rapid Bake setting gives the best results), select size of loaf and type of crust, and press Start. A couple of minutes after mixing has begun, lift the lid of the machine briefly and scrape down the sides of the pan with a plastic spatula to ensure even mixing. Close the lid once again.

4 Once the baking cycle has finished, remove the bread pan from the machine and turn the loaf onto a wire rack to cool. Serve in slices.

308 ▣Italian tomato bread

PREPARATION TIME *15 minutes* **COOKING TIME** *varies according to breadmaker*
MAKES *1 medium loaf (serves 10–12)*

1⅓ cups milk (at room temperature)
2 tablespoons sun-dried tomato oil (from a jar of sun-dried tomatoes)
2 tablespoons olive oil
2 eggs, lightly beaten
½ cup fresh Parmesan cheese, finely grated

¾ cup sun-dried tomatoes in oil (drained weight), patted dry and chopped
3 cups gluten-free wholewheat bread flour
2 tablespoons superfine sugar
1 teaspoon salt
1 sachet (¼oz) fast-action dried yeast

1 Please note, breadmakers vary, so add the ingredients to the bread pan in the order specified in your instruction booklet (if this differs from the instructions given here). Place the milk in a bowl, add the oils and eggs, and whisk together until well mixed.

2 Pour the milk mixture into the breadmaker pan. Sprinkle the Parmesan cheese over the milk, followed by the sun-dried tomatoes. Sprinkle over the flour, covering the liquid, cheese, and tomatoes completely. Sprinkle the sugar evenly over the flour, then add the salt. Make a small indent in the center of the flour and add the yeast.

3 Close the lid, set the machine to the program recommended in the manual (usually Rapid Bake setting gives the best results), select size of loaf and type of crust, and press Start. A couple of minutes after mixing has begun, lift the lid of the machine briefly and scrape down the sides of the pan with a plastic spatula to ensure even mixing. Close the lid once again.

4 Once the baking cycle has finished, remove the bread pan from the machine and turn the loaf onto a wire rack to cool. Serve in slices.

309 ▣Cheese and mustard bread

PREPARATION TIME *15 minutes* **COOKING TIME** *varies according to breadmaker*
MAKES *1 medium loaf (serves 10–12)*

3 cups gluten-free white bread flour
½ cup gram (garbanzo) flour
1¼ cups water
2 eggs, beaten
4 tablespoons olive oil
3 tablespoons gluten-free wholegrain mustard

¾ cup mature cheddar cheese, finely grated
1 tablespoon superfine sugar
1½ teaspoons salt
2½ teaspoons fast-action dried yeast

1 Please note, breadmakers vary, so add the ingredients to the bread pan in the order specified in your instruction booklet (if this differs from the instructions given here). Mix the flours together and set aside. Place the water in a bowl, add the eggs, oil, and mustard, and whisk together until well mixed.

2 Pour the water mixture into the breadmaker pan. Sprinkle over the cheese, then sprinkle over the flours, covering the liquid completely. Sprinkle the sugar evenly over the flour, then add the salt. Make a small indent in the center of the flour and add the yeast.

3 Close the lid, set the machine to the program recommended in the manual (usually Rapid Bake setting gives the best results), select size of loaf and type of crust, and press Start. A couple of minutes after mixing has begun, lift the lid of the machine briefly and scrape down the sides of the pan with a plastic spatula to ensure even mixing. Close the lid once again.

4 Once the baking cycle has finished, remove the bread pan from the machine and turn the loaf onto a wire rack to cool. Serve in slices.

310 🍞Spiced honey loaf

PREPARATION TIME *20 minutes, plus cooling* **COOKING TIME** *50–60 minutes* **MAKES** *1 loaf (serves 8)*

½ cup light soft brown sugar
¾ stick butter
½ cup thick-set honey
1½ cups gluten-free all-purpose flour
A pinch of salt

1 teaspoon gluten-free baking powder
2 teaspoons ground ginger
1 egg, beaten
⅔ cup milk

1 Remove the kneading blade from the bread pan and grease and line the base and sides of the pan. Place the sugar, butter, and honey in a saucepan and heat gently until melted, stirring. Remove the pan from the heat and cool slightly.

2 Sift the flour, salt, baking powder, and ginger into a bowl and make a well in the center. Mix together the egg and milk and pour into the center of the dry ingredients together with the melted honey mixture. Beat together using a wooden spoon until smooth and thoroughly mixed. Pour into the pan.

3 Place the bread pan in position in the machine and close the lid. Select the Bake Only setting and enter 50 minutes on the timer. Press Start. After baking, a cake tester inserted in the center of the loaf should come out clean. If the loaf requires further baking, select the same program as before and enter a further 5–10 minutes on the timer, or until the loaf is cooked.

4 Remove the bread pan from the machine using oven gloves, then let stand for 5 minutes, before turning the loaf onto a wire rack to cool. Serve warm or cold in slices.

VARIATIONS *Use light corn syrup in place of honey. Use ground cinnamon in place of ground ginger.*

311 🍞Sticky spiced loaf

PREPARATION TIME *20 minutes, plus cooling* **COOKING TIME** *50–60 minutes* **MAKES** *1 loaf (serves 8)*

½ cup light soft brown sugar
¾ stick butter
⅓ cup light corn syrup
¼ cup molasses
1½ cups gluten-free all-purpose flour
A pinch of salt

1 teaspoon gluten-free baking powder
2 teaspoons ground pudding spice
1 teaspoon ground ginger
1 egg, beaten
⅔ cup milk

1 Remove the kneading blade from the bread pan and grease and line the base and sides of the pan. Place the sugar, butter, syrup, and molasses in a saucepan and heat gently until melted, stirring. Remove the pan from the heat and cool slightly.

2 Sift the flour, salt, baking powder, and ground spices into a bowl and make a well in the center. Mix together the egg and milk and pour into the center of the dry ingredients together with the melted syrup mixture. Beat together using a wooden spoon until smooth and thoroughly mixed. Pour into the pan.

3 Place the bread pan in position in the machine and close the lid. Select the Bake Only setting and enter 50 minutes on the timer. Press Start. After baking, a cake tester inserted in the center of the loaf should come out clean. If the loaf requires further baking, select the same program as before and enter a further 5–10 minutes on the timer, or until the loaf is cooked.

4 Remove the bread pan from the machine using oven gloves, then let stand for 5 minutes, before turning the loaf onto a wire rack to cool. Serve warm or cold in slices.

VARIATION *Use ground cinnamon in place of ginger.*

312 📖Apricot and cranberry loaf

PREPARATION TIME *20 minutes* **COOKING TIME** *1–1¼ hours* **MAKES** *1 loaf (serves 10)*

1½ cups gluten-free all-purpose flour	1 cup ready-to-eat dried apricots,
2 teaspoons gluten-free baking powder	chopped
1 stick butter, diced	1 cup dried cranberries
½ cup light soft brown sugar	2 eggs, beaten
Finely grated zest of 1 small orange	⅔ cup milk

1   Remove the kneading blade from the bread pan and grease and line the base and sides of the pan. Sift the flour and baking powder into a bowl, then lightly rub in the butter. Stir in the sugar, orange zest, and dried fruit. Add the eggs and milk and mix together until thoroughly combined. Spoon the mixture into the pan and level the top.

2   Place the bread pan in position in the machine and close the lid. Select the Bake Only setting and enter 60 minutes on the timer. Press Start. After baking, a cake tester inserted in the center of the loaf should come out clean. If the loaf requires further baking, select the same program as before and enter a further 10–15 minutes on the timer, or until the loaf is cooked.

3   Remove the bread pan from the machine using oven gloves, then let stand for 5 minutes, before turning the loaf onto a wire rack to cool. Serve warm or cold in slices.

VARIATIONS *Use golden raisins or dried cherries in place of cranberries. Use the finely grated zest of 1 lemon in place of orange zest.*

CHAPTER 7
Bread dishes

As well as being delicious in its own right, bread can also be used as a versatile ingredient in many sweet and savory dishes. Some of the classic, everyday recipes in this chapter will be familiar to you, whereas other more adventurous recipes may be less so.

We include a tempting selection of tasty recipes, all of which use bread as an ingredient. We also include a small selection of recipes that use gluten-free bread as an ingredient, to appeal to those with a sensitivity to gluten.

Choose from basic recipes such as Croûtons, Melba Toast, or Hot Garlic Bread, as well as tasty snacks including French Onion Soup, Broiled Vegetable Bruschetta, or Mushroom Pâté. Children will love Chicken and Sesame Nuggets, Tuna Melts, or Spiced Beef and Carrot Burgers. Or you can select from a range of sweet treats such as Spiced Apricot Bread and Butter Pudding, Treacle Lattice Tart, or Brown Bread Ice Cream.

313 Croûtons

PREPARATION TIME *10 minutes* **COOKING TIME** *5–10 minutes* **SERVES** *4–6*

3–4 thick slices of day-old white bread   **Sunflower oil, for shallow-frying**

1 Trim the crusts from the bread slices and discard. Cut the bread into ½-inch cubes.
2 Heat a ½-inch depth of oil in a skillet until hot. Add the bread cubes and cook over a medium heat, turning continuously, until crisp and golden.
3 Remove the croûtons from the oil using a slotted spoon and drain on paper towels. Serve warm or cold.

VARIATIONS *Croûtons can be made in advance, cooled, and stored in an airtight container until ready to use. Use flavored bread such as sun-dried tomato bread or herb bread to make croûtons. Other types of bread such as wholewheat bread also make good croûtons. Add 1 crushed garlic clove to the oil for extra flavor.*

314 Oven-baked croûtons

PREPARATION TIME *10 minutes* **COOKING TIME** *15 minutes* **SERVES** *4–6*

3–4 thick slices of day-old sun-dried tomato bread   **Sun-dried tomato oil (from a jar of sun-dried tomatoes), for coating**

1 Preheat the oven to 200°C/400°F/gas mark 6. Trim the crusts from the bread slices and discard. Cut the bread into 1-inch cubes, then toss the bread cubes in the oil, coating them all over.
2 Place the bread cubes in a single layer on a cookie sheet or in a shallow roasting pan and bake for about 15 minutes, or until crisp and golden all over, turning once.
3 Remove from the oven. Drain the croûtons on paper towels and serve warm or cold.

VARIATIONS *Use sunflower, olive, or chili oil in place of sun-dried tomato oil. Use olive bread and olive oil or walnut bread and walnut oil in place of sun-dried tomato bread and oil.*

315 Parmesan croûtons

PREPARATION TIME *10 minutes* **COOKING TIME** *5–10 minutes* **SERVES** *4–6*

3–4 thick slices of day-old white regular or gluten-free bread
Sunflower oil, for shallow-frying
     ¼ cup fresh Parmesan cheese, finely grated

1 Trim the crusts from the bread slices and discard. Cut the bread into ½-inch cubes.
2 Heat a ½-inch depth of oil in a skillet until hot. Add the bread cubes and cook over a medium heat, turning continuously, until crisp and golden.
3 Remove the croûtons from the oil using a slotted spoon and drain on paper towels. While still warm, toss the croûtons in the Parmesan cheese, coating them all over. Serve warm or cold.

316 Melba toast

PREPARATION TIME *10 minutes* **COOKING TIME** *10 minutes* **SERVES** *4–6*

**4 thick slices of white or
wholewheat bread**

1 Preheat the broiler to high. Broil the bread slices on both sides. Quickly cut off and discard the crusts using a serrated knife, then slide the knife between the broiled edges and split each slice horizontally in half.
2 Cut each piece of bread into 4 triangles, then place them under the broiler again, uncooked-side uppermost, and broil until golden and crispy and the edges begin to curl.
3 Serve immediately or let cool, then store in an airtight container until ready to use. Warm through in the oven before serving.

VARIATION *Sprinkle the cut sides of toast with a little finely grated fresh Parmesan cheese, before broiling again, if desired.*

317　French toast

PREPARATION TIME *10 minutes* **COOKING TIME** *10–15 minutes* **SERVES** *2–4*

4 slices of white regular or gluten-free bread	A good pinch of freshly grated nutmeg or ground cinnamon
2 eggs	½ stick butter
⅔ cup milk	1–2 tablespoons sunflower oil
	Superfine sugar, for sprinkling

1　Trim the crusts from the bread slices and discard. Cut each slice of bread into 4 even fingers. Beat the eggs, milk, and nutmeg or cinnamon together in a bowl. Dip the bread fingers into this mixture, coating them all over.

2　Melt half the butter with 1 tablespoon oil in a large, heavy-bottomed skillet. When the butter is foaming, add half the bread fingers and fry until golden brown, turning once.

3　Remove the bread fingers from the pan, drain on paper towels, and keep hot. Add the remaining butter to the pan with more oil, if needed. Add the remaining bread fingers and fry as before, then drain.

4　Serve the French toast hot, sprinkled with a little superfine sugar

.

318　Hot garlic bread

PREPARATION TIME *15 minutes* **COOKING TIME** *15–20 minutes* **SERVES** *8–10*

1 large French baguette	3 cloves garlic, crushed
1–1½ sticks butter, softened	Sea salt and freshly ground black pepper

1　Preheat the oven to 180°C/350°F/gas mark 4. Using a bread knife, cut the loaf crosswise into 1-inch thick slices, almost to the base of the loaf.

2　Cream the butter in a bowl until soft, then add the garlic and salt and pepper to taste, and beat together to mix.

3　Spread the garlic butter liberally between each bread slice, then wrap the loaf loosely in foil and place on a cookie sheet.

4　Bake the loaf for 15–20 minutes, or until hot and the butter has melted into the bread. Serve warm, cut into slices.

319　Cheesy garlic bread

PREPARATION TIME *15 minutes* **COOKING TIME** *15 minutes* **MAKES** *2 loaves (each loaf serves 4–6)*

1 stick butter, softened	1 cup cheddar cheese, grated
3 cloves garlic, crushed	2 French sticks, each about 12 inches in length
2 tablespoons finely chopped fresh parsley	

1　Preheat the oven to 200°C/400°F/gas mark 6. Place the butter, garlic, and parsley in a bowl and beat together until well blended. Stir in the cheese and mix well.

2　Using a bread knife, make deep cuts across each loaf, at regular intervals (about ½ inch apart), almost to the base of the loaves. Spread some cheese mixture over each side of the bread slices. Wrap each loaf loosely in foil and place on a cookie sheet.

3　Bake the loaves for 10 minutes, then open up the foil and bake for a further 5 minutes, or until the cheese and butter mixture is melted, and the bread is crisp. Serve warm, cut into slices.

320 Broiled vegetable bruschetta

PREPARATION TIME *15 minutes* **COOKING TIME** *15 minutes* **SERVES** *4 (makes 8 bruschetta)*

1 red or yellow bell pepper, seeded
  and sliced into strips
1 zucchini, halved and thinly sliced
  lengthwise
1 red onion, thinly sliced
2 large plum or vine tomatoes,
  thickly sliced
1 tablespoon olive oil, plus extra
  for drizzling

2 teaspoons (gluten-free) wholegrain
  mustard
Sea salt and freshly ground black
  pepper, to taste
1 ciabatta loaf, cut into 8 equal portions
  (or 8 slices from a large French
  baguette) or 8 slices of gluten-free
  bread
1 clove garlic, halved
Shredded fresh basil leaves, to garnish

1 Preheat the broiler to high and line the broiler rack with foil. Place the bell pepper,
   zucchini, onion, and tomatoes in a large bowl. Whisk together the oil, mustard, and
   seasoning, then drizzle this mixture over the vegetables and toss gently to mix.
2 Spread the vegetables in a single layer on the broiler rack. Broil for 4–5 minutes on each
   side, or until lightly browned. Set aside and keep warm. (If your broiler pan is not big
   enough to broil all the vegetables at one time, do this stage in 2 batches and keep the
   first batch of broiled vegetables warm while cooking the second batch.)
3 Toast the bread slices on both sides under the broiler and, while still hot, rub the garlic
   halves over one side of each piece of toast. Divide the broiled vegetables between the
   toast slices, piling them onto the garlicky sides.
4 Drizzle a little olive oil over each slice of bruschetta, garnish with shredded basil, and
   serve immediately with a mixed leaf salad.

321 Tuna and tomato bruschetta

PREPARATION TIME *25 minutes* **COOKING TIME** *10 minutes* **SERVES** *8 (makes 16 bruschetta)*

8oz French stick or baguette (about half
  a large baguette), cut into 16 even
  slices
2 tablespoons olive oil
1 clove garlic, crushed
7oz can tuna in brine or spring water,
  drained
¾ cup canned corn kernels (drained
  weight)

½ red bell pepper, seeded and chopped
2 tablespoons chopped fresh chives
3–4 tablespoons mayonnaise
Freshly ground black pepper, to taste
4 small vine tomatoes, each cut into
  4 slices
Chopped fresh parsley or small
  watercress sprigs, to garnish

1 Preheat the oven to 200°C/400°F/gas mark 6. Place the bread slices on a large cookie
   sheet. Combine the oil and garlic in a small bowl, then lightly brush the tops of the bread
   slices with the oil mixture.
2 Bake for about 10 minutes, or until lightly browned and crisp. Transfer to a wire rack and
   let cool.
3 Flake the tuna into a bowl, then add the corn, red bell pepper, chopped chives,
   mayonnaise, and black pepper and mix well. Spoon some tuna mixture onto each toasted
   bread slice, flattening the mixture slightly.
4 Place 1 tomato slice on top of the tuna mixture, then garnish with chopped parsley or
   watercress sprigs. Arrange on a serving platter and serve immediately with a mixed baby
   leaf salad.

VARIATIONS *Use 2–3 scallions, thinly sliced, in place of corn kernels. Use 1 ciabatta loaf (about
10oz) in place of the French stick. Use canned pink salmon in place of tuna. Use chopped fresh
parsley or basil in place of chives.*

322 Smoked salmon bruschetta

PREPARATION TIME *20 minutes* **COOKING TIME** *5 minutes* **SERVES** *4 (makes 8 bruschetta)*

1 ciabatta loaf, cut into 8 equal slices,
   or 8 thick slices of gluten-free bread
2 tablespoons olive oil
1 clove garlic, crushed (optional)
½ cup full-fat cream cheese
1–2 tablespoons chopped fresh mixed

herbs (such as parsley, chives, and dill)
Sea salt and freshly ground black
   pepper, to taste
8 thin slices of smoked salmon
8 fresh watercress sprigs
12 cherry tomatoes, halved

1 Preheat the broiler to high. Place the bread slices on the rack in a large broiler pan. Mix
   together the oil and garlic, if using, then lightly brush this mixture over one side of the
   bread slices. Toast the bread slices on both sides under the broiler until golden.
2 Mix together the cream cheese, chopped herbs, and seasoning, then spread this mixture
   over the oil-brushed side of each piece of toast. Top each with a slice of smoked salmon,
   a sprig of watercress, and 3 tomato halves.
3 Serve immediately with a lightly dressed mixed watercress and lettuce salad.

VARIATIONS *Use flavored cream cheese, such as garlic and herbs or sun-dried tomato cream
cheese, in place of mixing the cream cheese and fresh herbs. Use French baguette in place of
ciabatta bread. Use smoked trout fillets or thin slices of prosciutto or Parma ham in place of
smoked salmon.*

323 Bread soup (Pancotto)

PREPARATION TIME *25 minutes* **COOKING TIME** *30 minutes* **SERVES** *6*

½ cup extra-virgin olive oil
2 onions, thinly sliced
3 fat cloves garlic, crushed
4 beef tomatoes (about 2lb in total
   weight), skinned, seeded, and
   chopped
6¼ cups vegetable or beef stock
1 cup dry white wine

Sea salt and freshly ground black
   pepper
6 thick slices of wholewheat bread,
   crusts removed
½ cup fresh Parmesan cheese,
   finely grated
3 tablespoons chopped fresh basil
Small fresh basil sprigs, to garnish

1 Heat the oil in a saucepan, add the onions and garlic, and sauté for about 5 minutes, or
   until softened and lightly golden. Add the tomatoes, stock, wine, and seasoning and mix
   well.
2 Bring to the boil gently, then reduce the heat, cover and simmer for 20 minutes, stirring
   occasionally.
3 Tear the bread into ½-inch pieces, then stir the bread into the soup. Simmer for a further
   5 minutes, then remove the pan from the heat, and stir in the Parmesan cheese and
   chopped basil.
4 Set the soup aside for at least 30 minutes. Serve warm or at room temperature (do not
   chill). Ladle into soup bowls to serve and garnish with basil sprigs.

324 French onion soup

PREPARATION TIME *20 minutes* **COOKING TIME** *1 hour 5 minutes* **SERVES** *6*

¾ stick butter
2lb onions, thinly sliced
1 tablespoon superfine sugar
2 tablespoons all-purpose flour
1 cup dry white wine

6¼ cups vegetable or beef stock
Sea salt and freshly ground black
  pepper
6 slices of bread from a French baguette
½ cup gruyère cheese, grated

1   Melt the butter in a large saucepan. Add the onions and sauté for about 5 minutes, or until softened. Sprinkle over the sugar and continue cooking over a low heat, stirring occasionally, for about 25 minutes, or until the onions are soft, golden, and caramelized.

2   Sprinkle the flour over the onions and cook for 1 minute, stirring continuously. Stir in the wine and let it bubble until reduced by half, then stir in the stock and seasoning. Bring to the boil, stirring, then reduce the heat, cover, and simmer for about 35 minutes, stirring occasionally.

3   Meanwhile, make the gruyère cheese croûtes. Preheat the broiler to high. Broil the baguette slices under the broiler on one side, turn them over and sprinkle the gruyère cheese evenly on top of each slice. Cook under the broiler until the cheese has melted.

4   Ladle the soup into warmed bowls and float a gruyère croûte on top of each portion of soup. Serve immediately.

VARIATION *If desired, once the soup is cooked, cool slightly, then purée about one third of the soup in a blender until smooth. Return the puréed soup to the soup in the pan and reheat gently before serving. Alternately, purée all the cooked soup and reheat before serving.*

325 Chèvre en croûte

PREPARATION TIME *10 minutes* **COOKING TIME** *10–15 minutes* **SERVES** *6*

1–2 tablespoons extra-virgin olive oil
1 small clove garlic, crushed
6 slices (each about ½ inch thick) of
   French baguette

4oz goat's cheese (chèvre) log (with
   rind), sliced into 6 even slices
Freshly ground black pepper
Fresh herb sprigs, to garnish

1 Preheat the oven to 180°C/350°F/gas mark 4. Combine the oil and garlic in a small bowl, then brush this mixture over both sides of each baguette slice. Place on a cookie sheet and bake for 5 minutes.

2 Remove from the oven, then place one slice of goat's cheese on each baguette slice. Sprinkle with a little black pepper.

3 Return the toasts to the oven and bake for a further 5–10 minutes, or until the cheese is soft and spongy.

4 Garnish with herb sprigs and serve warm with a mixed leaf salad.

326 Pepper and pesto pitta pizzas

PREPARATION TIME *15 minutes* **COOKING TIME** *10–15 minutes* **SERVES** *4*

4 white or wholewheat pitta breads
3 tablespoons ready-made green pesto
   sauce
4 scallions, finely chopped

4oz roasted bell peppers in oil, drained,
   and cut into thin strips
1 cup gouda cheese, grated
Fresh herb sprigs, to garnish

1 Preheat the oven to 180°C/350°F/gas mark 4. Place the pitta breads on a cookie sheet. Spread the pesto sauce evenly over the top of each pitta.

2 Scatter the scallions over the top of the pitta breads, then arrange the bell pepper strips over the scallions. Sprinkle the cheese over the top.

3 Bake the pizzas for 10–15 minutes, or until the cheese is melted. Cut each pitta pizza in half, garnish with herb sprigs, and serve hot with a lightly dressed, mixed leaf salad.

327 Chicken and zucchini muffin

PREPARATION TIME *10 minutes* **COOKING TIME** *10 minutes* **SERVES** *1*

1 small zucchini, thinly sliced
   lengthwise
1–2 teaspoons olive oil
1 white or wholewheat English muffin
Softened butter, for spreading

Sea salt and freshly ground black pepper
⅓ cooked small chicken breast half (hot
   or cold), sliced
1 tablespoon tomato salsa
Fresh herb sprig, to garnish

1 Preheat the broiler to high. Place the zucchini slices on the rack in a broiler pan and lightly brush all over with oil. Broil for several minutes on each side until lightly browned, but still slightly firm. Remove from the broiler and keep warm.

2 Cut the muffin in half horizontally and toast under the broiler on both sides. Spread the cut-side of both muffin halves with a little butter.

3 Top one muffin half (buttered-side up) with the zucchini slices and season with salt and pepper. Place the chicken over the zucchini and spoon the tomato salsa on top. Place the other muffin half on top, buttered-side down.

4 Cut the muffin in half, garnish with the fresh herb sprig, and serve immediately with a mixed dark leaf salad.

328 Cheese-chili French bread pizzas

PREPARATION TIME *30 minutes* COOKING TIME *20 minutes* SERVES *8*

8oz can bruschetta topping
2 tablespoons tomato paste
1 clove garlic, pressed
1½ cups mushrooms, chopped
2 tablespoons bottled sliced green
   jalapeño chilies, drained and finely
   chopped
2 tablespoons chili oil
1 large French baguette cut into 4 equal
   portions (each portion about 4oz in

weight), each portion then cut in half
   horizontally
1 red bell pepper, seeded and diced
5oz cooked chorizo sausage, thinly
   sliced
1½ cups mozzarella cheese, grated
⅓ cup fresh Parmesan cheese,
   finely grated
Chopped fresh parsley or cilantro,
   to garnish

1   Preheat the oven to 200°C/400°F/gas mark 6. Grease a large cookie sheet and set aside.
    Combine the bruschetta topping, tomato paste, garlic, mushrooms, and chilies in a bowl.
2   Brush a little chili oil over the cut-side of each baguette half, then spread the bruschetta
    topping mixture evenly over the oil-brushed side of each baguette base.
3   Scatter the red bell pepper and chorizo over the top. Sprinkle the grated mozzarella over
    the chorizo, then sprinkle the Parmesan over the top.
4   Transfer to the cookie sheet and bake for about 20 minutes, or until the cheese is melted.
    Sprinkle with chopped parsley or cilantro and serve with a mixed green salad.

VARIATIONS *Use pepperoni in place of chorizo. Use zucchini in place of mushrooms.*

329 Pepperoni muffin pizzas

PREPARATION TIME *25 minutes* COOKING TIME *15 minutes* MAKES *8 muffin pizzas*

4 white or wholewheat English muffins,
   cut in half horizontally
8 tablespoons tomato pizza topping
   sauce (such as tomato with herbs)
1 clove garlic, crushed
2 vine-ripened or plum tomatoes,
   seeded and chopped

½ cup pepperoni, chopped
1½ cups button mushrooms, thinly sliced
1 cup mozzarella cheese, grated
2 tablespoons chopped fresh parsley

1   Preheat the oven to 200°C/400°F/gas mark 6. Grease a large cookie sheet. Place the
    muffin halves, cut-sides uppermost, in a single layer on the cookie sheet.
2   Combine the pizza topping sauce and garlic in a small bowl, then spread some of this
    sauce over the top of each muffin half. Scatter the tomatoes, pepperoni, and mushrooms
    over the tomato sauce. Sprinkle the mozzarella evenly over the top.
3   Bake the muffin pizzas for about 15 minutes, or until the cheese is melted and golden, and
    the muffins are crisp and lightly browned around the edges.
4   Remove the pizzas from the oven and sprinkle a little chopped parsley over each one, to
    garnish. Serve hot or cold with a mixed baby leaf salad.

VARIATIONS *Use white or wholewheat baps in place of muffins. Use lean smoked ham or cooked
chorizo sausage in place of pepperoni. Use chopped scallions or canned (drained) corn kernels in
place of mushrooms. Use cheddar or red leicester cheese in place of mozzarella.*

330 Classic club sandwich

PREPARATION TIME *10 minutes* COOKING TIME *5–6 minutes (for bacon)* MAKES *1 sandwich*

2 slices of bacon
2 slices of wholewheat bread
1 slice of white bread
Softened butter, for spreading
2 tablespoons mayonnaise

1 tomato, sliced
Sea salt and freshly ground black pepper
A few mixed crisp salad leaves
½ cooked chicken breast half, sliced
4 stuffed green olives, to garnish

1 Preheat the broiler to high. Broil the bacon for 5–6 minutes, or until cooked and crispy, turning once. Keep hot. Toast the bread slices on both sides, under the broiler.
2 Butter both slices of wholewheat toast on one side only and butter the white toast on both sides. Spread mayonnaise over the buttered side of both wholewheat slices.
3 To assemble the sandwich, place a slice of wholewheat toast, buttered-side up, on a chopping board. Top with the bacon slices, then place the tomato slices over the bacon. Season with salt and black pepper. Top with the slice of white toast, then arrange the salad leaves and chicken over the toast. Top this with the second slice of wholewheat toast, buttered-side down.
4 Press the sandwich together lightly and cut into quarters. Push a toothpick into each sandwich quarter to hold it together and place a stuffed olive on top of each toothpick, to garnish. Serve immediately.

VARIATION *Use untoasted bread slices to make this sandwich, if desired.*

331 Pan bagna

PREPARATION TIME *20 minutes, plus 3 hours chilling* COOKING TIME *n/a* SERVES *4*

1 large French baguette (about 1lb in total weight)
1½ tablespoons extra-virgin olive oil
2 ripe plum tomatoes, thinly sliced
Sea salt and freshly ground black pepper
1 small yellow bell pepper, seeded and thinly sliced

1 small red onion, thinly sliced
½lb piece fontina or taleggio cheese, thinly sliced
12 pitted black olives, sliced
3 tablespoons fresh basil leaves, shredded

1 Slice the loaf in half lengthwise and brush the cut sides well with olive oil. Lay the tomato slices on one cut-side of the loaf and season well with salt and pepper.
2 Top with the bell pepper slices, then the onion slices, and finally top with the cheese slices. Scatter the sliced olives over the cheese, then sprinkle the basil over the top.
3 Replace the top half of the loaf, cut-side down, and press the halves gently together. Wrap in foil or plastic wrap and chill in the refrigerator for at least 1 hour and preferably for about 3 hours, to allow the flavors to develop.
4 Unwrap and slice across into 4 portions to serve. Alternately, slice across diagonally into thick slices to serve.

VARIATIONS *Use gouda cheese in place of fontina or taleggio. Top the cheese with thinly sliced lean smoked or unsmoked cooked ham, if desired.*

332 Croque monsieur

PREPARATION TIME *10 minutes* **COOKING TIME** *4–6 minutes* **SERVES** *4*

About ½ stick butter, softened, for spreading
8 thin slices of white regular or gluten-free bread

4 slices of lean smoked cooked ham
4 slices of gruyère or Dutch cheese
Freshly ground black pepper, to taste
Fresh flat-leaf parsley sprigs, to garnish

1 Preheat the broiler to high. Butter one side of each bread slice. Use the bread slices to make 4 sandwiches, making each sandwich with a slice of ham and a slice of cheese inside, seasoned with black pepper. Press well together.
2 Toast the sandwiches under the broiler until golden-brown on both sides, turning once.
3 Cut the sandwiches in half diagonally, garnish with parsley sprigs, and serve immediately.

333 Welsh rarebit

PREPARATION TIME *15 minutes* **COOKING TIME** *10 minutes* **SERVES** *4*

1 cup cheddar cheese, grated
1 cup gruyère cheese, grated
2–3 teaspoons French or Dijon mustard
1 egg, beaten
2 tablespoons beer

A good pinch of cayenne pepper
Sea salt and freshly ground black pepper
4 thick slices of bread
Softened butter, for spreading
Chopped fresh parsley, to garnish

1 Preheat the broiler to high. Combine the two cheeses in a bowl, then reserve 3–4 tablespoons and set this aside. Add the mustard, egg, beer, cayenne pepper, and salt and black pepper to the cheese in the bowl and mix well.
2 Toast the bread on both sides under the broiler, then spread the toast with a little butter. Spoon the cheese mixture on to the buttered sides of the toast, dividing it between each one and spreading it evenly, making sure all the edges are covered. Sprinkle over the reserved cheese and broil until lightly browned and bubbling.
3 Sprinkle the rarebits with chopped parsley and serve immediately on their own or with a mixed dark leaf salad.

334 Tuna melts

PREPARATION TIME *10 minutes* **COOKING TIME** *5 minutes* **SERVES** *2*

3½oz can tuna in brine, spring water or oil, drained and flaked
2 tablespoons mayonnaise
1–2 scallions, finely chopped
1 tablespoon finely chopped seeded red bell pepper
1 tablespoon chopped fresh chives

Freshly ground black pepper, to taste
About 3 tablespoons butter, softened
4 slices of white or wholewheat bread
½ cup gruyère or emmental cheese, grated
Fresh herb sprigs, to garnish

1 Preheat the broiler to medium. Place the tuna, mayonnaise, scallions, red bell pepper, chopped chives, and black pepper in a small bowl and mix well. Set aside.
2 Spread butter over one side of each slice of bread. Spread the tuna mixture over the top of 2 slices of bread, buttered-side up. Sprinkle the cheese over the tuna mixture, then place the remaining 2 slices of bread, buttered-side down, on top to make 2 sandwiches.
3 Butter the top of the 2 sandwiches, then place them on the rack in a broiler pan and broil for 1–2 minutes, or until lightly browned on top.
4 Turn the sandwiches over and spread the untoasted side with butter. Place under the broiler for a further 1–2 minutes, or until the bread is lightly browned, and the cheese is beginning to melt.
5 Garnish with herb sprigs and serve immediately with a mixed green salad.

335 Spiced bean picnic loaf

PREPARATION TIME *25 minutes* **COOKING TIME** *1–1¼ hours* **SERVES** *8–10*

14oz can red kidney beans
1 tablespoon olive oil
1 onion, finely chopped
1 clove garlic, crushed
2 cups chestnut or brown cap
   mushrooms, finely chopped
1 teaspoon each of ground cumin,
   ground cilantro, and garam masala

7oz can corn kernels, drained
1½ cups cheddar cheese, grated
2½ cups fresh wholewheat bread crumbs
2 eggs, beaten
2 tablespoons chopped fresh parsley
   or cilantro
Sea salt and freshly ground black
   pepper

1   Preheat the oven to 180°C/350°F/gas mark 4. Grease a 2lb loaf pan and set aside. Place the kidney beans and their juice in a pan and heat gently until hot, stirring occasionally. Drain the beans, rinse in hot water, and drain again. Place the beans in a bowl and mash them while still warm. Set aside.

2   Heat the oil in a skillet, add the onion and garlic, and sauté for about 5 minutes or until softened. Add the mushrooms and sauté for 2–3 minutes, then add the ground spices and sauté for 1 minute.

3   Combine the mashed beans, the onion mixture, and all the remaining ingredients and mix well. Spoon the mixture into the pan and level the top.

4   Bake for 1–1¼ hours, or until firm and lightly browned on top. Cool the loaf in the pan for a few minutes, then turn onto a wire rack. Serve warm or cold in slices with a mixed leaf salad and fresh crusty bread.

336 Stuffed roast bell peppers

PREPARATION TIME *35 minutes* COOKING TIME *30 minutes* SERVES *4*

1 tablespoon olive oil
1 red onion, thinly sliced
1 zucchini, finely chopped
2 cups button mushrooms, sliced
1 clove garlic, crushed
14oz can chopped tomatoes
1 tablespoon tomato paste
½ cup pine nuts

2–3 tablespoons chopped fresh basil
Sea salt and freshly ground black pepper
4 large bell peppers (2 red and 2 yellow)
½ cup mature cheddar cheese, grated
3 tablespoons fresh white or
    wholewheat regular or gluten-free
    bread crumbs
Fresh basil sprigs, to garnish

1   Preheat the oven to 180°C/350°F/gas mark 4. Heat the oil in a pan, add the onion, zucchini, mushrooms, and garlic, and sauté gently for 5 minutes.
2   Stir in the tomatoes and tomato paste, then bring to the boil, reduce the heat and simmer, uncovered, for 10–15 minutes, or until the mixture has thickened slightly. Remove the pan from the heat and stir in the pine nuts, chopped basil, and salt and pepper to taste.
3   Meanwhile, cut the bell peppers in half lengthwise and remove and discard the seeds. Blanch the bell pepper halves in a pan of boiling water for 3 minutes. Drain well.
4   Place the bell pepper halves, cut-side up, in a shallow baking dish and spoon some vegetable mixture into each one, dividing it evenly. Cover with foil and bake for 20 minutes.
5   Remove the foil. Combine the grated cheese and bread crumbs and sprinkle some of this mixture over each bell pepper half. Bake, uncovered, for a further 5–10 minutes, or until the cheese is melted and bubbling.
6   Garnish with basil sprigs and serve immediately with fresh crusty French bread and a mixed dark leaf salad.

337 Tasty nut loaf

PREPARATION TIME *25 minutes* COOKING TIME *50–60 minutes* SERVES *8–10*

1 tablespoon olive oil
6 shallots, finely chopped
1 leek, washed and chopped
2 cloves garlic, crushed
2 stalks celery, finely chopped
½lb mushrooms, chopped
15oz can lentils, rinsed and drained
1 cup mixed nuts, such as hazelnuts,
    cashew nuts, and almonds, finely
    chopped

1 cup fresh white or wholewheat
    regular or gluten-free bread crumbs
½ cup mature cheddar cheese, grated
1 egg, beaten
3–4 tablespoons chopped fresh mixed
    herbs
Sea salt and freshly ground black
    pepper
Fresh herb sprigs, to garnish

1   Preheat the oven to 190°C/375°F/gas mark 5. Grease and line a 2lb loaf pan and set aside. Heat the oil in a saucepan, add the shallots, leek, garlic, celery, and mushrooms, and sauté gently for 10 minutes, or until softened.
2   Add the lentils, mixed nuts, bread crumbs, cheese, egg, chopped herbs, and seasoning and mix thoroughly. Transfer the mixture to the pan and level the top.
3   Bake for 50–60 minutes, or until the loaf is lightly browned and firm to the touch. Cool slightly in the pan, then turn the loaf onto a serving plate, and garnish with herb sprigs. Serve warm or cold in slices with fresh crusty bread and a mixed baby leaf salad.

VARIATIONS *Use fresh Parmesan cheese in place of cheddar. Use 1 red or regular onion in place of shallots.*

338 Mushroom pâté

PREPARATION TIME *30 minutes, plus cooling and chilling* **COOKING TIME** *45–60 minutes*
SERVES *8–10*

1lb chestnut mushrooms, sliced
1 red onion, chopped
2 cloves garlic, crushed
1 red bell pepper, seeded and diced
2 tablespoons vegetable stock
2 tablespoons dry white wine
14oz can red kidney beans, rinsed
   and drained

1 egg, beaten
1 cup fresh wholewheat or white bread
   crumbs
1 tablespoon chopped fresh thyme
1 tablespoon chopped fresh rosemary
Sea salt and freshly ground black
   pepper
Fresh herb sprigs, to garnish

1 Preheat the oven to 180°C/350°F/gas mark 4. Grease and line a 2lb loaf pan and set
   aside. Put the mushrooms, onion, garlic, red bell pepper, stock, and wine in a saucepan.
   Cover and cook gently for about 10 minutes, or until the vegetables are softened, stirring
   occasionally.
2 Remove the pan from the heat and cool slightly, then purée the mixture together with the
   kidney beans, in a blender or food processor, until smooth.
3 Transfer the purée to a bowl, add the egg, bread crumbs, and chopped herbs and mix well.
   Season with salt and pepper to taste. Spoon the mixture into the pan and level the top.
4 Bake the loaf for about 45–60 minutes, or until lightly set and browned on top. Place on a
   wire rack and let cool completely in the pan.
5 Once cool, cover and refrigerate for several hours. Turn the pâté onto a serving plate.
   Garnish with herb sprigs and serve in slices with fresh crusty bread or toast and a mixed
   green salad.

339 Herby mushroom loaf

PREPARATION TIME *30 minutes, plus cooling and chilling* **COOKING TIME** *1 hour* **SERVES** *8–10*

4 tablespoons vegetable stock
1 onion, chopped
2 cloves garlic, crushed
2 stalks celery, chopped
¾lb closed cap mushrooms, sliced
¾lb chestnut or brown cap mushrooms,
   sliced

3–4 tablespoons chopped fresh mixed
   herbs
3 tablespoons ruby port
Sea salt and freshly ground black
   pepper
1½ cups fresh wholewheat bread crumbs
2 eggs, beaten
Fresh herb sprigs, to garnish

1 Preheat the oven to 180°C/350°F/gas mark 4. Grease and line a 2lb loaf pan and set
   aside. Place the stock, onion, garlic, and celery in a saucepan. Cover and cook gently for
   10 minutes, stirring occasionally.
2 Stir in the mixed mushrooms, cover and cook gently for 10 minutes, stirring occasionally.
   Remove the pan from the heat, add the chopped herbs, port, and seasoning, and mix well.
   Set aside to cool slightly, then place the mixture in a blender or food processor and blend
   until smooth.
3 Transfer the mixture to a bowl, add the bread crumbs and eggs, and mix well. Adjust the
   seasoning, transfer to the pan, and level the top.
4 Bake the loaf for about 1 hour, or until set and lightly browned on top. Remove from the
   oven and set aside to cool completely in the pan.
5 Once cool, cover and refrigerate for several hours before serving. To serve, carefully turn
   the loaf onto a serving plate and garnish with herb sprigs. Serve in slices with fresh crusty
   bread or toast.

340 Scallops au gratin

PREPARATION TIME *35 minutes* COOKING TIME *15–25 minutes* SERVES *4*

½ stick butter
4 shallots, finely chopped
2½ tablespoons all-purpose flour
1¼ cups milk
½ cup gruyère cheese, grated
Sea salt and freshly ground black
  pepper

8 large fresh scallops, shelled and
  cleaned, shells scrubbed and reserved
2 cups fresh white or wholewheat bread
  crumbs
2 tablespoons chopped fresh parsley
1 lemon, cut into 8 wedges
Fresh parsley sprigs, to garnish

1 Preheat the oven to 200°C/400°F/gas mark 6. Melt 2 tablespoons butter in a saucepan, add the shallots, and sauté for about 5 minutes, or until softened but not browned. Remove the shallots from the pan using a slotted spoon, place on a plate, and set aside.
2 Place 1½ tablespoons butter in the pan with the flour and milk. Heat gently, whisking continuously, until the sauce comes to the boil and thickens. Simmer gently for 2–3 minutes, stirring occasionally. Remove the pan from the heat, then stir in the cheese. Add seasoning to taste.
3 Spoon a little of the cheese sauce into the base of each scallop shell, then lay a scallop on top. Spoon some shallots around each scallop, then cover with the remaining sauce.
4 Combine the bread crumbs and chopped parsley, then sprinkle this mixture over the sauce. Melt the remaining butter and drizzle a little over each scallop.
5 Bake the scallops for about 15–25 minutes, or until they are just cooked. Garnish with lemon wedges and parsley sprigs and serve.

341 Stuffed mushrooms

PREPARATION TIME *25 minutes* COOKING TIME *15 minutes*
SERVES *4 (makes 8 stuffed mushrooms—serve 2 mushrooms per person)*

8 large field or flat mushrooms
2 tablespoons olive oil
1 small red onion, finely chopped
1 clove garlic, crushed
1 small zucchini, finely chopped
½ small red bell pepper, seeded and
  finely chopped
1 cup fresh white or wholewheat
  regular or gluten-free bread crumbs

2 tablespoons chopped fresh basil
1 tablespoon chopped fresh oregano
  or marjoram
Sea salt and freshly ground black
  pepper
¾ cup fresh Parmesan cheese,
  finely grated
Fresh herb sprigs, to garnish

1 Preheat the oven to 180°C/350°F/gas mark 4. Grease a shallow baking dish or cookie sheet and set aside. Remove the stalks from the mushrooms and chop them finely.
2 Heat the oil in a skillet, add the mushroom stalks, onion, garlic, zucchini, and red bell pepper, and sauté for about 5 minutes, or until softened.
3 Remove the pan from the heat and stir in the bread crumbs, chopped herbs, and seasoning. Place the mushroom caps, hollow-side up, in the dish or on the cookie sheet.
4 Spoon some of the onion mixture into each mushroom cap, dividing it evenly between each one, then sprinkle some Parmesan cheese over the top of each mushroom.
5 Bake for about 15 minutes, or until the mushrooms are tender and the cheese is melted and lightly browned. Garnish with herb sprigs and serve warm.

VARIATIONS *Use chopped fresh flat-leaf parsley or cilantro in place of the basil. Use mozzarella cheese in place of the Parmesan.*

342 Cheese and leek potato cakes

PREPARATION TIME *40 minutes* **COOKING TIME** *25 minutes* **SERVES** *4 (makes 8 potato cakes)*

2lb potatoes, peeled and diced
1 tablespoon sunflower oil
2 leeks, trimmed, washed and thinly
   sliced (about 8oz trimmed weight)
1 teaspoon Dijon mustard
1 cup mature cheddar cheese, grated

1 teaspoon dried herbes de Provence
Sea salt and freshly ground black pepper
All-purpose flour, for shaping
1 egg, beaten
About 1½ cups fresh white or
   wholewheat bread crumbs

1. Preheat the oven to 200°C/400°F/gas mark 6. Grease a cookie sheet and set aside. Cook the potatoes in a saucepan of boiling water for about 15 minutes, or until tender. Drain well and set aside.
2. Meanwhile, heat the oil in a skillet, add the leeks and sauté over a fairly high heat for about 8 minutes or until cooked. Remove the pan from the heat and set aside.
3. Crush the potatoes in their pan, then add the leeks, mustard, cheese, dried herbs, and seasoning and mix well. Divide the mixture into 8 equal portions.
4. Using floured hands, roll each portion into a ball, then press down on each ball to make a flat cake about 1-inch thick and about 2¾ inches in diameter. Brush each cake all over with beaten egg, then sprinkle with bread crumbs to coat evenly.
5. Place the potato cakes on the cookie sheet and bake for about 25 minutes, or until golden brown and crisp, turning once. Serve hot with a fresh mixed seasonal salad.

343 Chicken and sesame nuggets

PREPARATION TIME *15 minutes* **COOKING TIME** *20 minutes* **SERVES** *4–6*

1lb 2oz skinless, boneless chicken
   breast halves
2 eggs, beaten
2 cups fine fresh wholewheat bread
   crumbs

¼ cup sesame seeds
3 tablespoons chopped fresh mixed
   herbs (such as parsley, chives,
   oregano and basil)
3 tablespoons all-purpose flour

1. Preheat the oven to 200°C/400°F/gas mark 6. Grease a cookie sheet and set aside. Cut the chicken into 1-inch cubes and set aside. Beat the eggs with 2 tablespoons water in a dish. Mix together the bread crumbs, sesame seeds, and chopped herbs in a separate dish, and place the flour in a third dish.
2. Dip the chicken cubes firstly in the flour, then in the beaten egg mixture and finally in the bread crumb mixture, ensuring that each piece of chicken is well coated.
3. Place the chicken nuggets on the cookie sheet and bake for about 20 minutes, or until cooked, golden brown and crispy, turning once. Serve hot or cold with a tasty dip or salsa.

VARIATIONS *Use turkey breast in place of chicken breast. Use 1 tablespoon dried mixed herbs in place of fresh herbs.*

344 Spiced beef and carrot burgers

PREPARATION TIME *15 minutes* **COOKING TIME** *10–15 minutes* **SERVES** *4*

1lb lean ground beef
2 carrots, coarsely grated
1½ cups mushrooms, finely chopped
1 large onion, finely chopped
1 cup fresh wholewheat or white
 bread crumbs
2 tablespoons tomato paste

1 egg, lightly beaten
1 clove garlic, crushed
2 teaspoons ground cumin
2 teaspoons ground cilantro
1 teaspoon hot chili powder
Sea salt and freshly ground black
 pepper, to taste

1 Preheat the broiler to medium. Place all the ingredients in a large bowl and mix together thoroughly. Shape the mixture into 4 round, flat burgers, using your hands.
2 Place the burgers on the rack in a broiler pan and broil for about 10–15 minutes, or until the burgers are lightly browned all over and cooked to your liking, turning once.
3 Serve the cooked burgers in white, wholewheat or malted grain baps, topped with salad and fresh salsa or catsup.

VARIATIONS *Use lean ground lamb or pork in place of beef. Use 4–6 shallots in place of onion.*

345 Beef and bean burgers

PREPARATION TIME *20 minutes* **COOKING TIME** *10–15 minutes* **SERVES** *4*

1 cup lean ground beef
1 onion, finely chopped
1 clove garlic, crushed
14oz can red kidney beans, rinsed,
 drained, and mashed
1 cup fresh white or wholewheat bread
 crumbs
1 medium carrot, coarsely grated

1 egg, beaten
1 teaspoon ground cumin
1 teaspoon ground cilantro
1 teaspoon chili powder
3 tablespoons chopped fresh parsley
Sea salt and freshly ground black
 pepper
1–2 tablespoons sunflower oil

1 Place the ground beef, onion, garlic, kidney beans, bread crumbs, carrot, egg, ground spices, chopped parsley, and seasoning in a bowl and mix together thoroughly. On a lightly floured worktop, shape the mixture into 4 round patties and flatten them slightly.
2 Heat the oil in a skillet, add the burgers and cook over a medium heat for about 10–15 minutes, or until lightly browned all over and cooked to your liking, turning once.
3 Serve the cooked burgers in wholewheat or white baps, topped with salad leaves, tomato slices, and catsup.

VARIATIONS *Use lean ground lamb in place of beef. Use canned black-eye beans in place of kidney beans. Use zucchini in place of carrots.*

346 Zucchini and bacon pasta medley

PREPARATION TIME *15 minutes* COOKING TIME *20 minutes* SERVES *4–6*

1 cup dried fusilli pasta
Sea salt and freshly ground black pepper
½ stick butter
2 leeks, washed and sliced
2 zucchini, sliced
1 cup rindless bacon, chopped
4½ tablespoons all-purpose flour
3¾ cups milk

1½ cups mature cheddar cheese, grated
3 tablespoons chopped fresh flat-leaf
   parsley
3 tablespoons fresh wholewheat or
   white bread crumbs
3 tablespoons finely grated fresh
   Parmesan cheese
Fresh parsley sprigs, to garnish

1 Preheat the oven to 200°C/400°F/gas mark 6. Lightly grease a baking dish and set aside. Cook the pasta in a large saucepan of lightly salted, boiling water for 10–12 minutes, or until just cooked or *al dente*. Drain thoroughly, keep warm and set aside.

2 Meanwhile, melt 2 tablespoons butter in a skillet, add the leeks and zucchini and sauté for 5 minutes. Add the bacon and sauté for a further 5 minutes, or until the vegetables and bacon are cooked. Add to the drained pasta, toss to mix, then set aside and keep hot.

3 Put the remaining butter, flour, and milk in a pan and heat gently, whisking continuously, until the sauce is thickened and smooth. Simmer gently for 2–3 minutes, stirring.

4 Remove the pan from the heat and whisk in the cheddar cheese, chopped parsley, and seasoning. Pour the cheese sauce over the pasta mixture and stir gently to mix well. Transfer to the baking dish.

5 Mix the bread crumbs and Parmesan cheese together and sprinkle over the pasta. Bake for about 20 minutes (or place under a preheated broiler for several minutes) until golden brown on top and bubbling. Garnish with parsley sprigs and serve with a mixed salad.

347 Easy three-cheese macaroni

PREPARATION TIME *15 minutes* COOKING TIME *15 minutes* SERVES *4*

1 cup dried short-cut macaroni
Sea salt and freshly ground black pepper
½ stick butter
½ cup all-purpose flour
3 cups milk
2 teaspoons Dijon mustard
1½ cups cheddar or pecorino cheese,
   grated

1 cup mozzarella cheese, finely diced
1 cup fresh Parmesan cheese, finely
   grated
4 tablespoons fresh wholewheat or
   white bread crumbs
Fresh herb sprigs, to garnish

1 Grease a baking dish and set aside. Cook the macaroni in a large saucepan of lightly salted, boiling water for 8–10 minutes, or until just cooked or *al dente*. Drain thoroughly, keep warm and set aside.

2 Meanwhile, melt the butter in a separate pan, then stir in the flour and cook gently for 1 minute, stirring. Gradually whisk in the milk, then add the mustard and cook, whisking continuously, until the sauce is thickened and smooth. Simmer gently for 2–3 minutes, stirring.

3 Remove the pan from the heat and stir in the cheddar or pecorino cheese, the mozzarella, ½ cup Parmesan, and salt and pepper to taste. Add the cooked pasta to the cheese sauce, mix well, then transfer the mixture to the baking dish.

4 Preheat the broiler to high. Mix the remaining Parmesan with the bread crumbs and sprinkle evenly over the macaroni cheese. Place under the broiler for a few minutes, or until golden brown and bubbling.

5 Garnish with herb sprigs and serve with seasonal vegetables such as green beans and baby corn.

VARIATION *Use wholegrain or French mustard in place of Dijon mustard.*

348 Garden vegetable pasta bake

PREPARATION TIME *25 minutes* **COOKING TIME** *20 minutes* **SERVES** *4*

1 cup dried short-cut macaroni
Sea salt and freshly ground black pepper
8oz small broccoli florets
8oz zucchini, sliced
½ stick butter
½ cup all-purpose flour
3¾ cups milk

1½ cups mature cheddar cheese, grated
1 teaspoon Dijon mustard
2 tablespoons chopped fresh parsley
3 tablespoons fresh white or
    wholewheat bread crumbs
Fresh parsley sprigs, to garnish

1 Preheat the oven to 200°C/400°F/gas mark 6. Grease a baking dish and set aside. Cook the macaroni in a saucepan of lightly salted, boiling water for about 10 minutes, or until just tender. Drain thoroughly, keep warm and set aside.

2 Meanwhile, cook the broccoli and zucchini in a saucepan of boiling water for 3–4 minutes, or until just tender. Drain well and keep warm.

3 Place the butter, flour, and milk in a saucepan and heat gently, whisking continuously, until the sauce comes to the boil and thickens. Simmer gently for 2–3 minutes, stirring.

4 Remove the pan from the heat and stir in 1¼ cups cheese, the mustard, chopped parsley, and seasoning. Add the macaroni and vegetables and stir gently to mix. Transfer to the baking dish.

5 Mix the remaining cheese and bread crumbs together and sprinkle over the macaroni.

6 Bake for about 20 minutes, or until golden brown and bubbling. Garnish with parsley sprigs and serve with fresh crusty bread and a mixed garden salad.

VARIATIONS *Use sliced mushrooms in place of the zucchini. Use gruyère cheese in place of cheddar.*

349 Fishcakes with tomato salsa

PREPARATION TIME *15 minutes, plus 30 minutes chilling* COOKING TIME *20–25 minutes*
SERVES *2–4*

For the fishcakes
1 leek, washed and finely chopped
1 cup cold, cooked mashed potatoes
3½oz can pink salmon, drained or flaked
1 tablespoon chopped fresh parsley
A squeeze of fresh lemon juice
Sea salt and freshly ground black
 pepper
1 egg, beaten

About 1½ cups fresh wholewheat
 bread crumbs, for coating
Sunflower oil, for frying

For the tomato salsa
3 plum tomatoes, skinned, seeded,
 and finely chopped
1 tablespoon tomato catsup
1 tablespoon chopped fresh parsley

1 To make the fishcakes, cook the leek in a small pan of boiling water for about 10 minutes, or until tender. Drain well and squeeze out any excess water.
2 Mix the mashed potatoes with the leeks. Add the salmon, chopped parsley, lemon juice, and seasoning to the potato mixture and mix well.
3 On a lightly floured worktop, shape the mixture into 8 fish shapes or small round patties and flatten them slightly. Dip each fishcake in the beaten egg and then in the bread crumbs, coating them all over. Place on a plate, cover and refrigerate for 30 minutes.
4 Heat a little oil in a large skillet, add the fishcakes and cook over a medium heat until crisp and golden on both sides, turning once.
5 Meanwhile, make the tomato salsa. Combine the chopped tomatoes, tomato catsup and chopped parsley in a bowl, mixing well. Season to taste with salt and pepper.
6 Serve the fishcakes with the tomato salsa spooned alongside. Serve with baked potatoes and seasonal vegetables such as baby carrots and peas.

350 Fish goujons with herby sauce

PREPARATION TIME *20 minutes, plus 15 minutes chilling* COOKING TIME *10–15 minutes* SERVES *4*

For the fish goujons
1lb skinless, boneless cod or haddock
 fillet, cut into thin strips
2 tablespoons plain white flour
About 1¼ cups natural or wholewheat
 dry bread crumbs
1 teaspoon dried mixed herbs
2 eggs, beaten
½ stick butter

For the herby sauce
1½ tablespoons butter
2½ tablespoons all-purpose flour
1¼ cups milk
½ cup mature cheddar cheese, grated
1 teaspoon Dijon mustard
3 tablespoons chopped fresh mixed
 herbs (such as parsley, oregano,
 thyme and chives)
Sea salt and freshly ground black pepper
Fresh herb sprigs, to garnish

1 Make the fish goujons. Dip the fish strips in the flour, covering them completely, then shake off any excess flour. Mix together the bread crumbs and dried herbs and set aside. Dip the floured fish strips in the beaten egg, then roll in the bread crumb mixture, coating the fish strips completely. Place on a plate and chill in the refrigerator for 15 minutes.
2 Melt the butter in a large skillet, add the fish and cook over a medium heat for 8–10 minutes, or until cooked and golden brown, turning occasionally.
3 Meanwhile, make the herby sauce. Put the butter, flour, and milk in a saucepan. Heat gently, whisking continuously, until the sauce is thickened and smooth. Simmer gently for 2–3 minutes, stirring.
4 Remove the pan from the heat, stir in the cheese, mustard, and chopped herbs and season to taste with salt and pepper.
5 Serve the fish goujons with the herby sauce alongside and garnish with herb sprigs. Serve with seasonal vegetables such as new potatoes and green beans.

351 Baked stuffed trout

PREPARATION TIME *20 minutes* COOKING TIME *30–40 minutes* SERVES *4*

1 tablespoon olive oil
1 small onion, finely chopped
1½ cups fresh shiitake or oyster mushrooms, finely chopped
½ cup fresh white or wholewheat bread crumbs
¼ cup hazelnuts or almonds, finely chopped
Finely grated zest of 1 small lemon
1 tablespoon chopped fresh parsley
Sea salt and freshly ground black pepper
4 rainbow trout, each weighing about 10oz, gutted and cleaned, with heads and tails left on
Juice of 2 lemons
Fresh parsley sprigs, to garnish

1 Preheat the oven to 180°C/350°F/gas mark 4. Heat the oil in a saucepan, add the onion and mushrooms and sauté for about 5 minutes, or until softened.
2 Remove the pan from the heat, add the bread crumbs, chopped nuts, lemon zest, chopped parsley, and seasoning, and mix well.
3 Spoon some of the bread crumb mixture into each trout, dividing it evenly between each one. Place the trout side-by-side in a shallow baking dish and drizzle the lemon juice over the fish.
4 Cover with foil and bake for 30–40 minutes, or until the fish is cooked and the flesh just flakes when tested with a fork.
5 Garnish with parsley sprigs. Serve with baked potato wedges and seasonal vegetables such as broccoli florets and baby carrots.

VARIATIONS *Use button mushrooms in place of shiitake or oyster mushrooms. Use walnuts or pistachios in place of hazelnuts.*

352 Chicken cordon bleu

PREPARATION TIME *25 minutes, plus 20 minutes chilling* COOKING TIME *30–40 minutes* SERVES *4*

4 skinless, boneless chicken breast halves (about 1¼lb in total weight)
4 thin slices of gruyère or gouda cheese
4 thin slices of lean smoked cooked ham
4 sage leaves (optional)
Sea salt and freshly ground black pepper
1 egg, beaten
2 cups fresh white bread crumbs
2 tablespoons butter
2 tablespoons sunflower oil

1 Place each chicken breast between 2 sheets of waxed paper and pound to a thickness of about ⅛ inch using a rolling pin.
2 Place 1 slice of cheese on one half of each of the flattened chicken breasts and top with 1 slice of ham. Shred the sage leaves, if using, and sprinkle over the ham. Season with salt and pepper.
3 Fold the plain half of each chicken breast over the filling to enclose it completely. Secure each one with 1–2 wooden toothpicks.
4 Dip each folded chicken breast in beaten egg, then dip into the bread crumbs, ensuring each one is covered completely. Place on a plate and chill in the refrigerator for 20 minutes.
5 Heat the butter and oil in a large skillet until the butter is melted. Add the stuffed chicken breasts and cook gently for about 30–40 minutes, or until the chicken is thoroughly cooked and the bread crumb coating is crisp and golden, turning occasionally.
6 Remove the chicken from the pan and drain on paper towels. Serve immediately with baked potatoes and char-broiled mixed vegetables.

353 Cheese and broccoli strata

PREPARATION TIME *30 minutes, plus 30 minutes standing* **COOKING TIME** *1 hour* **SERVES** *4–6*

2 tablespoons butter	**4 eggs**
1 onion, finely chopped	**2½ cups milk**
10oz small broccoli florets	**2 tablespoons chopped fresh chives**
¼lb green beans, halved	**2 tablespoons chopped fresh parsley**
7oz can corn kernels, drained	**1 cup mature cheddar cheese, grated**
Sea salt and freshly ground black pepper	**Fresh herb sprigs, to garnish**
9 thick slices of white bread, crusts removed and slices cut in half	

1   Grease a deep baking dish and set aside. Melt the butter in a skillet, add the onion and sauté for about 5 minutes, or until softened.

2   Meanwhile, cook the broccoli and green beans in a pan of boiling water for 3–4 minutes, or until just tender. Drain well, then stir into the sautéed onion together with the corn, and season to taste with salt and pepper.

3   Arrange 6 of the bread slice halves side by side in the baking dish. Top with half of the broccoli mixture. Repeat the layers of bread and broccoli, then finish with a layer of bread.

4   Whisk together the eggs, milk, and chopped herbs, and season to taste. Pour the egg mixture evenly over the layered bread and vegetables, then sprinkle the cheese over the top. Set aside for 30 minutes, to let the bread soak up some of the liquid.

5   Meanwhile, preheat the oven to 180°C/350°F/gas mark 4. Bake the bread pudding for about 1 hour, or until set, puffy and golden brown. Garnish with herb sprigs and serve with oven-roasted mixed vegetables such as zucchini, bell peppers, and mushrooms.

354 Golden gruyère bread pudding

PREPARATION TIME *25 minutes, plus 30 minutes standing* **COOKING TIME** *40 minutes* **SERVES** *6*

2 cups milk	**Sea salt and freshly ground black pepper**
⅔ cup light cream	**8oz French baguette, cut into 1-inch thick slices**
3 eggs	
¼ cup fresh Parmesan cheese, finely grated	**About 2 tablespoons butter, softened**
1 teaspoon paprika	**2 cups gruyère cheese, grated**
	Fresh herb sprigs, to garnish

1   Grease a 3½-pint baking dish and set aside. Pour the milk and cream into a bowl. Add the eggs, Parmesan cheese, paprika, and seasoning and whisk together until well mixed. Set aside.

2   Thinly spread one side of each bread slice with a little butter. Place half of the bread slices, buttered-side up, in the baking dish, then sprinkle two-thirds of the gruyère cheese over the bread. Top with the remaining bread slices, buttered-side up.

3   Pour over the egg and milk mixture and press the bread gently into the milk. Sprinkle over the remaining gruyère cheese, then set aside and let stand for 30 minutes, to let the bread absorb most of the liquid.

4   Meanwhile, preheat the oven to 200°C/400°F/gas mark 6. Place the dish in a roasting pan and pour enough boiling water into the pan to come halfway up the sides of the dish.

5   Bake the pudding for about 40 minutes, or until puffed up, lightly set and deep golden brown. Cover loosely with foil toward the end of the cooking time if the top is browning too quickly. Garnish with herb sprigs and serve hot with a selection of seasonal vegetables such as peas, carrots, and green beans.

VARIATIONS *Use emmental cheese in place of gruyère. Use country-style bread in place of French baguette. Use milk in place of cream.*

355 Traditional bread sauce

PREPARATION TIME *10 minutes, plus 30 minutes infusing* **COOKING TIME** *15 minutes* **SERVES** *4–6*

4 whole cloves	**About ¾ cup fresh white regular or**
1 small onion, peeled	**gluten-free bread crumbs**
6 peppercorns	**1 tablespoon butter, diced**
1 small bay leaf	**Sea salt and freshly ground black pepper**
1 fresh thyme sprig	**Freshly grated nutmeg (optional)**
1¼ cups milk	**2 tablespoons light cream**

1 Press the cloves into the whole onion. Place the clove-studded onion in a saucepan with the peppercorns, bay leaf, fresh thyme, and milk. Bring gently to the boil, then remove the pan from the heat and set aside to infuse for 30 minutes.
2 Strain the milk into a clean pan. Discard the onion, spices, and herbs. Stir the bread crumbs into the milk, then bring gently to the boil and simmer for 5–10 minutes, or until thickened, stirring.
3 Stir in the butter until melted, then season to taste with salt and pepper. Add a little grated nutmeg, if desired. Stir in the cream just before serving. Serve hot with traditional roast turkey and all the trimmings.

356 Stuffing mixes

PREPARATION TIME *15 minutes* **COOKING TIME** *30–40 minutes*
Each quantity of stuffing serves 4–6

Shallot and cranberry	**1 cup fresh or frozen (defrosted)**
2 tablespoons butter	**cranberries**
3 shallots, finely chopped	**2 tablespoons chopped fresh cilantro**
3 cups fresh wholewheat	**Sea salt and freshly ground black pepper**
bread crumbs	**1 egg, beaten**

1 Melt the butter in a pan, add the shallots and sauté for about 5 minutes, or until softened.
2 Transfer the sautéed shallots to a bowl. Add the bread crumbs, cranberries, chopped cilantro, seasoning, and egg and mix well. Let cool.
3 Use the stuffing to stuff whole medium-sized birds such as chicken, duck, or turkey. Weigh the stuffed bird and calculate the cooking time according to the recipe.
4 Alternately, put the stuffing mixture into a greased baking dish and dot the surface with butter (about 1oz). Bake in a preheated oven at 180°C/350°F/gas mark 4 for 40 minutes, or until cooked and lightly browned. This stuffing is also good with roast lamb.

Lemon, herb, and hazelnut	**1 tablespoon chopped fresh thyme**
2 tablespoons olive oil	**Finely grated zest of 1 lemon**
1 red onion, finely chopped	**⅓ cup toasted hazelnuts, finely chopped**
1 clove garlic, crushed	**Sea salt and freshly ground black**
2 cups fresh white or wholewheat	**pepper**
bread crumbs	**1 small egg, beaten, to combine**
2 tablespoons chopped fresh flat-leaf	
parsley	

1 Heat the oil in a pan, add the onion and garlic and sauté for about 5 minutes, or until softened.
2 Transfer the onion mixture to a bowl and let cool. Once cool, add the bread crumbs, chopped herbs, lemon zest, hazelnuts, and seasoning. Add enough egg, mixing to bind the ingredients together.
3 Serve as suggested in steps 3 and 4 of the stuffing recipe above, but bake for only 30 minutes, or until cooked and lightly browned. This stuffing is also good with roast pork.

357 Apricot bread and butter pudding

PREPARATION TIME *15 minutes, plus 30 minutes standing* **COOKING TIME** *45 minutes* **SERVES** *4–6*

6 medium slices of white or wholewheat bread
½ stick butter, softened
⅔ cup ready-to-eat dried apricots, finely chopped

3 tablespoons light soft brown sugar
1½ teaspoons ground cinnamon
2 eggs
2½ cups milk

1   Lightly grease a baking dish and set aside. Spread one side of each bread slice with butter, then cut each slice into 4 triangles. Arrange half of the bread triangles in the base of the baking dish, buttered-side up. Sprinkle the apricots over the top.

2   Mix together the sugar and cinnamon and sprinkle half of this over the apricots. Arrange the remaining bread triangles over the top, buttered-side up, then sprinkle with the remaining sugar and spice mixture.

3   Beat together the eggs and milk and pour evenly over the bread. Set aside for 30 minutes to let the bread absorb some of the liquid.

4   Meanwhile, preheat the oven to 180°C/350°F/gas mark 4. Bake the bread pudding for about 45 minutes, or until lightly set and golden brown. Serve warm or cold on its own or with custard, cream or ice cream.

VARIATION *Use golden raisins or raisins in place of dried apricots.*

358 Traditional bread pudding

PREPARATION TIME *25 minutes, plus 20 minutes soaking* **COOKING TIME** *50 minutes* **SERVES** *6*

2 cups milk	**½ cup golden raisins**
½ stick butter, diced	**½ cup dried currants**
½ cup soft brown sugar	**2 teaspoons ground pudding spice**
⅓lb leftover (stale) brown wholewheat	**2 eggs, lightly beaten**
bread (crusts removed), diced	**1½ tablespoons raw brown sugar**

1   Grease a 11 x 7-inch shallow baking dish or baking pan and set aside. Pour the milk into a saucepan, add the butter and soft brown sugar, then heat gently, stirring, until the mixture just comes to the boil.

2   Place the bread cubes in a bowl, then pour over the milk mixture and stir to mix well. Let soak for about 20 minutes, or until the bread has absorbed all of the liquid, stirring occasionally.

3   Meanwhile, preheat the oven to 180°C/350°F/gas mark 4. Add the golden raisins, dried currants, pudding spice, and eggs to the bread mixture and beat to mix well.

4   Transfer the mixture to the baking dish or pan and level the top. Bake the pudding for about 50 minutes, or until set and golden brown. Sprinkle with raw brown sugar, cut into squares and serve hot or cold.

VARIATION *Use dried blueberries or chopped ready-to-eat dried apricots in place of golden raisins or dried currants.*

359 Yummy chocolate bread pudding

PREPARATION TIME *25 minutes, plus 30 minutes standing* **COOKING TIME** *45 minutes* **SERVES** *4–6*

4oz semisweet chocolate, broken into	**2 tablespoons cocoa powder, sifted**
squares	**2 tablespoons superfine sugar**
¾ stick butter, softened	**3 eggs**
6 medium slices of white bread	**Grated semisweet chocolate, to serve**
⅔ cup raisins	**(optional)**
2½ cups milk	

1   Grease a 7-cup baking dish and set aside. Place the chocolate and 2 tablespoons butter in a small heatproof bowl. Place the bowl over a saucepan of simmering water and leave until the mixture is melted and combined, stirring one or two times. Remove from the heat.

2   Thickly spread one side of each slice of bread with the remaining butter. Spread the melted chocolate mixture on top. Cut the bread into small triangles or squares. Place one third of the bread triangles, chocolate-side up, in the baking dish.

3   Sprinkle with half the raisins. Top with another third of the bread triangles, then sprinkle with the remaining raisins. Top with the remaining bread triangles, chocolate-side up.

4   Pour ⅔ cup milk into a saucepan and heat gently until almost boiling. Remove the pan from the heat, then whisk the cocoa powder and sugar into the hot milk until well mixed. Pour the hot chocolate milk into a jug and whisk in the remaining cold milk.

5   Beat the eggs and chocolate milk together, then strain into the dish over the bread. Let stand for 30 minutes, so the bread absorbs some of the liquid.

6   Meanwhile, preheat the oven to 180°C/350°F/gas mark 4. Bake the bread pudding for about 45 minutes, or until lightly set. Sprinkle with grated chocolate, if desired, and serve with cream, crème fraîche, or Greek-style plain yogurt.

VARIATIONS *Use sliced brioche or fruit bread in place of white bread. Use golden raisins, dried cherries, or chopped ready-to-eat dried apricots in place of raisins.*

360 Apple and cinnamon brown betty

PREPARATION TIME *25 minutes* **COOKING TIME** *50 minutes* **SERVES** *6*

3 tablespoons butter
3 cups fresh white or wholewheat
    regular or gluten-free bread crumbs
2lb cooking apples, peeled, cored and
    thinly sliced

½ cup superfine sugar
1 tablespoon apple juice
2 teaspoons ground cinnamon
1–2 tablespoons raw brown sugar

1 Preheat the oven to 200°C/400°F/gas mark 6. Grease a deep 7½-cup ovenproof soufflé dish (about 7 inches in diameter). Melt the butter in a skillet over a medium heat, add the bread crumbs and cook for about 5 minutes, or until the crumbs are crisp and golden, stirring. Remove the pan from the heat and set aside.

2 Place the apples in a bowl, add the superfine sugar, apple juice, and cinnamon. Toss to mix.

3 Spoon one-quarter of the bread crumb mixture over the base of the soufflé dish, spreading it evenly. Spoon half of the apple mixture into the dish and cover with another quarter of the bread crumb mixture.

4 Spoon the remaining apple mixture and any juices over the bread crumbs, then finally cover with the remaining bread crumbs. Sprinkle with the raw brown sugar.

5 Cover the dish with foil and bake for 20 minutes. Remove the foil and bake for a further 30 minutes, or until the apples are tender and the topping is golden brown. Serve hot on its own or with whipped cream, ice cream, or custard.

VARIATIONS *Use other prepared sliced fresh fruits such as pears or plums in place of apples. Use ground ginger in place of cinnamon.*

361 Treacle lattice tart

PREPARATION TIME *25 minutes* **COOKING TIME** *35 minutes* **SERVES** *8*

9oz ready-made shortcrust pastry
1 cup light corn syrup
2 tablespoons butter
Finely grated zest and juice of 1 lemon

7oz fresh white or wholewheat
    bread crumbs
A little milk, for glazing

1 Preheat the oven to 190°C/375°F/gas mark 5. Roll out the pastry on a lightly floured worktop and use it to line a 10-inch loose-bottomed tart pan. Set aside. Reserve the pastry trimmings.

2 Gently heat the syrup in a saucepan with the butter and lemon zest and juice, until melted and combined, stirring. Remove the pan from the heat, then stir in the bread crumbs, mixing well. Spoon the bread crumb mixture into the pastry case and level the top.

3 Roll out and make strips from the left-over pastry trimmings and place these over the tart in a lattice pattern (twisting them as you go, if desired), brushing the ends with milk so they stick to the pastry case. Brush the pastry lattice with a little milk, if desired.

4 Bake the tart for about 35 minutes, or until the pastry is golden brown and the filling is just set. Cool in the pan for a few minutes, then turn onto a serving plate. Cut into slices and serve warm or cold with whipped cream, ice cream, or custard.

362　Brown bread ice cream

PREPARATION TIME *20 minutes, plus freezing* **COOKING TIME** *10 minutes* **SERVES** *4–6*

2½ cups fresh wholewheat bread
　crumbs
⅓ cup light soft brown sugar
2 cups ready-made cold custard
　(regular or low-fat)

⅔ cup Greek-style plain yogurt
Finely grated zest and juice of 1 lemon
¼ cup confectioners' sugar, sifted
Thinly pared lemon zest, to decorate

1　Preheat the oven to 200°C/400°F/gas mark 6. Grease a cookie sheet. Spread the bread crumbs over the cookie sheet and sprinkle the brown sugar over the top. Bake for about 10 minutes, stirring occasionally, until the sugar caramelizes and the bread crumbs are crisp. Remove from the oven and set aside to cool. Once cool, break up the crumbs roughly with a fork and set aside.

2　Combine the custard, yogurt, finely grated lemon zest and juice, and confectioners' sugar in a bowl, mixing well. Pour the mixture into a chilled, shallow plastic container, spreading it evenly. Cover and freeze for about 1½–2 hours, or until the mixture is mushy in consistency.

3　Turn the mixture into a chilled bowl and beat with a fork or whisk to break down the ice crystals. Fold in the toasted bread crumbs evenly. Return the mixture to the container and freeze until firm.

4　Transfer the ice cream to the refrigerator for about 30 minutes before serving, to soften slightly. Serve in scoops. Decorate with thinly pared lemon zest and serve with chocolate wafers or scrolls or fresh fruit such as raspberries.

VARIATION *Use heavy cream, whipped until it forms soft peaks, in place of the Greek-style yogurt, if desired.*

363 Summer pudding

PREPARATION TIME *30 minutes, plus chilling* **COOKING TIME** *10 minutes* **SERVES** *6–8*

1lb 2oz mixed summer fruits such as
blackcurrants, blueberries,
loganberries, redcurrants, and
cherries (pitted)
⅔ cup superfine sugar
2¼ cups raspberries

2 tablespoons crème de cassis
(blackcurrant) or framboise
(raspberry) liqueur
8 medium slices of wholewheat or white
bread (one day old), crusts removed
Fresh redcurrant sprigs and mint leaves,
to decorate

1   Place the mixed fruits in a saucepan with the sugar and 5 tablespoons water. Bring gently
    to the boil, stirring until the sugar has dissolved, then simmer gently for about 5 minutes,
    or until the juices begin to run and the fruit is just tender. Remove the pan from the heat,
    stir in the raspberries and liqueur and set aside.
2   Cut a round from one slice of bread to fit the bottom of a 5-cup pudding bowl and use this
    to line the bottom of the bowl. Cut the remaining bread slices in half, reserve 4 halves for
    the top and use the rest to line the sides of the bowl, making sure the bread fits snugly
    together, leaving no gaps.
3   Reserve about ½ cup of the fruit juices, then spoon all the fruit and remaining juices into
    the bread-lined bowl. Cover the top of the fruit completely with the reserved bread slices,
    pressing down lightly and shaping the bread to fit.
4   Cover the pudding with a saucer that is small enough to just fit inside the top of the bowl,
    then set a 1lb weight (a large can of food is ideal) on top of the saucer. Cool, then chill in
    the refrigerator for about 8 hours or overnight.
5   Remove the weight and saucer and loosen around the edges of the pudding using a round-
    bladed knife. Place a serving plate on top of the bowl, hold the two firmly and invert the
    pudding onto the plate, shaking the bowl sharply two times to release the pudding.
6   Spoon a little of the reserved juices over the pudding, concentrating on pale patches, then
    decorate with redcurrant sprigs and mint leaves. Cut into wedges to serve and spoon any
    remaining juices over each portion. Serve with whipped cream or crème fraîche.

364 Raspberry monmouth pudding

PREPARATION TIME *25 minutes* **COOKING TIME** *45 minutes* **SERVES** *6*

1 cup milk	**⅓ cup raspberry jelly**
2 cups fresh white bread crumbs	**3 eggs, separated**
2 tablespoons butter, softened	**½ cup superfine sugar**
Finely grated zest of 1 lemon	**Sifted confectioners' sugar, to dust**

1   Preheat the oven to 140°C/275°F/gas mark 1. Grease a 5-cup baking dish and set aside. Pour the milk into a saucepan and heat gently until almost boiling. Remove the pan from the heat.
2   Place the bread crumbs in a bowl and pour over the hot milk. Stir in the butter and lemon zest and set aside to cool slightly.
3   Spread the raspberry jelly evenly over the base of the baking dish and set aside.
4   Add the egg yolks to the bread crumb mixture and mix well. In a separate bowl, whisk the egg whites until stiff, then whisk in the superfine sugar.
5   Gently fold the whisked egg whites into the bread crumb mixture. Spoon the bread crumb mixture evenly over the layer of jelly.
6   Bake in the oven for about 45 minutes, or until the pudding is set and pale golden. Remove from the oven, cool slightly, then dust with sifted confectioners' sugar. Serve warm.

VARIATIONS *Crush 1¼ cups fresh raspberries with 3 tablespoons superfine sugar and spread over the base of the dish in place of raspberry jelly, if desired. Use the finely grated zest of 1 small orange in place of lemon zest.*

365 Traditional christmas pudding

PREPARATION TIME *30 minutes* **COOKING TIME** *5–6 hours initial steaming, plus 2–4 hours further steaming* **MAKES** *1 pudding (serves 6–8)*

4 cups fresh white bread crumbs	**⅓ cup candied peel**
½ cup all-purpose flour	**½ cup flaked or chopped almonds**
2 cups shredded suet	**Finely grated zest and juice of 1 lemon**
1¼ cups light soft brown sugar	**1 apple/carrot, peeled, cored, and grated**
1¼ cups golden raisins	**4 eggs, beaten**
1¼ cups dried currants	**3 tablespoons sherry, rum or brandy**

1   Grease a 6¼–6½-cup heatproof pudding bowl, line the base with non-stick baking paper and set aside. Place the bread crumbs, flour, suet, sugar, golden raisins, dried currants, candied peel, almonds, lemon zest and juice, and grated apple or carrot in a large bowl and stir until well mixed.
2   Add the eggs to the fruit mixture together with the sherry, rum, or brandy and mix thoroughly.
3   Fill the bowl with the mixture, pressing down well. Cover the top of the pudding with a disc of waxed paper, then cover the bowl with waxed paper and foil, pleat them in the center and secure under the rim with string.
4   Place the bowl in the top of a steamer. Steam the pudding over a pan of gently simmering water for 5–6 hours (remember to top up the boiling water periodically so that the pan doesn't boil dry).
5   Remove the steamed pudding from the steamer and set aside to cool completely. Once cold, re-cover the pudding with fresh waxed paper and foil and store in a cool, dry, dark place for 6–8 weeks.
6   On Christmas Day, steam the pudding, as before, for 2–4 hours. Turn the pudding onto a warmed serving plate, cut into wedges and serve with brandy butter or brandy sauce.

Index

A

apple
    and apricot scone wedges 144
    and cinnamon brown betty 234
    and cinnamon pull-apart 101
    and cinnamon scone round 143
    ginger muffins 201
    loaf, spiced 149
    scone round, spiced 200
apricot
    and almond ring 84
    bread and butter pudding 232
    chelsea buns, spiced 92
    and cranberry quick bread 207
    and date breakfast loaf 152
    and lemon muffins 165
    Mini apricot scones 145
    and golden raisin quick bread 153
    and walnut quick bread 189
    zesty muffins 200

B

bacon
    and cheese bread 43
    and stilton pull-apart 139
    Blue cheese and bacon quiche 114
    Cheese and bacon bread 182
    Cheesy bacon muffins 169
    Classic club sandwich 218
    Zucchini and bacon pasta medley 226
Bagels 70, sesame 183
bananas
    Banana bread 198
    Banana chip muesli loaf 186
    Banana and date loaf 153
    Banana and honey loaf 150
    Banana pecan muffins 162
    Banana raisin bran loaf 156
    Chocolate banana bread 157
    Gingered banana bread 152
    Wholewheat banana muffins 165
Bannock, Selkirk 102
Barley bread 34
Barm brack 103
basil
    Tomato and basil tear 'n' share 138
    Tomato and fresh basil loaf 45
beans
    Beef and bean burgers 225
    Mushroom pâté 222
    Spiced bean picnic loaf 220
beef
    Beef and bean burgers 225
    Spiced beef and carrot burgers 225
Beer bread 130
Blackberry streusel muffins 168
Blini with smoked salmon 121
Bloomer 29
blueberries
    Blueberry wedges 146
    Fresh blueberry muffins 160
    Lemon blueberry loaf 187
Braided herb bread 37
Braided three-seed ring 33
Bread and butter pudding, apricot 232
bread pudding
    Traditional bread pudding 233
    Yummy chocolate bread pudding 233
Brioche 74
    Orange and cinnamon brioche 75
    Sally lunn 97
broccoli, Cheese and broccoli strata 230
bruschetta
    Broiled vegetable 213
    Smoked salmon 214
    Tuna and tomato 213
Buchty 77
Buckwheat and rice bread 193
burgers

Beef and bean 225
    Spiced beef and carrot 225
Buttermilk scones 140

C

carrots, Spiced beef and carrot burgers 225
celery
    Celery and walnut loaf 133
Challah 80
Chapatis 109
cheese
    Bacon and cheese bread 43
    Bacon and stilton pull-apart 139
    Blue cheese and bacon quiche 114
    Caraway cheese loaf 40
    Cheddar, herb, and onion bread 129
    and bacon bread 182
    and broccoli strata 230
    and celery loaf 132
    and date bread 130
    and grain cobb 41
    and herb tear 'n' share 105
    and leek potato cakes 224
    and mustard bread 205
    and olive bread 183
    and pineapple squares 138
    and poppyseed bread 42
    and seed bread 195
    and sesame seed cobb 41
    Cheese-chili French bread pizzas 217
    Cheesy bacon muffins 169
    Cheesy garlic bread 212
    Cheesy onion cornbread 192
    Cheesy pear scones 140
    Croque monsieur 219
    Easy three-cheese macaroni 226
    Festive cheese and fruit scone ring 143
    Garlic bubble ring 68
    Golden cheddar twists 65
    Golden cheesy breads 43
    Gruyère cheese twists 134
    Golden gruyère bread pudding 230
    Hot cheese triangles 137
    Mini parmesan scones 140
    Parmesan herb bread 194
    Parmesan herb twist 134
    Parmesan sesame swizzle sticks 135
    Pesto parmesan pull-apart 104
    Quick cheese and herb bread 132
    Rustic cheesy herb bread 129
    Welsh rarebit 219
    Wholewheat cheese scones 141
Chelsea buns 91
    Spiced apricot chelsea buns 92
cherries (fresh, dried, or candied)
    Cherry coconut scones 145
    Cherry and cranberry swirls 101
    Cherry and hazelnut twists 71
    Cherry kirsch savarin 74
    Cherry and walnut muffins 167
Chèvre en croûte 216
chicken
    Chicken cordon bleu 229
    Chicken and zucchini muffin 216
    Chicken and sesame nuggets 224
    Classic club sandwich 218
chilies
    Cheese-chili French bread pizzas 217
    Chili cornbread 192
chocolate
    Chocolate banana bread 157
    Chocolate bread 57
    Chocolate hazelnut loaf 85
    Double chocolate chip muffins 163
    Marbled chocolate quick bread 188

Mini chocolate chip muffins 169
    Pains au chocolat 93
    Yummy chocolate bread pudding 233
Christmas fruit bread 79
Christmas pudding, Traditional 237
Ciabatta 11, 49
    Rosemary ciabatta rolls 179
cinnamon
    Apple and cinnamon brown betty 234
    Cinnamon raisin whirl 87
    Cinnamon golden raisin loaf 199
    Cinnamon swirls 95
club sandwich, Classic 218
coconut, shredded, unsweetened
    Cherry coconut scones 145
    Coconut bread 54
corn syrup, light
    Treacle lattice tart 234
cornbread
    Cheesy onion cornbread 192
    Chili cornbread 192
    Country-style cornbread 131
Cornish saffron bread 88
Cottage loaf 30, 175
cranberries
    Cranberry and orange spirals 100
    Cranberry and walnut loaf 56
    Spiced cranberry whirls 96
Croissants 93
Croque monsieur 219
Croûtons 210
Crown loaf 32
    Festival fruit crown loaf 81
Crumpets 118
Currant bread 52

D

Damper bread 130
Danish pastries 12, 94
dates
    Date and muesli quick bread 154
    Date and walnut loaf 150
Devonshire splits 89
Doughnuts 98
Drizzled Danish apple braid 86
Drop scones 120
Dutch gingerbread 153

E

Easter bread, Greek 82
Easter bread ring 83

F

Farmhouse wholewheat loaf 25
Farmhouse loaf 174
Festival fruit crown loaf 81
Festive cheese and fruit scone ring 143
Festive fruit snails 96
fish dishes
    Baked stuffed trout 229
    Blini with smoked salmon 121
    Fish goujons with herby sauce 228
    Fishcakes with tomato salsa 228
    Smoked salmon bruschetta 214
flat breads 107-123
    Moroccan 113
    North African 112
    Pepper and pesto pitta pizzas 216
    seeded 112
Flowerpot bread 35
focaccia
    Focaccia breads 116
    Sun-dried tomato & olive focaccia 117
    Tomato focaccia 181
Fougasse 76
French bread 178
    baguettes 47
    toast 212
Fruit and nut snack bread 105
Fruit and nut swirls 147

Fruit and spice pinwheels 95
Fruit and spice scones 199
Fruit and spice swizzle sticks 100
Fruit and spice quick bread 155
Fruitburst twists 147
Fruited bran loaf 148
Fruited breakfast braid 56
Fruity hazelnut quick bread 157

G
garlic
    Cheesy garlic bread 212
    Garlic bubble ring 68
    Garlic and cilantro naan 109
    Hot garlic bread 212
ginger
    Apple ginger muffins 201
    Dutch gingerbread 153
    Ginger quick bread 196
    Gingered banana bread 152
    Golden gingerbread 149
Gluten-free white loaf, Basic 202
Gluten-free wholewheat bread 202
Golden gruyère bread pudding 230
Greek black olive bread 48
Greek easter bread 82
Griddle scones 118
Grissini 67
Gruyère cheese twists 134

H
ham
    Chicken cordon bleu 229
    Croque monsieur 219
    Ham and spinach pinwheels 136
    Smoked ham and mustard twists 135
Hawaiian fruit bread 189
hazelnuts
    Fruity hazelnut quick bread 157
herb breads
    Braided 37
    Cheddar, herb, and onion bread 129
    Cheese and herb tear 'n' share 105
    Flowerpot bread 35
    Fresh herb bread 203
    Garden herb bread 184
    Herb baguettes 46
    Herbed olive bread 204
    Herby mushroom loaf 222
    Herby polenta bread 182
    Malted grain herb round 32
    Parmesan herb bread 194
    Parmesan herb twist 134
    Potato bread 34
    Potato bread rolls 62
    Quick cheese and herb bread 132
    Rustic cheesy herb bread 129
honey
    Banana and honey loaf 150
    Honey oatmeal bread 55
    Honey wheat bread 129
    Spiced honey loaf 206
Hot cross buns 90

I
ice cream, Brown bread 235
Italian tomato bread 205

K
Kugelhopf 77

L
Lardy cake 12, 97
Lavash 111
leeks, Cheese and leek potato cakes 224
lemon flavored breads
    Apricot and lemon muffins 165
    Blueberry and lemon muffins 201
    Lemon blueberry loaf 187
    Lemon drizzle loaf 198
    Lemon fruit twist 84

Lemon frosted bun round 89
Lemon and golden raisin whirls 148
Sugared lemon loaf 154

M
Malted fruit loaf 151
Malted grain bread, Home-style 25
Malted grain herb round 32
Malted golden raisin loaf 186
Malted wheat bread 174
Malted wholegrain cobb 27
Marbled chocolate quick bread 188
Mediterranean olive bread rolls 181
Melba toast 211
Milk loaf 31, 175
mincemeat
    Mincemeat and apple ring 88
Monkey bread 80
Moroccan bread, seeded 50
Moroccan flat breads 113
muffins
    Apple bran 161
    Apple ginger 201
    Apricot and lemon 165
    Banana pecan 162
    Blackberry streusel 168
    Blueberry and lemon 201
    Cheesy bacon 169
    Cherry and walnut 167
    Chicken and zucchini 216
    Double chocolate chip 163
    English 118
    English wholewheat 184
    Fresh blueberry 160
    Fruity breakfast 162
    Glazed fruit and orange 164
    Mini chocolate chip 169
    Mini maple pecan 166
    Mini orange and date 167
    Pear and golden raisin 161
    Pineapple oatmeal 168
    Poppyseed 160
    Raisin and orange 159
    Raspberry wholewheat 164
    Spiced apple 159
    Wholewheat banana 165
    Zesty apricot 200
Multigrain harvest loaf 28
mushrooms
    Herby mushroom loaf 222
    Mushroom pâté 222
    Stuffed 223

N
Naan bread 108
    Garlic and cilantro naan 109
    spiced 109
North African flat breads 112

O
Oatcakes 122
olives
    Cheese and olive bread 183
    Greek black olive bread 48
    Herbed olive bread 204
    Mediterranean olive bread rolls 181
    Olive potato bread 49
    Onion, olive, and chive bread 131
    Tomato and olive soda bread 127
onions
    Onion, olive, and chive bread 131
    Onion, olive, and oregano calzone 114
    Red onion and rosemary pizza 195
orange flavored breads
    Cranberry and orange spirals 100
    Glazed golden raisin and orange muffins 164
    Frosted orange loaf 187
    Mini orange and date muffins 167
    Orange and cinnamon brioche 75

Orange and date muffins 167
Raisin and orange muffins 159

P
Pains au chocolat 93
Pan bagna 218
Pancetta, pepper, and olive pizza 115
Pancotto 214
Panettone 82
Paradise braid 81
Parathas 110
Parmesan croûtons 210
Parmesan herb bread 194
Parmesan herb twist 134
Parmesan sesame swizzle sticks 135
pasta dishes
    Easy three-cheese macaroni 226
    Garden vegetable pasta bake 227
    Zucchini and bacon pasta medley 226
pears (dried)
    Cheesy pear scones 140
    Pear and golden raisin muffins 161
pecans
    Banana pecan muffins 162
    Mini maple pecan muffins 166
    Mini orange and date muffins 167
    Pecan scroll 87
Pepperoni muffin pizzas 217
peppers, bell
    Pepper and pesto pitta pizzas 216
    Stuffed roast bell peppers 221
pesto
    Pepper and pesto pitta pizzas 216
    Pesto parmesan pull-apart 104
    Pesto whirl bread 53
    Pesto whirls 137
Petit pains au lait 64
Pikelets 118
pineapple
    Pineapple oatmeal muffins 168
Pitta bread 113
pizzas
    Cheese-chili French bread pizzas 217
    Pancetta, pepper, and olive 115
    Pepper and pesto pitta pizzas 216
    Pepperoni muffin pizzas 217
    Red onion and rosemary pizza 195
Plain oven scones 139
polenta, Herby polenta bread 182
potato breads
    Olive potato bread 49
    Potato bread 34
    Refrigerator rolls 61
Potato cakes 122
    Cheese and leek potato cakes 224
Pretzels 122
Prune and hazelnut quick bread 156
Pugliese 11, 46
Pumpernickel 50
Puris (Pooris) 110

Q
quick breads
    Apricot and cranberry loaf 207
    Apricot and golden raisin loaf 153
    Apricot and walnut 189
    Banana and date 153
    Banana and honey 150
    Banana raisin bran loaf 156
    Chocolate banana bread 157
    Cinnamon golden raisin loaf 199
    Date and muesli 154
    Date and walnut loaf 150
    Frosted orange 187
    Frosted raisin loaf 158
    Fruit and spice 155
    Fruity hazelnut 157
    Ginger quick bread 196
    Hawaiian fruit bread 189

Lemon blueberry loaf 187
Lemon drizzle loaf 198
Malted fruit loaf 151
Malted golden raisin loaf 186
Marbled chocolate 188
Prune and hazelnut 156
Seeded fruit and nut 197
Sticky spiced loaf 206
Tropical quick bread 197

R
raisins
Frosted raisin loaf 158
Raisin and orange muffins 159
raisins, golden
Cinnamon golden raisin loaf 199
Glazed golden raisin and orange
muffins 164
and hazelnut bread 44
Lemon and golden raisin whirls
148
Malted golden raisin loaf 186
Pear and golden raisin muffins
161
raspberries
Raspberry monmouth pudding
237
Raspberry wholewheat muffins
164
Rich fruit scones 142
rolls
Breakfast 58
Bridge 59
Butter 63
Dinner 59
Floury white baps 66
Grissini 67
Linseed 64
Malted country 61
Mediterranean olive bread 181
Panini 63
Petit pains au lait 64
Plain crusty white 58
Poppyseed clover leaf 71
Potato bread 62
Quickie bread 62
Refrigerator 61
Rosemary ciabatta 179
Rustic wholewheat 60
Scottish baps 66
Soft wholewheat 60
Sun-dried tomato 178
rosemary
Red onion and rosemary pizza
195
Rosemary ciabatta rolls 179
Roti (West Indian) 111
Rum babas 76
Rye bread
Farmer's 38
Rustic 38-9
Rye and caraway bread 39
Seeded rye bread 176
Spiced rye bread
Rye crispbreads 123

S
saffron, Cornish saffron bread 88
Sally lunn 97
sandwiches, Classic club 218

sauces
herby sauce 228
tomato salsa 69, 228
Traditional bread sauce 231
Sausage and salsa pasties 69
Scallops au gratin 223
scones
Apple and apricot scone wedges
144
Apple and cinnamon scone round
143
Blueberry wedges 146
Cheesy pear scones 140
Cherry coconut scones 145
Drop scones 120
Festive cheese and fruit scone
ring 143
Fresh strawberry scones 144
Fruit and spice scones 199
Griddle scones 118
Mini apricot scones 145
Mini parmesan scones 140
Orchard scone wedges 145
Plain oven scones 139
Rich fruit scones 142
Spiced apple scone round 200
Wholewheat cheese scones 141
Wholewheat fruit scones 142
Scots black bun (Scotch bun) 102
seeded breads
Braided three-seed ring 33
Caraway cheese loaf 40
Caraway seed bread 176
Cheese and poppyseed braid 42
Cheese and seed bread 195
Cheese and sesame seed cobb 41
Linseed rolls 64
Mixed seed loaf 204
Poppyseed clover leaf rolls 71
Poppyseed knots 185
Poppyseed muffins 160
Pumpkin bread 51
Pumpkin seed bread 36
Savory sesame loaf 44
Seeded flat bread 112
Seeded fruit and nut quick bread
197
Seeded knots 70
Seeded Moroccan bread 50
Seeded rye bread 176
Sesame bagels 183
Sesame breadsticks 67
Sesame ring breads 69
Six-seed bread 177
Sunflower seed loaf 177
Selkirk bannock 102
Singin' hinnie 121
Smoked ham and mustard twists 135
Soda bread, home-style 126
Soft grain cobb 31
soups
Bread soup (Pancotto) 214
French onion 215
Soy bread 40, 194
Spelt bread 33
spiced breads
Fruit and spice scones 199
Fruit and spice swizzle sticks
100
Fruit and spice quick bread 155

Golden raisin and spice
pinwheels 95
Spiced apple muffins 159
Spiced apple scone round 200
Spiced apricot chelsea buns 92
Spiced bean picnic loaf 220
Spiced cranberry whirls 96
Spiced honey loaf 206
Spiced naan bread109
Spiced rye bread 52
Spiced walnut bread 54
Sticky spiced loaf 206
Sticky fruit buns 90
Sticky spiced loaf 206
Stollen 78
strawberries, Fresh Strawberry
scones 144
Stuffing mixes 231
Summer pudding 236
Sweet potato bread 36

T
Tasty nut loaf 221
Teacake fingers 99
Teacakes 98
toast
French toast 212
Melba toast 211
tomatoes
Italian tomato bread 205
Sun-dried tomato & olive focaccia
117
Sun-dried tomato bread 180
Sun-dried tomato rolls 178
Tomato and basil tear 'n' share
138
Tomato and fresh basil loaf 45
Tomato focaccia 181
Tomato and olive soda bread 127
Tuna and tomato bruschetta 213
Treacle lattice tart 234
Traditional loaf 29
Tropical quick bread 197
Tsoureki 79
tuna
Tuna melts 219
Tuna and tomato bruschetta 213

W
walnuts
Rustic walnut bread 37
Spiced walnut bread
Welsh bara brith 103
Welsh rarebit 219
Wheat tortillas 116
Wheaten bread 128
white bread, basic 22, 172
wholegrain cobb, malted 27
wholewheat bread 22, 173
Basic 22, 173
Home-style 173
Quick country 26
Wholewheat fruit scones 142
Wholewheat soda round 126

Z
zucchini
Chicken and zucchini muffins 216
pasta medley 226
Rustic zucchini loaf 45

Author's acknowledgements

My special thanks go to my husband, Robbie, for his continued support and encouragement with this book and for his tireless tasting of many of the recipes. My sincere thanks also go to Sarah Bradford and Bev Saunder for all their dedicated hard work testing recipes, and to Gwen Whiting for her help with typing recipes.

I would like to thank Julia Charles at Duncan Baird Publishers for approaching me and asking me to write this book, and for her continued support throughout this project. I would also like to thank Megan Smith for her creative design, Rachel Connolly for her diligence and thorough editing work, Bridget Sargeson for her hard work and patience preparing and styling all the recipes for photography, and William Lingwood for his beautiful food photographs throughout the book.

United We Solve

Math Problems for Groups

Grades 5–10

Tim Erickson

Illustrated by   Rose Craig

Cover by   Sally Noll

eeps™ MEDIA

eeps media, 1996

Author:	Tim Erickson
Illustrator:	Rose Craig
Cover artist:	Sally Noll
Translators:	Harold Asturias, Ronda Calef
Editors and advisors:	Pam Beck, Grace Dávila Coates, Ruth Cossey, Meg Holmberg, Barbara Shulgold, Jean Stenmark, and Bob Whitlow
Proofreader:	Barbara Shulgold

eeps media is the educational publishing imprint of Epistemological Engineering ("helping you know how you know what you know…since 1987"), but it's easier to spell. We are consultants, writers, and curriculum developers in mathematics, technology, and conflict resolution.

For additional information or volume sales, contact us:

eeps media
5269 Miles Avenue
Oakland, CA 94618-1044
(510) 653-3377 (i.e., 653-eeps)
(510) 428-1120 fax
publications@eeps.com
http://www.eeps.com

For single copies, call us or your favorite educational catalog.

ISBN 0-9648496-0-7

8 7 6 5 4 3   02 01 00 99

First Printing, December 1995.
Third printing, June 1999.